Game Art Complete

Game Art Complete

All-in-One: Learn Maya, 3ds Max, ZBrush, and Photoshop Winning Techniques

Edited by

Andrew Gahan

AMSTERDAM • BOSTON • HEIDELBERG • LONDON
NEW YORK • OXFORD • PARIS • SAN DIEGO
SAN FRANCISCO • SINGAPORE • SYDNEY • TOKYO

Focal Press is an imprint of Elsevier

Focal Press is an imprint of Elsevier.
30 Corporate Drive, Suite 400, Burlington, MA 01803, USA
Linacre House, Jordan Hill, Oxford OX2 8DP, UK

 Recognizing the importance of preserving what has been written, Elsevier prints its
books on acid-free paper whenever possible.

Library of Congress Cataloging-in-Publication Data
Gahan, Andrew.
  Game art complete: all-in-one: learn Maya, 3ds Max, zBrush, and Photoshop winning
    techniques / Andrew Gahan.
    p. cm.
    Includes index.
  ISBN 978-0-240-81147-5 (pbk. : alk. paper) 1. Computer games—Design. 2. Computer
    animation. 3. Computer graphics. I. Title.
  QA76.76.C672.G32 2008
  794.8'1536—dc22   2008036474

British Library Cataloguing-in-Publication Data
A catalogue record for this book is available from the British Library.

ISBN: 978-0-240-81147-5

For information on all Focal Press publications
visit our website at www.books.elsevier.com

08 09 10 11 12 5 4 3 2 1

Printed in Canada

Contents

Introduction

The purpose of this book is to give artists and modelers who may be new to 3D modeling and animation, or who may want to expand their skill set, an overview of the four main programs with some tutorials to get them started.

We will take you through a series of tutorials, covering the following topics:

- Character concepts
- Anatomy
- Low-poly asset modeling in 3ds Max
- Normal maps, including CrazyBump
- Creating texture maps from photographs
- Alpha maps
- Color theory
- Maya's interface
- Creating a low-poly character in Maya
- Production pipelines
- Introduction to ZBrush
- Workflow
- Rigging a character
- Facial expressions
- Shading and texturing
- Low- to high-poly modeling
- Complex mapping and textures
- UVTool

I will be introducing you to a number of authors, all specialists in their fields, who will in turn introduce you to Photoshop, 3ds Max, Maya, and ZBrush. These are the four main programs used in 3D modeling, game development, TV, design, architecture, print media, and many other industries. Understanding the basics of all of these programs will save you a lot of time when developing new ideas for your work.

We will be kicking off with some basic modeling techniques using 3ds Max and Photoshop, written by myself, and by getting to grips with normal maps with David Wilson, one of the senior lecturers from the University of Derby in the UK. These initial four chapters take the complete beginner in modeling for games to a competent level where they can be producing final artwork for current games.

We will then move onto two chapters on concept art and anatomy with Jason Patnode. These chapters have been added to the book to get artists and designers to start thinking about how they start to create concept art; in this case, specifically concept art for characters. There is also a good introduction to anatomy to help every artist to create great-looking designs that can be modeled.

We will discuss preparing for texture creation in great detail, with Luke Ahearn covering all aspects including shape and form, light and shadow, as well as the general usage and creation of game textures.

We then move onto some Maya character modeling with Jean-Marc Gauthier and Jason Patnode, looking at some different techniques and approaches, including the introduction of ZBrush.

It's important to know that there are a number of different methods and techniques for creating similar pieces of work in multiple software packages, and we hope to give you quite a thorough introduction to the most popular ones in this book.

Then we continue with some character rigging, facial expressions, texturing and shading to almost complete the picture, with us ending with a mega build in 3ds Max of a low- to high-poly character, including baking the high-res details onto the low-res model and creating all the texture maps with Tom Painter.

It was really difficult to pick the best parts of each software package to focus on, so we decided upon this general approach with a slight bias to looking at characters. It would be impossible to cover every aspect of game art creation for every genre of game on every platform in just one book, so we have focused on the core strengths of each software package and will introduce you to all of them.

This book can be picked up at any chapter, so feel free to jump in and out wherever you like. Try looking at all of the software packages and try to be disciplined enough to continue with a good working knowledge of them all.

There are lots of different game developers all over the world and they all favor different software packages. The ones defined and explained in this book are the core for almost all developers, so if you can gain a good working knowledge of all of them before you decide to specialize, you may create more opportunities for yourself in the future.

Good luck with your modeling and development and remember to have fun with it.

Now let me introduce you to the authors.

Luke Ahearn, *3D Game Textures: Create Professional Game Art Using Photoshop* (ISBN-10: 0240807685)
Luke has been a professional game developer since 1992. He has served in lead positions such as designer, producer, and art director on seven published game titles, including *Dead Reckoning* and *America's Army*, and has worked as a background artist at EA. He has authored numerous books on game

development and ran his own computer game company for ten years. Currently, he is the art director and a partner of ICPU.

Luke contributed Chapter 7 to this book.

Cheryl Cabrera, *An Essential Introduction to Maya Character Rigging* (ISBN-10: 0240520823)

Cheryl is an Autodesk Certified Instructor in Maya and has been a professor in the Animation Department of the School of Film and Digital Media at the Savannah College of Art and Design since 2001. She has a background in education and acting, and in addition to her work in 3D, she is an exhibiting painter and has participated in numerous group and solo exhibitions in the United States. Her award-winning students have been featured in animation festivals worldwide and work throughout the gaming and entertainment industry.

Cheryl contributed Chapters 12, 13, 14, and 15 to this book.

Andrew Gahan, *3ds Max Modeling for Games: Insider's Guide to Game Character, Vehicle, and Environment Modeling* (ISBN-10: 0240810619)

Andrew joined the games industry in 1992 as an artist and has subsequently worked at all levels of the industry throughout his career. Roles have included senior artist, lead artist, art manager, art director, art outsource manager, and producer. He is currently working on the MotorStorm series for PlayStation 3 at Evolution Studios/Sony Computer Entertainment.

Andrew contributed Chapters 1, 2, and 3 to this book.

Jean-Marc Gauthier, *Building Interactive Worlds in 3D: Virtual Sets and Pre-visualization for Games, Film & the Web* (ISBN-10: 0240806220)

Jean-Marc, director of Tisch Asia Animation and the Digital Arts MFA program in Singapore, is an assistant art professor at New York University, Tisch School of the Arts. Jean-Marc teaches interactive 3D animation and game production. He creates interactive projects crossing the borders between arts, sciences, architecture, animation, virtual spaces, games, and museum installations. His interactive media art works have been presented at venues internationally, including New York's American Museum of the Moving Image, Institute of Fine Arts, and Chelsea Art Museum, File Festival (Brazil), Ars Electronica Festival (Austria), Daegu Art Center (South Korea), Cite des Sciences Villette-Biennale Numérique (France), Le Cube (France), MAMAC (France).

Jean-Marc's recent entertainment projects include *Cold Stone Dead Serious*, a 3D interactive game for a theater play; NightHawks, a gaming installation interacting with a large audience inside a public park; and Aphrodisias, a virtual archeology immersive display in a museum. He has collaborated on numerous educational and scientific visualization projects, including immersive environments for visually impaired people; the Dynamic Virtual Patient, a visualization browser for the human body; the Brain Project, a 3D interactive navigation of the brain; and an interactive tool for exploring the genetic diversity of the world's 10,000 bird species.

Gauthier has written several books on creating interactive animation and the production of real-time 3D games, including *Creating Interactive 3D Actors and Their Worlds* (Morgan Kaufman, 2001), *Building Interactive Worlds in 3D: Virtual Sets and Pre-Visualization for Games, Film & the Web* (Focal Press, 2005). The author thanks Miro Kirov. Gauthier's website is www.tinkering.net.

Jean-Marc contributed Chapter 8 to this book.

Tom Painter, Contributor to *3ds Max Modeling for Games*

Tom would waste many a sunny day on his ZX spectrum and Amiga, and by the time he was a teenager, he had developed a serious addiction to *Street Fighter 2*. Encouraged by his father, he decided that he would pursue a career in games.

After his studies, he got his first break in the games industry as a pixel artist working at Tiertex on Nintendo Game Boy Advance titles. When Tiertex dissolved, he joined Evolution Studios as an environment artist for the World Rally Championship (WRC) series of games on the Sony PlayStation 2.

In 2005, he moved to Pandemic Studios in Australia to work on *Destroy All Humans! 2*. He changed roles to become a character artist working on Saboteur and two top-secret titles in progress (project B and project Q). He recently founded Big Man Production, a specialist-character production company working for clients in the videogame and advertising industries.

Tom contributed Chapter 16 to this book.

Jason Patnode, *Character Modeling with Maya and ZBrush: Professional Polygonal Modeling Techniques* (ISBN-10: 0240520343)

Jason has worked at such companies as LucasArts, Activision, and Pixar. Currently he is working as a freelance artist and instructor. He has written multiple books on Maya and has a new Maya/Z-brush modeling book available.

Jason contributed Chapters 5, 6, 9, 10, & 11 to this book.

David Wilson, Contributor to *3ds Max Modeling for Games*

David spent the last three years involved in the production of *MotorStorm* (Evolution Studios), a critically acclaimed game that has been celebrated for its game play and graphical excellence. He has significant next-generation experience, and the work he has produced in recent years is the current benchmark for real-time graphics in the games industry.

He has also worked remotely as a freelance artist for clients internationally, building assets for games such as *Need for Speed Underground*.

He is currently using his game production experience on a BA (Honors) undergraduate degree course in Computer Games Modeling and Animation at the University of Derby, UK.

He is enjoying the opportunity to work with people who have raw enthusiasm about games and are at the beginning of their journeys in games development. He wants to shape the way that students understand games and develop the relevant skill sets needed by the next generation of artists.

David contributed Chapter 4 to this book.

Thanks also to:

- Everyone at UVLayout (http://www.uvlayout.com).
- Ben Cloward, for the use of the shaders (http://www.bencloward.com).
- Ryan at CrazyBump (http://www.crazybump.com).

CHAPTER 1

Creating a Box Using 3ds Max

Introduction to Modeling

This first tutorial is designed to get complete beginners up to speed on the basics of modeling using primitive objects and applying textures in the simplest way. In the games industry we lay out the textures in a slightly different way than in this tutorial. You'll learn that technique in Chapter 2, which covers more complex mapping techniques, but to get any complete beginners through their first complete object build, I have explained the most straightforward method first. This chapter also introduces you to some of the preferences, settings and shortcuts that will speed up your modeling and give you better results.

Setting Up 3ds Max

To begin with, we'll start with some basic settings for 3ds Max. Go to Customize > Preferences > Files. Enable Auto Backup, set number of Auto Backup files to 9, and set Backup Interval (minutes) to 10, then click OK.

Next we'll set up the units we'll be modeling in; these vary from studio to studio, but in this tutorial, one unit equals 1 cm. Go to Customize, Units setup… and select Metric, then click OK.

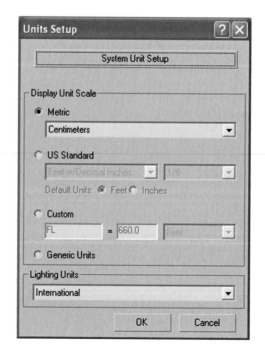

We will now begin to model a simple object. First, we'll create a primitive object and scale it to approximately the correct dimensions. We will then apply texture maps to the object, UVW map it and then do some quick renders of it using 3ds Max's built in scan-line renderer.

If you don't understand what I mean by "UVW map," search for the term using the new InfoCenter, or press F1 for help and search for the term "Unwrap UVW Modifier"—it explains everything you need to know about this. This goes for anything you don't understand, or aren't sure of—just search through the help feature, and it will all be explained to you. Feel free to browse the help, too. You'll find lots of cool things that would otherwise take you many years to find out on your own.

Creating a Cardboard Box

First, we're going to create the box (Create > Standard Primitives > Box) and set the dimensions to 45 × 45 × 50. If your box is being displayed in wireframe in any of your viewports, just right-click in the viewport and press the F3 key.

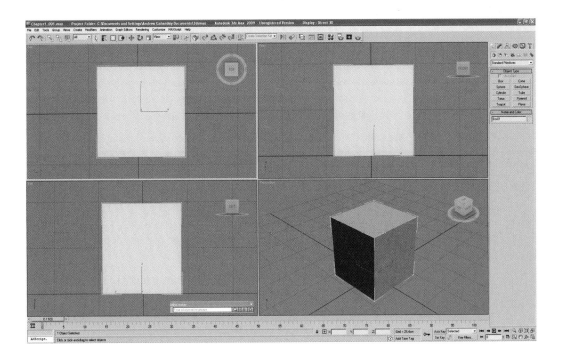

With the box selected, right-click it and select "Convert to editable mesh" from the Quad menu.

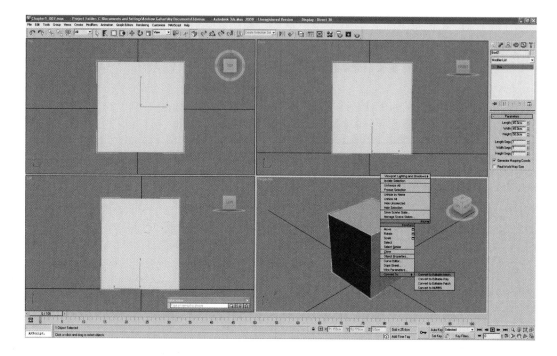

Now you need to save your progress. Always name your files with a relevant name to make it easier to find your assets later. As this is the first save file, we'll create a few folders to store all the files that you'll be working on while using this book. Go to save the file (File > Save as…), create a folder called Game Art Complete, and then create another folder inside the one you've just created, called Chapter 1. Now save your file as Cardboard box1.max or Chapter1_001.max.

We have completed the modeling part of this tutorial. Now we have to apply the texture maps to the faces of the box and our first asset will be complete.

3ds Max Shortcuts

There are a few viewport configurations to help you to speed up the mapping of the box. Go to Modify, click the Configure Modifier Sets button, and select Show Buttons from the menu.

This action displays a set of buttons beneath the Modifier List rollout menu that can be configured to include all your most often used modifiers. Set the Total Buttons value to 10 and add Edit Mesh, UVW Map, and Unwrap UVW to the buttons, as we will use these modifiers the most in the first few chapters of the book. Do this by finding the modifier on the alphabetized list and drag it onto the button. To find a modifier on the list easily, just keep typing the first letter from it on the keyboard, and you will cycle through all the modifiers with that letter (for example, press E for Edit Mesh). Then click OK to close the Configure Modifier Sets window.

Texture Mapping Your Box

With your box still selected, go to Selection, click Element, and select the box. This should highlight all the faces (press F2 to toggle the highlighted selection).

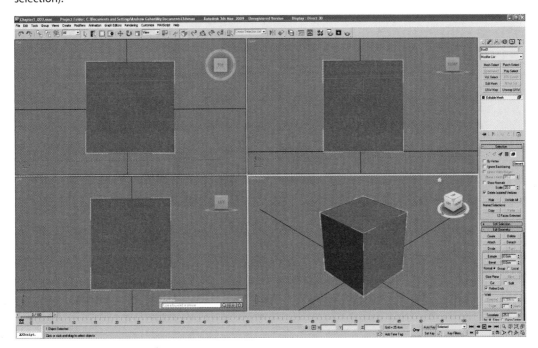

Now click UVW Map from your newly created modifier set and check Box Mapping from the Parameters menu.

Next, right-click UVW Map in the Modifier stack and select Collapse All from the pop-up menu, then click Yes—you want to continue at the prompt, as we don't need to preserve the stack in this instance.

With your box still selected, click on the Material Editor (on the top tool bar) and change the standard material to a multi-sub object material as shown, clicking OK to discard the old material. If you keep the old material by accident, don't worry—it doesn't matter either way in this instance, as we are creating new ones.

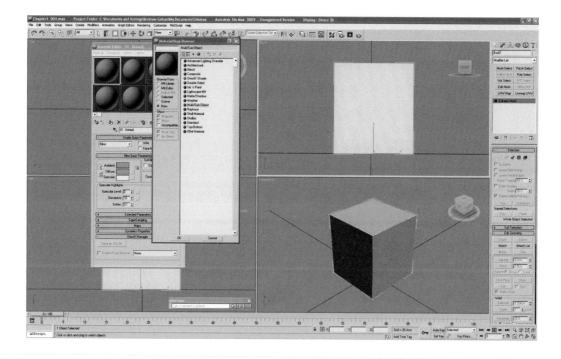

To keep this first tutorial simple, I have already prepared the texture maps that you'll be using from photographs. In Chapter 3, we will cover this process in a lot of detail, showing how to take photographs, how to modify them in Photoshop, and how to apply them to models.

To add the textures into the material editor, select the material ID from the vertical list and load in the texture map for each side of the box. Although there are ten materials displayed in the editor, we'll just use the first six listed Material #2 through to Material #7 in my case. Yours could have different names, depending on how you have used 3ds Max previously. Don't worry if your names don't match mine at this point, as they can be renamed.

Click on the first material in the list, next to ID 1 (Material #2 in my case) and assign a Bitmap material to it. To do this, click the small square button on the right of "diffuse" in Blinn Basic Parameters, select Bitmap from the top of the pop-up menu, and click OK.

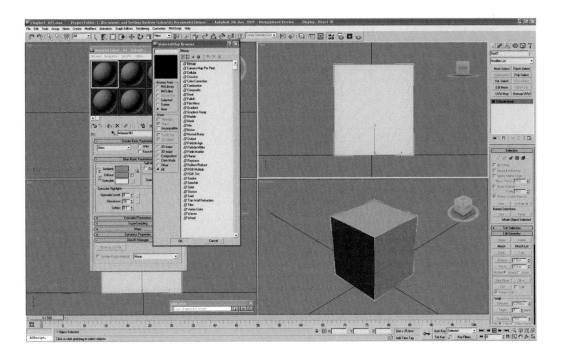

Now load Box1_top.jpg from \Chapter 1\Textures\, which you should have downloaded from the Web site. If you haven't downloaded the source files already, go to www.GameArtComplete.com and follow the instructions for downloading the files you'll need.

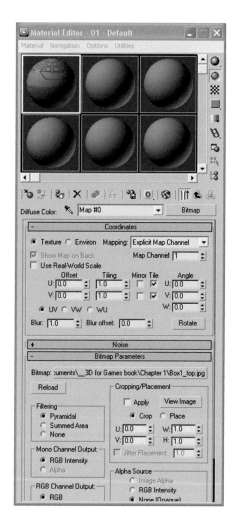

There are two ways to assign the next material to ID 2. The first way is to click on the Go To Parent button, then click the Go Forward To Sibling button (as shown here).

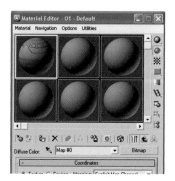 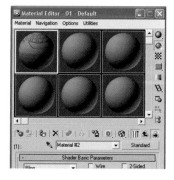

The second method is to click the Go To Parent button twice, then select the second material in the list (as shown in the figure).

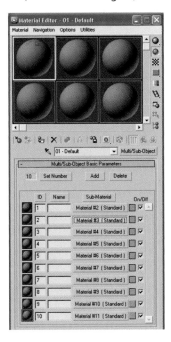

Then repeat the process of clicking the small square button to the right of "diffuse" in Blinn Basic Parameters, selecting Bitmap from the top of the pop-up menu, and clicking OK.

As you assign each material a texture map, click the Show Standard Map in Viewport button 🌐, so that when you Assign Material to Selection the textures are visible on the object.

Repeat this process for ID 2 through ID 6, loading the remaining five texture maps into the material editor and ending with Box1_base.jpg being assigned to ID 6.

Here's how they should be assigned:

ID 1—Material #2—Box1_top.jpg
ID 2—Material #3—Box1_sid1.jpg
ID 3—Material #4—Box1_ sid2.jpg
ID 4—Material #5—Box1_ sid3.jpg
ID 5—Material #6—Box1_ sid4.jpg
ID 6—Material #7—Box1_base.jpg

Remember that your Material number may differ from the numbers I have. As long as you match the ID (number)—for example, ID 1 goes with the corresponding texture map, in this case Box1_top.jpg—then you'll be okay. Also *make sure* that you remember to select Show Standard Map in Viewport 🌐.

Now that we have assigned texture maps to all of the materials, we will apply the material set to the box and apply the material IDs to the faces of the box, allowing us to see the texture maps.

With the box still selected as an editable mesh, click the Assign Material to Selection button 🗷 to assign the material set that you've just set up to the box you're mapping. At this point, you should see that a lot of the box's faces now have texture maps on them. These currently correspond to the default face IDs, which are not necessarily the ones we want, so let's go through and check each face of the cube individually to make sure that the correct texture map is applied to the correct face on the box.

For this model, we must do this carefully, as some of the packaging tape on the box wraps around onto the adjacent faces. Look out for mistakes when you complete the model.

To get the correct map onto the correct face, first select the face of the box that is on the top of the box in the perspective viewport. Go to Selection and select Polygon. Scroll down from selection until you get to the Surface Properties rollout box and in Material, make sure that Set ID: is set to 1.

In the perspective view, select the polygon on the left-hand side and assign the ID to 4. Depending on how the box mapping oriented each of the box faces when we mapped it, the texture map may not be oriented the correct way round. If this is the case, we'll need to modify the UVW Mapping coordinates to correct it.

From the Modifier List, click the button Unwrap UVW, which adds the Unwrap UVW modifier to the modifier stack. Below the modifier stack, adjust the vertical scrolling menu until you find Parameters. Once you have found the Parameters section, click Edit. The Edit UVW window will pop open.

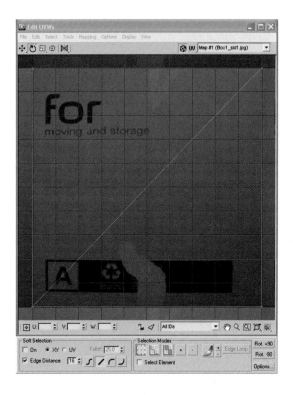

From the pull-down menu at the top right of the new Edit UVW window, click on the rollout and select Map#1 (Box1_sid1.jpg). Now we need to select all of the vertices (left click, drag bounding box around all vertices, then release the left mouse button). You'll know if you've gotten them all as they all change to a red color (see image).

Now we need to rotate all the vertices to the correct orientation on the cardboard box, but first press A to activate the Angle Snap shortcut. We rotate the vertices (select Rotate at the top left of Edit UVW window) until the text on the texture map is the right way up on the cardboard box model in the viewport.

There are a few options that I like to set to help me to see the map more clearly when doing this type of mapping. At the bottom right-hand corner of the Edit UVW window, click Options…. This step brings up some extra settings for editing the UVWs. Uncheck Tile Bitmap, and set brightness to 1, which is useful in that it will help you see the texture sheet a lot more clearly. This option can also be set from the top menu, by selecting Options > Preferences (Ctrl + O) and adjusting it in the Display Preferences menu.

Next, right-click Unwrap UVW in the modifier stack and select Collapse All, then select Yes to clear the stack.

Now we'll continue mapping the rest of the cardboard box. Left-click on Editable Mesh in the Modifier Stack and press the 4 key on the keyboard (the shortcut to Select Polygon). The other useful shortcuts of this type are: 1 = Select Vertex, 2 = Select Edge, 3 = Select Face, 4 = Select Polygon, and 5 = Select Element.

With Edit Polygon selected, select the other visible front polygon in the perspective view.

Repeat the mapping and unwrapping procedure on the second side that you can see in the perspective viewport, but this time, set the ID of the face of the box to ID 3.

To see what you are doing more clearly in each of the viewports, right-click on the name of the viewport and select Smooth and Highlights from the pop-up window.

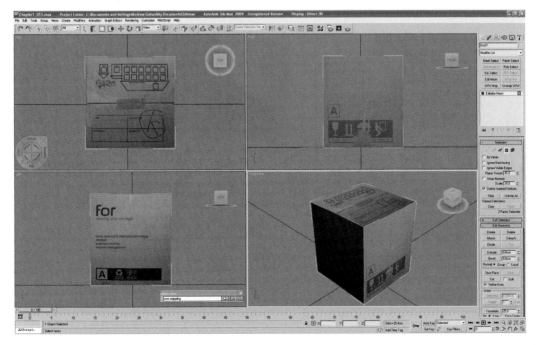

On this occasion, the second box side texture map on my model is the correct way up, so there is no need for me to unwrap the UVs. If yours doesn't match this, repeat the previous process.

To help you to see the model more clearly, while in the Perspective view, click on the Maximize Viewport Toggle (bottom right of interface), which shows just the Perspective view, allowing you to see your model a lot more clearly. Now click on Arc Rotate Selected (to the left of the Maximize Viewport Toggle) and rotate the object so that you can clearly see the rear two sides of the cardboard box. You can also close the material editor or minimize it for a good look at all sides too. Feel free to have a play with the new floating controllers (in the top right) of each viewport to change your view, too.

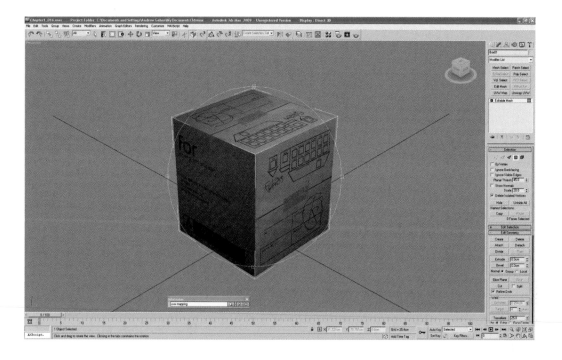

Select the polygon on the left and assign it ID 2. If the texture map is not oriented correctly, quickly right it by following the mapping procedure from mapping the first side of the box (Unwrap UVW > Edit > Select Map#2 box_sid1.jpg, select vertices, rotate to correct orientation).

Collapse the stack again, press 4 and select the fourth side to map. This time, set the ID to 5 and adjust the UVW mapping, if necessary, so that it matches the example.

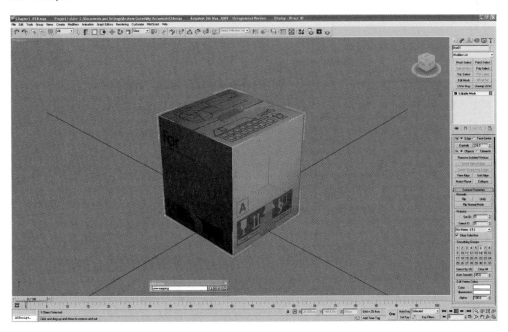

Finally, rotate the Perspective view (Arc Rotate Selected button) and select the bottom polygon of the cardboard box. Set the ID to 6 and adjust the mapping if necessary. On this side of the box, pay close attention to the packaging tape on the texture map and make sure that it lines up correctly with the tape wrapping around onto the sides of the box. Once you're happy with it, that's it—you're done. Congratulations on completing this model!

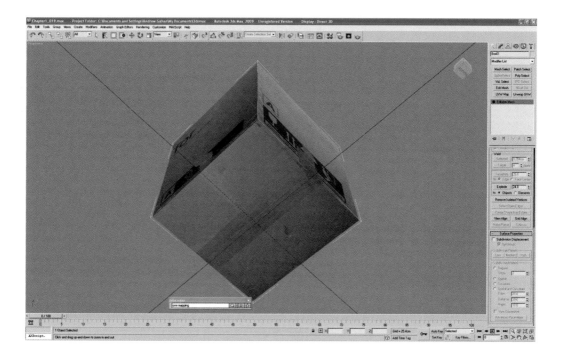

Common Problems

When building assets like this one, always make sure that all of the texture maps are all the same size and resolution. Differences in resolution have a massive impact on the quality of your finished model, and even if the maps are supplied to you, always check their size and color depth to make sure that they match where they should.

With models using continuing patterns that wrap around the object, make sure that they line up correctly on all sides.

Rendering Your Model

To produce quick renders of your model for an object database or for a progress portfolio, first we need to set up the environment.

At the top of the screen select Rendering then Environments and Effects from the drop-down menu, or press 8 for the shortcut. For this type of quick render, I usually set the Global Lighting Ambient to around 150, the Tint to approximately 200, with the intensity at 0.5 and the background color set to something neutral or close to white (around 230). In this case, as I'll be using the render just to put in a progress portfolio, I'll be using 230 for the background as it'll help the object stand out and it'll be a lot less messy to print in color.

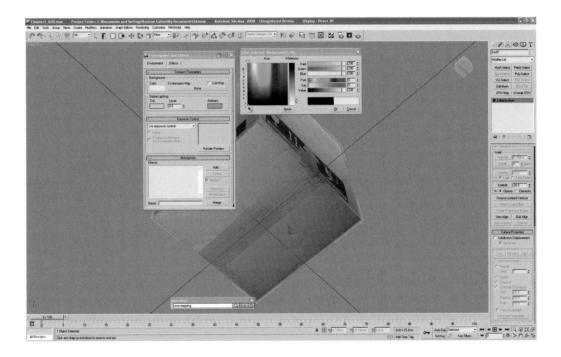

Once you're happy with the settings, close the Environment and Effects window and rotate the viewport until you're satisfied that the view is showing off the best of the model. I like the detail in the cardboard on the top of the box and I also like the staple details with the rips on the sides so they will be most prominent in my render.

Go to Rendering > Render or type F10 as a shortcut, opening up the parameters for the scanline renderer. In Output Size, click the 800 × 600 button and click on the Render button (bottom right of parameters popup). You should now have a render of your cardboard box. If you want a render that is of a slightly higher resolution, instead of clicking the 800 × 600 button, click the Image Aspect lock button and type in 1920 (or whatever size you like) and press Return and then the render button. You can render images at any size you like.

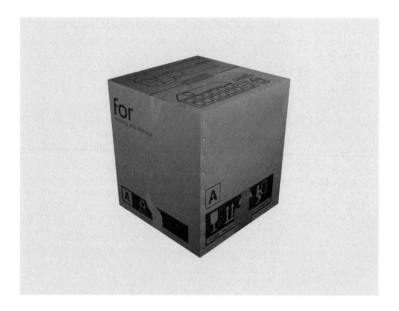

Try adjusting the Ambient light, Tint, and Background color settings until you render an image that you're happy with. But keep the render nice and clean if it's for a portfolio. You can always add it to a themed style sheet in Photoshop for your final portfolio later. Keeping it clean will enable you to make any style changes later on a lot more easily.

Moving On to Chapter 2

In the next chapter, we will be building a slightly more complex asset. You will learn how to lay out the texture map, making the most of the available area and we will also look at a slightly more complex method of laying out the UVs for the texture. We will be using some new tools to create the new asset including Slice, Extrude, and Scale, and we will be producing another render for your portfolio.

Well done, for getting to the end.

Creating an Oil Drum Using 3ds Max

Modifying Primitive Objects and UV Mapping

Congratulations, you're at Chapter 2 already! Hopefully, you've managed to complete the first tutorial without encountering any problems. If you skipped the tutorial, try to at least flick through it, so that you know what we've covered, especially the 3ds Max setup information and the UVW mapping. As we have to cram so much into this one book, we will not be repeating things. Because of this, I advise you to complete the tutorials so that you don't miss anything, even if you know what you are doing. There could be something important that you miss, which could cause problems for you later on if you don't understand it.

On to the second tutorial. This time we will be creating another primitive object and using a lot of different actions, including: Editable Poly, Select and Uniform Scale, loading background images, keyboard shortcuts, object properties (see-through and backface cull), Boolean (Cut & Union), deleting faces, and Target Weld for vertices.

Let's get started. For this tutorial, we will use some reference photos (already provided in the Chapter 2 download from the Web site www.GameArtComplete .com) to build a fairly simple model. It will involve slightly more modeling than the first tutorial and a little more complex mapping. We will use the reference photos as a guide to model from, and we will use them again to create the texture map.

First, open up 3ds Max and start with a new scene (File > New, select the new all, and click OK). The first thing we need to do is load the first photo into 3ds Max to use as a guide. While in the top viewport, press Alt+B to import a background image.

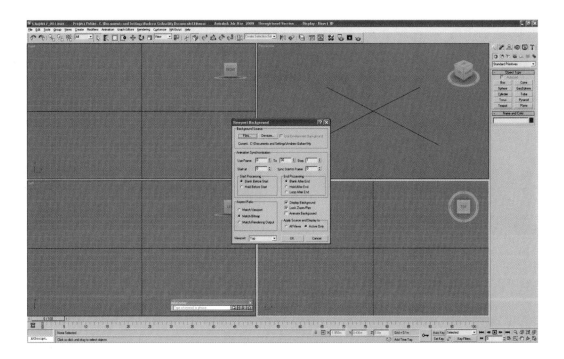

Make sure that you check the options Match bitmap, Display background, and Lock zoom/pan. From Files, open Img_0301.jpg from \Chapter 2\Textures\ from the download on the Web site, then click OK. You could also create a flat plane of polygons and map the image to it for reference.

You should now see the photograph of the top of a dirty plastic barrel in your Top viewport. Go to Create > Geometry, make sure that Standard Primitives is selected, and click on Cylinder. Then click in the Top viewport, approximately in the center of the barrel in the photo, and create a Cylinder that is about the circumference of the barrel. Don't worry about the height at this point, as we will adjust it in a moment. Next, set the parameters to 12 Sides and 3 Height Segments. Click Select and Rotate and rotate the cylinder so that the top and bottom edges are horizontal as shown in the figure.

Now maximize the Top viewport (Alt+W) so that the top view is full-screen.
Go to Modify and right-click on Cylinder and convert to Editable Poly.

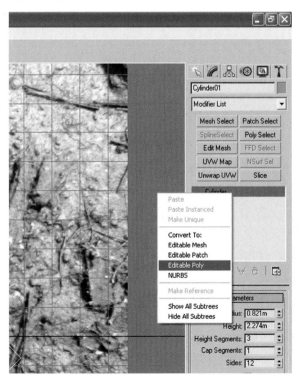

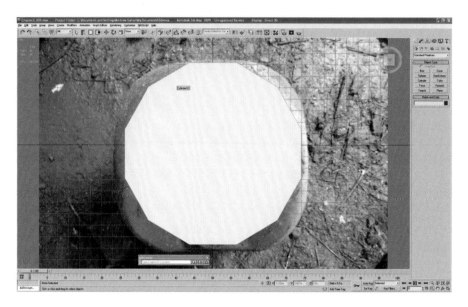

Feel free to modify the cylinder so that it matches the photograph more closely (as pictured in *Chapter2_004.tif*) using Select and Uniform Scale and Select and Move from the top toolbar. Click Editable Poly and select Vertex, if it's not already selected. We need to make the cylinder slightly squarer to match the photo, by selecting groups of vertices and moving them either horizontally or vertically. The completed shape doesn't have to be perfect, so don't spend too much time getting the form right. I used Select and Uniform Scale and selected four groups of vertices at a time. When you're finished, the object should look roughly like this image:

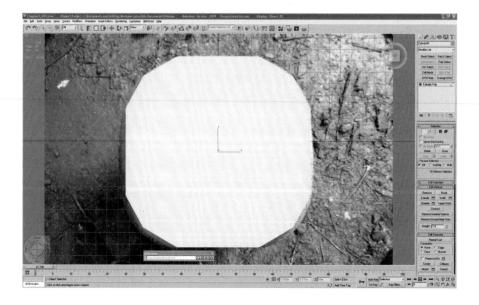

Click Alt+W again to reveal the other viewports, and we'll open up another image to use as a guide. While still in the Top viewport, click Alt+B and uncheck Display Background (because we are finished with that image).

Right-click on the Front viewport and zoom out from the barrel using Zoom Extents (in the bottom-right corner) and the left mouse button. If you aren't sure what any of the buttons on the toolbar are, just hover the mouse over them for a second and a pop-up dialog box will tell you. We've zoomed back from the image slightly; now we need to import another background image (Alt+B). Load in Img_0300.jpg from \Chapter 2\Textures\ (downloaded from the Web site); this time, uncheck Lock Zoom/Pan and then click OK.

As this photograph was taken from a different angle to the model we're building, I've unchecked Lock Zoom/Pan to let me rotate the object and zoom in and out. This will allow me to set the right height for the cylinder, which we'll now call the "barrel." Click Select and Rotate from the top toolbar, and rotate the barrel 90 degrees, so that it lies on its side. If angle snap is off, turn it on (press the A key) before starting to rotate the barrel. You should be left with something that looks like this:

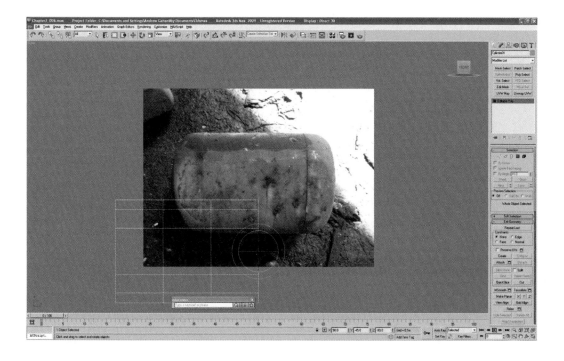

Using Select and Move, as well as Select and Uniform Scale, move the barrel over the photograph and set the height of it, so that it looks like this:

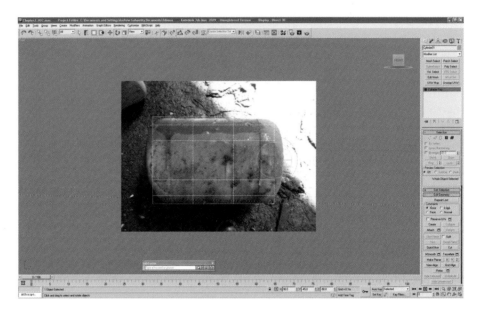

We have the basic dimensions of the barrel, so we can start to model the details and make it look a bit more realistic. As this is a low-poly object, we won't be adding lots of details—just enough to round off the edges and add the handle shape on the top. The rest of the detail will come from the texture map.

We need to create the slight curves to the top and bottom of the barrel. To do this, we will scale the center vertices on the x-axis. Click Editable Poly, go back to the Front viewport, and drag-select the center vertices. Click Select and Uniform Scale and drag them out so that they look something like this:

Click Editable Poly again to turn it off. Click Select and Rotate and rotate the barrel back 90 degrees into the upright position that it was in earlier. Click Alt+B and turn off Display Background. Finally, click Zoom Extents All (Shift+Ctrl+Z).

If you like, you can click in each viewport and click F3 to toggle Wifeframe/ Smooth + Highlight and also click F4 to toggle View Edged Faces, so that you can see your work far more clearly. For details on the other shortcuts on the F (function) keys and all the preset shortcuts in 3ds Max, go to Customize > Customize User Interface and scroll down the list to see what the default hotkeys are. You can also assign your own here. If you make any changes, remember to save the settings.

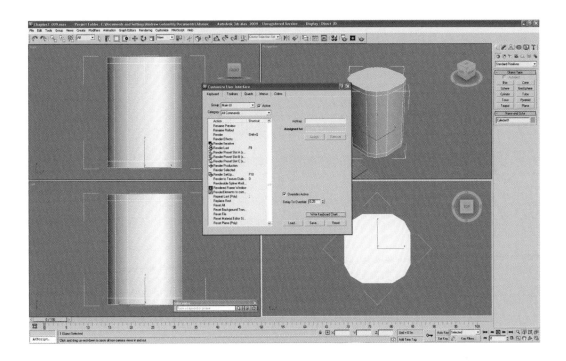

Let's get moving. In the Front viewport, type 1. This selects Vertex in Editable Poly (try pressing the keys 2, 3, 4, and 5, one at a time to see how these work as shortcuts). Type Alt+W and then drag-select all of the very top row of vertices and then Ctrl+drag-select the very bottom row of vertices. Click T for Top viewport and click Z for Zoom Extents.

Click Select and Uniform Scale and scale the vertices in to give a slight bevel to the top and bottom of the barrel. If you drag toward the center of the barrel when scaling, look at the coordinates at the bottom of the screen (just right of center). Drag until you hit 90%, which should look about right. Again you don't have to be especially accurate on this.

Click F to go to the Front viewport and scale the same set of vertices a little on the y-axis until your barrel looks something like this:

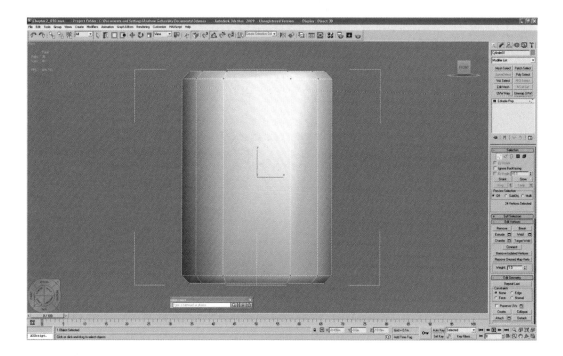

There are two ways we can go with the build at this point. We could leave the model as it is now and create a texture map for it, and call that complete (which would be reasonable for a low-poly object), or we can model some detail on the top. In this case, we'll model the detail on the top, as I want to show you a really cool tool called Boolean.

Type T to select the Top viewport, then F3 to see the wireframe of the barrel. Click Create > Standard Primitives > Cylinder and make sure that Height Segments is set to 1 and Sides is set to 12. Click right in the center of the barrel and create a cylinder that is about half as wide as the barrel. Now type F for the Front viewport and then Shift+Ctrl+Z to Zoom Extents. You should now have the barrel and also a cylinder in the scene. Click Select and Move, and move the cylinder up so that it intersects with the top of the barrel, something like this:

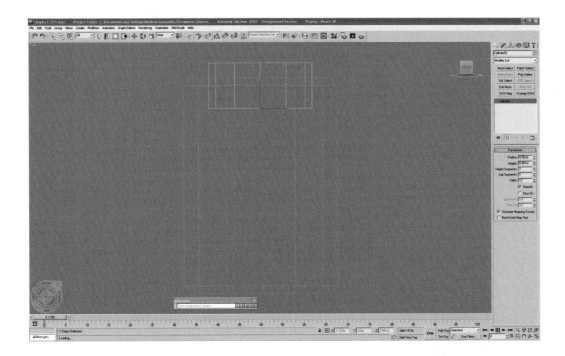

Remember to save your work regularly as you model. It's really easy to get swept away with the progress, and you can spend many hours on something—only to lose it all in a crash. Try to save regularly and have the autoback function set (see Chapter 1). We all usually only remember to save just as our computers crash, which is obviously too late.

Performing the Boolean

Let's move onto Boolean. Select the barrel and press P (for the Perspective viewport) and F3 if the meshes aren't Smooth and Highlight–shaded. Click Create. Where Standard Primitives is displayed, click on the rollout menu and select Compound Objects.

You should see Morph, Scatter, Conform, ShapeMerge, some others, and Boolean. Boolean is a powerful tool and can be quite confusing until you get the hang of it. First, you need two objects: it works best with solid "closed meshes"; that is, where there are no holes in the mesh. These are called

Operand A and Operand B—think of these as Shape A and Shape B. There are four different types of Boolean in 3ds Max 2009: Union, Intersection, Subtraction, and Cut. If you search for "Boolean Compound Object" in the 3ds Max 2009 help (F1) or the InfoCenter, it explains what all these are in detail. It is well worth reading the explanation and then creating two objects in a different file and playing with the different types to see what results you can get.

For this model, we will be using Cut. With the barrel still selected, click Cut from the Operation selection on the right of the workspace, then click Pick Operand B (choose the other shape), and then click to select the cylinder, as shown here:

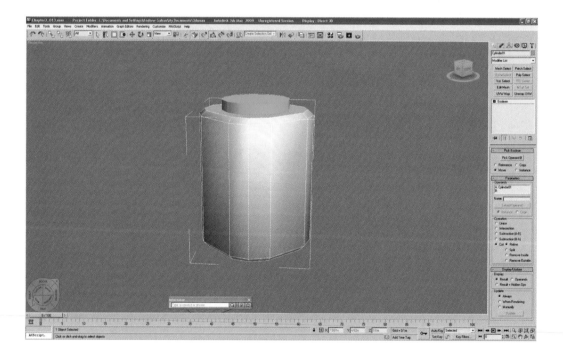

This step will cut the barrel with the shape of the cylinder, but leave you with a solid mesh.

To finish off the Boolean work, click on Modify, right-click on Boolean, and select Edit Mesh.

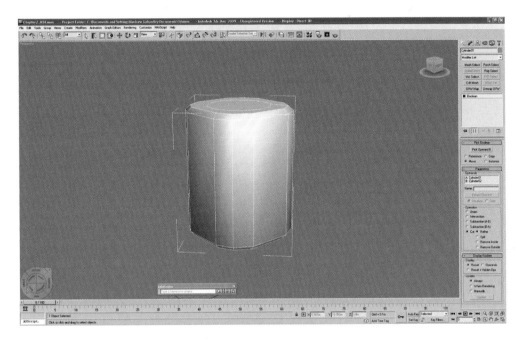

Fixing Your Mistakes

One of the most important parts of modeling something that you haven't modeled before is that you may not build it perfectly from start to finish and you may have to modify your work. This approach can be a lot quicker than going back to a save file or (even worse) rebuilding something. If you've followed the tutorial accurately up to this point, you will have made a small mistake that was deliberately included on the last action. Before we performed the Boolean, it would have made progressing easier if we had rotated the cylinder that we were using to cut, so that the top and bottom edges were horizontal. Rather than going back to a previous save file, we'll just fix it at the polygon level.

First, you need to be in the Top viewport. Make sure that the barrel is still selected and type 4 to go into polygon mode. To make sure that you have the center polygons selected, press F2 (Shade Selected Faces Toggle) to display what you've got selected. If you don't have a mouse with a scroll wheel, it's a good idea to get one, as the wheel can be used to zoom in and out of the scene.

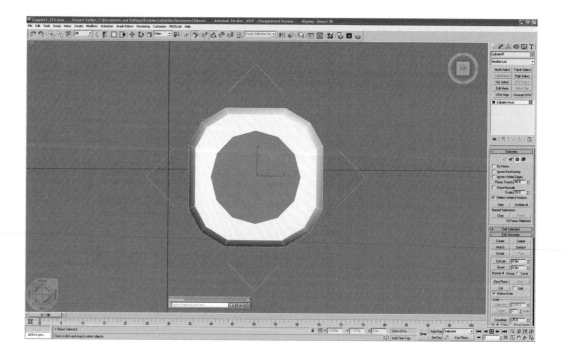

We need to rotate the polygons only a small amount, but looking at the barrel, it's impossible to see which way it should be. So we need to have a look at the edges of the polygons. Press 2 and drag-select the whole barrel. This step will show you how to find all the hidden edges.

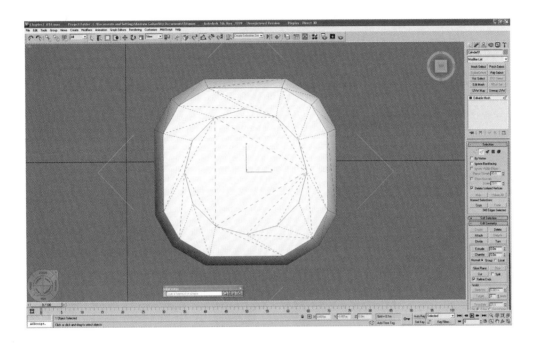

There are two ways to line the polygons up the way we want them. The first is to select just the edges we want to rotate and then rotate them, but the quicker way is to press 4, make sure the center polygons are selected, and rotate them, making sure that angle snap (A) is on.

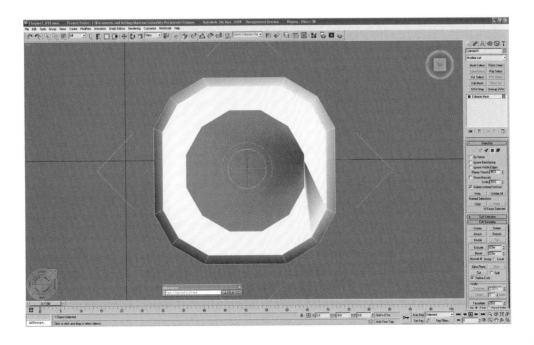

As you can see by the shadows that have appeared on the surface (smoothing), we have turned some of the polygons so that they now overlap. We just need to type 2 to modify the edges again and then select Turn from the Edit Geometry toolbar on the right.

Then we just need to click on the edges that are cutting through the corners of the central circle of polygons on the top of the barrel, turning them so that the polygons no longer overlap. If you see any other particularly long and thin triangles, you might want to turn the edges of those too, to tidy up the mesh.

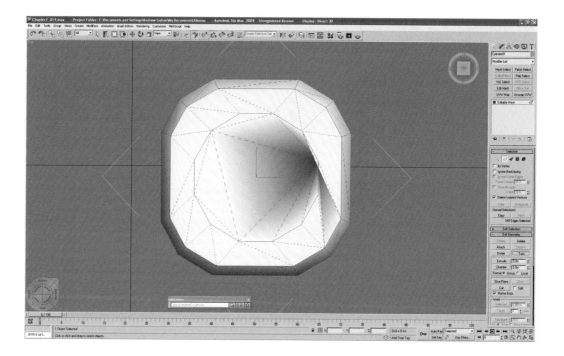

Next we will add the final details to the top of the barrel. First, let's extrude the center polygons to create the dip in the top of the barrel; then, we'll create a simple handle form.

Press P to jump into the Perspective window, then Z (Zoom Extents) so that you can see what you're doing. Buttons like Zoom Extents (Z) have a small triangle in the corner to show that they have multiple options. Left-click and hold on the triangle and the various options will be made available. In this case, there are two options: Zoom Extents and Zoom Extents Selected. I usually prefer Zoom Extents Selected, as it zooms into the selected part of the model only, usually making it easier to work. Have a look at all the other buttons and get familiar with what they do—getting up to speed with these early will save you a lot of time.

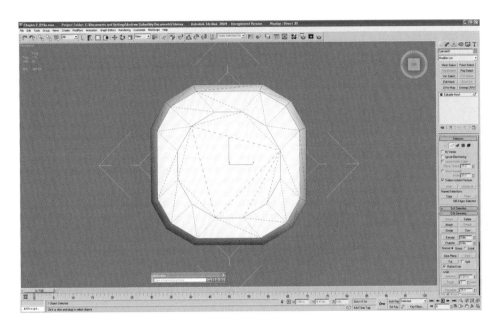

Next, we need to Extrude the top center polygons to create the sunken
form of the top of the barrel. Still in Editable mesh, select Extrude from Edit
Geometry, then click on the center polygons (select them if they have been
unselected) and drag the mouse toward you. This will create the extrusion.
Obviously if you had clicked and pushed forwards when extruding, you would
have created the same form, but as an addition to the geometry rather than a
subtraction. Next, just scale the polygons to create the indentation on the top.

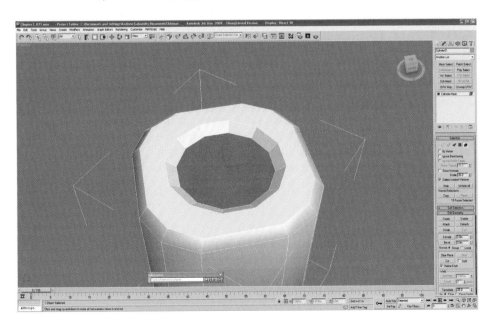

Now, we need to create a handle. We'll use Boolean again, as it's nice and quick. From the Top viewport, create a new cylinder in the center of the barrel. Give it eight sides and one height segment, and rotate it so that the top and bottom edges are horizontal. Then convert it to an Editable Mesh and scale it to the rough shape of a handle. Make sure that the handle shape intersects with the barrel shape as we will be using Union, but also that it stays in the center of the barrel and doesn't overlap the sloped edges of the indent. Just before you perform the Boolean, select the barrel instead of the handle. As before, select Create > Compound Objects > Boolean and make sure that Union is selected, click Pick Operand B, and then click to select the handle. Don't worry if the barrel suddenly changes color. It is just picking up the material from the cylinder (meaning that you didn't select the barrel before picking the handle as the Operand B). If this happened, just undo and try again. As we'll be texture-mapping the barrel, the color of the base material doesn't matter, but you may pick up some properties from the handle that could affect the way we map the barrel, so make sure you have the barrel selected before you click Operand B.

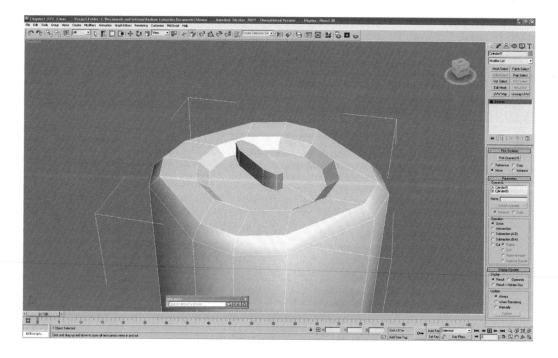

As we left a small gap between the handle and the edge of the barrel on the top of the barrel, let's join that up next. First select Modify, then right-click Boolean and convert to Editable Mesh. As we're not sure what the Boolean has done to the mesh let's have a look by going to Edge select (press 2) and drag-selecting all the edges on the top of the barrel (or using Ctrl+A). As you can see, there are a few really thin polygons around where we join the handle and the barrel together, so let's clean them up by selecting Edit Geometry and Turn. We'll turn each of the long edges until we get something that looks like this:

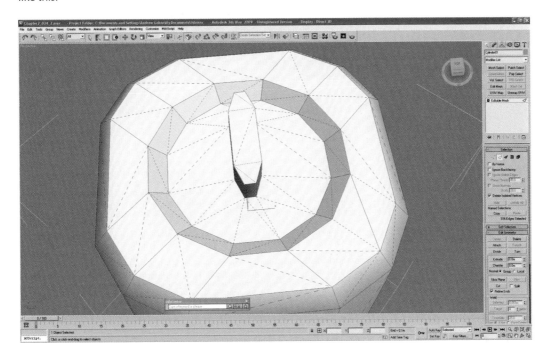

Remember to confirm that Ignore Backfacing is selected so that you don't accidentally turn edges on the back of the object by mistake. Errors like this can be quite time-consuming to fix if they go unnoticed, as you won't really want to use Undo if you've done a lot of modeling. Extra care should also be taken when welding vertices, as the errors can be difficult to undo if unnoticed.

Now we're going to weld a couple of vertices to make the handle look a little more realistic and like the reference. First, select Edit from the main toolbar at the top of the screen and select Object Properties to open a pop-up box. In Display Properties, check Backface Cull and click OK. By checking Backface Cull, all the polygons will be displayed only as one-sided. Next, we need to delete a few polygons and weld the vertices to fill the hole. If you weld the vertices first, you may unknowingly create some inner-facing polygons. Not only will these affect the smoothing on the object, but they can also make some of the UVW unwrapping confusing. Now let's delete the unwanted polygons. Rotate the barrel until you can clearly see the far side of the handle. We're looking to delete the three faces that make up the join between the handle and the edge of the barrel. Type 3 to select Face Selection and make sure that you can see which faces you have selected. Select the three faces and click Del to delete them.

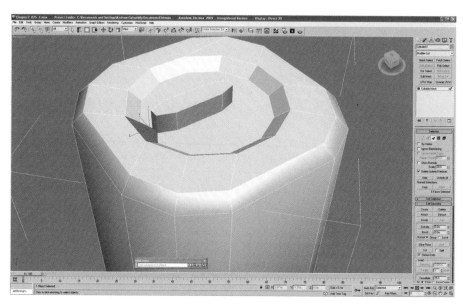

Next, we need to fill the gap by target-welding the vertices. Hit 1 to go to Vertex selection, and select Target from the Weld menu. Select the vertices on the open edge of the handle and drag them onto the vertices of the edge of the barrel. If the vertices seem to be sliding on a single axis, press F8 and then try again; you should now be able to move the vertices on multiple axes. Even without clicking F8, if you were to drag the cursor onto the correct vertex to weld, it would still have done it correctly. If you rotate the barrel around, enabling you to see the back of the handle to complete the weld accurately, you should end up with a shape like this:

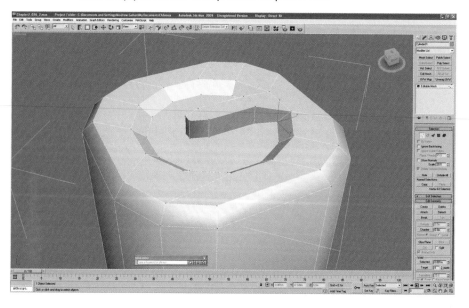

Now that we have the basic form of the top of the barrel, we need to compare it to the reference photo again and manipulate the top vertices so that they match the photo. Type T for Top viewport and then Alt+B to load up the background image. Select Img_0301.jpg \Chapter 2\Textures\ (from the Web site download), select Lock/Zoom Pan and Display Background, and click OK.

There are a couple of different ways in which we can manipulate the model and still see the reference photo. One is by pressing F3 to toggle wireframes, and the other is to set the image so that it is see-through. With the object selected, right-click on it to open up the Options fly-out. In Transform (bottom right), select Object Properties, select See-Through from the Display Properties, and click OK. This option changes the look of the object, enabling you to see both the polygons as well as the reference photo behind it. Now we just need to match up the vertices with the photo using Select and Move and also Select and Uniform Scale. To accurately select the lower vertices to taper the handle, jump into Perspective view and select them individually before returning to the Top viewport to spread them out.

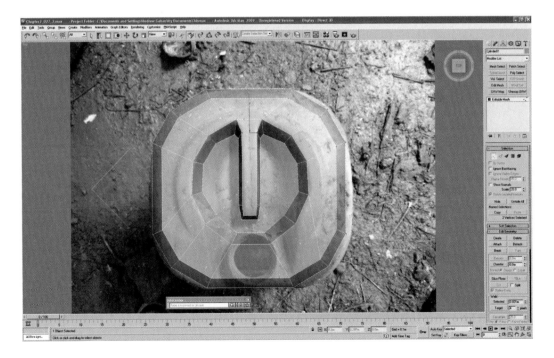

The last part of modeling that we need to complete before we start texture-mapping is the flattened area around the spout. In the Front viewport (shortcut F), make sure that the top of the handle is flush with the top of the barrel and that the vertices are laid out as shown.

Press F3 and rotate the barrel forwards slightly. Select the two edges on the top of the barrel nearest to you and move them down so that they are level with the indent on the top of the barrel. Once we've selected the edges, we need to jump back to the Front view (shortcut F) so that we can see how far we need to move them down. Hit F3 to make this easier. Moving these edges down has highlighted how a few of the edges need to be turned so that the curves on the barrel look more realistic.

Press F2 and then Ctrl+A to display all the edges. Have a look to see whether you can improve some of the curves by turning edges. This isn't important; it just improves the form of the model when viewed from some acute angles.

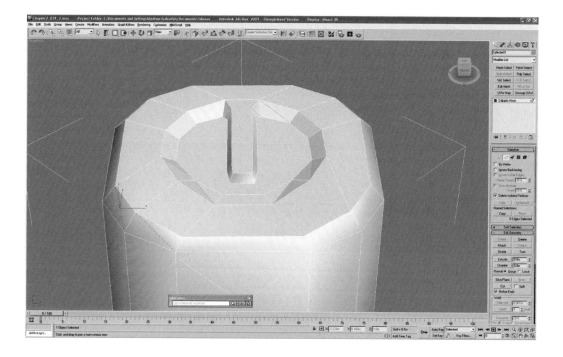

Now we need to move onto texture-mapping the barrel. This time we will be using just one texture map to map the whole of the barrel. Again, the texture map has been created from the reference photos, but this time all the photos have been blended together in Adobe Photoshop as they would be for use in a game. We'll cover creating textures from photos in the next tutorial, but for this one, use the texture map that I've already created.

First of all, let's get rid of the background image and return the barrel to solid shading (Alt+B, uncheck Display Background Image, click OK. Then right-click on the barrel, select Object Properties, uncheck See-Through, and click OK).

Next we need to open up the Material Editor (on the top toolbar or click M). Then click the map button next to Diffuse in Blinn Basic Parameters. In Blinn Basic Parameters, click on the box next to Bitmap to load the texture and select Drum001_004.jpg in \Chapter 2\Textures\ (from the Web site download) and click Open. Next, click Assign Material to Selection; you should see the texture map applied to the barrel object.

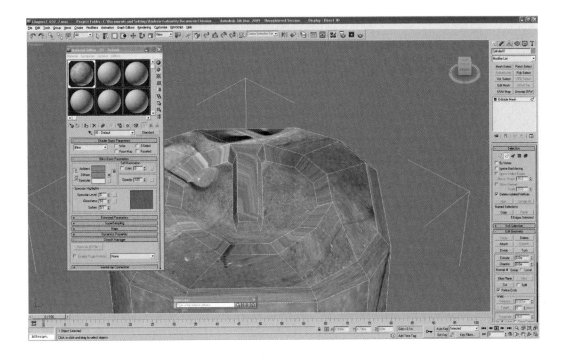

You can now close the Material Editor. At this point, although we have applied the texture map to the object, the only mapping coordinates on the barrel are from when you initially created it, so we need to apply new ones. We'll map the sides of the barrel first, and then we'll map the top and bottom.

Go to the Front viewport (F) and Zoom Extents so that you can see the whole barrel. If the top of the handle is sticking out above the barrel, select the vertices and drag them down so that they are level with the top of the barrel.

Select Editable Mesh, if it isn't selected already, and then select Edit Polygon (shortcut 4). Drag select all of the barrel's side faces, including the small bevels on the top and bottom. Take care not to select the extra polygons that make up the handle detail on the top.

Next, click UVW Map from the modifier list (refer to Chapter 1 if you haven't completed it) and check Cylindrical in Parameters > Mapping. On this model, we will try to wrap the top mapping over smoothly from the sides, so we also need to check Flip in the V Tile Mapping parameters. Press F3 and go to Perspective view to see what you have.

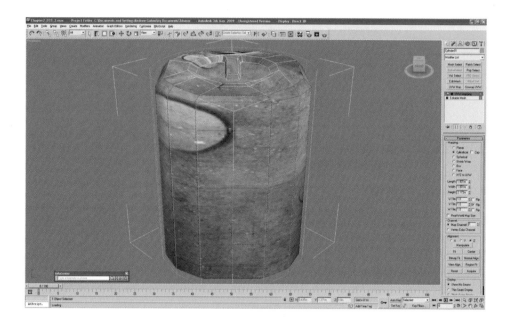

Although the mapping looks really rough and there seem to be parts of the barrel map everywhere, we should at least see the texture map wrapping continually around the sides of the cylinder.

Next, we're going to slightly rotate the mapping on the sides of the barrel so that the top and the sides line up. Rotate your view around the barrel so that the handle is pointing away from you, and then click on UVW Mapping in the

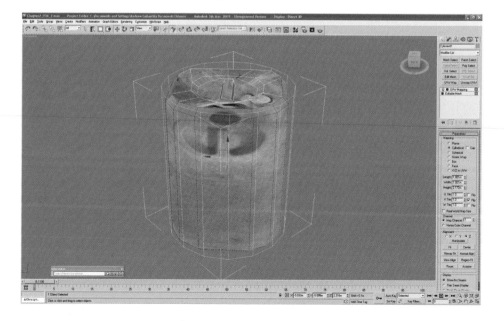

modifier stack to select the sub-tree (which will turn yellow to indicate the mode change). Then choose Select and Rotate and rotate the mapping (not the model) until the handle on the map roughly lines up with the handle on the model (even though it is below it).

Next, we'll adjust the UVW coordinates so that the top and bottom details on the texture map are no longer seen on the sides of the barrel. Select Unwrap UVW from the modifier list and then select Edit from the Parameters rollout. The Edit UVW box should appear on screen.

Now go to the top right-hand corner, open up the drop-down menu, and select the texture map, which is map #1 in the list. This step shows the texture map and also how the polygons are laid out on it.

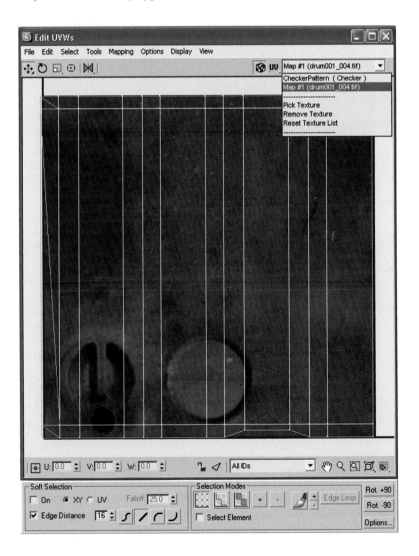

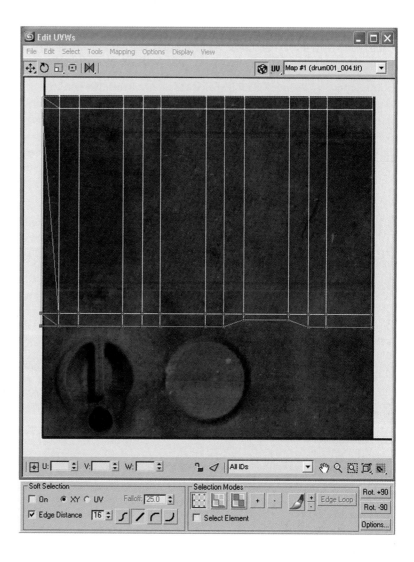

We now need to move some of the vertices around in the Edit UVW window so that the texture map fits our barrel model a little better. First, select the bottom two rows of vertices in the window and move them vertically up just past the top details on the texture map. If you hold Shift down while you move them, they will move in a straight line up or across.

You can close the Edit UVW window now and have a look at your barrel. You should now see that the sides of the model are mapped. All we have to do is map the top and bottom and we're pretty much done.

As the top and bottom mapping will be pretty much the same, we can use one planar map to apply mapping coordinates to both the top and bottom. We will then unwrap them separately as we have just done.

Now we will add Edit Mesh to the stack from the Modifier List (the button above UVW Map; refer to Chapter 1 if it isn't there). Then press 4 to edit polygons, and from the top menu, choose Edit > Select Invert (Ctrl+I) to select all the remaining polygons to map. You should now have all the polygons on the top and bottom of the barrel selected.

We now need to go to Top viewport (shortcut T) and click UVW Map and make sure that Planar is selected in the Mapping Parameters.

Scroll down the right-hand side to Alignment and select View Align. The texture map will be aligned to the Top viewport, not the model's transform. Select Fit (still in Alignment) so that the texture fits to the selected polygons only, with no overlap.

Finally, in Mapping, as we know that the top and bottom only take a small amount of the texture page, we can set the U Tile to 0.3 and the V Tile to 0.3. This step makes unwrapping the UVs a bit easier, as they are now closer to their final position. You should now see the texture map for the top of the barrel almost aligned.

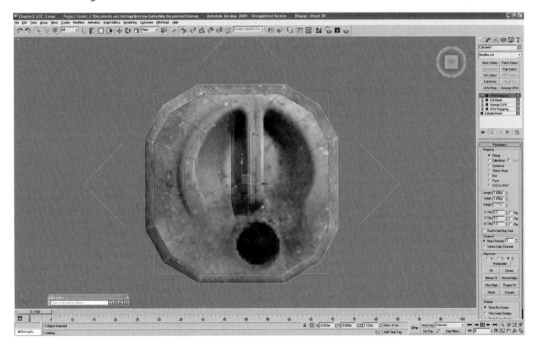

Select Unwrap UVW (from the modifier list), then select Edit and pick Map #1 from the drop-down menu in the Edit UVW window that appears. Using Zoom Region, we need to get in close to the vertices so that we can adjust the UVs accurately. Click Ctrl+A to select all the vertices. Now we can scale them up so that they fit the rough shape of the barrel a little better. Don't worry too much about getting them pixel perfect-at this point—we can always fine-tune them later. You should end up with something like this:

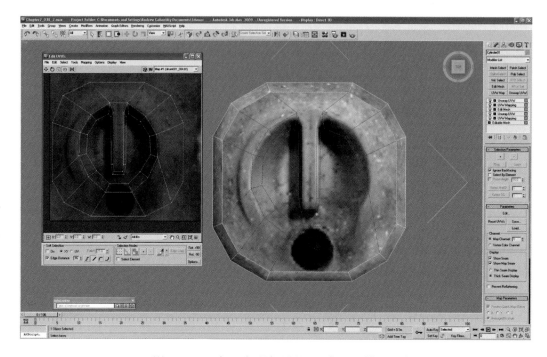

We can now close the Edit UVW window and have a look at what we have so far. To really see what we've got, we need to add another Edit Mesh to the Modifier stack and press F4 so that we can see the joins in the mapping between the top of the barrel and the sides.

Without using programs like Maxon's BodyPaint 3D (http://www.maxon. net), it is extremely difficult to create textures that wrap seamlessly around 3D models, so don't worry too much if you can see a slight edge. Most imperfections like this will never be seen in a game, so we don't dwell on them. If however, you are working at a studio and this problem arises … well, you know what to put on your purchase request.

Now we're in the home stretch. All we need to do is adjust the UVs on the bottom of the model and we're done—or almost done.

Jump into the Front viewport and deselect all the polygons on the top of the barrel (hit F and then Ctrl + Alt + Z) and deselect the polygons on the top of the barrel (click Select Object and while holding Alt, drag and deselect the top polygons). Click P for perspective view, rotate the barrel so that you can see the bottom polygons, and we'll map the last part.

Once again, select Unwrap UVW from the modifier list, select Edit (from Parameters), and select Map #1 from the drop-down menu in the Edit UVW window that appears. All we need to do now is to slide the vertices along to the right to match up with the bottom of the barrel, and we're almost done. Now click Ctrl + A to select all the vertices, and move them into place using the Move tool.

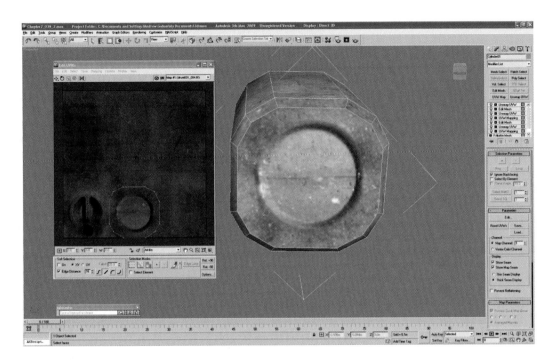

Once again, close the Edit UVW window, apply an Edit Mesh to the model, and press F4 so that you can see the model fully mapped. If there are any areas that look stretched, select the polygons and edit the UVW unwrapping until you are happy. Render the model in the same way that you rendered the cardboard box from Chapter 1, print it, and add it to your portfolio.

Congratulations! You've completed the second chapter and I hope that you learned a few new techniques. With the skills that you've learned so far, you should be able to make almost any low-poly object. So well done—you're on your way.

CHAPTER 3

Creating Texture Maps from Photographs Using Photoshop

In this tutorial, I cover the basics of creating texture maps from photographs. We will be creating the type of texture maps that we used in the cardboard box and plastic barrel tutorials. We will then create some alpha maps and a model to put one of the maps on to.

Camera

The first thing to consider when taking photographs to be used for texture map creation or reference is what camera to use. When I was in charge of camera equipment at Evolution Studios, almost every time someone new asked to sign a camera out, I was asked, "Which camera can I take?" My response was always, "Which camera do you know how to use?" All too often, when given a choice of cameras, most people will take the most expensive, or the one with the most megapixels, or the one with the biggest lens. Well you would too, wouldn't you? But there is absolutely no point if you don't know how to use it.

So we need to take some photos to use as reference. If you don't have a digital camera, and you're serious about doing 3D professionally, you should probably think about buying one. You don't need to fork over thousands on 12-megapixel SLRs; a decent compact digital camera will do, at least for now. As I've been doing this professionally for fifteen years, I have a few to choose from, but one of my favorites is a little Canon Digital IXUS. These ultra-compact cameras are great because they have a flash and a reasonable zoom, and they are small enough to put in the pocket of your jeans, so you will never miss a photo opportunity. I always carry a Canon IXUS with me wherever I go.

Photo Shoot

Ideally, you should try to take reference photos on a neutral day. A light overcast day is ideal, as it means that you won't have any shadows on your photograph. England is great for this, but if you live in one of the sunnier areas of the world, pick a time when there aren't long shadows across everything that you want to photograph. Taking photos in bright light or where there are a lot of shadows on the subject matter can mean that you have to do a lot of retouch work (sometimes many days' worth), as you'll need to go through and retouch every image you want to use as a texture. It may be worth postponing the photo shoot to another day, if you can, to prevent this kind of extra work.

One final point to consider when you are taking reference photos is that if you see something that is really good and you can't miss taking a photo of it, remember to take more than one shot. When you see a great photo opportunity, it's a terrible shame to stop the car and take the shot, only to find out when you get home that it wasn't properly exposed or that you shook the camera, or whatever. If it's worth stopping for to take one shot, it's worth taking a few, just to make sure.

There is a fantastic book written by Luke Ahearn called *3D Game Textures: Create Professional Game Art Using Photoshop* (Focal Press, ISBN-10: 0-240-80768-5). If you are new to modeling or creating texture maps, I highly recommend that you buy this for your bookshelf. It covers most aspects of creating texture maps and how to use them, in far more detail than I can do in one chapter here.

Creating the Cardboard Box Texture Map

On to the texture creation for a cardboard box. I chose this model for its simplicity. The model has only six polygons, which we will map with six separate texture maps. I have included a number of photographs of boxes that I have taken in fairly good condition. These can be downloaded from the Web site, under \Chapter 3\Source Files\box photos\6photos.jpg

As in the first tutorial, we are not too concerned with laying out all the sides of the box on one texture sheet; we're just quickly throwing the textures out, for you to get modeling quickly.

If you can, take some photos of something yourself, instead of using the ones provided on the disc. This is a great habit to get into, and you'll learn far more by completing the whole exercise yourself. You'll also be able to add this model to your portfolio if you use your own photos.

From whatever source, you should have six photos of a box-like object. You may have decided to take photos of a cereal box, a DVD player, or even a piece of furniture, but as long as you have some photos of a square or rectangular object, we can progress.

Next, upload the first photograph into Photoshop and drag some rough guide lines around the straight edges of the box. We're going to use these to make sure the box is square when creating the texture. Then using the Rectangular Marquee tool, I select an area around the box in the photo and crop the image. Make sure that you don't crop to the guidelines—we need a little extra to play with.

With the cropped area still selected, use Edit > Transform > Skew to line up the edges of the box roughly with the guide lines. Once you're satisfied that the box texture is approximately squared and that the Skew modifier hasn't distorted the image, crop it at the guidelines.

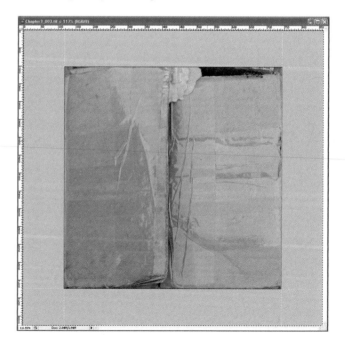

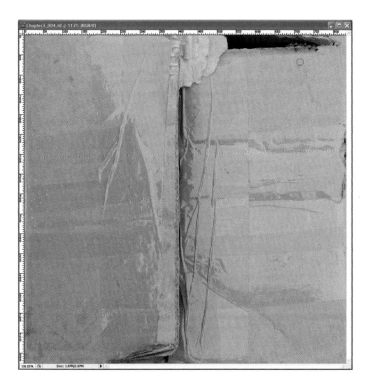

If the box has slightly rounded corners, use the Clone Stamp tool or the Healing Brush tool to tidy up the edges and corners of the image. Then go to Image > Image Size and rescale the image to a size that we can use in a game.

In this case, I've selected 256 × 256 pixels. This size might be considered fairly large for a lot of game engines, for such a small asset, but as this will be primarily for a portfolio composition, let's keep it quite high. You don't have to scale the proportions down at all, but it helps to make scenes more believable if all the pixels in the scene are approximately the same size.

To explain this a little more, if your next asset to be built were half the size of this box, you would probably want to use a texture map that is half the size. That way, if they are positioned next to each other in the scene, one won't look like it's at a higher resolution than the other.

After repeating this exercise with all the other photos of the box, you should be left with a set of six new texture maps. You could speed up this process by taking only a photo of the top of your box and a photo of one of the sides and then using only two textures on the box that you build. This is a great trick for texture memory usage in a game (you'll use much less texture memory) and you'll also be able to complete the build in a fraction of the time.

Here are the completed textures:

Top

Bottom

Side 1

Side 2

Side 3

Side 4

Creating the Barrel Texture Map

First, open up the reference photos from \Chapter 3\Source Files\Barrel Photos\ (from the Web site download) in Adobe Photoshop. You will definitely need Photoshop for this part of the texture creation process, as you'll have to use some of Photoshop's tools to create the seamless blends. You should see that we have a top and bottom for the barrel and also four side photos.

What we are going to try to do is to recreate the key parts of the barrel from the photographs provided and fit it all neatly onto a 1024 × 1024 texture page. This time, instead of cropping each photograph and using the resulting image for each side of the model as we did with the cardboard box, we're going to blend key parts of some of the photographs together to make something that looks believable and is also laid out neatly. In the games industry, it's very important to have very efficient texture pages. An efficient texture page uses up as much of the page as possible and does not have lots of gaps or unused space that the model doesn't use.

As you can see from this flower image, there is the least amount of texture map waste around the flower as possible (shown in green). This is a good example of minimizing waste on a texture sheet. Although there is quite a lot of waste (shown in green), it is the least amount possible to produce the right effect.

There are a few different ways that you can create texture maps for models like this, but here is the method that I think is most appropriate for this exercise. First of all, we need to think about how the barrel texture can be laid out or unwrapped. We want to represent the key components of the photos, and we want the barrel to look as realistic as possible when we finish.

For this model, I think that there should be three main parts to the texture map: the top, the bottom, and the sides. To make the model look realistic when it is mapped, we want as few joins on the texture map as possible, as all of the edges on this model are rounded. If we were modeling an asset like the cardboard box again, this issue wouldn't matter, as the joins on each of the sides are hidden by the corners and also by the smoothing groups. But for this model, we'll need to treat the edges differently.

Although the barrel shape has flat sides, its corners are rounded, so in this instance we should consider mapping the sides with cylindrical mapping. This means that the texture for this part of the model needs to "tile" (that is, to wrap seamlessly around the model). With this in mind, we will dedicate most of the texture page to the sides, but we'll also make sure that it covers the top area of the texture completely (from left to right) so that we can use the Offset tool in Photoshop. This approach will enable us to tile the texture and thus to seamlessly map all the sides on the barrel.

To keep the texture resolution roughly even across the model, allow the top and bottom of the barrel around 30% of the height of the texture page as shown in the figure.

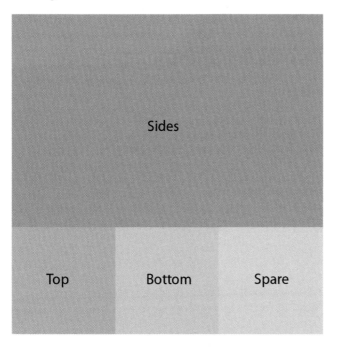

Dividing up the texture map in this way should give us plenty of room for the top and bottom details and also enable us to tile the side's part of the map easily in Photoshop. It does, however, leave us a small spare area. We can use this for any extra details that we haven't thought of yet, or maybe a label or some other feature not on the source photo. Dividing up the texture page in this way will mean that we will not be using each side of the barrel directly from the photograph. As texture pages need to be either square (512 × 512) or divisible by two (1024 × 512), we would have to cram and stretch the four sides of the barrel into this area, which wouldn't really work, as it would cause distortions.

A texture that is divisible by two could be used, which would give us plenty of room for the four sides and the top and bottom, but again, we would still be stretching the photo reference to use the texture page efficiently, so we will opt for the first layout, as it is closer to the reference.

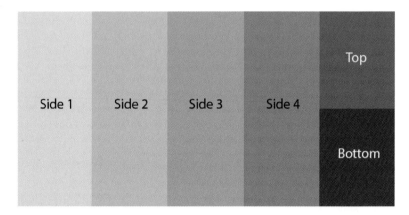

Obviously, if you never intend to put your texture maps into a game engine, you could make them any size or shape you like. The best way to do this is to model your barrel, then take screen grabs or wireframe renders of the front, sides, top, and bottom, and use them as a guide for your map. There are also other plug-ins and tools that help, but these are the simplest methods to get you started.

Let's get started with the texture map creation. First, open up the reference photos from \Chapter 3\Source Files\Drum Photos\ (from the Web site download), and copy and paste the components that you'd like to see on your texture map into a new Photoshop file. Once you have the main components for the sides, crop the image and save it out. Next, flatten the image by going to Layer > Flatten Image. This step should give you a nice canvas to start to work on.

Next, use a combination of the Clone Stamp tool (shortcut S) and the Healing Brush tool (J) to cover up the parts of the texture map that we don't want. Start with the really dark areas and the lines that don't line up by replacing them with the more generic parts that we do want. If you have an older version of Photoshop, you'll probably just have the Clone Stamp tool. Don't worry—you'll do just fine using that.

If you haven't used these tools before, here are some basic instructions. Start by holding down Alt and left-clicking the area of the texture map that you want to clone from, then just left-click and hold to paint over the area that you want to change. Experiment with the opacity settings of the tools for varied effects.

One thing to watch out for when creating texture maps with these tools is not to repeat obvious areas of the texture. This sort of repetition really stands out and ruins the illusion of your model being real. Any bright spots or dark creases should only exist once, or be completely removed. The horizontal lines around the barrel should be removed too as we'll add these back in later.

As you can see from this image, after only a few minutes of cloning and healing, the texture map is starting to take shape.

Continue this process until you have eliminated all the areas of the texture map that we don't need and you have a fairly generic barrel texture. If the Healing tool is taking a long time to calculate, just resize the image so that it is smaller and use slightly shorter brushstrokes; this should improve the update speed.

Let's make sure that the image tiles. To do this, we use the Offset tool in Photoshop: Filter > Other > Offset…and select an offset so that the join mark is roughly in the center of the image.

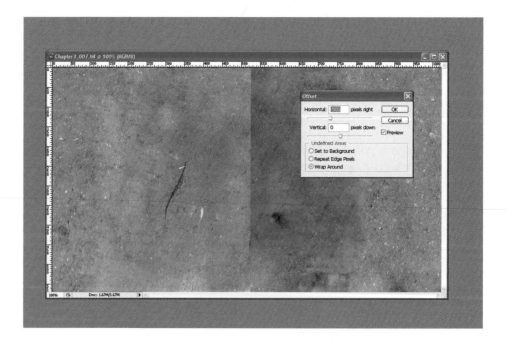

Use the same Heal and Clone tools to remove the join line down the center of the texture map. Once the join is removed, we can either leave the texture map as it is or offset it back to its original position. I always like to offset it back, but there's no need, as this texture map now tiles on the horizontal axis. Once finished, you should end up with something like this:

Now we need to add the other details of the texture map. As we didn't create the first part of the texture page with any size considerations, let's do that next. We need to start to lay out the texture map so that the new components will be in the right place and at the right scale. We need to create a new image to lay out our map, so create a new file measuring 1024 × 1024 pixels. Go to Edit > Preferences and set the rulers to measure in pixels, then press Ctrl + R to show the rulers, if they are not already displayed. We next need to create a few guidelines to help us with the proportions of the rest of the texture. To do this, click on the ruler on the left-hand side of the image and drag a guide out to 341 pixels. Just drag it out to approximately 341 pixels, and use the Move tool (V) along with the Zoom tool (Z) to make it accurate. Do this again from the left margin to 682 pixels and again from the top margin to 682 pixels. This should give you perfectly measured guidelines to fit the top and bottom of the barrel on the texture map.

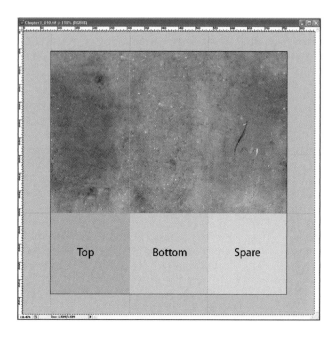

Next, cut out the top and bottom of the barrel from the photo reference and lay them out in the gaps on the texture map.

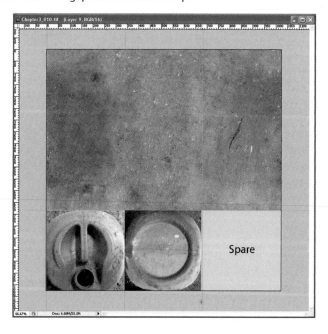

Then clone and heal the areas around the top and bottom of the barrel so that they blend into the surrounding area. You can adjust these joins once you have the texture mapped onto the model. We might make these areas slightly lighter or darker, depending on their corresponding edge on the model. We then fill in the blank space on the map with base texture, or we can choose to leave it blank, so that we know there is some spare room on the texture map, should we come back to this model in the future to make changes or add details.

Finally, we need to create a new layer and draw the dark and light lines across the sides to suggest that there is extra detail where there isn't—and our texture page is complete.

Creating Alpha Maps

"Alpha maps" are partially transparent maps used for 3D models that need to create the illusion of complexity without having lots of polygon detail. One of the most popular uses for alpha maps is foliage (trees, bushes, and plants). For instance, when creating the illusion of lots of trees in an in game environment, if we were to model and texture every leaf on a tree, not only would it take the artist a long time, but it would also be expensive for the 3D engine to run. If you needed to show thousands of trees in a game, then the problems would be thousands of times worse. Alpha maps do not come without cost, but they are usually preferable than this approach, called "poly modeling," where thousands of instances of the model are to be used.

So, to create an alpha map from a photo, we first need to take the reference image. It can be really useful if the photo is taken with a neutral background to the image. Good examples include taking a photo of a tree against the sky, holding up a white sheet behind a bush, or even just photographing leaves against a white foam board. Obviously, smaller items like chocolate bar wrappers or leaves can just be scanned, but remember to make sure that they are clean before you scan them. We don't have to use a photograph to create alpha maps; we can also create them from scratch in Photoshop or a similar graphics package.

Once you have the reference image to create the alpha map from, remove all of the extra pixels on the photograph that you don't want to be included on the image. For this step, I use Photoshop again. Open the image in Photoshop. (If you are using an application other than Photoshop, you should really think about upgrading, as it is the industry-standard package for this type of work.) Once you have the photograph loaded up, create a duplicate layer of the image. I always create an extra "empty" layer beneath my duplicated background layer, which I fill in neon pink or green so that I can clearly see what I am taking away and what parts of the photograph remain.

Remove the parts of the photograph that you do not want to see on the 3D model in the alpha map. I tend to use the Magic Wand tool or the Eraser tool for this. There are a number of plug-ins for Photoshop that help to do this, such as Fluid Mask 3 from Virtus, but the Magic Wand and Eraser tools work well enough for most artists.

Once you have the flower cut out, use the Magic Wand tool to select the empty area. Go to Select > Inverse so that you now only have the flower selected. Finally, use Select > Modify > Contract, and contract by 1 pixel. The reason we are reducing the selection by 1 pixel is to prevent a halo on the areas around the edges of the alpha.

Create a new layer with a white background (RGB 255,255,255) and fill the selected area in black (RGB 0,0,0). The white area of this layer will be the part of the texture we see in a game on the alpha map, and the black area will be the transparent part. The RGB values are important when creating alpha maps, as 0,0,0 is completely invisible and 255,255,255 is completely opaque, so if you were to choose values between, they would be semi-transparent.

We now need to copy this whole layer (Ctrl+A and then Ctrl+C) and then copy it into an alpha channel in the Channels tab (next to the Layers tab). To do this, click the Channels tab and then click on the tiny arrow on the right-hand side, just right of the Paths tab. This will open up a fly-out box. Click New Channel on the fly-out box and name the channel Alpha 1 (it may default to this). Now paste the alpha information into this channel by using Ctrl+V. The final thing to do is to invert this channel so that the flower part is white. To do this, go to Image > Adjustments ≥ Invert or just use the shortcut Ctrl+I. Our alpha channel is complete. Now we need to save the image as Flower.tga.

It's important to save this image with a TGA extension, as it is a lossless format, but more importantly, TGAs support the alpha content of the file via the alpha channels, which will be picked up in 3 ds Max. You could also use PNG or DDS for your alpha maps, but they are not as straightforward and therefore aren't covered here.

Alpha Maps in 3ds Max

To view this map in 3 ds Max, create a simple primitive object and apply our Flower.TGA texture map to it. Open up Max, go to Create > Box, and then create a box of any dimensions, then hit Z to Zoom Extents All. With the box still selected, go to Modify > UVW Map and select Box from the mapping parameters.

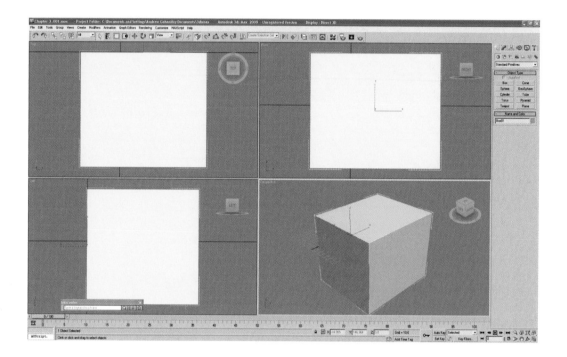

Next, open up the Material Editor (shortcut M), click Diffuse > Bitmap and then load \Chapter 3\Source Files\Flower.TGA (from the Web site download). Still in the Material Editor, click the Assign Material to Selection and Show Map in Viewport buttons and you should see the flower image mapped neatly on all sides of the box.

Next, click the Go To Parent button in the Material Editor and open up the Maps rollout menu. Check the box on the left of Opacity and then click the None button to the right to open the Material/Map Browser window. Double-click Bitmap and open up the Flower.TGA file as before. This time, in the Bitmap Parameters select Alpha in the Mono Channel Output box. This basically tells 3 ds Max that we want to alpha this bitmap. Go to Rendering (press F10) and then click the Render button; you should see our flower alpha map clearly rendered against the background (which I have made light gray).

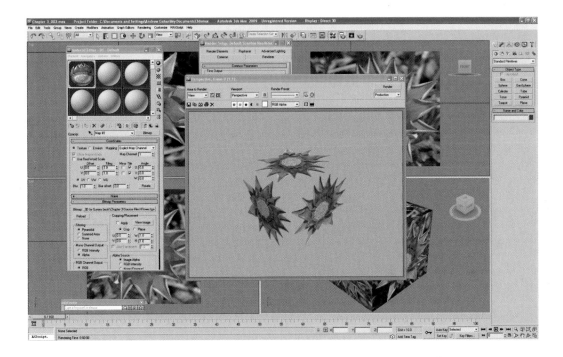

Alpha maps can be used on models with any number of polygons. As long as you take care to lay out the UVs properly, you can work with any number of polygons and bitmaps, just like any other type of modeling. Alpha maps can also be separate files to the diffuse texture and don't need to be in an alpha channel defined within the TGA file. They can be other file formats, too. The reason we use TGA (or DDS) for alphas is that we don't need to define and load a separate alpha map into the game engine, which makes it more economical, but it also means that we don't load up the wrong alpha map or delete or modify it by accident.

Next, we'll create another alpha mapped model to be used in one of your scenes later on.

Creating a Tiling Alpha Map

For this exercise, we will create another texture map from a photograph, but this time we'll make it tile in both the x- and y-axes. We need to start with some source material. We're going to make some chicken wire from this reference photo:

As you can see, it's not the greatest reference photo in the world, but often you have to make do with what you can get your hands on, and this is a good example of making something good from very little.

Start to build up a reference library of your own by filing good reference images when you find or take them. This habit will help you immensely if you turn professional. Most artists that I know have a secret stash of photos that they've taken throughout the years of stuff that they've either needed in the past or that they think will come in handy at some point.

Common models like traffic cones and street signs often come in handy for populating all sorts of virtual worlds, so if you take a good set of reference photos once, they can serve you for many years. Construction vehicles like diggers and tractors come in handy too—not to mention generic trees and plants. As you travel around, keep your camera handy and build up your collection. Remember to organize your photos so that you know where everything is, or even meta-tag them so that you can search them like a database.

Let's move on with the texture map. Just like with the flower alpha map, make a copy of the background layer and add a brightly colored layer in between so that you can see what you're erasing. Take out all the areas of the map that you don't need. For this particular map, it's probably best if we just use the Eraser tool (E) instead of the Magic Wand tool, as the pixels we want to delete are closely matched in color to the ones we want to keep.

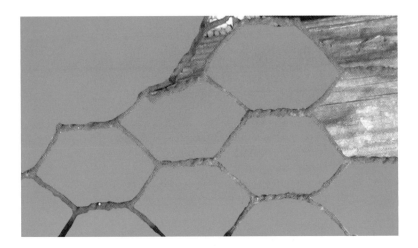

Keep on erasing until all you have left is the chicken wire part of the texture. Create a new image measuring 512 × 512 pixels and paste our piece of chicken wire on it. Using all the tools we've used before (Copy and Paste, Clone, Skew, Offset…), keep working on the texture until you have a basic tiling pattern.

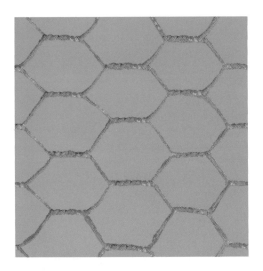
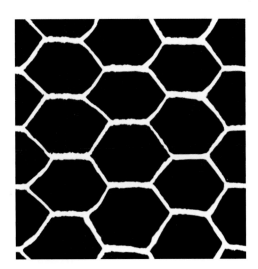

Use the same techniques as earlier to create the alpha version of the texture and add it to the alpha channel of a TGA file or save it as a separate alpha TIF file.

It's good practice at this point to fill in the bright neon color with one a little closer to the chicken wire color; this step will help prevent halos or green pixels from showing on the model if your alpha map does not match perfectly.

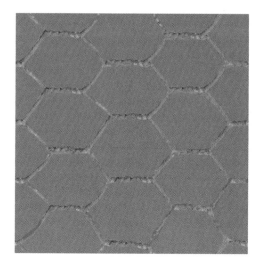

Finally, we need to create a chicken wire model onto which we will map the texture. Here is the texture mapped onto a simple box, tiled ten times in both the U and the V.

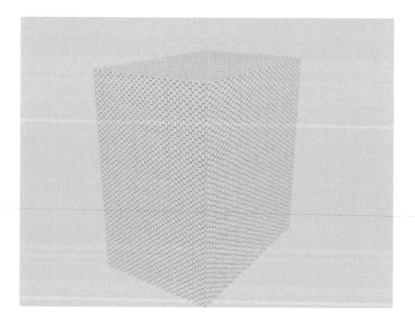

Congratulations! You've now completed Chapter 3—well done. You should now have the ability to create most primitive objects in 3ds Max and also to create texture maps for them in Photoshop.

At this point, feel free to move on or to play around with what you have learned so far. And don't feel that you have to rush on to Chapter 4. You will probably retain all the stuff you've learned so far much better if you go over it a few times, so maybe before you move on, practice what you've learned and reread these first few chapters—it might help speed you along in the long run.

The next chapter is written by Davie Wilson, a lecturer from Derby University in the United Kingdom. In it, he covers the theory and construction of normal maps.

CHAPTER 4

Creating Normal Maps Using Photoshop and Crazy Bump

Introduction

A "normal map" is the latest buzzword for artists creating assets for next-generation videogames. These maps are used to increase the level of detail and fidelity in modern videogames. Creating a normal map is an additional process that increases the amount of time to create an asset. Normal maps are applied to a model like a texture, but a common mistake is to treat them as conventional textures. There are a number of reasons why your approach to creating and applying normal maps should be different from conventional model construction and texturing. This chapter explains the concept of normal mapping and how to create and implement normal maps efficiently and effectively.

There is more than one type of normal map. We will focus on the most common type used for games development. This is a "tangent-based normal map," or "tangent map." You can identify this type of normal map easily, as it is mostly blue in color.

It's All in the Lighting

An object appears three-dimensional because of how it is lit. The contrast between the parts of the objects that are lit and the parts that are in shadow define the form.

The shapes in the following figure are the same; the shape on the left has no lighting attributes, whereas the shape on the right has lighting and shading applied, and it is quite clear to see that the shape has a three-dimensional form.

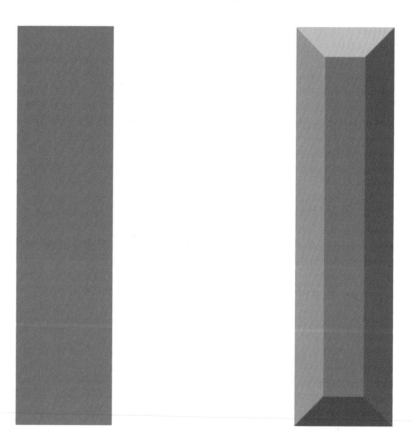

The Role of the Normal Map

Having an understanding of how games are lit will help you to understand how to use normal maps. Game lighting tries to replicate real lights in an economical and simplistic way.

Each surface on a model has a normal direction (imagine a perpendicular line extending from the surface of the polygon). See the following figure.

If the normal map is aligned with the direction of the light, it receives the maximum light value. However, if the surface is facing the opposite direction, it receives no lighting values and therefore is in shade.

Modern games that implement normal maps use a "per-pixel" lighting engine. In a per-pixel lighting engine, normal maps are used to describe the normal direction of each pixel of an object. They do this by using Red, Green, and Blue channels in the texture to store a directional value that describes their normal direction in either x, y, or z. The following example is a normal map that represents a hemisphere.

The red and green channels use a grayscale value ranging from black to white to represent the normal direction along the x- and y-axes. In a tangent map, the blue channel can represent only a positive value, so the grayscale value represented ranges from 50% gray to white.

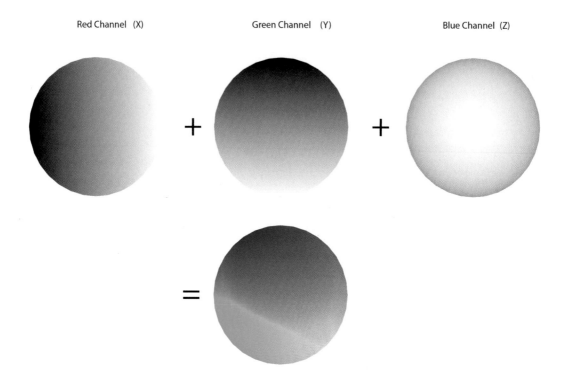

Red Channel (X)   Green Channel (Y)   Blue Channel (Z)

When these values are combined they create a normal direction for each pixel applied to the model. This is interpreted by the lighting engine as to how the surface should be represented when lit. These details react to lighting in real time as if they are actually modeled into the surface. The detail of a normal map is restricted only by the resolution of the pixels applied to the model and the compression used in the texture.

Using Normal Maps in Practice

There are two main types of detail that normal maps are used to represent; these can be categorized as follows.

High-Frequency Detail

These are small surface details like scratches, lumps, and bumps. These are typically produced from images using an automated process, because modeling this type of detail would be time-consuming.

Low-Frequency Detail

This type of detail describes the overall form of a complex object that typically can be projected as surface normal information onto the UVs of a game resolution object of less detail. The resulting normal map gives this object the appearance of having a higher level of detail to describe its form. This process is time-consuming, as two models have to be created to produce the final result, so it is usually reserved for organic or feature assets. For this reason, this technique is popular when creating characters.

These techniques can be combined to create more complex normal maps that are created in a realistic timescale.

Creating a Weathered Door with a Tiled Normal Map

The following tutorial will focus on how to create a normal map for a simple scene asset. The important difference between this type of object and a character is mainly time. When making games, you are always working with a deadline. A character that is central to the action could take anywhere up to a couple of months to create; it would undoubtedly be constructed in high resolution first, and the details from this model would be projected onto a game resolution version using a normal map; it would have a complex shader network with many texture maps. In contrast, an environment or scene asset would be part of a collection of assets and therefore would not have the same level of time allocated to it.

In this exercise, we will create a door with some panel detailing. This door is part of a dilapidated warehouse scene, so it must look relatively scruffy. This is straightforward to model and texture and it serves as a good host for the type of normal mapping process common for a simple game asset. By the end of this tutorial, you will have created a door with a tiled normal map that will have been created using a combination of surface transfer techniques, as well as by generating normal mapping detail directly from bitmaps. In reality, given that this door is meant to be weathered, I would probably choose to not tile it, but instead would make the texture unique. However, this exercise demonstrates the process of tiling a normal map on a simple object well, and this is a valuable lesson to learn for your own projects.

Following are some reference photos of a door; these can be found in \Chapter 4\images\ref\ (downloadable from the Web site). The first task is to look at the details.

The door on page 76 will be used to help create the detail for the normal map. The image above will be used as reference for the weathered and distressed look of the door that will be applied to the final model.

Let's create a normal map for this door. The door has a natural repeating form; therefore, it is relatively easy to create a repeating tiled texture. The following figure is a good example of high-frequency detail. The grain of the wood would take far too long to model; and because this detail does not form any complex shapes in the surface, it is an ideal candidate for automatic generation from the photographic reference.

The following figure is an example of low-frequency and high-frequency detail combined.

To get the best representation of the panel relief, this detail should be modeled and then projected onto a game detail surface. This type of detail would be very hard to replicate using an automated process.

The following figure shows a quick test of the effect of converting an image into a normal map, to qualify our reasons for using two different processes to create the door.

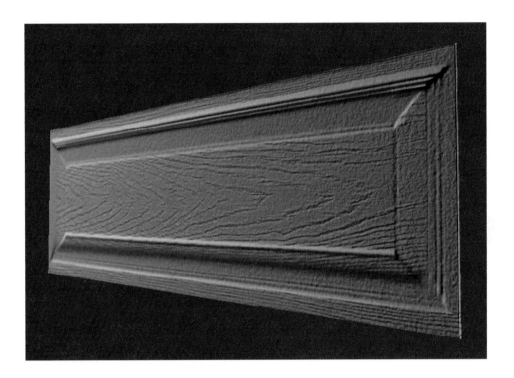

This preview is taken form Ryan Clark's Crazy Bump software (we will discuss this later). The normal map has been generated from the following image.

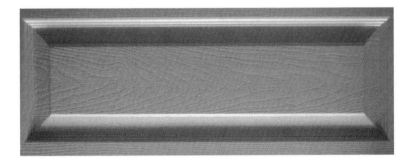

As you can clearly see, the high-frequency detail has transferred really well. The low-frequency detail is more confused as to how it should be displayed. This process interprets highlights and shadows as height information. This does not work very well on any forms that go beyond simple surface detail, as these tend to have shadows baked into the texture. This is why modeling these shapes in 3ds Max and combining them together at the end will give us the best result. With that in mind, let's open 3ds Max.

Creating a Reference Model

First, we'll create a reference box that defines the size of the door (it's important that we get a good idea of the scale of the object that we want to create). We'll apply a reference-tiled texture to it. This process will allow us to see where any extra faces need to be added to allow the texture to tile correctly. Follow these steps:

- Open 3ds Max.
- Go to File > New.
- Create > Standard Primitives > Box.
- Drag a box in the Front viewport.
- Set the following values in the Parameters rollout. The values are approximately the size of a door in millimeters.
  - Length: 2000
  - Width: 800
  - Height: 50

Applying a Texture

A template of the texture is created from a photo of the door. We will use this as a guide for laying out our UVs to tile correctly. It is just for layout, so it's saved as a JPEG with the dimensions 1024 × 512. It is advisable to use power of two textures, as that is what will be used in the final game texture. Also, I recommend making the textures double the size that they are expected to be for the game; this allows you more options for changing them if necessary.

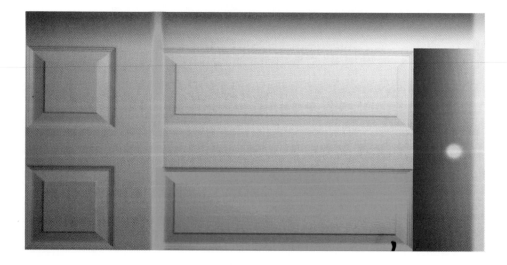

The above texture is the reference tile that will be used as a template for our normal map. To check whether it will correctly tile when complete (see below), it is color-coded, so that it is easy to see how it should tile. When tiled across the model you should end up with something that looks like this:

Although this looks like a bit of a mess, it is useful to lay out the tile in Photoshop and create markers that will help define UV layout. These markers help with orientation and scale. They show where seams will occur, so I can plan to blend those areas. I will apply this to the reference model that we have created to show how the door should look when the UVs are correctly placed. Preparation time here prevents fundamental mistakes from being made later.

Apply a Material

First, press the M key to call up the Material Editor. In the available material slot, open the Maps box (by clicking on the plus sign). Click on the diffuse map slot to open the material map browser. Click on the bitmap. Now navigate to the folder containing the door_fulltile.jpeg image from \Chapter 4\images\ (downloadable from the Web site). Click Open. In the Material Editor, your texture should be applied to a material slot. To view it on your door model, click on the Show Standard Map in Viewport button (it should be highlighted yellow when active).

Now select the material in the slot and drag it onto your door shape. You should now have your material displayed on the reference door object like this:

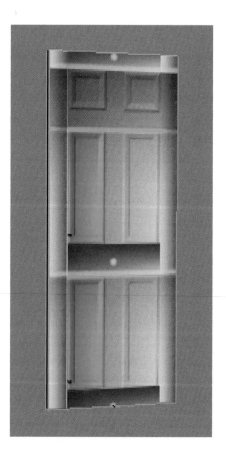

We can now use this material to help create the actual door model.

Creating the Door Model

We will split the model into parts, which will allow it to tile more convincingly. This is more work than just applying a texture over the whole mesh but will save us texture space.

Create a copy of the model. Hold down Shift and move the model to one side (in the Front viewport). Right-click on the model and select Convert to > Convert to editable mesh. Apply a blank material to this mesh (this will make it easier to work with). In the Modify panel, rename box02 to Door. In the Selection drop-down, click Vertex mode.

In the Front viewport, set the top row of vertices and pull them down level with the point on the reference mesh where the tile repeats, as shown in the figure.

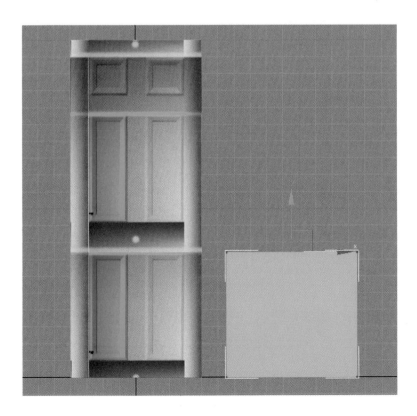

Switch to Face Mode. Select the top face of the box (it may be easier to do this in the Perspective viewport). Under Edit geometry, click Extrude and pull up the face level to the top of the reference box (as shown in the figure).

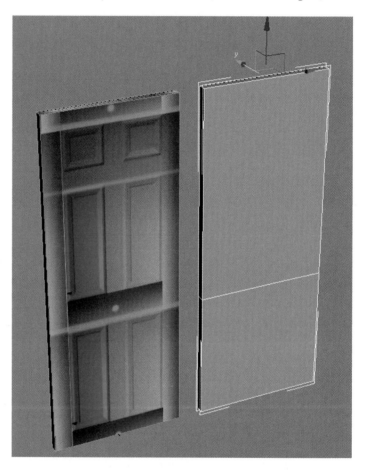

This will be your door. We now need to create a material for this model that has the untiled version of the texture to help us set up the UVs correctly. You can do this by applying the Door_setup.jpeg from \Chapter 4\images\ (downloadable from the Web site) image to the map slot in the current material that you have applied to the door model. This is the same method with which you created the full tile material previously.

Setting Up UVs

Go to the Modify tab. From the modifier list, add a UVW modifier and make sure that it is set to Box in the Parameters section. Right-click on the model and select Convert to > Convert to editable mesh. Under Selection, select Face Mode and select the largest face on the front of the door (the upper one).

Now select Unwrap UVW from the modifier list (by selecting Face, only this face will be affected by this modifier). Under Parameters, select Edit to bring up the Edit UVW panel. It will help if you set the background image to display the texture set in your material. This can be selected from the drop-down list in the top right-hand corner (the default is a checkered pattern).

Use the Move, Rotate, and Scale transforms to move the UVs to match the reference image. See below.

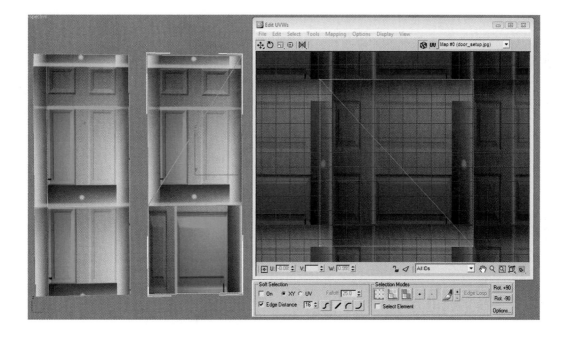

It may help to toggle Angle Snap to on (shown below).

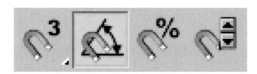

Now repeat this process for all the faces on the Door model.

For the edges of the door, I have reused the edge of the door texture. The seam is on the corner, so it will not matter if it repeats in that direction. Make sure that you try to keep the pixel resolution similar to that on the front of the door.

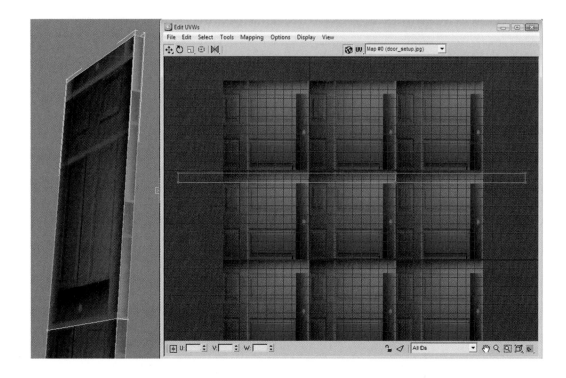

It is important that you do not mirror any UVs, as they will also reverse the normal map. Everything that should look like it is pointing out will be lit like it is pointing in.

Creating the High-Resolution Components

We first need to look at creating the low-frequency detail for the normal map for the door. For this, we need to create a new scene. Don't forget to save this scene first.

Select File > New. Create a plane and set the following parameters:

Length = 1024
Height = 512

These values represent the size of the texture that will be applied to this plane and ensure that you have the correct ratio for the normal map that is created.

Apply a material using the door_setup.jpeg to the plane (the material should be created the same way as before). This will form the reference plane for our low-frequency map.

Now we need to add some detail. In the Front viewport, create a new plane the size and position of one of the panel details. Move this smaller plane in front of the reference plane. Hit the F4 key to display the wireframe. This will make the following steps easier to see.

Select the new plane and apply a new material to it. In the Basic parameters, set the opacity to approximately 70% so that you can see the reference plane behind it. Right-click the plane and select Convert to > Convert to editable mesh. In the Selection section on the Modify tab, toggle Face Mode. Select the face of the plane. Click the Extrude button and extrude the face back toward the reference plane, like this: .

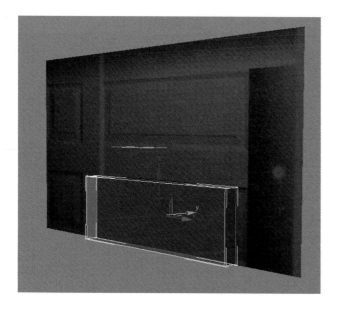

Now move and scale the face so that the edges replicate the form of the first ledge on the panel in the reference texture image. You may want to change the opacity of the material depending on the view in which you are working.

Repeat this technique by extruding the main face in and out and scaling it. It is usually a good idea to slightly overexaggerate the indentation, as this trick will make the normal map more prominent.

Note that you should avoid sharp angle changes, as they have a tendency to create strange artifacts in normal maps. You should have something that looks like this:

To create the square panel, make a copy of the panel you just made. Move the panel into position. Level with one edge. On the Modify tab, under Selection choose Vertex Mode.

Select the vertices on one side that are not aligned. Line them up with the reference image. You should now have something that looks like this:

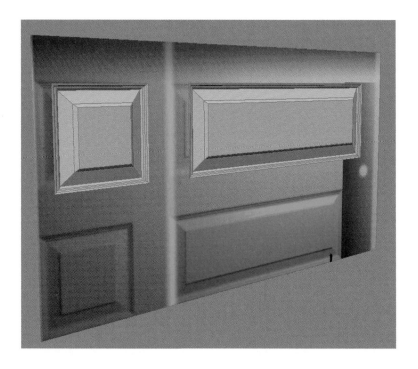

Creating the Low-Frequency Normal Map

First, name your panels Panel01 and Panel02. Rename your Reference plane to Ref01. Now make sure that panels 01 and 02 are aligned with each other and are both placed just in front of Ref01. Now press the 0 (zero) key; this shortcut calls up the Render to Texture dialog box. You can also find this under Rendering > Render to Texture. Under General Settings, pick a folder that you would like all your rendered assets to be placed in. Select Low01. This should show up under the Objects to Bake section. Check Enable under Projection Mapping. Then click the Pick button. Select your two panel objects.

Under Mapping Coordinates, make sure that Use Existing Channel is selected and the channels are set to 1; this will make sure that the texture coordinates on the Low model will be used for basis of your normal map. Under Output, click the Add button. The Add Texture Elements dialog box will pop up. Select Normals Map. As you can see from the list, you can bake out all manner of things using this technique. For now, we will concentrate on the normal map.

You will now have some new options under Output. These are specifically for the output of the normal map. First, give it a name and select File Type. TGAs or TIFFs are the best choices, as they have no compression. Next, set the size of the texture. The measurements given here are in pixels:

Width 1024
Height 512

Click Render. What is rendered does not look like a normal map. Don't worry— it isn't a normal map. If you open the folder that you specified in General Settings, your normal map will be in there. Mine looks like this:

You will notice a lot of pink; this is nothing to worry about. There was no surface to transfer in this space, so the surface transfer process has not worked correctly in this area. We won't be using it, though, so it doesn't matter.

Finishing the Low-Frequency Normal Map

The next part of this tutorial is based in Adobe Photoshop. We will be creating and organizing the elements that will make up the final normal map. This is not a Photoshop tutorial, and these results can be created in any good piece of image manipulation software. For the purpose of this tutorial, however, the operations referred to are in Photoshop.

Open Photoshop. Open your low-frequency normal map. Open the Door_setup.jpg file from \Chapter 4\images\ (from the Web site download). This will be used as a template for arranging your normal map to follow the UVs that have been set up correctly.

Cut out the panel elements in the normal map using the rectangular marquee select tool and paste them onto new layers in the Door_setup image. You can then move them into the correct positions.

Setting up some guides that follow the major sections of the door is a good idea, as this image will become the main reference for creating the final normal map. To access the guides, you must make sure that both Extras and Rulers are selected in the View menu. If you drag out from a ruler, a guide is dragged along with your mouse pointer. The guides make it easier to consistently snap to these areas with other tools selected.

You can make copies of and move elements of a normal map. You cannot rotate these, though, as the color relates directly to their orientation. You should end up with some that look like this:

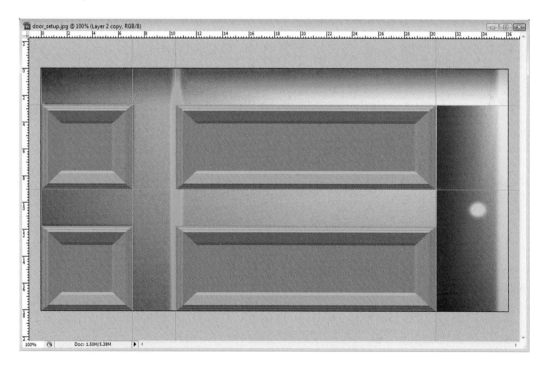

Now we should make a neutral (flat) background color for these elements to sit in. Create a new layer and fill it with a color with the following RGB values:

R 128
G 128
B 255

These values match a perfectly neutral or flat surface normal color. The background layer should fit behind all the panel details. It should look like this:

At this point, let's preview what has been created so far. Save your file as door_setup_normal.psd. Flatten this image (Ctrl+Alt+E) and save as Door_LowF_normal.tif.

Ryan Clark's Crazy Bump is a very useful tool for previewing normal maps as well as producing them. At the time of print, this program was in beta and may therefore have changed from how it is described here. You can download it from the following Web site: http://www.crazybump.com. Once installed, open Crazy Bump. Click the Open button in the bottom left corner. Choose File > Open Normal Map. Browse to and open Door_LowF.tif.

You will be presented with two windows. The main window shows you the normal map and gives you options for editing it. The smaller window is the Crazy Preview window. This should default to having your normal map applied to a cuboid. If this is not the case, you can change it to a cuboid in the bottom right-hand corner drop-down.

Follow the instructions on the screen to rotate the cuboid and the light. This step will give you an idea of how well it has worked. You can already see that constructing this type of detail using this process works a lot better than trying to generate it automatically from a bitmap. It should look something like this (note that the example is offset slightly to view it better):

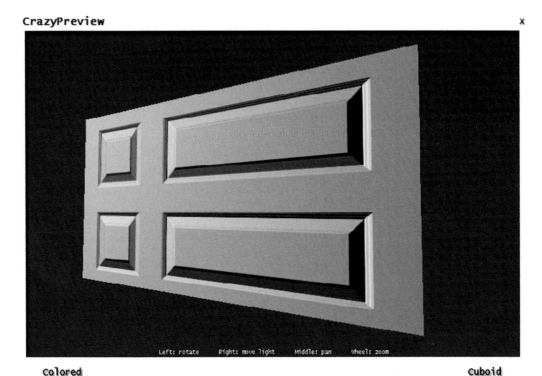

Creating the High-Frequency Normal Map

Next, we'll create the high-frequency bitmap that will be converted into a normal map. We will create a grayscale bitmap that represents the grain of the door. To do so, open Photoshop.

Once again we will use the Door_setup image as a starting point. First, we need to get some reference for the grain on the door. This reference will be taken from the original door reference photos gathered (we benefit from the door being virtually white). Hide all the layers with the other normal map parts on. You won't need these for this section. As before, you have to manipulate the images into place to fit the template.

When creating a bump map for auto-generation, you need to remember that they are generated using grayscale values. If you want something to stick out, it has to be between 50% gray and white. If you want it to be recessed, then it must go the opposite way. You should end up with something like this:

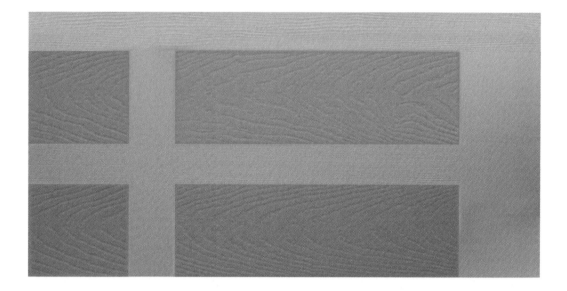

The inner panels have been made darker so that they will appear recessed. I have made a note of all the areas where the texture needs to tile and overlaid and blended sections so that the texture can be repeated. The good thing about creating normal maps this way is that you can set them up to tile very easily using this method. It is important to note that this step must be done at this stage, because when the normal map is created, it will no longer behave like a conventional texture, and editing it will be time-consuming and prevent it from working correctly.

If you have to hand-edit the normal map, you should work on each color channel individually. Remember that the lighting information is stored in each channel in the following ways:

- Red is lit from left to right
- Green is lit from top to bottom
- Blue represents depth

It is also important to note that depending on your video card, you may need to invert the green channel for it to work correctly. The best way to make sure is to try it both ways to determine the correct method for your card.

Once you have edited the map, use NVIDIA's Normal Map filter to renormalize the normal map so that it will display correctly. The Normal Map filter can be downloaded from here: http://developer.nvidia.com/object/photoshop_dds_plugins.html. To use this filter, make sure that your normal map is flattened and selected. Under filters, choose NVIDIA tools > NormalMapFilter. Under Alternative Conversions, select Normalize Only. This step ensures that each channel adds up to 1, which basically means that it will work correctly as a normal map.

When you are happy with the result, save it as Door_HighF_setup.tif. Open Crazy Bump. Click the Open button. Select File > Open photograph. Browse to and select Door_HighF_setup.tif. You will be instructed to wait as it generates a normal map preview. In the main Crazy Bump window, you will see a representation of your normal map. In the Crazy Bump Preview window, you will see the normal map applied to a cuboid.

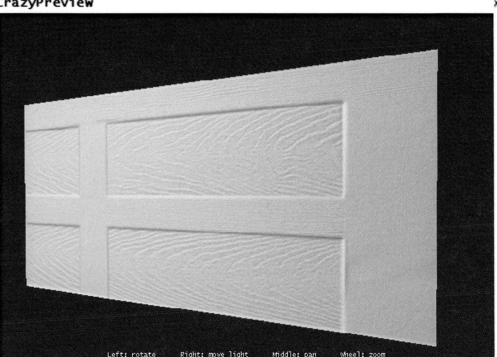

As you can see, all the detail comes through as it should. By making the panels darker, these areas already appear recessed. We will now add the low-frequency map to this model to help define these forms. In the main Crazy Bump window select, Open Normals Mixer. A Normals Mixer dialog box will open. Select Add Another Map. Select File > Normals and browse to and select the low-frequency normal map that you created (door_lowf_normal.tiff). You should end up with something that looks like this in the Crazy Bump preview:

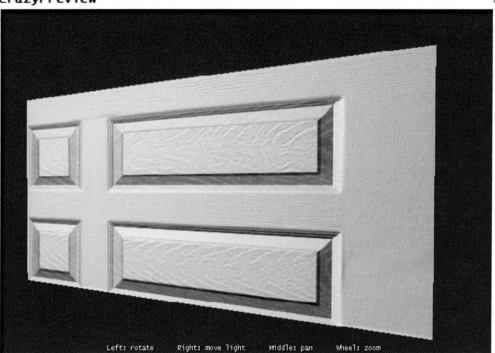

When both maps are combined, you get an idea of the effect the normal map will have on the model in game. It is possible to combine maps and generate normal maps in Photoshop using the NVIDIA Normal Map filter and using overlay layers, but I prefer this tool, as it gives good artistic feed back in real time. You always know that these maps will work properly, as they will always be normalized.

You could experiment further with the values in Crazy Bump to get something that suits your purpose. In the Normals Mixer, you can control the strength of both maps. In the main menu there are a number of controls that can change the look of your normal map. Feel free to experiment until you get the result you want. When you are happy with your normal map, click the Save button.

Select Save to File and save the as Door_Normal.tif. It should look something like this:

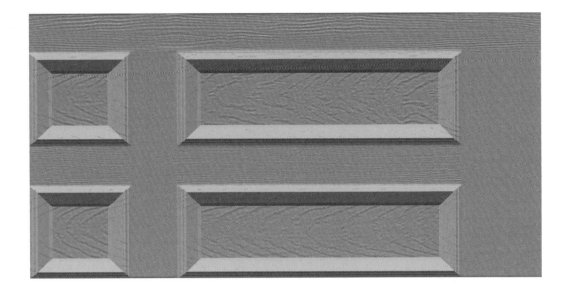

View in 3ds Max

Now that we have created a normal map, we want to see it on the door we have created. Let's begin by opening 3ds Max. Open the Door file that has a complete set of UVs applied.

Open the Material Editor and select a vacant slot. Under Blinn Basic Parameters, select the diffuse color swab (default is gray). This will call up the Color Selector. I am selecting an off-white to display the door. I have used the following values:

- Red 245
- Green 243
- Blue 228

Apply this to the door.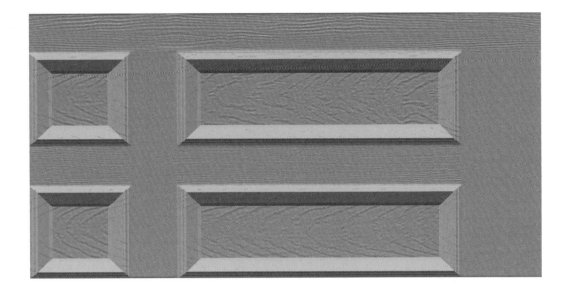

Click and hold over the blue checked box, select the pink checked box, and make sure that it is toggled on to display (yellow highlight). This step will allow the material to use hardware rendering, which is necessary to display the normal map correctly on your graphics card. Under Maps, select the bump slot and make sure that the amount is set to 100 (default is 30). From the Browser menu, select Normal Bump. Under the Normal Bump Parameters select the bump slot.

From the browser select Bitmap, then browse to and select Door_Normal.tif.

You should now have something in your viewport that looks like this . . .

Congratulations—you have created a tiled normal-mapped asset using a combination of next-gen techniques. The way we have tiled this normal map works in our favor: any seams that you have should be able to be tiled in the same axis. Otherwise, you will get strange artifacts around the seams.

Creating the Final Look of the Door

Our door is very clean-looking and would be totally out of place in the dilapidated warehouse scene it belongs in. The geometry and UVs are in place for a full door, so now it will be easy to edit this door to look like sections are missing. However, we will first apply a diffuse texture to the model to give it a weathered, bare look.

I have created this textured from a weathered wood reference image, using the normal map as a guide. I have not added lots of baked-in shadow information (a practice often seen in textures created for games). The reason for this is that the normal map describes the form of the object, so it is not needed.

When this is applied, the door will look older and more weathered, and appropriate for a warehouse-style environment.

Moving On from This Lesson

Now that you have created a full door, you can go on to create variations of this door by removing sections to create doors with panels missing, or pieces of wood that can be littered throughout the scene.

Summary

Here is a summary of what we now know about normal mapping:

- Normal maps create more work for the artist. Always consider whether you actually need one.
- Tangent maps are used mostly in games.
- Normal maps are used to describe both low- and high-frequency detail. Different production techniques are used to produce these effects. Combining these effects is the quickest way to get good results.
- Spending time preparing a UV layout saves you time in the long run.
- Tiled textures can be more work to prepare, but give you more resolution/save texture space.
- Do not flip UVs; doing so will make your normal map display incorrectly.
- Building individual details and combining them in image manipulation software is a quick way of developing complex low-frequency detail without long build and render times.
- Normal-mapped elements can be moved and scaled, but not rotated in image manipulation software.
- Avoid sharp angles, which can create strange artifacts in the normal map.
- The quality of the normal map is dependent on its resolution and compression.
- Normal maps cannot be edited like normal textures.
- Normal maps can display differently depending on the software and hardware used.
- Normal maps successfully tile along the same axis.
- You do not need to bake as much shadow information into your diffuse map when using normal maps.

CHAPTER 5

Concept Art

Concept art is a vital part of any production. Concept art allows an artist to design the look and feel of a movie, game, or character prior to moving into the expensive production stage.

After the story is approved, an artist is brought in to start delivering concepts. Concept art is the first visual created for a production. The artist can quickly and easily produce many different designs. Each design can go before the art director for approval, and if changes are needed, it's a very simple matter. It's much easier and more cost-effective to rework some concept art than it would be to have to redo an entire model. Color, lighting, and even the overall mood of a scene can be worked out by an artist with just pen and paper.

Even on smaller productions, it's very important to create concept art prior to moving into production. Work out the look of your character before moving into production, when changes would be expensive and time-consuming to perform.

FIG. 5-1 Tools of the concept artist: pencils, paper, grayscale pens, blue pencils, and so on.

Tutorial: Cleaning Up Concept Art

When sketching your concept art using paper and pencil, it's a good idea to use a nonphoto blue pencil (available at any art store) to rough out your character. Later, you can finalize the outline using a hard pencil or ink.

Scan your image at a sufficiently high resolution. Line art is typically scanned at 300 dpi for concept work. Use a higher resolution if you need to send it to be printed.

If you've scanned the image as black and white, you're all finished. The nonphoto blue should not register during the scanning process.

However, if you need to remove the blue in Adobe Photoshop, scan the image in color and load it into the program.

FIG. 5-2 Character concept.

1. In Adobe Photoshop, open the Channels window.
2. Deselect all channels except for blue. This step turns all of the blue pencil work invisible, leaving the gray outlines intact.

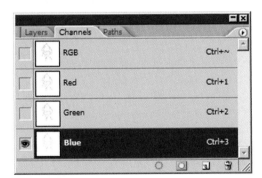

FIG. 5-3 Working with just the blue channel.

1. Click Select > All.
2. Click Edit > Copy.
3. Change to the green channel.
4. Click Edit > Paste. This will paste the clean pencil work into the green channel.
5. Repeat for the red and RGB channels.

105

FIG. 5-4 Final image with blue removed.

Adobe Photoshop is, of course, one of the more popular programs available
for the concept artist. I also enjoy using a program called ArtRage by Ambient
Designs, Ltd. Both programs have important roles in the concept artist's
toolbox: Photoshop for its unparalleled image editing tools and ArtRage for its
intuitive pencil options.

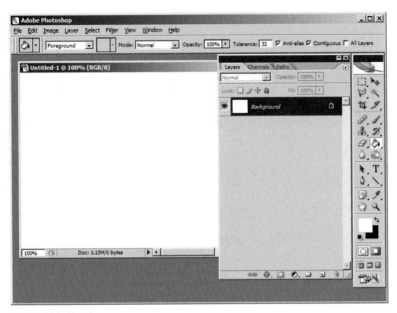

FIG. 5-5 Adobe Photoshop.

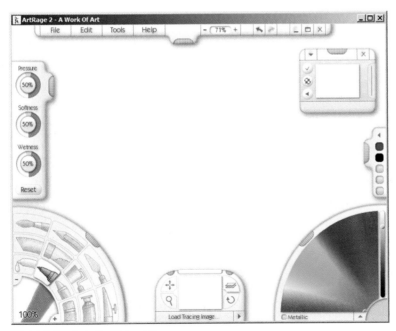

FIG. 5-6 ArtRage by Ambient Designs, Ltd.

FIG. 5-7 Concept art.

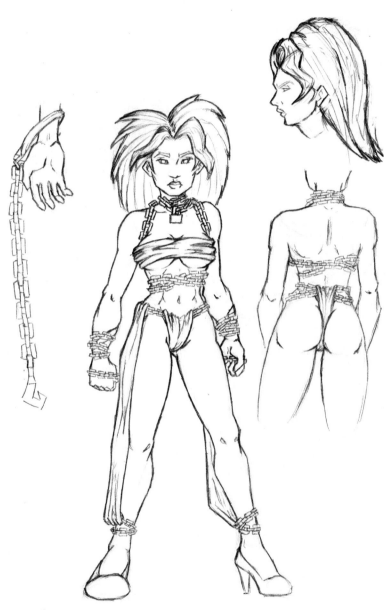

FIG. 5-8 Concept art.

FIG. 5-9

FIG. 5-10

FIG. 5-11

FIG. 5-12

CHAPTER 6

Anatomy

Anatomy

A basic understanding of anatomy is vital in creating believable characters. You don't have to go to medical school for four years, but be prepared to study some basic anatomy. Luckily, there are tons of resources available.

First, pick up some books on the subject. Although this chapter offers information on anatomy, it shouldn't take the place of books solely devoted to the subject.

My favorite anatomy books are:

- *Artistic Anatomy,* by Paul Richter, Watson-Guptill Publications (**Figure 6-1**)
- *Cyclopedia Anatomicae*, by Gyorgy Feher, Black Dog & Leventhal Publishers, Inc. (**Figure 6-2**)
- *An Atlas of Animal Anatomy for Artists*, by Frances A. Davis, Dover Publications (**Figure 6-3**)
- *Dynamic Anatomy,* by Burne Hogarth, Watson-Guptill Publications (**Figure 6-4**)

FIG. 6-1 *Artistic Anatomy.*

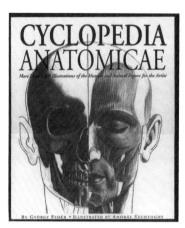

FIG. 6-2 *Cyclopedia Anatomicae.*

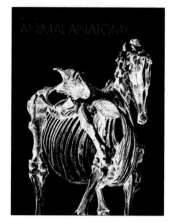

FIG. 6-3 *An Atlas of Animal Anatomy for Artists.*

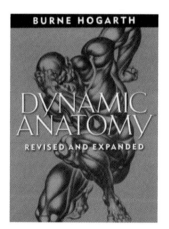

FIG. 6-4 *Dynamic Anatomy.*

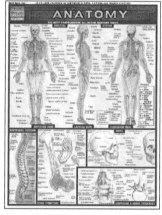

FIG. 6-5 Quickstudy Anatomy by BarCharts, Inc.

In addition to the books, I also recommend the Quickstudy Academic Charts by BarCharts, Inc. (**Figure 6-5**). These are great laminated charts that easily fit into a laptop case or folder. I always carry the charts for skeletal, muscular, and surface anatomy.

One of the best ways to study anatomy is to attend life drawing sessions. I recommend very strongly that you attend a weekly class to exercise your sketching. As you practice, you'll be able to picture more easily the human form in a variety of poses. Of course, the availability of classes differs depending on your location. Search the Internet to see what is available. Also, check local community colleges, which often have inexpensive art classes.

If you are unable to attend an art class, there are some Web sites available that provide very nice anatomy studies (**Figure 6-6**). My favorite of the anatomy

FIG. 6-6   Anatomy Web site.

Web sites is http://www.3d.sk. There are thousands of photos available, ranging from modeling poses to clothed humans and action poses—truly an invaluable resource if you are unable to attend life drawing classes.

The skeleton is the framework of a human. As such, it should be the first thing that you learn when you begin studying anatomy. Many artists make the mistake of skipping studying the skeleton, and their art suffers as a result. If the skeleton isn't learned, the resulting art can lack proper form; it tends to be a bit blobby.

What the artist should learn is where the main bony masses lie. These masses are prominent structures like the elbows, knees, pelvis, and so on. Of course, it's important to learn where bones like the vertebrae, femur, pelvis, and ulna are located. But even more important is studying how these bones affect the overlying muscles.

After learning the major bone structures (**Figures 6-7 through 6-10**), you'll be able to detail those sections properly in your art and your characters will have more life.

Characters are often designed in terms of height by a measurement representing a number of "heads"; that is, a multiple of the character's head height. For instance, the ideal male is generally thought to be eight heads high. A meek character might be six-and-a-half heads high, with the average male being around seven heads high. Of course, eight heads high is a generalization, but it does give you a good starting point when designing a new character.

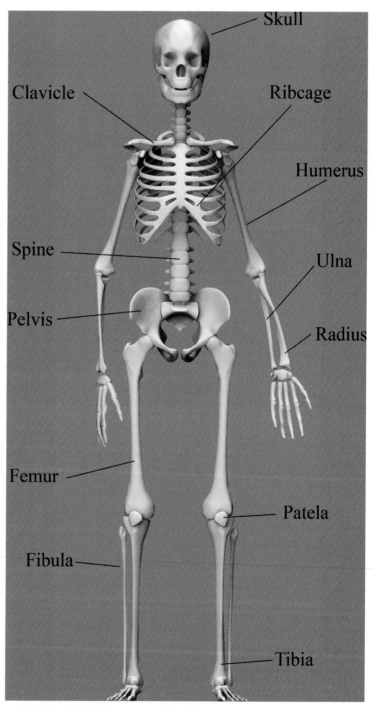

FIG. 6-7 Skeleton front.

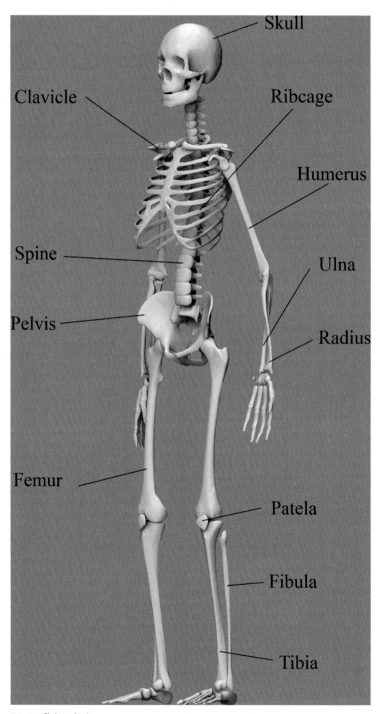

Skull

Clavicle

Ribcage

Humerus

Spine

Ulna

Pelvis

Radius

Femur

Patela

Fibula

Tibia

FIG. 6-8 Skeleton ¾ view.

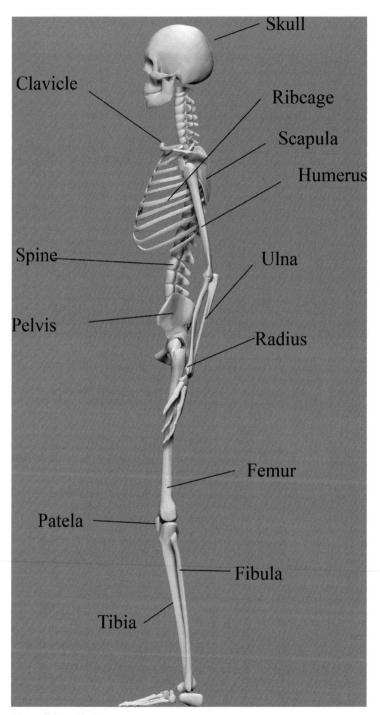

FIG. 6-9 Skeleton side view.

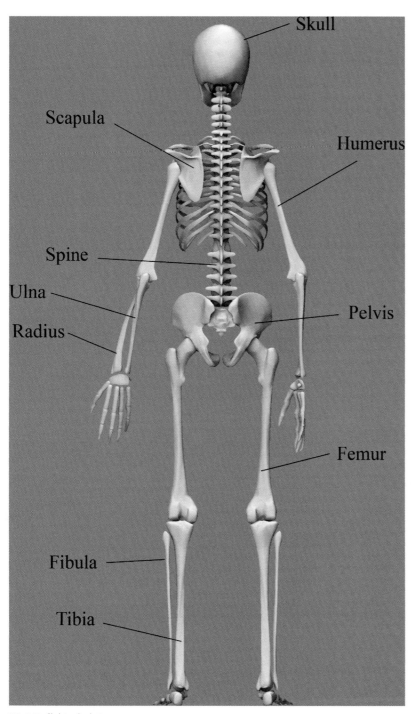

Skull

Scapula

Humerus

Spine

Ulna

Radius

Pelvis

Femur

Fibula

Tibia

FIG. 6-10 Skeleton back view.

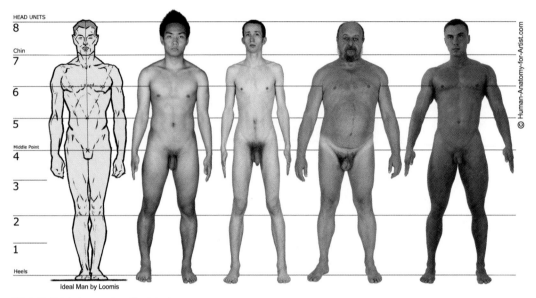

FIG. 6-11 Male body comparisons (front view).

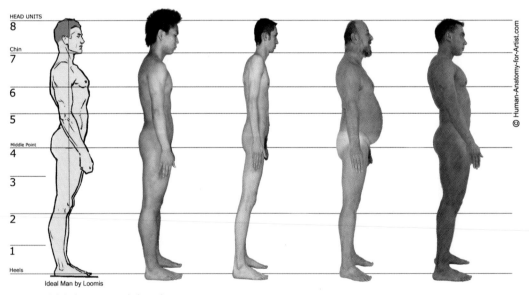

FIG. 6-12 Male body comparisons (side view).

Males typically have less body fat than females. The male pelvis is much narrower than that of a female. Males also have much wider shoulders. All of these factors should be taken into account in any original designs.

Notice how the different body types compare to the ideal male (**Figures 6-13 through 6-16**). Keep an eye on where the different bony masses lie.

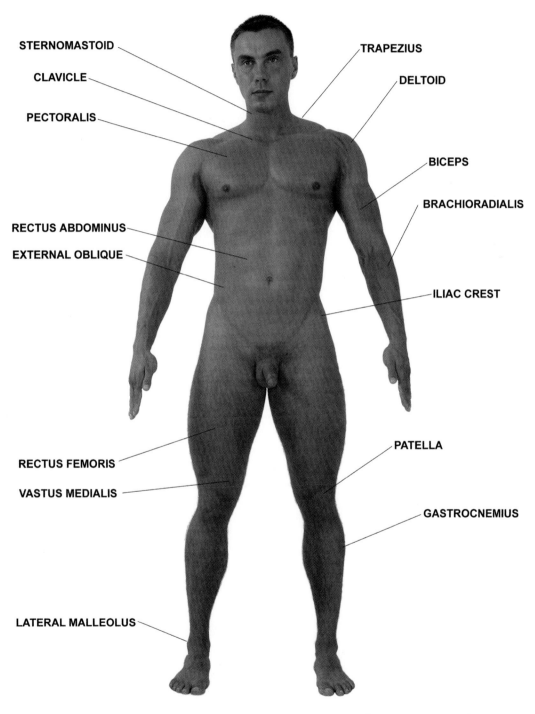

STERNOMASTOID

CLAVICLE

PECTORALIS

TRAPEZIUS

DELTOID

BICEPS

BRACHIORADIALIS

RECTUS ABDOMINUS

EXTERNAL OBLIQUE

ILIAC CREST

RECTUS FEMORIS

VASTUS MEDIALIS

PATELLA

GASTROCNEMIUS

LATERAL MALLEOLUS

FIG. 6-13 Male front view.

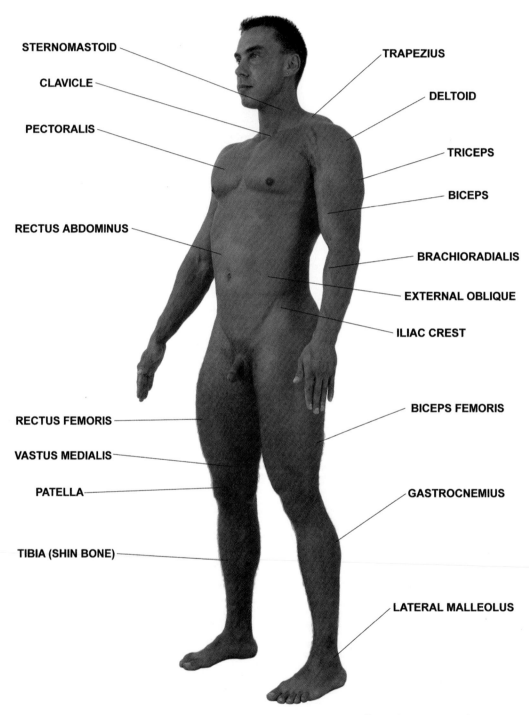

STERNOMASTOID

CLAVICLE

PECTORALIS

RECTUS ABDOMINUS

RECTUS FEMORIS

VASTUS MEDIALIS

PATELLA

TIBIA (SHIN BONE)

TRAPEZIUS

DELTOID

TRICEPS

BICEPS

BRACHIORADIALIS

EXTERNAL OBLIQUE

ILIAC CREST

BICEPS FEMORIS

GASTROCNEMIUS

LATERAL MALLEOLUS

© www.human-anatomy-for-artist.com

FIG. 6-14 Male ¾ front view.

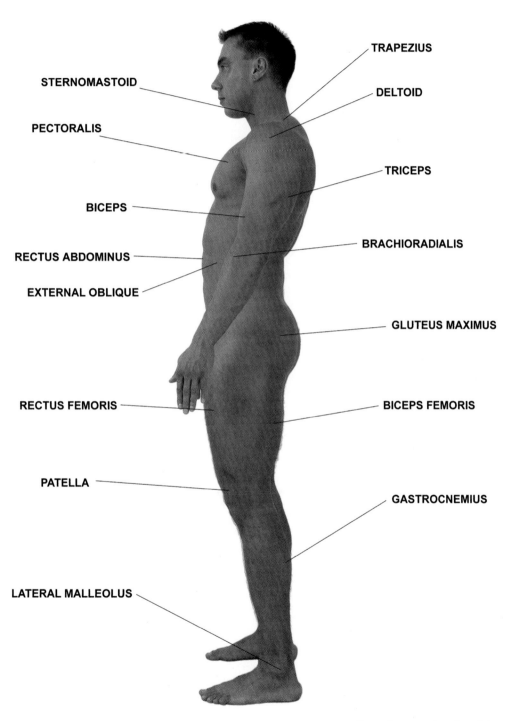

TRAPEZIUS

STERNOMASTOID

DELTOID

PECTORALIS

TRICEPS

BICEPS

BRACHIORADIALIS

RECTUS ABDOMINUS

EXTERNAL OBLIQUE

GLUTEUS MAXIMUS

RECTUS FEMORIS

BICEPS FEMORIS

PATELLA

GASTROCNEMIUS

LATERAL MALLEOLUS

© www.human-anatomy-for-artist.com

FIG. 6-15 Male side view.

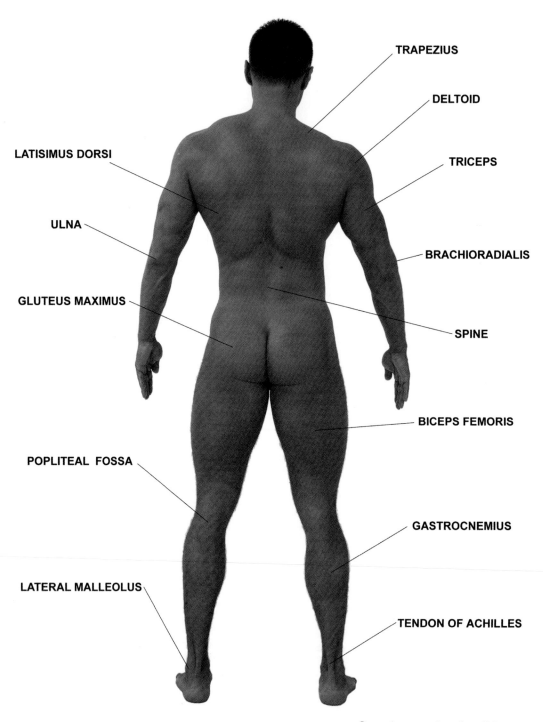

TRAPEZIUS

DELTOID

LATISIMUS DORSI

TRICEPS

ULNA

BRACHIORADIALIS

GLUTEUS MAXIMUS

SPINE

BICEPS FEMORIS

POPLITEAL FOSSA

GASTROCNEMIUS

LATERAL MALLEOLUS

TENDON OF ACHILLES

© www.human-anatomy-for-artist.com

FIG. 6-16 Male back view.

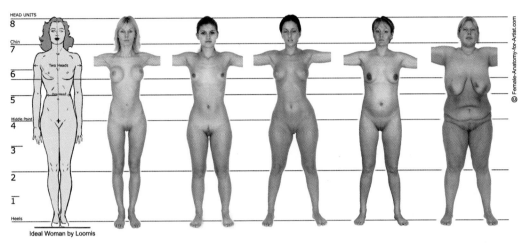

FIG. 6-17 Female body comparisons (front view).

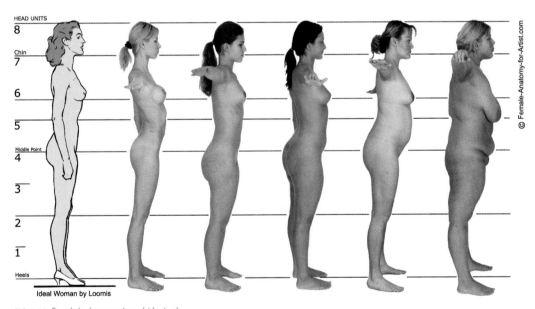

FIG. 6-18 Female body comparisons (side view).

The first thing to note about the skeletal anatomy of women is that the pelvis is wider and shallower than a man's (**Figures 6-19 through 6-29**). This is a good example of the bony structure I mentioned earlier. This is something the artist really needs to emphasize, or the character will not look right. Women also have narrower rib cages, and smaller, less angular jaw lines. The arms and legs of a female are also thinner and shorter than those of a male.

As with a male, the ideal female is usually depicted as being eight heads high, and the average woman between seven and seven-and-a-half heads high.

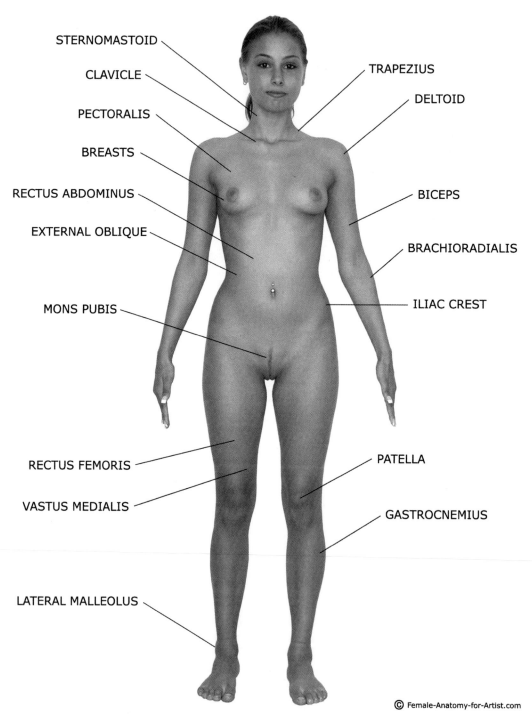

STERNOMASTOID

CLAVICLE

PECTORALIS

BREASTS

RECTUS ABDOMINUS

EXTERNAL OBLIQUE

MONS PUBIS

TRAPEZIUS

DELTOID

BICEPS

BRACHIORADIALIS

ILIAC CREST

RECTUS FEMORIS

VASTUS MEDIALIS

PATELLA

GASTROCNEMIUS

LATERAL MALLEOLUS

© Female-Anatomy-for-Artist.com

FIG. 6-19 Female front view.

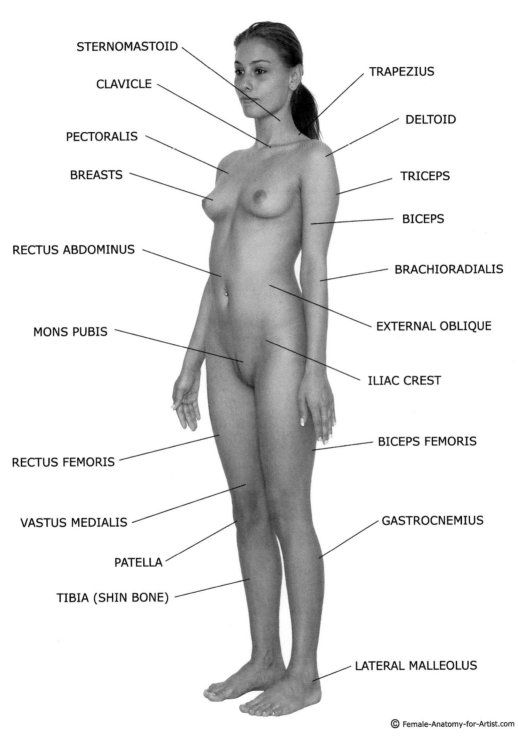

STERNOMASTOID

CLAVICLE

PECTORALIS

BREASTS

RECTUS ABDOMINUS

MONS PUBIS

RECTUS FEMORIS

VASTUS MEDIALIS

PATELLA

TIBIA (SHIN BONE)

TRAPEZIUS

DELTOID

TRICEPS

BICEPS

BRACHIORADIALIS

EXTERNAL OBLIQUE

ILIAC CREST

BICEPS FEMORIS

GASTROCNEMIUS

LATERAL MALLEOLUS

FIG. 6-20 Female ¾ front view.

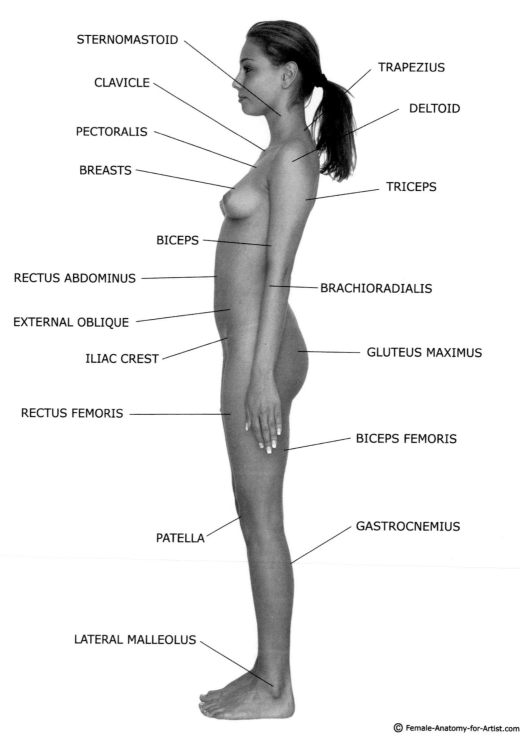

STERNOMASTOID

CLAVICLE

PECTORALIS

BREASTS

BICEPS

RECTUS ABDOMINUS

EXTERNAL OBLIQUE

ILIAC CREST

RECTUS FEMORIS

PATELLA

LATERAL MALLEOLUS

TRAPEZIUS

DELTOID

TRICEPS

BRACHIORADIALIS

GLUTEUS MAXIMUS

BICEPS FEMORIS

GASTROCNEMIUS

© Female-Anatomy-for-Artist.com

FIG. 6-21 Female side view.

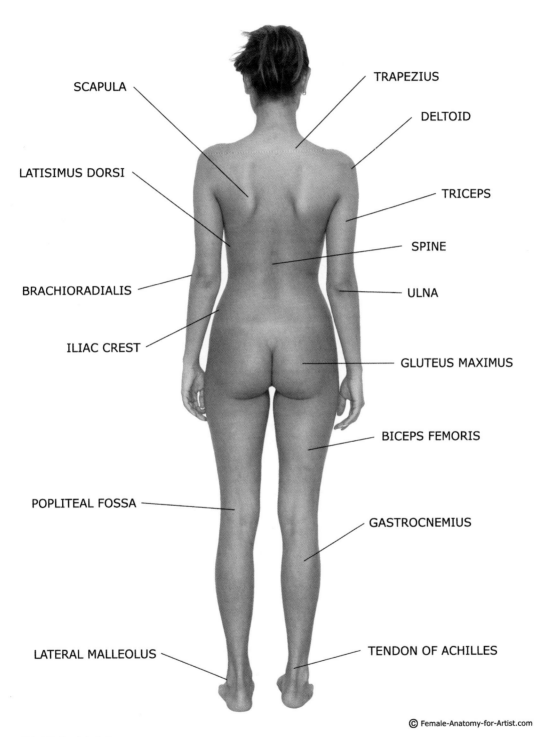

SCAPULA

TRAPEZIUS

DELTOID

LATISIMUS DORSI

TRICEPS

SPINE

BRACHIORADIALIS

ULNA

ILIAC CREST

GLUTEUS MAXIMUS

BICEPS FEMORIS

POPLITEAL FOSSA

GASTROCNEMIUS

LATERAL MALLEOLUS

TENDON OF ACHILLES

© Female-Anatomy-for-Artist.com

FIG. 6-22 Female back view.

FIG. 6-23 Male back.

FIG. 6-24 Male kneeling back view.

FIG. 6-25 Male kneeling front view.

FIG. 6-26 Male standing back view.

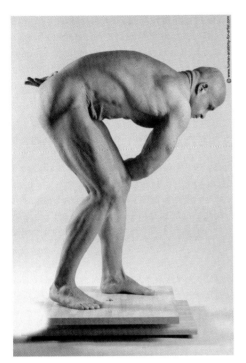

FIG. 6-27 Male standing front view.

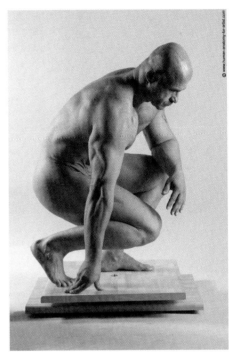

FIG. 6-28 Male kneeling.

FIG. 6-29 Female kneeling.

CHAPTER 7

A Basic (Game) Art Education

Art is born of the observation and investigation of nature.

Cicero
Roman author, orator, and politician (106 BC–43 BC)

Introduction

The basis of computer art is art itself, so before we dive into any technical issues, we must first discuss the most basic—yet most important—aspects of visual art. Although teaching you traditional fine art skills is beyond the scope of this book, it is critical to have an understanding of some basic aspects of visual art in order to create game textures. Fortunately, these basic aspects of art are fairly easy to present in book form. By studying these basics of art, you will learn to see the world as an artist does and understand what you see, and then you will be more able to create a texture set for a game world.

The basic aspects of visual art we will focus on are:

- Shape and form
- Light and shadow

- Texture
- Color
- Perspective

Learning to observe the basic visual aspects of the world around you is a strong beginning in the process of seeing the world like an artist, communicating with other artists, and creating great game textures. Technology is, of course, critical to the larger picture of game textures, but the actual basics of art is where great textures begin. Too often, would-be game artists are thrown into a discussion on tiling, or even game engine technology, when what is most important for the creation of game textures is the ability to understand what you are seeing in the real world and to recreate it on the computer. Often a texture artist is required to break a scene down to its core materials and build a texture set based on those materials, so learning this ability is essential. Although you don't need to have an advanced degree in art to create great textures, let's face it—almost anyone can learn what buttons to push in Photoshop, but the person who understands and skillfully applies the basics of art can make a texture that stands out above the rest.

There are many types of art and aspects of visual art that you should explore further in order to develop as a game artist. Some of the things you can study and/or practice are:

- Figure drawing
- Still-life drawing
- Photography
- Painting (oil, watercolor, etc.)
- Lighting (for film, still photography, the stage, or CG)
- Color theory and application
- Sculpture
- Drafting and architectural rendering
- Anatomy
- Set design

It is even worth the time to study other areas of interest beyond art, including science—particularly the behavior of the physical world. Light, for example, is becoming processed more and more in real time and not painted into the texture to the extent that it was just a few years ago. The more you understand and are able to reproduce effects such as reflection, refraction, blowing smoke, and so on, the more success you will find as a game artist. We presently have emerging technologies that reproduce the real world to a much greater extent than ever before, but it still takes an artist to create the input and adjust the output for these effects to look their best. The areas of study that will help you when dealing with real-world behaviors are endless. You can start by simply observing the world: how water drips or flows, the variations of light and shadow on different surfaces at different times of the day, how a tree grows from the ground. Straight like a young pine or flared at the base like an old oak—you will soon be staring at the cracks in the pavement and photographing the side of a dumpster while the world stares at you. An excellent book for this type of activity is *Digital Texturing & Painting* by Owen Demers (New Riders, 2001). You can also take tours of museums, architectural tours, and nature walks; join a photography club; or take a figure drawing class—there is no end to the classes, clubs, disciplines, and other situations that you can expose yourself to, and that will open up your mind to new inspirations and teach you new tools and techniques for texture creation. And, of course, playing games, watching movies, and reading graphic novels are the food of the game artist.

Chapter Overview

- Shape (2D) and Form (3D)
- Light and Shadow
- Texture: tactile vs. visual
- Color
- Perspective

There are many elements of traditional art, but we will narrow our focus to those elements that are most pertinent to texture creation. We will start with shape and form.

Shape and Form

A "shape" is a two-dimensional (height and width) outline of a form. Circles, squares, rectangles, and triangles are all examples of shape. Shape is what we first use to draw a picture before we understand such concepts as light, shadow, and depth. As children, we draw what we see in a crude way. Look at the drawings of very young children and you will see that they are almost always composed of pure basic shapes: triangle roof, square door, circle sun. Even as adults, when we understand shadows and perspective, we have trouble drawing what we see before us and instead rely on a whole series of mental notes and assumptions as to what we think we are seeing. There are exercises to help develop the ability to draw what we actually see. Most notably, the book *The New Drawing on the Right Side of the Brain* by Dr. Betty Edwards (Tarcher, 2001) offers many such exercises.

One of the most famous of these exercises involves the drawing of a human face from a photo. After you have done this, you then turn the photo upside down and draw it again. The upside-down results are often far better than the right-side-up results and your first try, because once you turn the image upside down, your brain is no longer able to make any mental assumptions about what you think you are seeing; you can see only what's really there. Your brain hasn't yet developed a set of rules and assumptions about the uncommon sight of an upside-down human face. One of the first skills that you can practice as an artist is trying to see the shapes that make up the objects that surround you. **Figure 7-1** has some examples of this, ranging from the simple to the complex. This is a very important skill to acquire. As a texture artist, you will often need to see an object's fundamental shape amidst all the clutter and confusion in a scene so that you can create the 2D art that goes over the 3D objects of the world.

FIG. 7-1 Here are some examples of shapes that compose everyday objects. These shapes range from simple to complex.

FIG. 7-2 Here are examples of shapes and forms. Notice how it is only shadow that turns a circle into a sphere.

"Form" is three-dimensional (height, width, and depth) and includes simple objects like spheres, cubes, and pyramids. See **Figure 7-2** for examples and visual comparisons. You will see later that as a texture artist, you are creating art on flat shapes (essentially squares and rectangles) that are later placed on the surfaces of forms. An example can be seen in **Figure 7-3**, as a cube is turned into a crate (a common prop in many computer games). When a shape

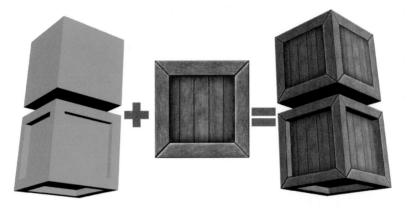

FIG. 7-3 A game texture is basically a 2D image applied, or mapped, to a 3D shape to add visual detail. In this example, a cube is turned into a crate using texture. A more complex 3D shape makes a more interesting crate, using the same 2D image.

FIG. 7-4 Here is an example of how shapes can be cut into an image and—with some simple layer effects—can then be turned into a texture in Photoshop.

is cut into a base material in Photoshop and some highlights and shadows are added, the illusion of form is created. A texture can be created rather quickly using this method. See **Figure 7-4** for a very simple example of a space door created using an image of rust, some basic shapes, and some standard Photoshop Layer Effects.

Of course, mapping those textures to more complex shapes like weapons, vehicles, and characters gets more complex, and the textures themselves reflect this complexity. Paradoxically, as the speed, quality, and the complexity of game technology increase, artists are actually producing more simplified textures in some cases. The complexity comes in the understanding and implementation of the technology. Don't worry—you will gradually be introduced to this complexity until it culminates with the sections on shader technology.

As in the previous section, you can practice looking for the forms that make up the objects around you. In **Figure 7-5**, you can see some examples of this.

FIG. 7-5 Here are some examples of the forms that make up the objects around you.

Light and Shadow

Of all the topics in traditional art, that of light and shadow is arguably the most important, due to its difficulty to master and its importance to the final work. Light and shadow give depth to and, as a result, define what we see. At their simplest, light and shadow are easy to see and understand. Most of us are familiar with shadow; our own shadow cast by the sun, making animal silhouettes with our hands on the wall, or a single light source shining on a sphere and the round shadow that it casts. That's where this book will start. Light and shadow quickly get more complicated, and the examples in this book will get more complex as well. The book will start with the ability to see and analyze light and shadow in this chapter, then move up to creating and tweaking light and shadow in Photoshop (using Layer Styles, for the most part), and finally, look at some basic hand-tweaking of light and shadow. If you wish to master the ability to hand-paint light and shadow on complex and organic surfaces, then you are advised to take traditional art classes in illustration, sketching, and painting.

We all know that the absence of light is darkness, and in total darkness we can obviously see nothing at all, but the presence of too much light will also make it difficult to see. Too much light blows away shadow and removes depth and desaturates color. In the previous section, we looked at how shape and form differ. We see that difference primarily as light and shadow, as in the example of the circle and a sphere. But even if the sphere were lit evenly with no shadows and looked just like the circle, the difference would become apparent when rotated around the vertical axis. The sphere would always look round if rotated, whereas once you began to rotate the circle, it would begin to look like an oval until it eventually disappeared when completely sideways.

In the previous example, where a shape was cut into an image of rusted metal and made to look like a metal space door using Photoshop Layer Effects, the highlights and shadows were faked using the various tools and their settings. In **Figure 7-6**, you can see the same door texture rotated from front to side. Notice the complete lack of depth in the image on the far right. The illusion is shattered.

FIG. 7-6 Here is the same door texture from the previous section. Notice the complete lack of depth as we look at it from angles other than straight on. The illusion of depth is shattered.

Understanding light and shadow is very important in the process of creating quality textures. We will go into more depth on this topic as you work through this chapter. One of the main reasons for dwelling on the topic is not only the importance of light and shadow visually, but also because many of the decisions that need to be made are based on whether light and shadow should be represented using texture, geometry, or technology. Making this decision intelligently in a serious game production involves the input and expertise of many people. Although what looks best is ideally the first priority, what runs best on the target computer is usually what the decision boils down to. So keep in mind that in game development, you don't want to make any assumptions about light and shadows—ask questions. It can be challenging to make shadows look good in any one of the situations. Too little and you lack depth; too much and the texture starts to look flat. Making shadows too long or intense is an easy mistake. And unless the game level specifically calls for that, on rare occasions, don't do it. Technology sometimes handles the highlights and shadows. This is challenging, because it is a new way of thinking that baffles many people who are not familiar with computer graphics. This method can also be a bit overwhelming, because you go from creating one texture for a surface to creating three or more textures that all work together on one surface. Naming and storing those textures can get confusing if you let it get away from you.

Overall, you want your textures to be as versatile as possible, and to a great degree, that includes the ability to use those textures under various lighting

FIG. 7-7 The crate on the left has conflicting light sources. The shadow from the edge of the crate is coming up from the bottom, is too dark, is too long, and even has a gap in it. The highlights on the edges are in conflict with the shadow cast on the inner panel of the crate, and they are too hot, or bright. The crate on the right has a more subtle, low-contrast, and diffuse highlight and shadow scheme and will work better in more diverse situations.

conditions. See **Figure 7-7** for an example of one texture where the shadows and highlights have been improperly implemented and one that has been correctly created. For this reason, we will purposely use highlight and shadow to a minimalist amount. You will find that if you need more depth in your texture than a modest amount of highlight and/or shadow, then you most likely need to create geometry or use a shader—or consider removing the source of shadow! If there is no need for a large electrical box on a wall, then don't paint it in if it draws attention to itself and looks flat. If there is a need and you are creating deep and harsh shadows because of it, you may need to create the geometry for the protruding element. You may find that as game development technology accelerates, things like pipes, doorknobs, and ledges are no longer painted into the texture but modeled in geometry. Many texture surface properties are no longer painted on. Reflections, specular highlights, bump mapping, and other aspects of highlight and shadow are now processed in real time.

One of the main benefits to creating your own highlights and shadows in your textures is that you can control them and make them more interesting as well as consistent. Nothing is worse than a texture with shadows from conflicting light sources: harsh, short shadows on some elements of the texture and longer, more diffuse shadows on others. See **Figure 7-8** for an example of this. The human eye can detect these types of errors even if the human seeing it can't quite understand why the image looks wrong. One of the artist's greatest abilities is not only being able to create art, but also being able to consciously know and verbalize what he is seeing. In **Figure 7-9**, you can see the various types of shadows created as the light source changes. This is a simple demonstration. If you ever have the opportunity to light a 3D scene or movie set, you will discover that the range of variables for light and shadow can be quite large.

Highlights also tell us a good bit about the light source as well as the object itself. In **Figure 7-10**, you can see another simple illustration of how different materials have different highlight patterns and intensities. These materials lack any texture or color and simply show the highlights and shadows created on the surface by one consistent light source.

FIG. 7-8 Here is a *really bad* texture created from two sources. Notice the difference in the shadows and highlights. The human eye can detect these errors, even if the human seeing it can't understand why the image looks wrong.

FIG. 7-9 With one light source and a simple object, you can see the range of shadows we can create. Each shadow tells us information about the object and the light source, such as location, intensity, and so on.

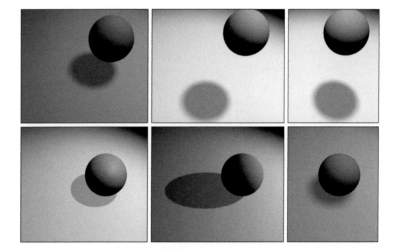

FIG. 7-10 With one light source and a simple object with various highlights on it, you can see that the object appears to be created of various materials. Keep in mind that what you are seeing is only highlight and shadow. How much does just this aspect of an image tell you about the material?

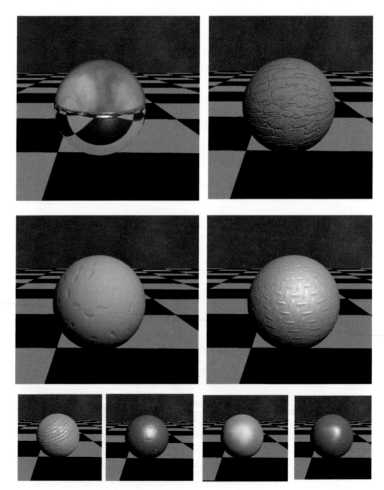

For a more advanced and in-depth discussion on the subject of light and shadow for 3D scenes, I recommend *Essential CG Lighting Techniques* by Darren Brooker (Focal, 2002).

Texture

In the bulk of this book, as in the game industry, we will be using the term "texture" to mean a 2D static image. What we refer to as textures in this book are also sometimes called materials, or even tile sets (from older games), but we will stick to the term "texture." The one exception in this book is that in this section we will talk about the word "texture" as it is used in traditional art: painting, sculpture, and so on. A side note: Keep in mind that vocabulary is very important and can be a confusing aspect of working in the game industry. There is much room for miscommunication. Different words can often mean the same thing, and the same words can often mean many different things. Acronyms can be especially confusing; RAM, POV, MMO, and RPG all mean different things in different industries. POV means "point of view" in the game industry and "personally owned vehicle" in the government, and also stands for "persistence of vision." So to clarify, the term "texture"—while usually meaning a 2D image applied to a polygon (the face of a 3D object)—in this section of this chapter, it refers to an aspect of an image and not the image itself. We draw this distinction for the following conversation on traditional art.

In traditional art, there are two types of texture: tactile and visual.

"Tactile texture" is when you are able to actually touch the physical texture of the art or object. Smooth and cold (marble, polished metal, glass) is as much a texture as coarse and rough. In art this applies to sculptures and the like, but many paintings have thick and very pronounced brush or palette knife strokes. Vincent van Gogh was famous for doing this. Some painters even add materials like sand to their paint to add more physical or tactile texture to their work.

"Visual texture" is the illusion of what the surface's texture might feel like if we could touch it. Visual texture is composed of fine highlights and shadows. As computer game texture artists, we deal solely with this aspect of texture. So, for example, an image on your monitor may look like rough stone, smooth metal, or even a beautiful woman, and if you try to kiss that beautiful woman, she is still just a monitor—not that I have ever tried that, mind you.

There are many ways to convey texture in a 2D piece of art. In computer games, we are combining 2D and 3D elements and must often decide which to use. With 2D, we are almost always forced to use strictly 2D imagery for fine visual texture. And although the faster processors, larger quantities of RAM, and the latest crop of 3D graphic cards allow us to use larger and more detailed textures and more geometry, a great deal of visual texture is still static—noticeably so to a trained artist. This limitation is starting to melt away as complex shader systems are coming into the mainstream of real-time games.

The real-time processing of bump maps, specular highlights, and a long list of other more complex effects are adding a depth of realism to our game worlds not even dreamed of in the recent past. **Figure 7-11**, you can see how in the 2D strip the object rotates but the effects stay static on the surface, while on the 3D strip, the object rotates and the effect moves realistically across the surface.

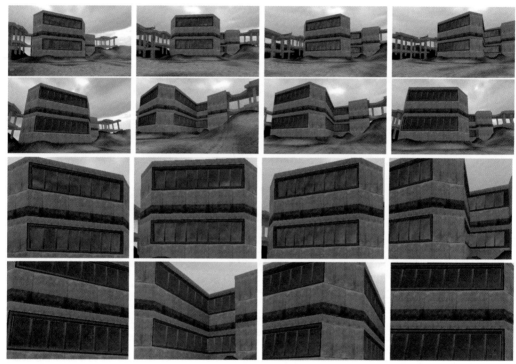

FIG. 7-11 Visual texture is composed of fine highlights and shadows. A shader allows for the real-time processing of visual texture, among other effects, and adds much more realism to a scene as the surface reacts with the world around it. In this example, I used a specular map. These effects are best seen in 3D, but you can see here that the windows in the building on the top row have a reflection of the sky in them and that reflection moves as the player does. The windows in the building on the lower row are painted textures and stay the same no matter where the player walks. The bottom two rows are close-ups to help you see the effect. If you pick one window in the close-up images and look closely, you will see that the cloud reflections are in different places in each frame.

The game artist's job is often to consider what tools and techniques are available and choosing which best accomplishes the job. We must often trade off between what looks good and what runs well. As you begin to paint textures, you will find that some of the techniques of traditional art don't work in the context of game texturing. A traditional artist usually does a painting that represents one static viewpoint, and can paint into it strong light sources and a great deal of depth, but that amount of depth representation

FIG. 7-12 There are several possibilities when dealing with overt depth representation. **Upper left:** the pipes are painted into the texture and totally lack any depth; notice how they dead-end into the floor. **Upper right:** restricting the players' ability to move around the texture can alleviate some of the problem. **Lower left:** adding actual geometry for the parts of the texture that cause the overt depth is the best solution if possible (this method uses less texture memory but more polygons). Finally, **lower right:** adding the actual geometry into the recess is an option that looks pretty interesting and actually allows for a reduction of geometry. The removal of polygons from the backsides of the pipes more than offsets the added faces of the recess.

goes beyond tactile texture and becomes faked geometry and looks flat in a dynamic, real-time 3D world. As mentioned earlier in this chapter, this will not work in a 3D game where a player can move about and examine the texture. Once again we must choose what to represent using a static 2D image, what can be processed in real time using a shader, and what must be represented using actual geometry. There are many solutions for this problem: among them are restricting the players' ability to move around the texture, removing the element of overt depth representation, or adding actual geometry for the parts of the texture represented by the overt depth representation (see **Figure 7-12**).

Color

We all know what color is in an everyday fashion: "Get me those pliers. No, the ones with black handles." "I said paint the house green—I didn't mean neon green!" That's all fine for the layman's discussion of color, but when you begin to speak with artists about color, you need to learn to speak of color intelligently, and that takes a little more education and some practice. You will also learn to choose and combine color. In games, as in movies, interior design, and other visual disciplines, color is very important. Color tells us much about the world and the situation we are in. While I was at CMP, we developed a massively multiplayer game that started in the town—saturated green grass, blue water, butterflies—you get the picture—this was a nice and safe place. As you moved away from town, the colors darkened and lost saturation. The grass went from a brighter green to a less saturated brownish-green. There were other visual clues as well. Most people can look at grass and tell if it is healthy, dying, kept up, or growing wild. Away from town, the grass was also long and clumpy, dying, and growing over the path. But even before we changed any other aspect of the game—still using the same grass texture from town that was well trimmed—we simply lowered the saturation of the colors on the fly and you could feel the life drain from the world as you walked away from town. As you create textures, you will most probably have some form of direction on color choice, but maybe not. You might need to know what colors to choose to convey what is presented in the design document and what colors will work well together.

This section lays out a simple introduction to the vocabulary of color, color mixing (on the computer), and color choices and their commonly accepted meanings. I decided to skip the complex science of color and stick to the practical and immediately useful aspects of color. Color can get very complex and esoteric; you would benefit from taking your education further and learning how color works on a scientific basis. Though this chapter will be a strong starting point, you will eventually move on from working with only the colors contained in the texture you are creating to how those colors interact with other elements in the world, such as lighting. To start with, however, a game texture artist needs the ability to communicate, create, and choose colors.

First, we will address the way in which we discuss color. There are many color models, or ways of looking at and communicating color verbally. There are models that concern printing, physics, pigment, and light. They each have their own vocabulary, concepts, and tools for breaking out color. As digital artists, we use the models concerning light, because we are working with colored pixels that emit light. A little later we will take a closer look at those color systems from the standpoint of color mixing, but for now we will look at the vocabulary of color. In game development, you will almost always use the RGB color model to mix color and the HSB color model to discuss color. You will see that Photoshop allows for the numeric input and visual selection of color in various ways. When you discuss color choices and changes and then enact them, you are often translating between two or more models. Don't worry; this is not difficult and most people don't know they are doing it.

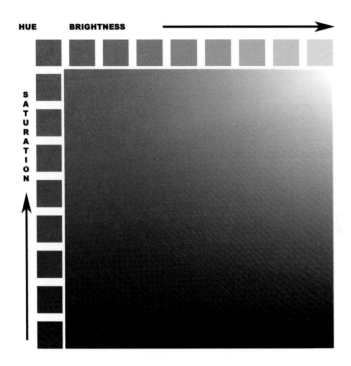

First, we will look at the HSB model, which stands for hue, saturation, and brightness, as this is the most common way for digital artists to communicate concerning color. These three properties of color are the main aspects of color that we need to be concerned with when discussing color. In **Figure 7-13**, you can see examples of these aspects of color:

- Hue is the name of the color (red, yellow, green).
- Saturation (or chroma) is the strength or purity of the color.
- Brightness (or value) is the lightness or darkness of the color.

Hue

Most people use the word "color" when referring to hue. Although there are many, many colors, there are far fewer hues. Variations of saturation and brightness create the almost unlimited colors we see in the world. Scarlet, maroon, pink, and crimson are all colors, but the base hue for all of these is red.

Understanding color and its various properties is best done with visual examples. The most often used method is the color wheel developed by Johannes Itten. We will look at the Itten color wheel a little later. In Photoshop you will recognize the Color Picker, which allows for various methods for choosing and controlling color, both numerically and visually. The Color Picker provides various ways to choose color, but the most commonly used is RGB (red, green, blue)—see **Figure 7-14**.

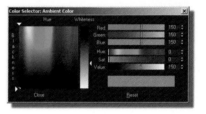

FIG. 7-14 Here are Color Pickers from various applications.

Saturation

Saturation is the amount of white in the color. In **Figure 7-15**, you can see the saturation of a color being decreased as white is added. If you have access to a software package like Photoshop and open the color picker, you can slide the picker from the pure hue to a less saturated hue and watch the saturation numbers in the HSB slots go down as the color gets less saturated. Notice how the brightness doesn't change unless you start dragging down and adding black to the color. Also, you may want to look down at the RGB numbers and notice how the red in RGB doesn't change, but the green and blue do.

100% saturation   **0% saturation**

FIG. 7-15 The saturation of the color red at 100% and decreasing to 0% by adding white.

Brightness

Brightness is the amount of black in the color. In **Figure 7-16**, you can see the brightness of a color being decreased. As in the previous example discussing saturation, you can open the Color Picker in Photoshop and this time, instead of decreasing the saturation, you can decrease the brightness by dragging down. You can look at the HSB and the RGB slots and see the brightness

100% brightness   **0% brightness**

FIG. 7-16 The brightness of the color red at 100% and decreasing to 0% by adding black.

numbers decreasing. Also notice that this time in the RGB slots the red numbers decrease, but the blue and green are already at zero and stay there.

Like most other aspects of color, brightness is affected by other factors. What colors are next to each other? What are the properties of the lights in the world? Another job of the texture artist is making the textures in the world consistent, which involves balancing the hues, saturation, and brightness of the color in most cases. **Figure 7-17** depicts an example of a texture that may have looked okay in Photoshop, but needed to be corrected to fit the scene. You can see that a great deal of contrast and intensity of color makes tiling the image a greater challenge.

FIG. 7-17 Here is an example of a texture that may have looked okay in Photoshop, but needed to be corrected to fit in the scene correctly. This is a subtle example. Notice the patch of exposed stone in the concrete on the building that repeats.

Color Systems—Additive and Subtractive

There are two types of color systems: additive and subtractive. Subtractive color is the physical mixing of paints, or pigments, to create a color. It is called "subtractive" due to the fact that light waves are absorbed (or subtracted from the spectrum) by the paint and only the reflected waves are seen. A red pigment, therefore, is reflecting only red light and absorbing all the others. In the subtractive system, you get black by mixing all the colors together—theoretically. It is a challenge to mix pigments that result in a true black or a vibrant color, which is one of the reasons that art supply stores have so many choices when it comes to paint. One of the advantages of working in the additive system is that we can get consistent and vibrant results with light.

We won't dwell on the subtractive system, as we won't be using it. The additive system works as light is added together (like on a computer screen) to create a color, so naturally we deal with the additive system because as computer artists, we are working with projected light. In **Figure 7-18**, you can see how the additive system works. I simply went into 3ds Max and created three spotlights that were pure red, green, and blue and created my own additive color wheel, or a visual representation of how the colors interact. Black is the absence of light (the area outside of the spotlights), white is all light (the center area where all three lights overlap each other)—the combination of red, green, and blue is the additive system. If you look at the Color Picker in Photoshop (**Figure 7-19**) you will see a vertical rectangle of color graduating from red through the colors and back to red. This allows you to select a hue and use the Color Picker Palette to change the value and intensity.

FIG. 7-18 The additive system works by adding lights. Black is the absence of light (the area outside of the spotlights), white is all light (the center area where all three lights overlap each other). The combination of red, green, and blue is the additive system.

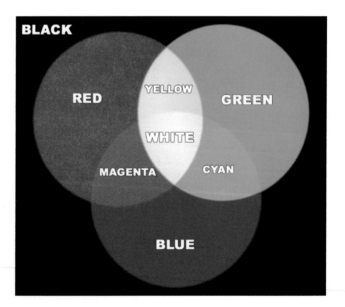

Primary Colors

The three primary colors in the additive color system are red, green, and blue (RGB). They are referred to as "primary" colors because you can mix them and make all the other colors, but you can't create the primary colors by mixing any other color. Many projection televisions use a system where you can see the red, green, and blue lenses that project the three colors (RGB) to create the image you see using the additive method.

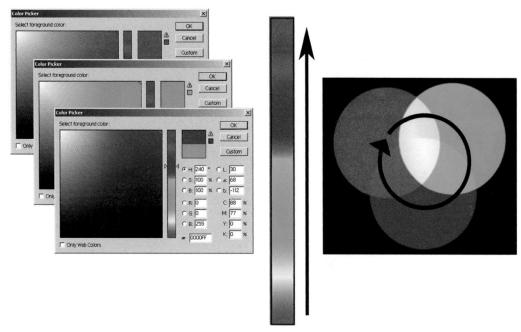

FIG. 7-19 The Color Picker in Photoshop has a vertical rectangle of color graduating from red through the colors and back to red. This allows you to select a hue and use the Color Picker Palette to change the value and intensity.

Secondary Colors

The secondary colors are yellow, magenta, and cyan. When you mix equal amounts of two primary colors together, you get a secondary color. You can see that these colors are located between the primary colors on the color wheel and on the Photoshop Color Picker vertical strip.

Color Emphasis

Color is often used for emphasis. Look at **Figure 7-20**. All things being equal, the larger shapes dominate, but the small shapes demand your attention once color is added. Of course, there are many other forms of emphasis that you can use in creating art, but color can be the most powerful—and the most overused. Ever come across a web page that has a busy background and every font, color, and emphasis devised by man splashed across it? There is almost no emphasis, as all the elements cancel each other out. Often, less is more.

In another example using a photograph, in **Figure 7-21**, you can see that in the first black-and-white photo, your eye would most likely be drawn to the dark opening of the doghouse and you would most likely assume that the subject of this picture is the doghouse. In the second version, the colorful flower draws the primary interest—it still competes with the doghouse entrance for

FIG. 7-20 The larger shapes dominate, but the small shapes demand your attention once color is added.

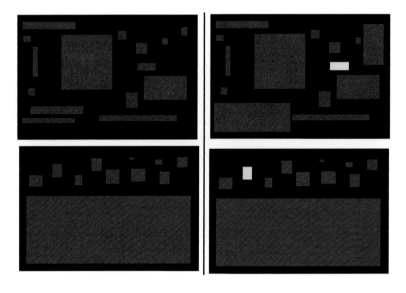

FIG. 7-21 Your eye is most likely drawn to the opening of the doghouse in the black and white photo, but add color, and the flower draws the primary interest.

attention, but you would probably make the assumption that the focus of this picture was the flower.

In a game scene, you can see the use of color drawing the attention of a player to an important item. Look at **Figure 7-22**. In the first version of the scene, you are drawn to the fire and then look around at all the items in the shadows. In the second version, the red crate draws your attention and clearly means something. Depending on the world logic of the game you are playing, that could simply mean that you can interact with the object, or it could mean that the item is dangerous. That decision brings us to our next topic: color expression.

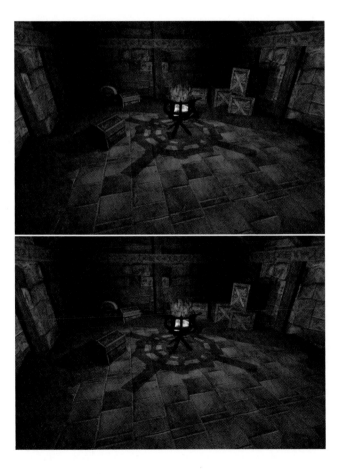

FIG. 7-22 In a room full of normal objects, the players' eyes will be drawn to the fire and then equally to the objects. In a room full of normal objects, a red crate draws attention, especially given the fact that there are other normal crates around it.

Color Expression or Warm and Cool Colors

When you start painting textures and choosing colors, you will want to know how they react together in terms of contrast, harmony, and even message. There is a lot of information on this topic and once again, Johannes Itten (the guy who did the color wheel) enters the picture.

Itten has provided artists with a great deal of information on how color works and how they work together. He was among the first to look at color not just from a scientific point of view, but from an artistic and emotional point of view. He was very interested in how colors made people feel. From his research, we get the vocabulary of "warm" and "cool" colors. We all are familiar with this convention, as it is mostly based on the natural world. When asked to draw a flame, we reach for the red or orange crayon, ice is blue, the sun yellow. Each warm and cool color has feelings commonly associated with it, both positive and negative. The brighter or more pure the color, the more positive the association. Darker and duller colors tend to have negative connotations associated with them.

The warm colors are red and yellow, and the cool colors are blue and green. Children will color the sun yellow and ice blue and use the black crayon to scratch out things they don't like. Traffic lights are hot when you should stop or be cautious (red and yellow) but cool when it is okay to go (green). Red and orange are hot and usually associated with fire, lava, coals. How many red and black shirts do you see at the mall? Red and black generally symbolize demonic obsession. Red by itself can mean royalty and strength as well as demonic symbolism. Deep red can be erotic. Yellow is a hot color like the sun, a light giver. Yellow is rich like gold as a pure color. A deep yellow (amber) window in the dark of a cold night can mean fire and warmth. But washed out or pale yellow can mean envy or betrayal. Calling a person yellow is an insult, meaning that he is a coward. Judas is portrayed as wearing yellow garments in many paintings. During the Spanish Inquisition, people who were considered guilty of heresy were made to wear yellow. Moving into green, we think of lush jungles teaming with life. As green washes out, we get a sense of dread and decay (zombie and orc skin). Vibrant green in a certain context can be toxic waste and radioactive slime. Blue in its saturated state is cold like ice, fresh like water and the sky. Darker blues are misery. Purple is mysterious and royal.

Keep in mind that color is context-sensitive. Water is generally blue; would you drink dark green water? But not just any blue will do. In the real world, if we come across water that is a saturated blue that we can't see through, we get suspicious. Was this water dyed? Are there weird chemicals in there? If anything lives in that, then what could it be?! Blood is generally red, but what if an enemy bled green? What if the game you are playing is about an alien race taking over earth and one of your companions bleeds green from an injury during combat? In a fantasy game, you might come across coins. Which coin do you take, the bright yellowish metal or gray-green metal? With no previous information on the color of coins in this world, most people would pick the brighter yellow. Look at **Figure 7-23**. What are some of the assumptions you might make about these three scenes?

Looking at color in this way may make it seem a bit mechanical, but it still takes a talented artist to make the right color choices. You can memorize all the information in the world, but it usually comes down to having a good eye and being able to convey that vision in your work and to your coworkers.

FIG. 7-23 These three scenes are the same, except for the ax. What questions and/or assumptions run through your mind looking at each version?

Perspective

We discussed earlier in this chapter that dramatic perspective (**Figure 7-24**) is usually not used in the creation of a game texture, although sometimes perspective is present and needs to be understood. In addition, understanding perspective is not only a valuable artistic tool to have available, but will also help you when you are taking digital reference images and cleaning and straightening those images.

FIG. 7-24 Although dramatic perspective is used in traditional art, it is not used in a game texture, but there is some notion of perspective—so it is best to understand the concept.

Perspective is the illusion that something far away from us is smaller. This effect can be naturally occurring, as in a photo, or it can be a mechanically created illusion in a painting. You can see samples of this in **Figure 7-25**. In 2D artwork, perspective is a technique used to recreate that illusion and give the artwork 3D depth. Perspective uses overlapping objects, horizon lines, and vanishing points to create a feeling of depth. You can see in **Figure 7-26** an image with the major lines of perspective as they converge on one point, called the "vanishing point." There are several types of perspective used to achieve different effects.

One-Point Perspective

One-point perspective is when all the major lines of an image converge on one point. This effect is best illustrated when looking down a set of straight railroad tracks or a long road (see Figure 7-25). The lines of the road and track,

FIG. 7-25 Perspective is the illusion that something far away from us is smaller. Are the street lights actually getting smaller in this image? Are the train tracks really getting closer together?

although we know they are the same distance apart, seem to meet and join together at some point in the far distance—the vanishing point. In one-point perspective, all the lines move away from you (the z-axis) and converge at the vanishing point. Vertical and horizontal or up and down and right and left lines (x and y) remain straight, as seen in **Figure 7-27**.

Two-Point Perspective

One-point perspective works fine if you happen to be looking directly at the front of something or standing in the middle of some railroad tracks, but what if the scene is viewed from the side? Then you shift into two-point perspective. Two-point perspective has two vanishing points on the horizon line. All lines, except the vertical, will converge into one of the two vanishing points. See **Figure 7-28**.

FIG. 7-26 In 2D artwork, perspective is a technique used to recreate that illusion and give the artwork 3D depth.

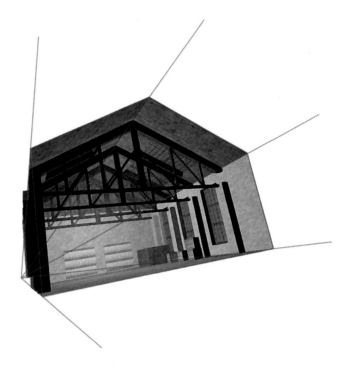

FIG. 7-27 In one-point perspective, all the lines that move away from the viewer seem to meet at a far point on the horizon. This point is called the "vanishing point."

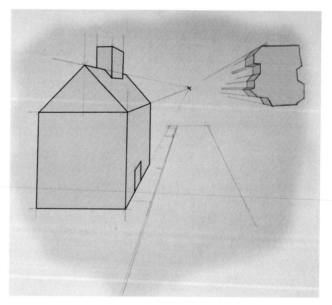

Three-Point Perspective

Three-point perspective is probably the most challenging of all. In three-point perspective every line will eventually converge on one of three points.

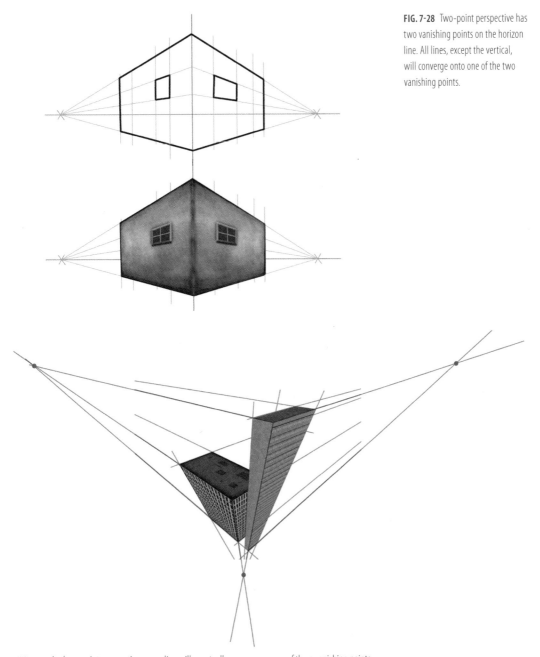

FIG. 7-28 Two-point perspective has two vanishing points on the horizon line. All lines, except the vertical, will converge onto one of the two vanishing points.

FIG. 7-29 In three-point perspective, every line will eventually converge on one of three vanishing points.

Three-point perspective is the most dramatic of all and can often be seen in comic books when the hero is flying over buildings or kicking butt in the alley below as the buildings tower above. **Figure 7-29** shows some three-point perspective.

159

From the texture artist's point of view, such as while photographing surfaces for game art, perspective can be the enemy.

Quick Studies of the World Around You

The following pages show some quick studies I did of random objects. I tried to work through each of them as a game artist might, to give you some quick and general examples of how a game artist might break them down. This is a general look and introduction to the thought process of recreating surfaces and materials in a digital environment. I covered all that was introduced in this chapter: shape and form, light and shadow, texture, color, as well as considering other aspects of the object or material. I didn't touch on perspective in these exercises because I wanted to limit the exercise to

FIG. 7-30 The upper left-hand image is a digital photo of some simple concrete stairs. You might have an art lead email you an image like this and tell you that she wants a texture based on these stairs. Fortunately, this is a rather simple form; not a lot of color or detail to distract us. Look at the simple recreation of the stairs to the right showing the basic light and shadow patterns on the stairs. The lower left image shows the 2D texture created in Photoshop to be applied to a 3D model of the stairs. If you look at the yellow stripe on the stairs and compare it to the stripe on the texture, you can see the highlights painted in the texture where the edge of the step is and the shadow under the lip of the edge. If you were able to examine the original digital image of the stairs closely, you would see an almost infinite amount of detail. Part of the texture artist's job is to know when to draw the line. Here I didn't include every scuff and mark from the original stair image, because it wouldn't work. I created this texture pretty quickly; given more time, I would experiment with the chips and wear on the edge of the steps to add more character.

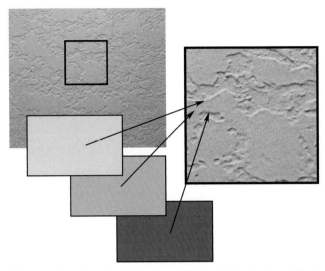

FIG. 7-31 This is a straight-on photo of an interior plaster wall. I included this obviously unexciting image to demonstrate that even in such a simple surface there can be complex highlight and shadow going on. Look at the color swatches of the highlight, shadow, and mid-tone. Notice that the colors are not simple black, white, and gray. The highlight is not pure white or light gray, but a very pale green. Look at the close-up of the image. You can clearly see the consistent behavior of light as it highlights the upper ridges of the plaster and shadow falls from the lower edges. Once you start studying such seemingly commonplace things, like a wall that you might walk by a hundred times a day, you will start to notice, understand, and remember how various lights, materials, and other factors affect a surface. Do you convey that simple raised pattern in the texture, using geometry, or a shader? Of course, that depends on many factors, but hopefully you can now start to know what questions to ask to determine the answers.

recreating 2D surfaces (textures), and perspective is not as critical as the other concepts in this chapter. In the following pages, **Figures 7-30 to 7-35** each have a caption that discusses the particulars of each study.

Conclusion

This chapter was an overview of the most basic, but critical, aspects of traditional art. Understanding the concepts in this chapter, and further exploring them on your own, will make you a much better texture artist.

FIG. 7-32 This image simply shows the world that I need to wash my car. Seriously, look at the various parts of complex objects, and you will see a variety of surface behaviors. Notice how the paint is highly reflective and mirrors the world around the car. The metal is not flat like a mirror, so notice the distortion of the reflected image. The windows, while reflecting the surrounding world as well, are translucent, so you can also see what's behind the window and on the other side of the car. The window also has a patina of dirt and spots on it. If you needed to recreate this as realistically as possible, you would have to take all those aspects into consideration and determine the best way to achieve the effect. Look at the close-up of the rim. You can see that the highlights are not mirror-like in their accuracy, but rather they are a diffuse notion of highlight. Looks simple to paint, but wheels rotate and will instantly look bad if not painted properly. Using a real-time process for highlights eliminates this problem. Although the tires are flat black and reveal only a faint notion of highlight, depending on the detail level, you may be dealing with complex mapping and shader effects here, too. While all of this seems obvious, taking the time to examine the object you are recreating and understanding what you are seeing and how to verbalize it helps when turning the object into game art. If you were to make materials or textures for this vehicle, you would need to know many things about the technology and how the car will be used in the game. Can we have real-time environmental reflections? Can we fake them using a shader? Do we have to carefully paint in a vague notion of metallic highlights that work in all situations the car may be in? And the windows. Can we do a translucent/reflective surface with an alpha channel for dirt? If the car is used in a driving game where the vehicle is the focus of the game and the player gets to interact up close and personal with the car, then I am sure a lot of attention will be given to these questions. But if this car is a static prop sitting on a street that the player blazes past, then over-the-top effects may be just a waste of development time and computer resources.

FIG. 7-33 This sewer intrigued me; a simple shape of a common item that many might overlook as not worthy of serious attention. Some may have the attitude that it is only a sewer grate, so make it and move on. But a shiny new sewer grate with clean edges would stand out in a grungy urban setting. Look at this sewer grate. It is made of iron and looks solid and heavy. It was probably laid down decades ago and has had thousands of cars drive over it, thousands of people walk over it, millions of gallons of rain water pour through it. On the image at the upper left, you can look at the iron and see how it is rusted, but so well worn that the rust is polished off in most places. Dirt has built up in the cracks between the grate, the rim, and the concrete. Even little plants have managed to grow. Look at the close-up at the upper right and you can see just how beat up this iron is and how discolored it has become. At the lower left, I desaturated and cleaned up a portion of the image to see just how the light and shadow are hitting it and to get a feel for the quality of the surface. In this image you can more clearly see the roughness of the cement and the metal, and although the circular grate looks round from a distance, up close there are no straight edges and smooth curves. All this detail can't be depicted 100% in a game texture, but knowing it's there and understanding what you are seeing will allow you to convey a richer version of the grate as you will learn to focus on those details that add realism and character. On the lower right is a texture I did, and you can see that I was able to quickly achieve a mottled and grungy look for the metal and the edges. There are a few places at the top where I started the process of eating away at the concrete and the metal a bit.

FIG. 7-34 The process behind this image is similar to the sewer in approach. Here I wanted to point out how a simple shape can be turned into an ornate hinge with little effort. The top image is the original digital photo of the hinge. I drew the shape of the hinge in Photoshop. You may notice that I drew the screws separately. This is because you need the shapes separately to work with them in Photoshop. In Photoshop I applied and adjusted the Layer Effects and then colored the hinge close to the overall color of the original. After that it was a matter of applying the right filters and doing some hand work to get the edges looking right.

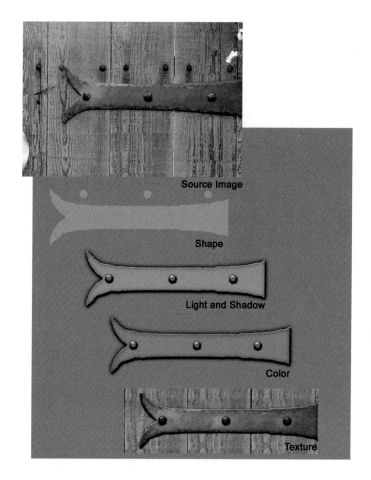

Source Image

Shape

Light and Shadow

Color

Texture

FIG. 7-35 This light switch is a common object that you may need to create. Instead of taking the time to clean up and manipulate a photo, you can just make one more quickly from scratch. The switch is composed of simple shapes with the Layer Effects applied. The wall behind the switch was a quick series of filters run to add a base for this exercise.

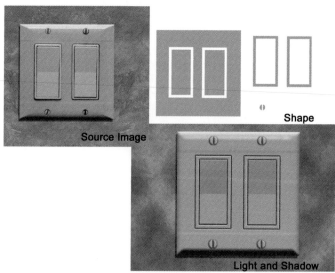

Source Image

Shape

Light and Shadow

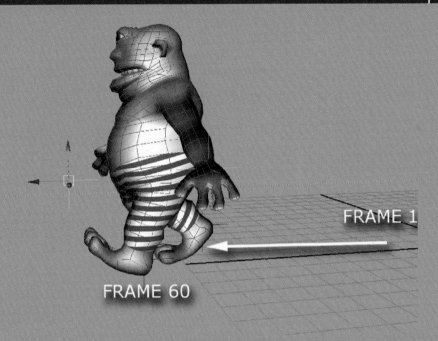

CHAPTER 8

FRAME 1

FRAME 60

The Basic 3D Kit Using Maya

The Roadmap

This chapter is an introduction to basic 3D modeling and animation in Maya and Virtools. "Basic 3D Kit" means that you will learn how to use a selection of creative tools that will get you up and running quickly using Maya. This chapter, designed to be fun and creative, will hopefully make you anxious to explore this amazing software.

The following tutorials, created in collaboration with Miro Kirov, show how to use Maya and Virtools for creating interactive models and animated characters. We hope that you will enjoy the process of producing 3D interactive content.

The first tutorial is a step-by-step introduction to modeling and animating Mr. Cyclop, an interactive character in Maya. The second tutorial shows how to create trees and grass in Maya using 3D paint tools and how to set up Mr. Cyclop inside the forest in Virtools. The last part of the tutorial shows how to add scripts to the character in Virtools.

The Making of Mr. Cyclop, An Interactive Character in Maya

Mr. Cyclop is a one-eyed mythological creature with a good and charming temperament. Mr. Cyclop is a goofy creature who enjoys playing inside a lush forest.

This tutorial covers step-by-step modeling, texturing, and animation of an interactive character, using two 3D applications: Maya and Virtools.

Maya will be used to build and animate the 3D content. Virtools will be used to add behaviors, including scripting an interactive environment using a keyboard, a mouse, or a game controller.

This tutorial shows how to create a goofy Mr. Cyclop using Subdivision Primitives, how to add textures, and how to animate the Cyclop's walk using skeletal structure and Inverse Kinematics systems.

Tour of Maya's Interface

Let's take a tour of the Maya interface (**Figure 8-1**):

- Maya, like other 3D applications, uses several modules called Modeling, Animation, Dynamics, and Rendering.

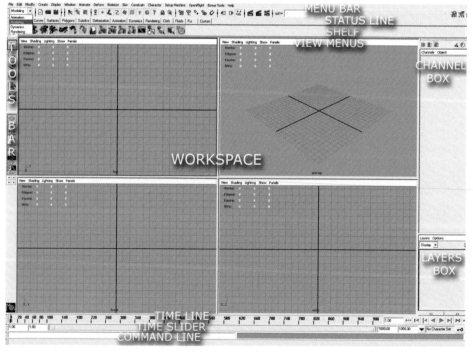

FIG. 8-1 Maya's interface.

- From top to bottom, you can find the menu bar, the Status Line, and the Shelf.
- The Workspace includes top, side, front, and perspective views.
- The mini Tools bar is located on the left side of the Workspace.
- The Channel box is on the right side of the Workspace.
- The Layers box is under the Channel box.
- In the lower part of the screen, you can find the Time Line, the Time Slider, and the Command Line.

Let's review the row of tools represented with icons located below the top menu.

The tools change according to the module selected in the Status Line box (Figure 8-2). Click on the box located on the left in the Status Line to see the different modules. We will use Modeling and Animation for this chapter.

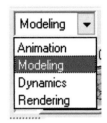

FIG. 8-2 The tools change according to the module selected in the Status Line box.

The first group of tools found in the menu bar includes buttons for the following commands: Create New Scene, Open a Scene, and Save the Scene.

The second group of items includes buttons for selection: Selection by Hierarchy, Selection by Object, and Selection by Components.

The third group of items includes buttons for selecting different components: Vertices, Lines, Polygons, and Curves.

The fourth group of items includes buttons for snapping tools: Snap to a Grid, Snap to a Curve, and Snap to a Surface.

The last group of items includes shortcut tools for rendering: Render, IPR Render, and Render Globals.

The Shelf can be customized to store your most frequently used tools.

Customizing the Shelf
Click on a tool in the menu bar while pressing Shift and Control simultaneously. You will see an icon of the selected tool added to the Shelf.

The Workspace is the place to preview your 3D content. You can customize the Workspace according to the type of views and rendering mode, including shading, texturing, or wireframe mode. You can toggle between the perspective view and the four (top, front, side, perspective) views by pressing the space bar. Each of the views has its own menu bar, including View, Shading, Lighting, Show, and Panels.

To navigate in the perspective view window, use the following commands:

- To rotate, use the Alt key and the left mouse button.
- To pan, use the Alt key and the middle mouse button.
- To zoom, use the right mouse button.

The Tool bar, located on the left side of the Workspace, includes the following tools, from top to bottom: Select, Lasso Select, Move, Rotate, Scale, Manipulator, and Current, which displays the tool that you are currently using. The Layout bar with icons for different views of the Workspace can be found under the Tools section.

The Channel box, located on the right side of the Workspace, contains information about 3D models selected in the Workspace and current transformations applied to the models. The Layer box contains information about the layers created for 3D objects and lets you work on each 3D object without affecting the others.

The Time Line displays the key frame numbers. The Animation Controls and the Time Slider help you browse through the Time Line.

The Command Line for Maya's scripting language (MEL) commands lets you script transformations of the 3D content.

The Help Line is located below the Command Line.

After exploring the basic elements of the Maya's Interface, you can start building your character. You will use a fast and accurate way to model a character called Subdivision Surfaces. This modeling technique allows the computer to calculate shapes as polygonal surfaces and to display a subdivided smooth approximation of surfaces. After the modeling phase, we will convert the model to a polygonal mesh. Let's start modeling.

Modeling

Start your project by creating a project folder and its subfolders, where your content will be saved.

Generating a New Project Folder

Go to the top menu and select, File > Project > New. In the dialog window, specify a name for your project, choose the location where it will be saved, and click on Use Defaults. Click Accept to close the window. See **Figure 8-3**.

To start creating the character, choose the modeling module. Go to the top menu, and select Create > Subdiv Primitives > Sphere.

Subdivision Surfaces has two modes: the PolygonProxy Mode, in which the shape can be manipulated as a polygonal mesh, and the Standard Mode, used for fine details.

We will use the PolygonProxy Mode for this tutorial (**Figure 8-4**).

Go to the top menu, and select Subdiv Surfaces > PolygonProxy Mode. The workspace displays a wireframe cube with its smooth approximation. Press key 5 to display the sphere in the shaded mode. Press key 3 to increase its smoothness.

Now let's select the cube by its components: vertex, line, and polygon.

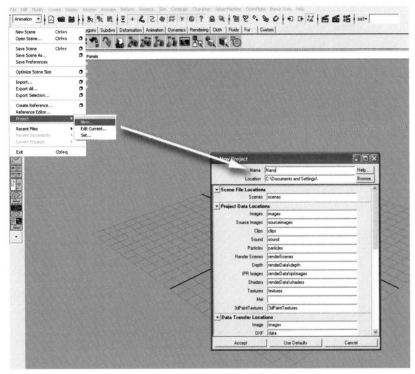

FIG. 8-3 Start your project by creating a project folder and its subfolders, where your content will be saved.

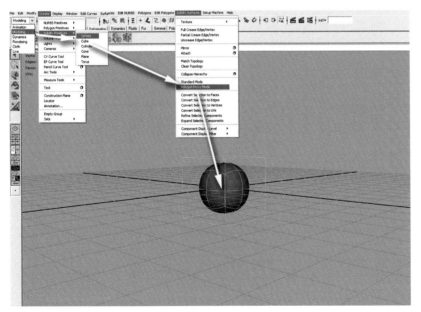

FIG. 8-4 To start modeling, choose the modeling module. Go to Create > Subdiv Primitives > Sphere. We will use the PolygonProxy Mode for this tutorial.

In the Status Line, click on the Select by Components button, then click on the Face button. The color of the cube changes to blue and a handle appears on each of the sides. Lines of bounding boxes are visible on the borders of the polygons.

To select the left side of the cube, click on the blue handle located on the left side of the cube. Press the Delete key. The 3D object looks like one-half of a sphere (**Figure 8-5**).

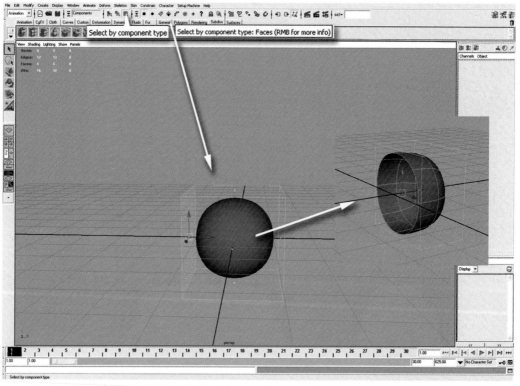

FIG. 8-5 To select the left side of the cube, click on the blue handle located on the left side of the cube. Press the Delete key. The cube now looks like one half of a sphere.

You can subdivide the polygons of the cube by selecting the Object Mode from the Status Line or by pressing the F8 key. The edges of the polygons turn green (**Figure 8-6**).

Go to Edit Polygons > Subdivide > Options. The Polygon Subdivide Face Options dialog window contains options for the Subdivide tools. Select subdivision level = 2 and click on Subdivide. Your model is similar to the one in the following illustration. First, you will be modeling only one side of the character. Later, you will mirror the other side of the 3D model.

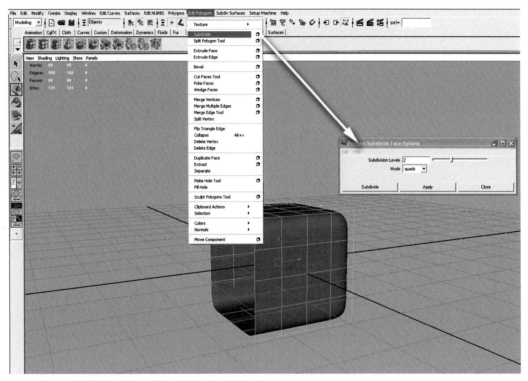

FIG. 8-6 You can subdivide the polygons of the cube. The edges of the polygons turn green.

This soft cube represents one half of the character's torso. You can use Move and Scale from the Tool bar to reshape the torso.

Go to the top menu bar, select, Polygon > Tools Options. Ensure Keep Faces Together is turned on.

In the Status Line, choose the Components Face mode. You can also press the F11 key. Select two polygons located on the right side.

Go to the top menu, and select Edit Polygon > Extrude Face. See Figure 8-7.

You just created a new polygon that remains connected with the rest of the character. The Manipulator tool is automatically activated. Click and drag the yellow arrow perpendicular to the selected polygons. You will notice that the smooth surface is changing shape locally (Figure 8-8). You have begun to create a new arm for your Cyclop.

Repeat the same operations for the left leg and the neck.

Let's play with selecting other components such as lines and vertices. You can select lines and vertices either from the icons of the Status Line or by pressing the F10 or F11 keys.

Let's model the character's limbs and face from the basic shape that you created (Figures 8-9 through 8-11).

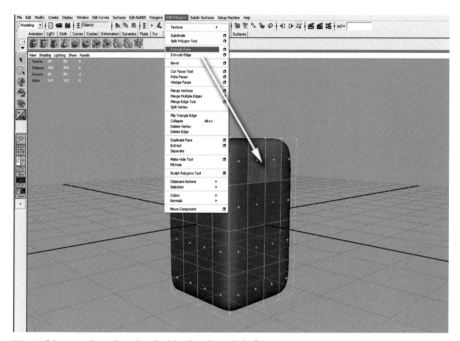

FIG. 8-7 Select two polygons located on the right side and extrude the faces.

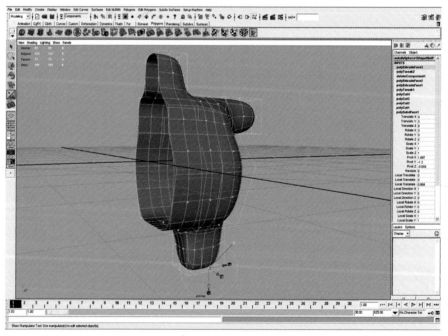

FIG. 8-8 Click and drag the yellow arrow from the Manipulator tool, perpendicular to the selected polygons. You will notice that the smooth surface is changing shape locally.

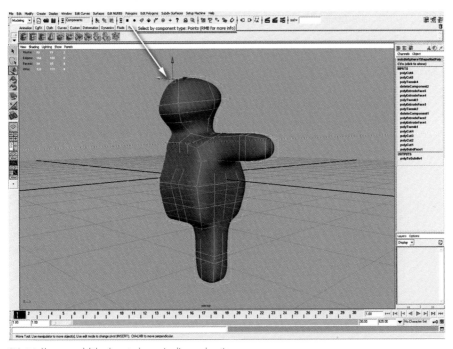

FIG. 8-9 You can model the character by moving lines and vertices.

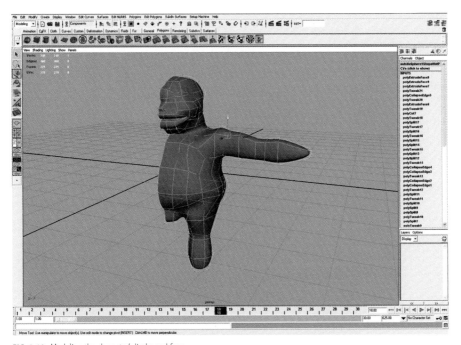

FIG. 8-10 Modeling the character's limbs and face.

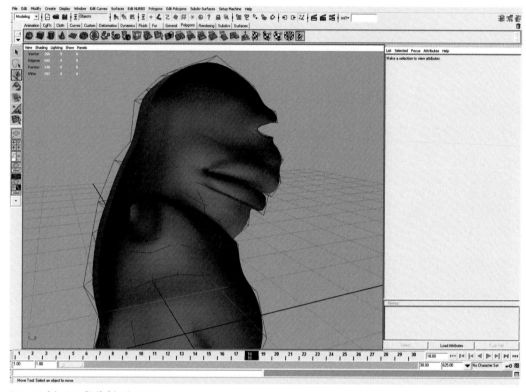

FIG. 8-11 Side view of half of the character.

Let's work inside the model to define the mouth and the eye socket.

Go to the top menu, and select Edit Polygons > Extrude Face. Select the Extrude Face tool or the Split Polygon tool to add more details.

To split a polygon, select Edit Polygons > Split Polygon Tool. Select the Split Polygon tool, and click and drag on the desired lines surrounding the polygon. This tool will let you create small details, such as the eyes, the nose, and the fingers (Figures 8-12, 8-13).

To create the fingers, select the polygon located on the edge of the hand. Split the polygon into five polygons in the area that will become the base of the fingers. Three fingers will be extruded from five polygons.

To finish the detail of the fingertip, go to the top menu and select Edit Polygons > Poke Faces. Move the vertex located in the middle of the polygon at the fingertip to add a nice finishing touch to the fingertips (Figure 8-14).

Repeat the same operation to create the thumb. Select the polygon on the side of the hand. Use the Extrude Face tool, move the new polygon, extrude again, and poke the face. Move the vertex located in the middle of the polygon at the fingertip to get a nice finish on the thumb (Figure 8-15).

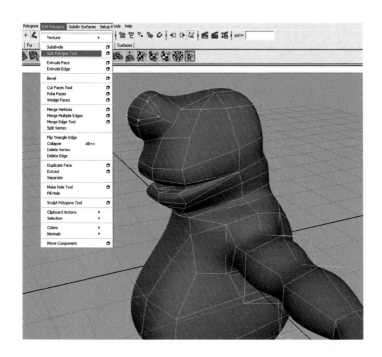

FIG. 8-12 The split polygons tool will let you create small details such as the eyes, the nose, and the fingers.

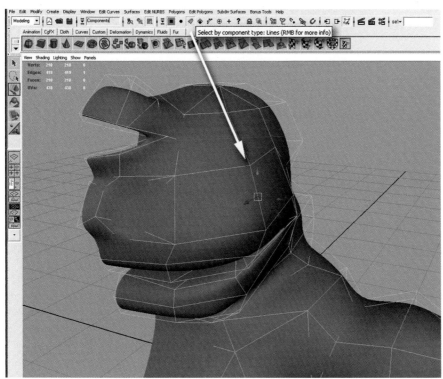

FIG. 8-13 Selecting the edge of a polygon.

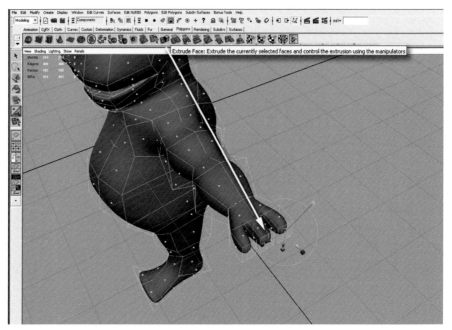

FIG. 8-14 To create the fingers, select the polygon located on the edge of the hand. Split the polygon into five polygons in the area that will become the base of the fingers. Three fingers will be extruded from five polygons. Move the vertex located in the middle of the polygon at the fingertip to add a nice finishing touch to the fingertips.

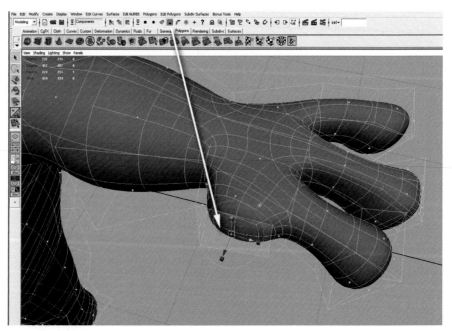

FIG. 8-15 Use the Extrude Face tool to create the thumb.

The same operations can be repeated for the leg and the toes (**Figure 8-16**).

Once you enjoy the look and feel of half of the character's body, you can convert the 3D model to a polygonal mesh.

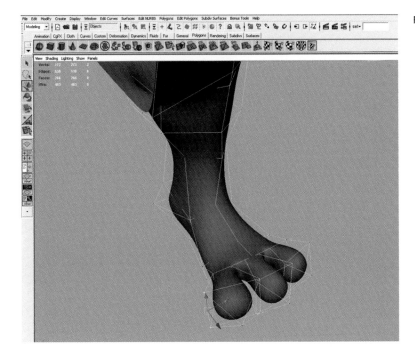

FIG. 8-16 Creating the toes.

Converting to a Polygonal Mesh

Go to the top menu bar, select Modify > Convert, and check on the Subdiv to Polygons option box. The box is on the right of the name of the tool. A dialog window will open. Select the Tessellation Method with Uniform.

The Adaptive Method option may increase the tessellation inside the detailed area, which would create too many polygons. We will choose the Uniform Method, because we want to keep down the number of polygons. Enter the following settings: Level = 1, the Division Per Face = 1, Replace Original Object = ON.

After conversion, you should have a shape made of interconnected polygons similar to the one you had before. Let's repeat the same modeling steps to add on more details for ears, nostrils, and wrinkles on the polygonal mesh (**Figures 8-17 through 8-19**).

Let's model the teeth (**Figure 8-20**).

Select the edges on the lips polygon located inside the mouth. Go to the top menu and select Edit Polygons > Extrude Edge. Move the newly created edges.

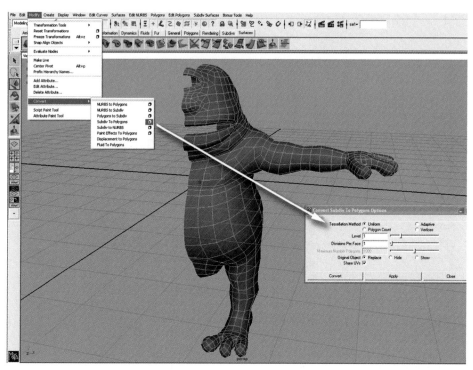

FIG. 8-17 Converting the 3D model to a polygonal mesh.

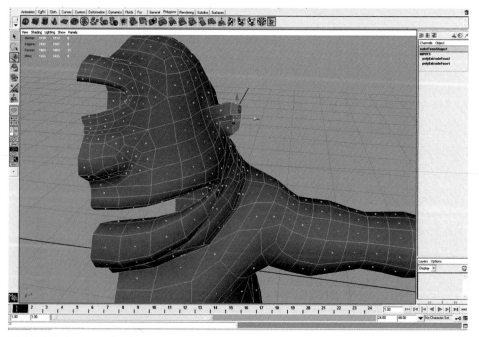

FIG. 8-18 Let's add more details to the ears.

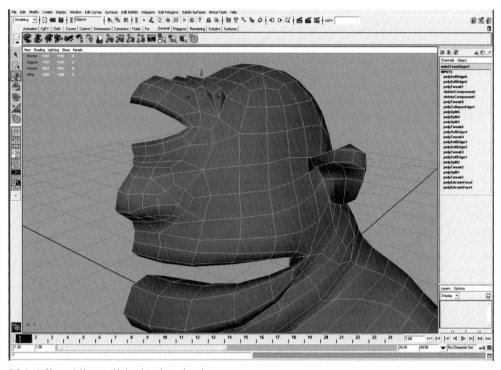

FIG. 8-19 More wrinkles are added to the polygonal mesh.

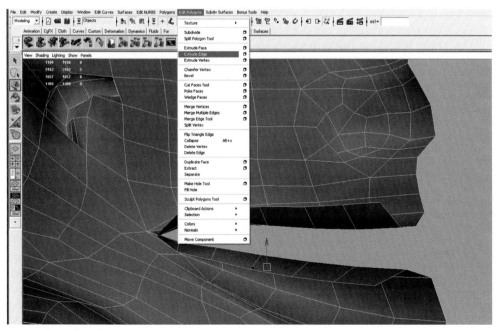

FIG. 8-20 Creating the teeth.

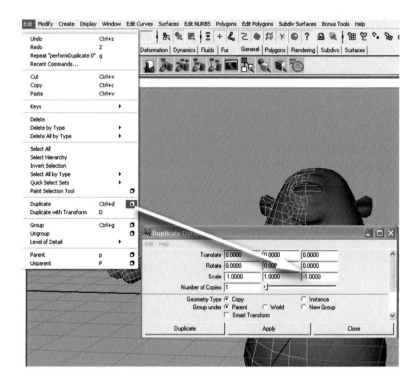

Because your modeling job is detailed enough, you are going to duplicate the other half of the body to create a whole character (**Figure 8-21**).

Creating the Other Half of the Character

Go to the top menu and select Edit > Duplicate Options.

In the dialog window, go to the column for the X axis, and change the scale value = −1. Click the Duplicate button. A complete mirrored clone is created. The edges of the two halves should slightly touch each other. If this is not the case, use the move tool to adjust one half.

Combining the Two Halves

Go to the top menu and select Polygons > Combine.

The color of the meshes changes from green and white to green, indicating that we have one surface (**Figure 8-22**).

The edges need to be welded together.

Welding the Edges Together

Select the edges of each of the halves by clicking on one edge on the left half and on one edge on the right side.

Go to the top menu and select Edit Polygons > Selection > Select Contiguous Edges. Both edges will have a brown color.

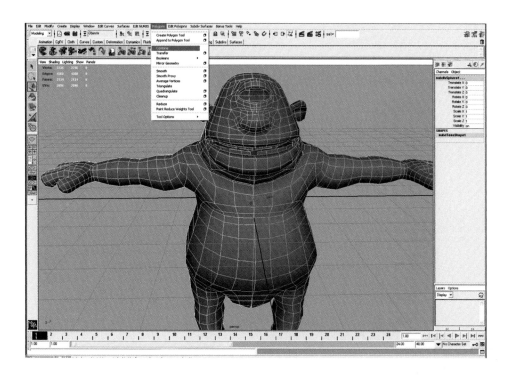

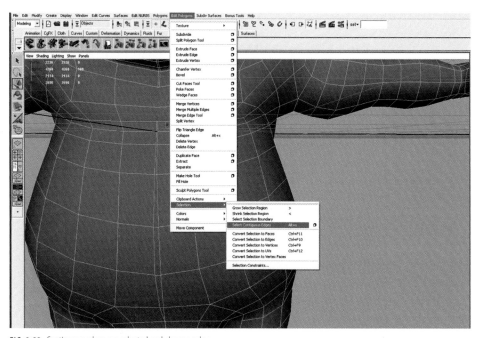

FIG. 8-22 Contiguous edges are selected and change color.

The next step is merging two surfaces into one continuous surface (**Figure 8-23**). Go to the top menu and select Edit Polygons > Merge Multiple Edges.

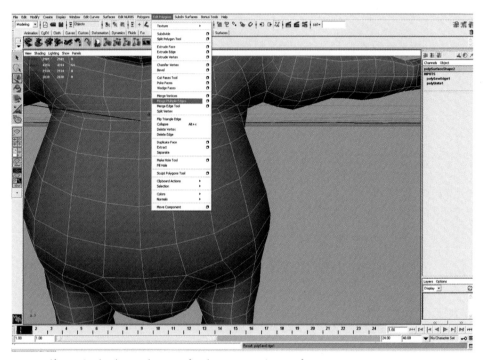

FIG. 8-23 After merging the edges together, two surfaces become one continuous surface.

Accidents on the surface of the mesh can be hard to detect. Gaps and holes can prevent some edges from being welded together.

Detecting Holes on the Surface of the Mesh

Go to the top menu and select Display > Polygon Components > Border Edges. Maya displays a thicker line around the contours of holes appearing in the mesh (**Figure 8-24**). In this example, the edges surrounding the mouth and the eye are obviously needed for our Cyclop character.

Closing Unwanted Holes and Gaps

Go to the top menu and select Edit Polygon > Merge Edge. Click on the first edge of the hole and on the corresponding edge on the other side. Press Enter, and repeat the same process until the surface is closed (**Figure 8-25**).

Let's model the eye (**Figure 8-26**).

Go to the top menu and select Create Polygon Primitives > Sphere. In the dialog window, specify the number of subdivisions along the height and around the y-axis = 10. Select Create.

Save your scene. Go to top menu and select File > Save Scene As.

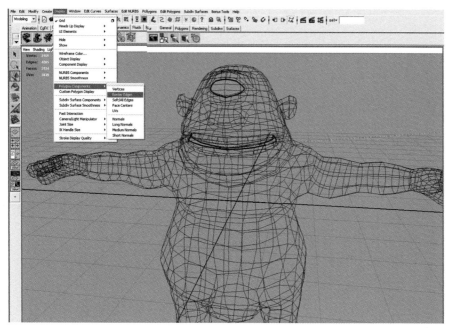

FIG. 8-24 Maya displays a thicker line around the contours of holes appearing in the mesh. In this example, the edges surrounding the mouth and the eye are needed for our Cyclop character.

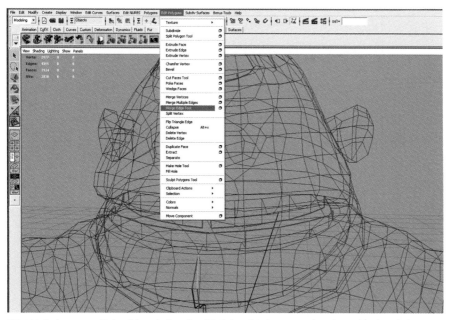

FIG. 8-25 To close gaps and holes, click on the first edge of the hole and on the corresponding edge on the other side. Press Enter, and repeat the same process until the surface is closed.

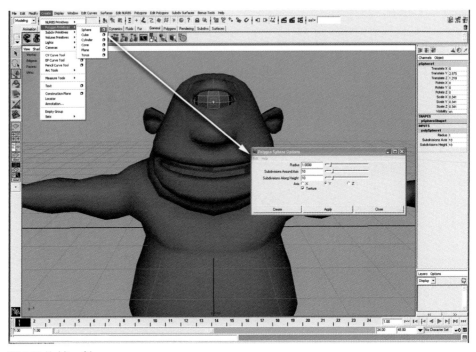

FIG. 8-26 Modeling of the eye.

Materials and Textures

Let's apply colors and textures to the character.

Opening the Hypershade Window

Go to the top menu and select Window > Rendering Editor > Hypershade. The Hypershade window contains the library of materials, textures, and utilities. 3D objects with surfaces require the creation of a material to receive a texture. When a new surface is created, Maya assigns a gray Lambert material by default to the surface.

You can customize your own materials and assign them to various surfaces of your project. In the case of this tutorial, we are using only image-based materials and textures. Maya can also use shaders, which are materials using code to describe the way the surface of the 3D model is rendered.

To create a new material for the eye, open the Hypershade window. (To open the Hypershade window, Go to the top menu and select Window > Rendering Editor > Hypershade.)

Go to the menu with materials and texturing tools found on the left side of the Hypershade window. Select Surface > Blinn. This material has a shinier surface, which is more appropriate for the skin than Lambert. The new material will be added to the library under the Material Tab. Double click on the Blinn material to open the Attribute Editor.

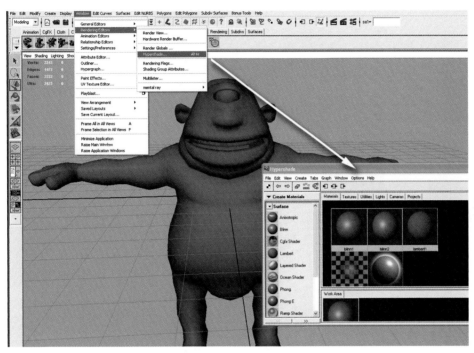

FIG. 8-27

The Attribute Editor lets you edit most of the information and attributes of any 3D object in the scene including shapes, cameras, lights, materials, and shaders. In this case, the Attribute Editor displays Color, Transparency, Bump Map, and other parameters for the material. The number of folders and options sometimes can be overwhelming, but we will use only a small number of parameters in these tutorials.

Let's start with adjusting the color for the character's eye (**Figure 8-28**).

To get the white color of the eye material, move the Color slider all the way to the right. Rename the material "eyeSG" after Blinn in the Attribute Editor.

You need to assign the material to the eye surface to update the color changes in the scene. To get a white sphere for the eye inside the Workspace, click with the middle mouse button over the material in the Hypershade window and drag it over the eye.

For Mr. Cyclop's body texture, go to Component Mode and select the polygons for the body; assign a Lambert shader from the Create Library. Repeat the same operation for the pants, and assign a new Lambert material.

For Mr. Cyclop's teeth texture, go to Component Mode and select the teeth polygons. This time you can choose a Blinn material. Press the middle mouse button and drag the material over the teeth.

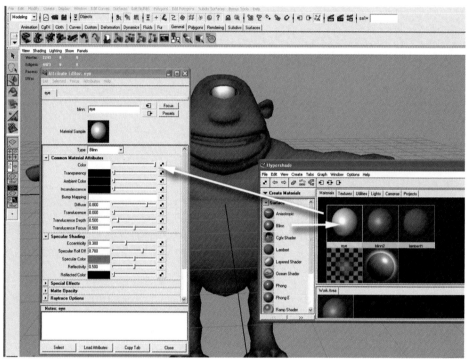

FIG. 8-28 Adjusting the color for the character's eye.

Let's specify the UV mapping coordinates for every vertex of every polygonal face to apply textures to your model. UV mapping defines the corresponding coordinates of every vertex of the surface on a 2D image. There are many ways to define the direction of UV mapping. You may use planar, cylindrical, or spherical mapping, according to the shape of the object. You will use four textures for your character: one for the eye, one for the body, one for the pants, and one for the teeth.

When creating textures, I suggest creating a 256 × 256 pixel image in Photoshop and saving your work as a JPEG texture.

Initializing the UV Mapping for the Eye

Go to the top menu and select Edit Polygons > Texture > Planar Mapping. Click on the check box located on the right of Planar Mapping. Using a texture with Planar Mapping on the surface of a 3D model has the same effect as projecting an image on a surface in front of the screen of a movie theater.

In the dialog window, check the options for Smart Fit and Fit to Bounding Box.

Select the perpendicular axis to the surface of the 3D model. In the case of the eye socket, the z-axis is selected. Click on Project, and the Projection Manipulator is displayed around the eye (Figure 8-29).

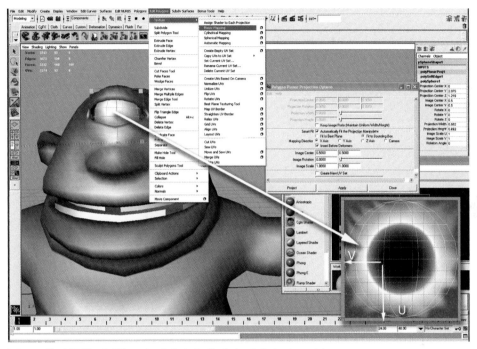

FIG. 8-29 After initializing the UV mapping, the Projection Manipulator is displayed around the eye.

Previewing in the Workspace, several versions of the texture applied to the 3D model help you to find the best axis.

Let's define UV mapping for the pants (see **Figure 8-30**). The type of projection is also Planar.

Now let's define UV mapping coordinates for the body (see **Figure 8-31**).

The type of projection will be cylindrical. In the case of planar mapping, an image is projected in a movie theater on a round object placed in front of the screen. The image appears stretched on the sides of the round object, but cannot reach the back of the object. In the case of cylindrical mapping, the image wraps around the round surface without deformation.

Although we are used to planar mapping, which is similar to the effect of a slide projector, cylindrical and spherical mapping cannot be recreated with a single projector in the real world.

Choosing Textures for the Surfaces of the Character

Go to Hypershader and double click on a material of your choice. A version of the Attribute Editor is displayed for each material.

On the right of the Attribute Editor, click on the check box icon on the right of the color slider. A new dialog window called Create Render Node opens. Click on the File button and upload an image of your choice by browsing through your files.

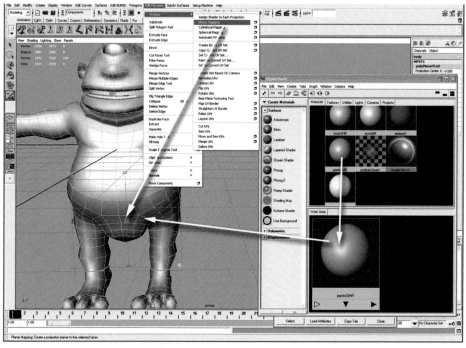

FIG. 8-30 Defining UV mapping for the pants.

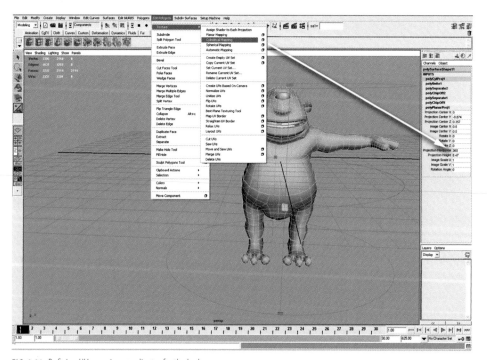

FIG. 8-31 Defining UV mapping coordinates for the body.

Viewing Your Texture in the Perspective Window

On top of the Workspace window, select Shading > Hardware Texturing. Assign all the textures to the different parts of the character (see **Figures 8-32, 8-33**). For the teeth, you also can apply texture and initialize the UV tool from the top menu. Go to Edit Polygon > Texture to display the texture on all faces of the selected polygons.

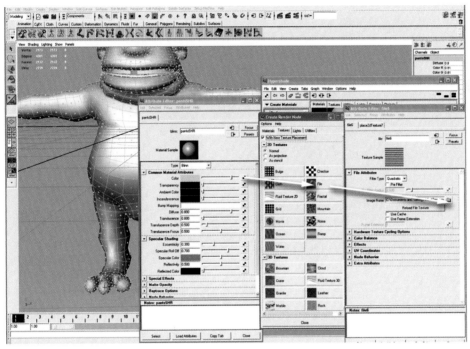

FIG. 8-32 Choosing textures for the surfaces of the character.

Important note:

Elements in the scene may have different points of origin, which is the center of the world, described as X,Y,Z = 0,0,0 in your coordinate system. This may create problems when you export the scene to Virtools. The solution to this problem is to assign the same point of origin for all 3D objects in the scene.

Select all the 3D objects by pressing Ctrl+A.

Go to Modify > Freeze Transformations. The location coordinates for all the elements in the scene become X,Y,Z = 0,0,0.

Save your scene.

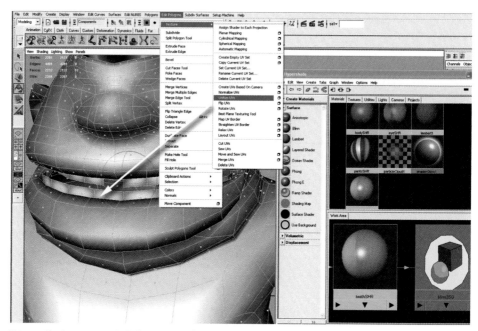

FIG. 8-33 Viewing your texture in the Perspective window.

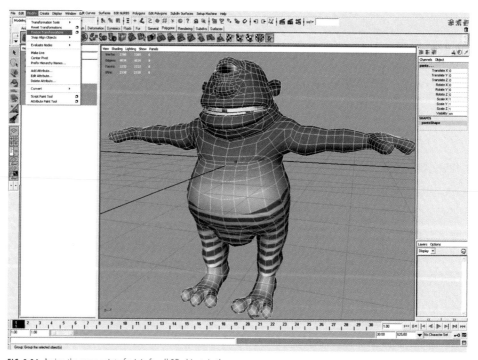

FIG. 8-34 Assign the same point of origin for all 3D objects in the scene.

Building a Skeleton with Inverse Kinematics

It is time to bring your champion to life. First, you will build an internal skeletal system that will control the body (see **Figure** 8-35).

Select the Animation module on the right of the Status Line. Go to the Main Menu and select Skeleton > Joint Tool. Start drawing in the front view the spinal skeleton, starting from the character's pelvis. To create bones, click once to create the first joint, then move your mouse to the location of the second joint and click a second time. A joint is created at every click. You can create five bones from the spine to the tip of the head. Repeat the same for the right arm starting with the collar joint. Repeat the same for the right leg starting in the hip area. You can adjust the joints by clicking on them and moving them to the right location.

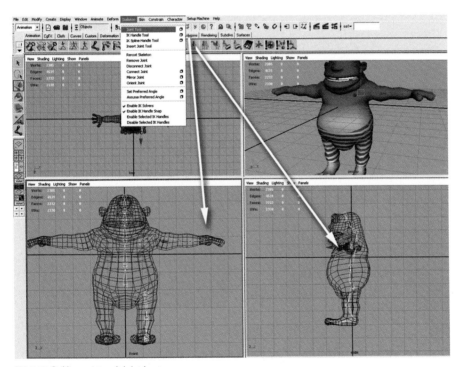

FIG. 8-35 Building an internal skeletal system.

Connecting the Bones for the Spine and for the Leg

First, click on the hip joint, then on the pelvic joint, while pressing the Shift key. Go to the top menu and select Skeleton > Connect Joint. Repeat the same to connect the arm-first-collar joint and the third spinal joint (see **Figure** 8-36).

You can mirror the right arm joints to create the left arm joints (see **Figure** 8-37).

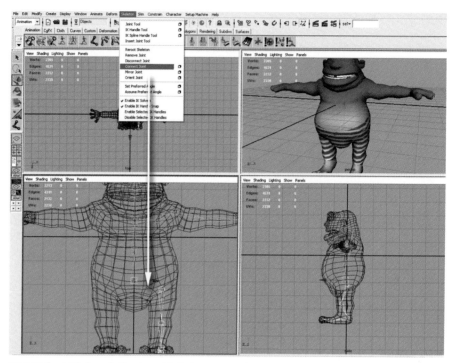

FIG. 8-36 Connect the bones for the spine and for the leg.

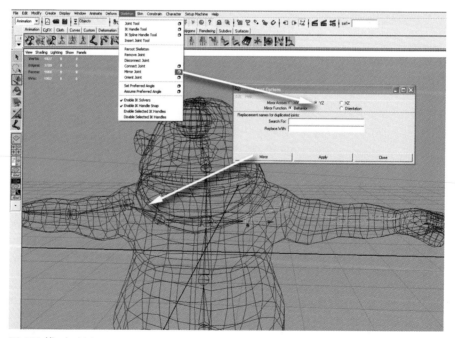

FIG. 8-37 Mirroring joints.

Mirroring Joints

Click on the collar joint, and then select Skeleton > Mirror Joint. Choose Mirror across Y, Z plane. Repeat the same operation for the right leg, starting with the hip joint.

After creating a full skeleton, go to Window > Outliner. Click inside the Outliner dialog window to view the nodes. Click on the first node to rename it "skeleton." Open the names for each chain of joints by clicking on the icons with plus signs next to the names of the nodes and rename them accordingly (see Figure 8-38).

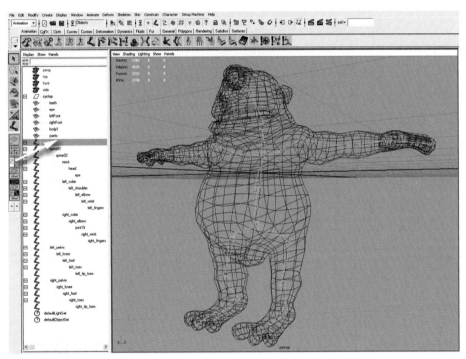

FIG. 8-38 Renaming the skeleton.

Binding the Surfaces with the New Skeleton

Select all surfaces for the eye and the body and also select the skeleton. Go to the top menu and select Choose Skin > Bind Skin > Smooth Bind (see Figure 8-39).

To test the binding process, select one of the joints and rotate it. The mesh should be stretched around the joint. In Figure 8-40, the shoulder area is stretched around the shoulder joint.

Adjusting Weight Maps with the Paint Skin Weight Tool

Go to the top menu and select Skin > Edit Smooth Skin. Check the box on the right of the menu item. Go to the dialog box with parameters for the joint,

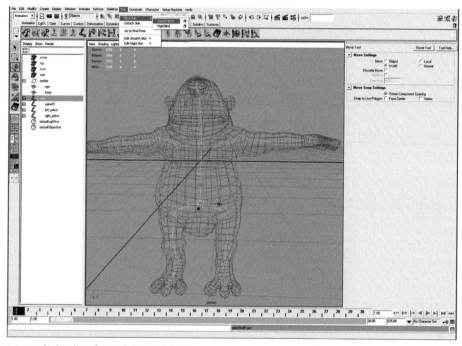

FIG. 8-39 Binding the surfaces with the new skeleton.

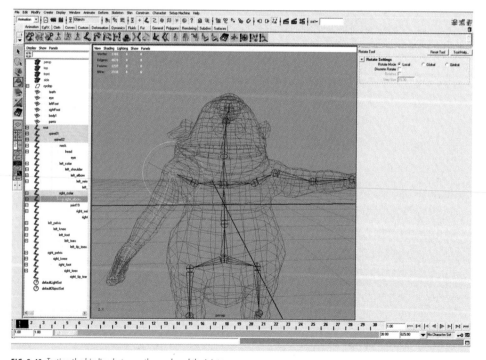

FIG. 8-40 Testing the binding between the mesh and the joint.

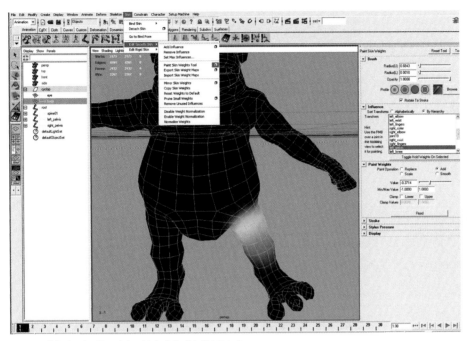

FIG. 8-41 Adjusting the skin weight with the Paint Skin Weight tool.

and click on different joints to see their respective influence on the skin of the character. Keep working only on the right half or the left half of the 3D model.

The color of the skin can change from white to black according to the intensity of the skin weight around the joint (see **Figure 8-41**). Painting around the joint with a brighter color increases the value of the attraction of the joint on the mesh. Painting a brighter skin weight increases the force of attraction of the joint on the mesh. Parts of the mesh around the joint move easily in places with a stronger force of attraction. Parts of the mesh located further away from the joint move with more resistance.

You can control the intensity of the attraction by changing the Min/Max Value from –1 to 1 and by turning on the Add button to paint over the skin.

Surfaces of body parts are not all affected by the motion of a joint. A skin weight with a dark color keeps meshes idle when a joint is moving.

For example, when you select the left collar joint, the skin weight for the head is black (see **Figure 8-42**). This explains why the head will remain idle when you move the left collar joint. Select various joints in the Outliner and rotate them to test your model.

Mirroring the Skin Weights to the Opposite Side

Move your model in the middle of the y-axis. Go to the top menu. See **Figure 8-43**.

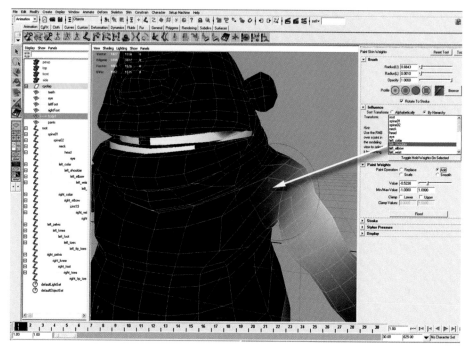

FIG. 8-42 When you select the left collar joint, the skin weight for the head is black. This explains why the head will remain idle when you move the left collar joint.

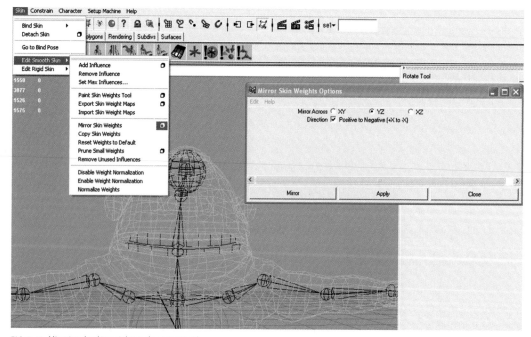

FIG. 8-43 Mirroring the skin weights to the opposite side.

First, select Skin > Bind Pose. Second, select Skin > Edit Smooth Skin > Mirror Skin Weights. Specify the right direction and a plane. If you work on the right side of the character, select Direction Positive to Negative.

In the workspace, run some tests by moving the joints with weight maps on the left and right sides. They should be identical.

Applying Inverse Kinematics to Your Skeleton

Inverse Kinematics (IK) is an animation technique inspired by string puppets in which a chain of articulations follows the animation of a single string attached to the end of the chain (see **Figure 8-44**).

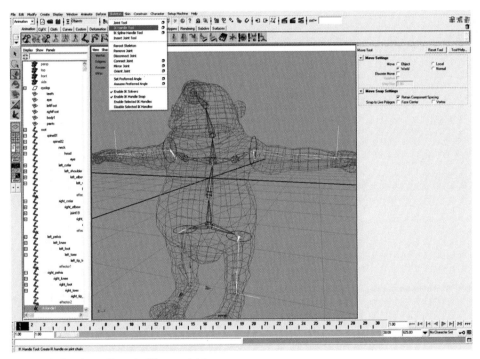

FIG. 8-44 Applying Inverse Kinematics (IK) to your skeleton.

A string, attached to the hand of a puppet, can connect a chain or joints including the lower arm, elbow, upper arm, and shoulder. Although only the last joint of the chain, the hand, is animated, the chain of joints follows the animation naturally. The IK technique allows you to animate only one joint located at the end of the chain of joints, instead of each joint of a skeleton.

You can use IK for animations controlled by real-time events. For example, one joint located in the palm of the hand can react to sounds produced by the viewer and move the arm in a realistic way.

To set up IK, go to the top menu, and select Skeleton > IK Handle.

First, click on the left shoulder joint. Second, click on the left wrist joint. Repeat the same operation for the right arm.

To set up IK for the legs, first, click on the left hip joint. Second, click on the ankle joint. Repeat the same for the right leg.

Locators can help you add constraints to the IK handles when joints are difficult to select and move around.

Creating Locators

Go to the top menu and select Create > Locators. Create five locators. Place four of them at the wrists and ankles. Place one locator for the body, in front of the model (see **Figure 8-45**).

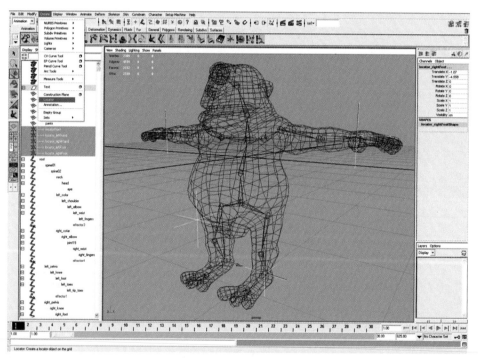

FIG. 8-45 Creating locators.

Constrain the Locators to the IK Handles

First, select the locator. Second, select the IK handle. See **Figure 8-46**.

Go to Constraint > Point. Select the box on the right side of the word. Select the following parameters in the Point Constraint Options dialog window: eight = 1, Add Targets ON. Select Apply.

Repeat the same steps for the locator in front of the body (see **Figure 8-47**). Select the following parameters: Offset, Z = −3. Select Apply.

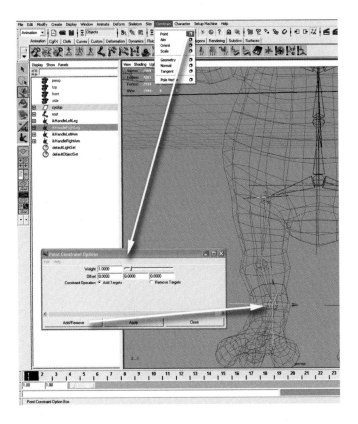

FIG. 8-46 Setting up the locators on the IK handles.

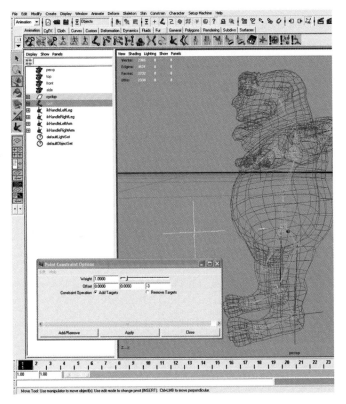

FIG. 8-47 Setting up the locator for the body.

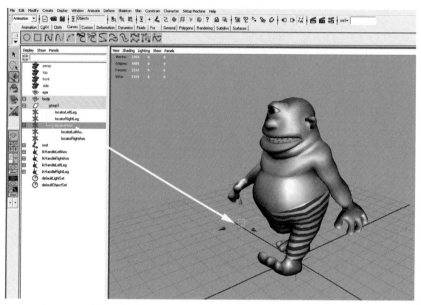

FIG. 8-48 Reorganizing the hierarchy of the nodes.

Before exporting the model to Virtools, you need to reorganize the hierarchy of the nodes (see **Figure 8-48**).

In the Outliner dialog box, select all of the locators and group them by pressing Ctrl+G. Rename the group "Locators."

In the Outliner dialog box, drag the locators called Left Arm and Right Arm on top of the locator called Body.

Figure 8-49 shows how the hierarchy should be reorganized after moving the Body locator.

Creating a Walk Animation

Let's create a looped animation of a walk for the Cyclop character. First, you will create a walk cycle that you later loop over and over again to create the illusion of a continuous walk. This method allows you to use a short walk animation that will be optimized for 3D interactive content. The walk cycle takes sixty frames. The first and the last poses are the same so the cycle can be repeated without any visible discontinuity. The following illustration shows how to move the limb locators for the first posture of the Cyclop.

Animating Mr. Cyclop
To key the first frame, first select the Body locator. Second, press Shift+W. Repeat the same operations with the other locators:

Select the Left Leg locator. Press Shift+W.

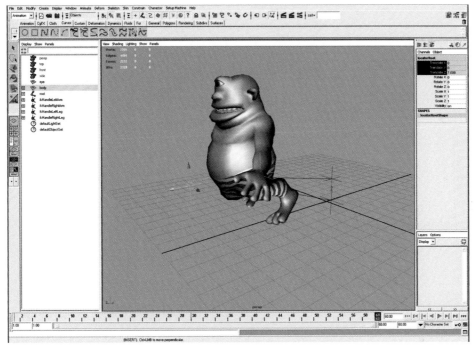

FIG. 8-49 This illustration shows how the hierarchy should be reorganized after moving the Body locator.

Select the Right Leg locator. Press Shift+W.

The posture of the character is recorded at frame 1.

Select the Body locator, and move the character 15 units ahead (see **Figure 8-50**). You can adjust the position of the leg locators to get a posture similar to the previous one.

You can specify the length of the animation in the End Time box located on the left of the Playback Animation Controls.

Move the Time Slider to frame 60, and record the posture by keying the locators again.

Go to the top menu, and select Animation > Animation Snapshot.

Specify time range = 1–60 and increment = 60. Press Snapshot. When you move the Time Slider back to the first frame you will notice that Maya took a snapshot of the character at frame 60.

Select the snapshot posture in the Perspective window. Display a wireframe version of the snapshot posture (see **Figure 8-51**).

Go to the top menu and select Display > Object Display > Template.

You can play back your animation (see **Figure 8-52**) by pressing the Play button located with the Playback Controls, in the lower right corner of your screen.

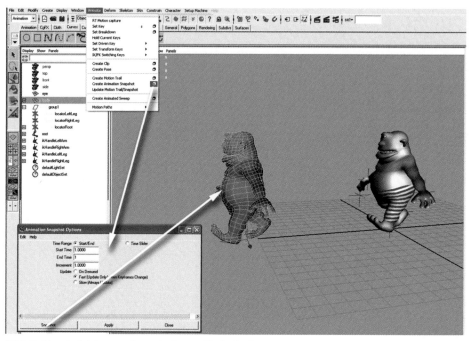

FIG. 8-50 Select the Body locator, and move the character 15 units ahead.

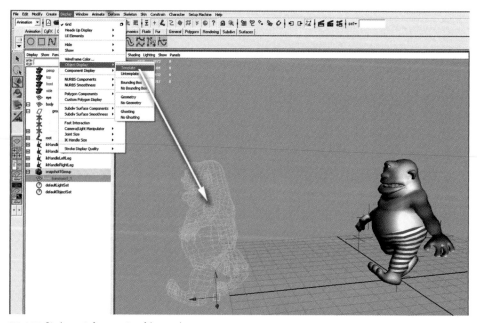

FIG. 8-51 Display a wireframe version of the snapshot posture.

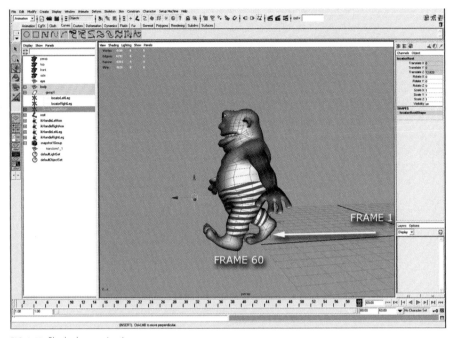

FIG. 8-52 Play back your animation.

When you record the posture at frame 30, the legs and arms will be in the opposite direction of the postures previously created at frame 1 and 60 (see Figure 8-53).

Creating Two More Postures

One posture is at frame 15, and the other one is at frame 45. Fine tune the bending of the feet at these two frames, and press the Shift+E keys to record the keyframe. See Figure 8-54.

The Graph Editor Helps You Tweak the Animation

Go to the top menu and select Window > Animation Windows > Graph Editor. Select the keyed locators, and in the Graph Editor choose View > Frame All. The curve is smooth by default. You can make it linear by clicking on the Linear Tangent button. Please remember to delete the snapshot posture that you previously created. See Figure 8-55.

Adding a Point Light to Your Scene

Go to the top menu and select Create > Lights > Point Light (see Figure 8-56). Save your work.

How to Export the Character to Virtools

Please make sure that the Virtools2Maya exporter plug-in is installed on the copy of Maya that you are using.

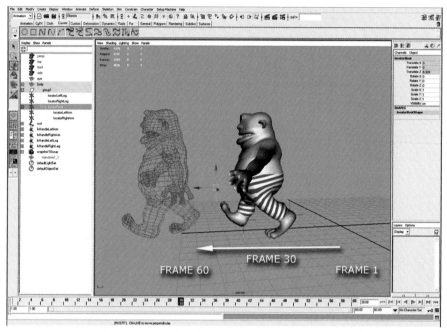

FIG. 8-53 When you record the posture at frame 30, the legs and arms will be in the opposite direction of the postures previously created at frame 1 and 60.

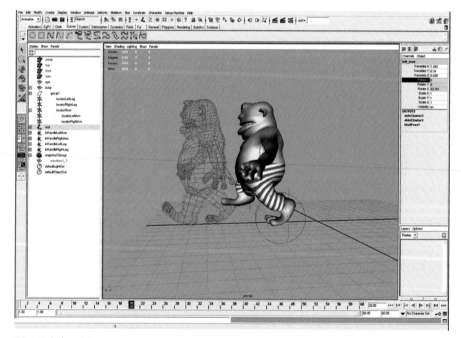

FIG. 8-54 Let's create two more postures.

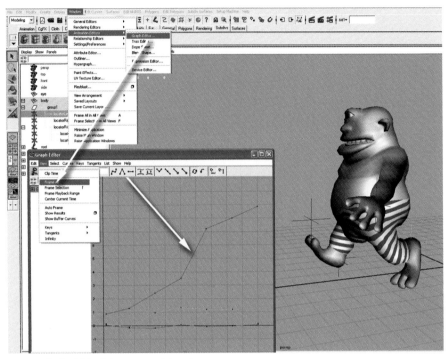

FIG. 8-55 The Graph Editor helps you to tweak the animation.

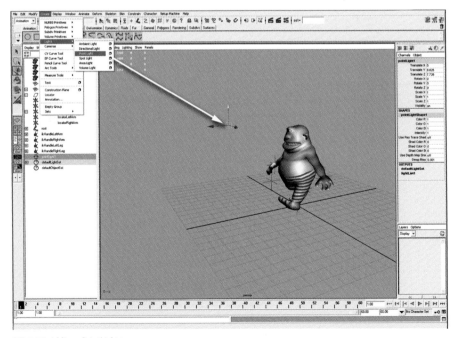

FIG. 8-56 Adding a Point Light to your scene.

To activate the plug-in, go to the top menu and select Window > Settings/ Preferences > Plug-in Manager.

Select and enable the plug-in.

Exporting the Character to Virtools

Go to the top menu, and select File > Export All. Select the box on the right side of the text. In the Export All Options dialog window, select the following parameters:

- Under File Type, select Virtools.
- Under Export Options, choose:
    - Type = Character
    - Hierarchy = Full
    - Export = All
    - Exported Objects = Meshes, Lights, Normals, Textures, Cameras
- Under Textures Options, choose Include Textures in File = ON.
- Under Animation Options, choose:
    - Enable Animation = ON
    - Start = 0
    - End = 60 frames
    - Sampling Step = 5
    - Frame Sampling = ON
- Next to Animate, check Meshes, Lights, Vertices, Cameras.
- Name your file "exporting file" and export.

What Did You Learn in This Tutorial?

This section showed you how to create a fully functional character in Maya and to export the character from Maya to Virtools (see **Figure 8-57**). The next section will take you step by step through the creation of a natural environment in Maya. You will be able to set up your character inside the environment and add interactivity in Virtools.

Creating a 3D Immersive Environment

This tutorial introduces you to Maya's 3D Paint Effects, allowing you to paint in 3D. A few strokes can paint trees, grass, or flowers. The paint strokes from your brush are converted into 3D objects inside a 3D space. Maya's ability to convert 3D Paint Effects to polygonal objects is helpful in creating content for interactive environments. This tutorial requires Maya 5.0 or higher.

You can control the strokes' shape, color, and density while painting on the horizontal grid plane of the perspective view or directly on other 3D objects.

Let's grab a brush and start to paint trees and grass in 3D. Let's create the ground for your forest.

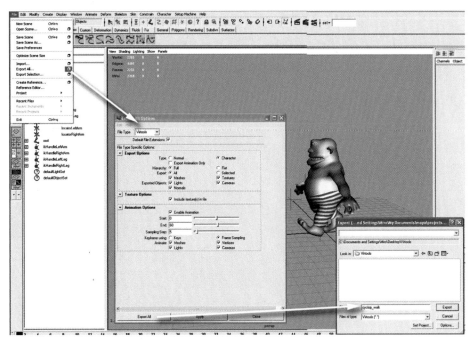

FIG. 8-57 Exporting your character to Virtools.

Creating the Ground

Open a new scene in Maya. Go to the top menu and select File > New Scene.

Select the Modeling module in the box located on the left of the Status Line.

Create a polygonal plane for the floor of your scene (see **Figure 8-58**). Go to Create > Polygon Primitives > Plane.

Painting the Trees

A library of Paint Effects can be found in the Visor module.

To open the Visor window, go to the top menu and select Window > General Editor > Visor. Multiple folders with preset brushes are available. You can select a variety of paint effects inspired by natural forms by clicking on the folder named trees (see **Figure 8-59**).

Resizing Your Brush
Go to the top menu and click on Paint Effects > Template Brush Settings. The Paint Effects Brush Settings dialog window opens. Select the Brush Profile. Set the Global Scale Slider = 2.0.

Go to the Visor dialog window. Select Trees or MeshTrees. On the left side of the Visor window, click on the icon of the MEL file called birchBlowingLight.mel.

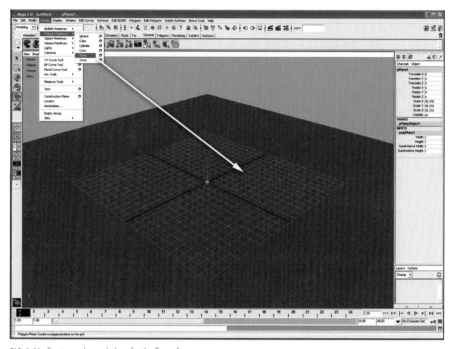

FIG. 8-58 Create a polygonal plane for the floor of your scene.

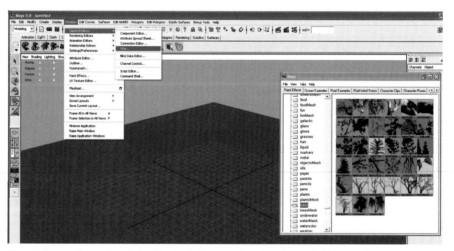

FIG. 8-59 You can select a variety of paint effects inspired by natural forms by clicking on the folder named trees.

Go to the Workspace, and click and drag the mouse pointer a short distance near the Origin center in the Perspective window.

Maya creates randomly generated lush trees with a realistic look. Render the scene to see the final result (see **Figure 8-60**).

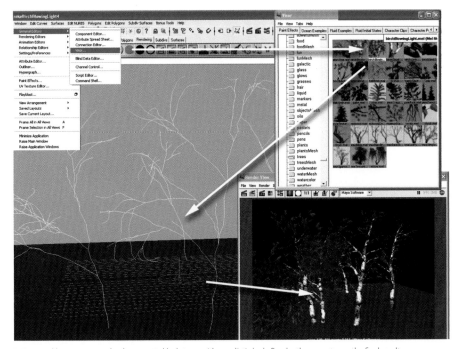

FIG. 8-60 Maya creates randomly generated lush trees with a realistic look. Render the scene to see the final result.

Painting Grass

Let's paint some 3D grass.

Go to the Visor dialog window. Select Grass on the left side of the Visor window, and click on the icon to choose the grass of your choice.

Important note:

Because you will convert the content from your 3D painting into polygonal meshes, you have to keep an eye on the number of polygons. The density of the brush strokes needs to be kept low.

Let's control the creation of your vegetation by tweaking parameters inside the Attribute Editor.

Tweaking Parameters for Your Brush Stroke in the Attribute Editor

Select the brush stroke and press Ctrl+A. In the Attribute Editor, check Sample Density and Tube Segments, which are the main parameters.

Two or three types of trees are needed for your scene in Maya. Once you import the trees in Virtools, you will clone them to create a whole forest (see Figure 8-61).

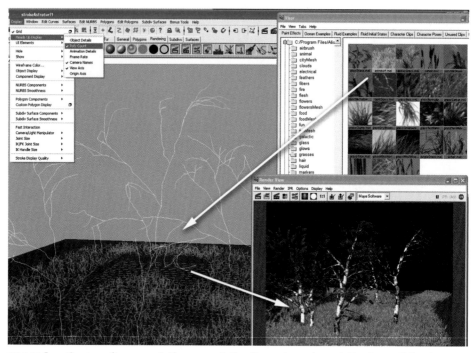

FIG. 8-61 Two or three types of trees are needed for your scene in Maya. Once you import the trees in Virtools, you will clone them to create a whole forest.

The limit for the total number of polygons created inside a scene is 50,000. To view the polygonal count, go to the top menu and select Display > Head Up Display > Poly Count. Check the number of Faces rendered in the scene.

Conversion of 3D Models to Polygonal Meshes

Let's convert the Paint Effects to 3D objects made of polygonal meshes (see **Figure 8-62**).

Converting the 3D Paint Effect to Polygonal Meshes
Select one of the strokes from the Outliner window or from the perspective view. Choose Modify > Convert > Paint Effects To Polygons. The output from the conversion is a high-resolution model with a high polygonal count.

Reducing the Number of Polygons

Let's see how Maya can help you reduce the polygonal count.

Select the Modeling module in the box located on the left of the Status Line.

Reducing the Number of Polygons for a Tree
Let's control the number of polygons for the tree (see **Figure 8-63**).

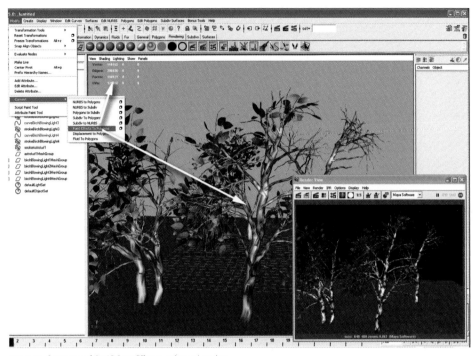

FIG. 8-62 Conversion of the 3D Paint Effect to polygonal meshes.

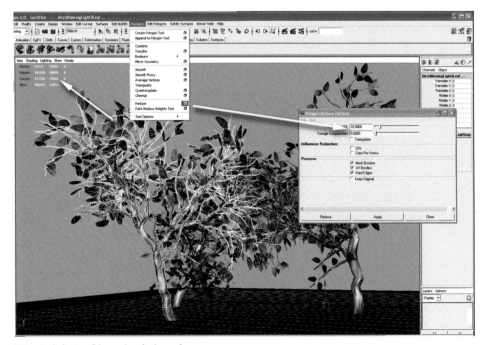

FIG. 8-63 Reduction of the number of polygons for a tree.

Go to Display > Heads on Display > Polygon Count. Go to the Rendering menu and select Paint Effect > Paint Effects Mesh Quality.

Decrease the number of polygons by moving the sliders to the left for Tube Sections and Segment, and check the number of polygons on the Polygon Count. You will notice that this operation can radically alter the shape of the model. In most cases, you will need to use the following polygon reduction to reduce the number of polygons while keeping the integrity of the 3D object.

Select a tree and choose Polygons > Reduce. Click on the box located on the right of the word to open the Polygon Reduce Options dialog window.

Enter the percentage of reduction. Go to Preserve. Check the following parameters, and keep Mesh Borders, UV Borders, Hard Edges. Click Reduce.

Keep reducing the polygon count until your tree has less than 15,000 polygons.

If you get a message saying "Cannot Reduce Polygonal Object with Non-manifold Geometry," go to the top menu, and select Polygons > Cleanup. Click on the box located on the right of the word to open the Polygon Cleanup Options dialog window.

Go to Other, and check non-manifold Geometry and Normals and Geometry. Press Clean Up, and repeat the reduction process.

Please note that another way to lower the polygon count is to make quadrangular meshes. Maya creates triangular meshes by default.

You have created a 3D tree made of two 3D models, the branches and the leaves. Before exporting to Virtools, you should combine the two models into one. Select all the branches and leaves for the tree and go to Modeling > Polygons > Combine.

Materials and Textures

Let's open the Hypershade window to assign materials to your 3D models.

To open the Hypershade window, go to the top menu, and select Window > Rendering Editor > Hypershade (see **Figure 8-64**).

Name the leaves material "LeavesSG." Name the trunk material "TrunkSG."

Selecting One Material in the Hypershade Window

Go to the main menu in Hypershade. Select Graph > Input and Output Connections. You will see a network of connections that Maya generated after converting the trees to polygons.

You are looking for more information about textures, so double-click on the texture icon and check the path of the texture that is used for the trees.

The file is stored in Program Files > Maya > Brushes > Trees > pine2LeafShader.

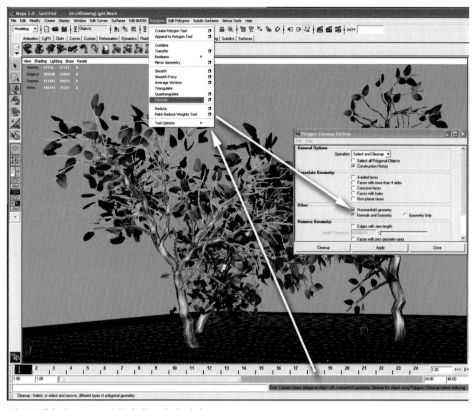

FIG. 8-64 Selecting one material in the Hypershade window.

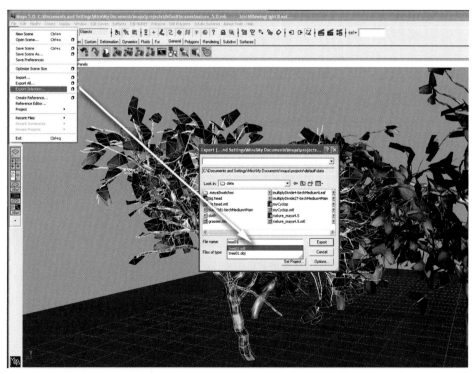

FIG. 8-65 Exporting the scene to Virtools.

The texture used for the leaves is called sideleaf.iff. For the bark of the tree, the texture is called wrapBark.iff.

Save your scene as "forest."

How to Export the Scene to Virtools

Maya will export your polygonal mesh data, plus the UV mapping information and shaders, generated during the conversion process.

You need to export each element one by one as one tree or one object, OBJ (object) files.

Exporting the Scene to Virtools

Select the object and go to File > Export Selection.

Point your file browser in the desired location (for example, the data folder located in the Virtools database). Assign a unique name, choose a file type (OBJ), and click export.

Let's export the elements of the scene to Virtools:

- Select one of the trees and go to File > Export Selection.
- In the exporting window, select Virtools.
- Check Default File Extensions.
- Under Export Options, select the following parameters:
    - Check Type = Normal
    - Hierarchy = Full, Export = Selected
    - Meshes and Normals are on

Setting Up the Scene in Virtools

Open Virtools. The 3D Layout window with a perspective view is on the left. The Building Blocks folders are on the right. The Schematics window is at the bottom. This window displays a network of connections between building blocks that is similar to the Hypergraph window in Maya. The Lever Manager is similar to the Outliner window in Maya.

You will create a Data Resource folder with subfolders to save your scene (see Figure 8-67).

Creating a Data Resource Folder

Go to Virtools top menu and select Resources > Create New Data Resource.

Name the Data Resource folder and save it. Virtools creates a file called Data_Ressource.rsc.

The files exported from Maya or from other 3D software applications can be saved in the subfolders inside the Data Resource folder. For example, a

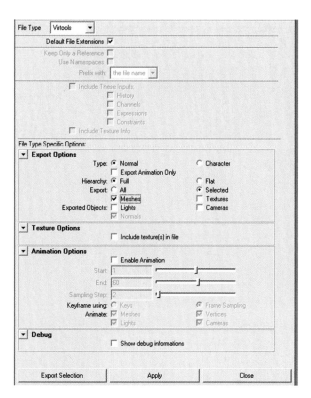

FIG. 8-66 The Virtools export dialog window.

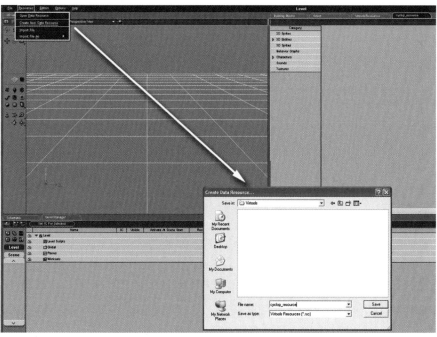

FIG. 8-67 Creating a Data Resource folder.

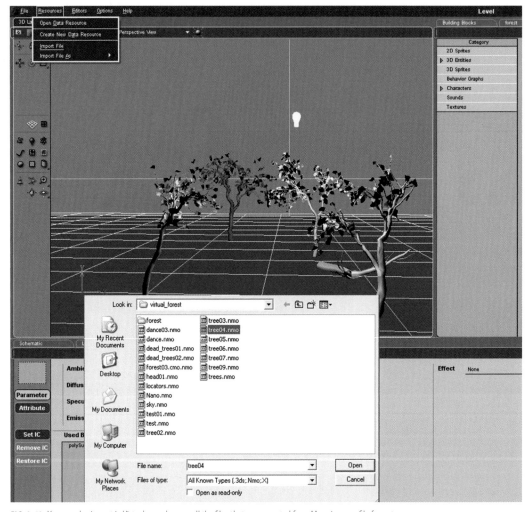

FIG. 8-68 You can also import in Virtools, one by one, all the files that you exported from Maya in .nmo file formats.

character will be saved in Data Resource folder > Character. A tree, which is a 3D object, will be saved in Data Resource folder > 3D Entity.

Accessing Your Assets Saved in the Data Resource Folder in Virtools
Go to the top menu, and select Resources > Open Data Resource. Select the Data_Resource.rsc file.

Please note that you can also import in Virtools, one by one, all the files that you exported from Maya in .nmo file formats (see **Figure 8-68**).

Importing .nmo Files One by One
Go to the top menu and select Resources > Import File.

Loading Textures from Maya in Virtools

In the Level Manager, go to Globals > Materials. Double-click on the name of material. The Materials Setup window shows materials from 3D objects in the scene.

Although most of the time Virtools loads 3D models with their textures in place, some textures may not be displayed automatically, which is the case with 3D objects created in Maya.

The following steps will help you to correct this situation.

Exporting Textures from Maya to Virtools
Let's export textures from Maya.

Textures in IFF format need to be converted to JPG format using the Maya FCheck converter.

Converting a Texture from Maya
Open the FCheck application from your desktop. Go to the Start Menu > Programs > AliasWavefront > Maya > Fcheck.

Go to the Fcheck menu, and select File > Open Image. Load the leaf and bark IFF files. Go to File > Save Image. Save as JPG file formats. The texture files are saved in the Data Resource folder > Textures folder that you previously created.

In Virtools, select the tab for the Data Resource folder located on the right of the 3D Layout window. Select the Textures shelf. The names of the textures that you previously saved will appear in the column to the right.

Loading a Texture in Virtools
Click on the name of a texture and drag it over the 3D Layout window or Level Manager window. The texture will automatically reside in the Level Manager window, under Level > Global > Textures shelf. When you save your file, assets referenced inside the Level Manager window will be saved with your project regardless of the presence of the Data Resource folder (see **Figure 8-69**).

If you don't see the Resource folder located on the right of the 3D Layout window in Virtools, you may need to load the Resource folder. Go to the top menu and select Resources > Open Data Resource. Select the Data_Resource.rsc file.

Sometimes, textures are missing on 3D objects viewed in the 3D Layout window. If the texture is missing from Level Manager > Textures, you need to import the texture again. If the texture can be located in Level Manager > Textures, you need to associate the texture to the 3D model again.

Reassigning a Texture to a 3D Object in Virtools
Go to the 3D Layout window, and right-click on various shades visible on the trees. In the drop-down menu, select Material Setup (see **Figure 8-70**).

FIG. 8-69 Loading a texture in Virtools.

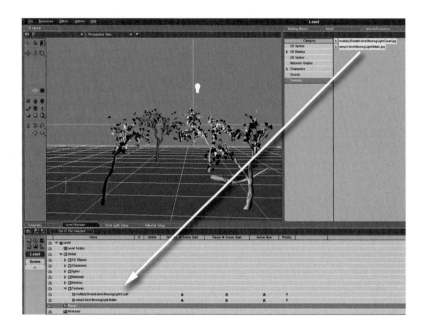

FIG. 8-70 Assign a texture to a 3D object in Virtools.

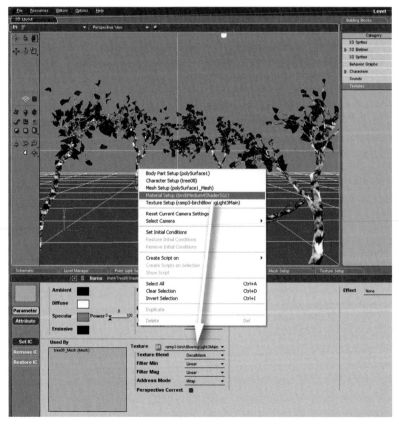

A Material Setup tab opens at the bottom of the 3D Layout window. The material is located in the lower part of the screen. Go to Texture, and select the appropriate texture for the material that you selected.

You are looking at trees inside a Virtools scene with the same look and feel of the trees that you created in Maya.

Creating a Skybox

Let's create a skybox for your scene in Virtools (see **Figure 8-71**).

Creating a Skybox

Go to the top menu and select Resources > Open Data Resource. Open the Virtools Resources folder installed with the application, which can be found on your hard drive at Program Files > Virtools > Documentation > VirtoolsResources.rsc.

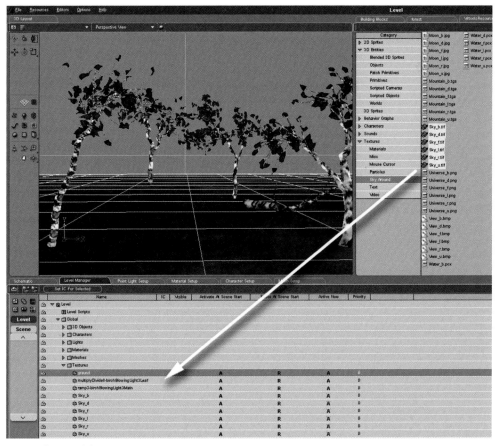

FIG. 8-71 Creating a skybox.

Go to the right of the 3D Layout window. A new tab called VirtoolsResources will appear next to your existing Data Resource. Check Virtools Resources > Textures > Sky Around Subfolder, and select the five textures in TIFF format. Drag the textures over the 3D Layout window or Level Manager window.

In the Building Blocks tab, select World Environment Folder > Background Subfolder. Select the Sky Around building block, and drag it over one of the cameras located in the Level Manager > Cameras. Please note that this building block can be connected to any 3D object in the world.

In the Sky Around window select the corresponding textures: sky_t for the top, sky_b for the bottom, sky_d for the back, sky_f for the front, sky_l for the left side, and sky_r for the right side of your environment (see **Figure 8-72**).

FIG. 8-72 Selecting textures for the Sky Around building block.

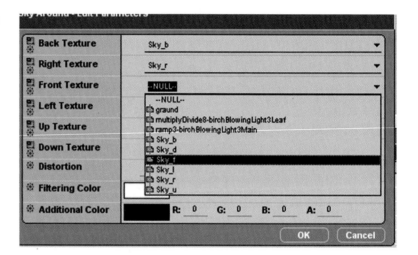

Run the program by clicking on the Play button located at the left corner of the Virtools window. Textures of the sky are projected around the scene.

Using Textures with Alpha Channels

You may notice that the textures for the leaves are unrealistic. A whole polygon is showing around the leaf texture. You can fix this problem by adding an alpha channel to the texture (see **Figure 8-73**). This channel will turn black areas of the texture transparent.

To add an alpha channel to your texture, go to the Level Manager and double-click on the leaf texture. The leaf texture tab will open under the 3D Layout window.

Select the following parameters:

- Check Color Key Transparency.
- Use the Color Picker to select the black color inside the leaf texture.
- Check the transparencies in your scene.

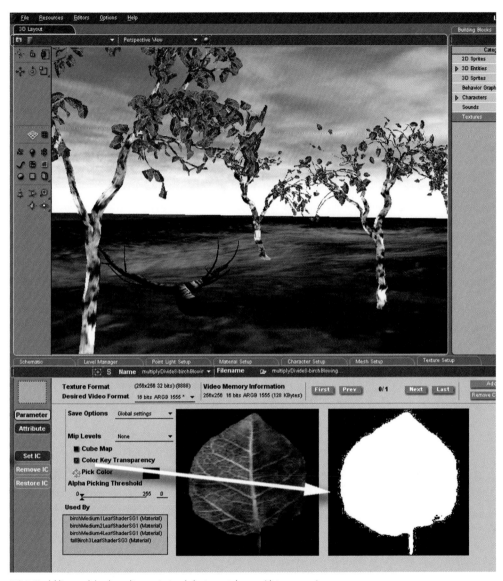

FIG. 8-73 Adding an alpha channel to your texture helps to create leaves with transparencies.

Importing a Character

Let's import Mr. Cyclop.mno, the character created in the previous tutorial (see
Figure 8-74).

Go to the top menu, and select Resource > Import File As > Character. Go to
the Level Manager. Check Characters > Cyclop subfolder, where you can find
Mr. Cyclop's body parts, bones, and animations.

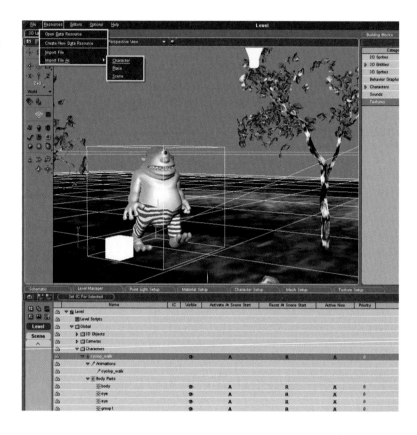

FIG. 8-74 Let's import
Mr. Cyclop.mno, the Maya character
created in the previous tutorial.

Please note that you need to export Cyclop as a character in Maya if you want to use Cyclop as a character in Virtools. If you can't get Virtools to recognize Cyclop as a character, go to Maya and repeat the steps from the earlier section "How to Export the Character to Virtools."

The Character Stands on the Floor

Let's make our character stand on the floor. This may be critical when your character stands on an uneven surface, such as a hill. The character is going to receive a force of attraction similar to gravity. You need to prevent the character from falling across the ground.

Let's see how you can declare that the ground is a Floor, add gravity to the scene, and keep the character standing on the ground.

Adding the Floor Attribute to the 3D Object Called Ground

Go to the Level Manager > Level > Global > 3D Objects > Ground. Ground is what we called the plane created in Maya earlier in this tutorial (see **Figure 8-75**).

Double-click on Ground. A new tab will open with the 3D Object setup. Click on the Attribute button. Click on the Add Attribute button.

FIG. 8-75 Adding the Floor attribute to the 3D Object called Ground.

The Add Attribute dialog box opens. Select Floor Manager > Floor. Click Add Attribute. Click Add Selected, and close the window.

Setting Up the Character on the Floor

Go to Building Blocks, located on the right side of 3D Layout. Select Characters > Constraint Folder > Character Keep on Floor (see **Figure 8-76**).

This building block looks for any obstacle or 3D Object with a floor attribute. The behavior will add gravity to the character and keep the character standing on the floor.

Please note that because the behavior is activated only during playback, the initial position of a character with Keep on Floor behavior should be slightly above ground.

The Character Walks

Let's get our character to walk around. Remember to set Initial Condition for your character before starting. The interactive animation setup for Mr. Cyclop has the following two steps.

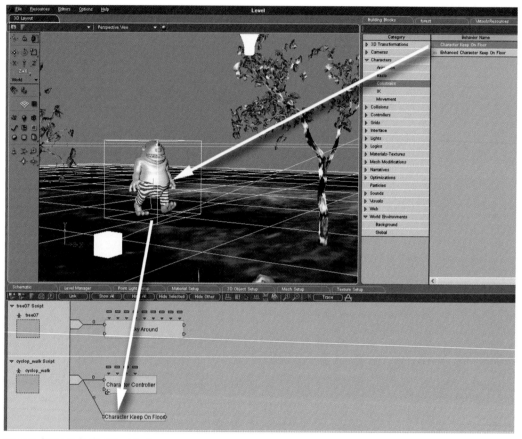

FIG. 8-76 Setting up the character on the floor.

Creating an Interactive Walk Animation for Mr. Cyclop
Go to Building Blocks, located on the right side of 3D Layout. Select Characters > Movement > Character Controller.

A Character Controller dialog window opens. Select Walk Animation = cyclop_walk animation. Click OK. See **Figure 8-77**.

Controlling the Walk Animation for Mr. Cyclop
Go to Building Blocks, located on the right side of 3D Layout. Select Controllers > Keyboard > Keyboard Controller.

Drag the Building Block over the character in 3D Layout. The character is highlighted with a yellow bounding box. The Keyboard Controller Building Block uses the numeric keys 8 and 6 for playing animations and the numeric keys 2 and 4 for turning the character to the right or to the left.

In this example, press 8 to trigger the walk animation.

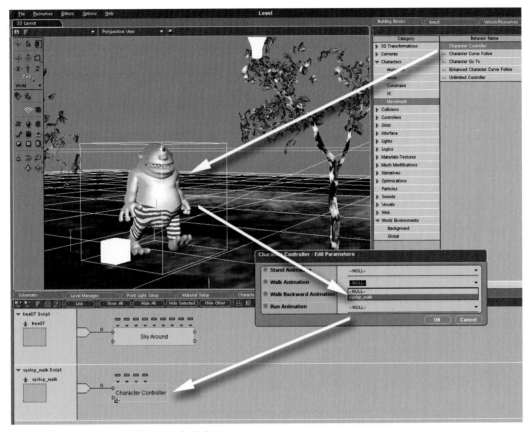

FIG. 8-77 Creating an interactive walk animation for Mr. Cyclop.

Play the application, and check the walk animation by pressing 8. Your Cyclop stays on the floor and walks. Press 2 and 4 to turn the Cyclop (see Figure 8-78).

To save your creation as a CMO file, go to File > Save Composition.

To bring the application into the Virtools Web player, you can publish a compressed VMO file embedded inside a Web page.

Go to File > Create a Web Page. Choose the window size for your 3D interactive content and select Preview in Browser.

Virtools generates a Virtools Web player file with the VMO extension, and a Web page with the HTML extension. The Web page contains the code to embed the Web player file.

So this is it! Congratulations on completing your interactive 3D application.

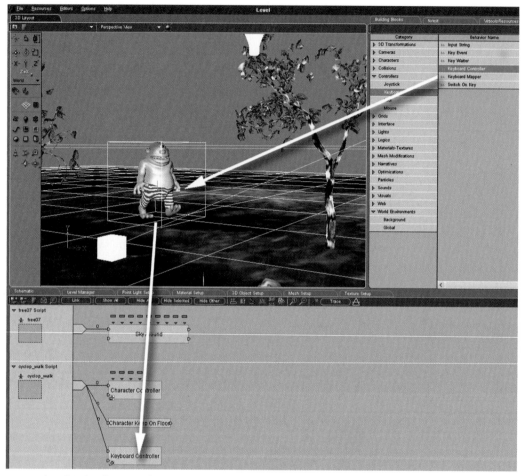

FIG. 8-78 Controlling the walk animation for Mr. Cyclop.

What Did You Learn in This Tutorial?

This tutorial showed you how to create a small forest in Maya and how to export 3D objects with their textures from Maya to Virtools. You learned how to set up an animated character inside a 3D interactive scene and how to get the character to walk around.

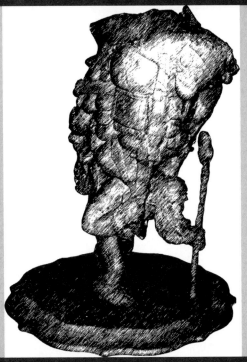

CHAPTER 9

Pipeline and Modeling Guidelines Using Maya

The "pipeline" is the path that assets travel to make it into a movie or game. It is important to have a solid, working pipeline in place before beginning production. Who is the first person to touch a model once the concept art is done? Where does a character go after it has been modeled? What happens if a model needs to go back for revisions? These are all questions that should be answered before any art is created.

Yes, it does add some extra work before you can get to the fun part of creation, but it will save countless hours during actual production. Though this chapter will be focusing on modeling, be aware that a pipeline encompasses all aspects of a production. At any given time, you should be able to locate art assets. Thus it is very important to become familiar with how production pipelines work (see **Figure 9-1**).

Concept art is the 2D designs created during preproduction. These consist of orthographic views, reference views, and character sheets. A character sheet typically portrays the character in a variety of poses.

From concept, the pipeline usually branches out for storyboards on the animation side and maquettes on the modeling side.

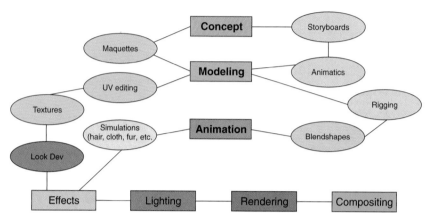

FIG. 9-1 A typical production pipeline.

Storyboards are somewhat related to animation. They are the story sequences as realized visually. The artist will compose the camera and place the characters on paper or 4″ × 6″ cards. If something doesn't look right at this stage—for instance, if a camera is too tight on a character or a character's pose is awkward—simply have the storyboard artist draw the frame again. It's much cheaper to work out the scene staging during the storyboarding phase than it would be during production.

After the storyboards are approved, they are given to the layout department to be made into animatics. Think of an animatic as a moving storyboard. During layout, the timing and spacing of the characters will be animated as well as the camera animation. The characters are generally low-polygon placeholders. Simple quick renderings or playblasts are fine. The goal is to fine-tune the timing and spacing for the characters and to get the camera animation in place. Working with simple placeholder objects allows for quick reviews and redos at this stage. This amounts to a huge cost-savings benefit.

The other branch from concept art is the maquette phase. A "maquette" (see **Figure 9-2**) is usually a clay model built for reference purposes. The more complex the character, the more likely there will be a maquette made. By allowing 3D modelers to handle a tiny statue that can be viewed from any angle, maquettes generally help for the creation of more lifelike characters. Some game companies, and almost every movie house, will have a maquette artist create a model. The 3D modeler may create the maquettes or at some larger companies there might be full-time maquette artists on staff.

Modeling is the creation of the object or environment mesh in 3D. As with all of the other stages, the type of work may be split into smaller subgroups. For example, one person may model props, another may model "hero" (a.k.a. "main") characters, and still another might work on just the environments. Whatever needs to be modeled, though, it is done during this stage.

FIG. 9-2 Maquette.

The focus of this book is a more general look at a number of aspects of the various software and techniques, but it is important to see how modeling fits into the pipeline. Typically, multiple people will work on the same model in different capacities, and that work is often done concurrently.

After modeling, an object can be textured and rigged concurrently.

During the texturing phase, a model needs to have the UV texture coordinate laid out. UVs are used to conform and hold the textures to an object. Maya creates UVs automatically, but these will almost always need to be changed. At many game companies the modeler lays out the UVs; at a larger film company, there might be a dedicated person working on the UVs. Proper UVs are vital for a model to look correct once textured, but be forewarned: UV editing can be a very time-consuming process.

Once the UVs are complete, the textures can be created. The UVs can then be brought into an image editing program like Adobe Photoshop to be used as a template when creating the textures.

"Rigging" is the process of preparing a model for animation (see **Figure 9-3**). There are many steps within the rigging phase. First a skeleton composed of joints and bones needs to be created. A skeleton in 3D functions the same as a skeleton in the real world; it acts as the framework for the body. In 3D the body that's the mesh is created by the modeler. The mesh needs to be bound and weighted to the joints so that the mesh will move with the skeleton.

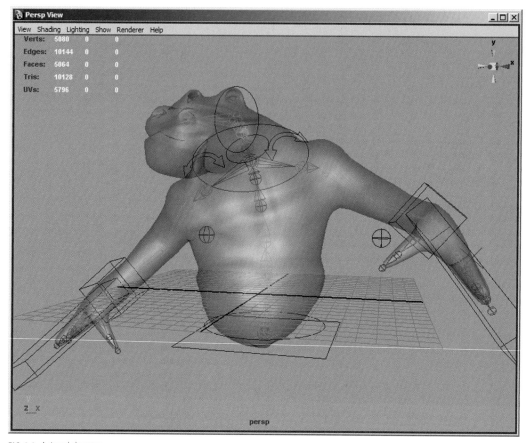

FIG. 9-3 A rigged character.

After the rigging is complete, any blendshapes needed are created. Blendshapes (also known as morph targets) can be used for facial animation or for correcting problematic mesh deformations. To help keep the art consistent, blendshapes are usually created by the same person that modeled the character.

The development of a "look" can begin at this time. Creating shading networks and designing lighting for the characters are all part of developing the look of a character.

The next step is to animate the character. Once animation is complete, fur, hair, and cloth simulations can be performed. From there, the assets move to the effects artists.

Once the animation is complete, final lighting is applied.

Finally, the character is exported into the game engine or sent to the render farm for final rendering. For film and video game cut-scenes, there is an added step after rendering. All of the elements need to be composited together.

This is an example of a very simple pipeline. On large productions, each of these jobs could be further broken down into separate tasks. However, even on large productions, the goal is to make the process of getting assets into the game or movie as pain-free as possible. Often times, a model will need to go through the pipeline multiple times (if something needs to be changed, for instance) and having a smooth process to facilitate this is vital.

Now that we can see how important it is to work within a pipeline, how can that be transferred over to Maya? Maya has very simple, yet complete project tools to help set up and manage your own pipeline. In Maya these are called "projects."

To set up a new project (see **Figure 9-4**), go to File > Project > New. In the Project Setting window (see **Figure 9-5**), type a name for the project and set a path.

Next, click Use Defaults. It's advised to always select Use Defaults, as this setting will allow Maya to organize all of the assets for the project. Click Accept.

You now have a new project and are ready to work.

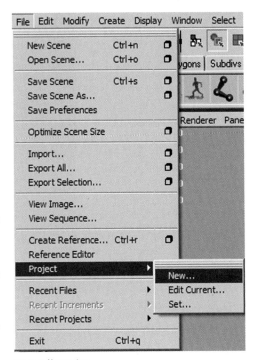

FIG. 9-4 New project.

For a long time, polygons were relegated mainly to videogame work. For that use, they excelled. The higher number of polygons needed to achieve

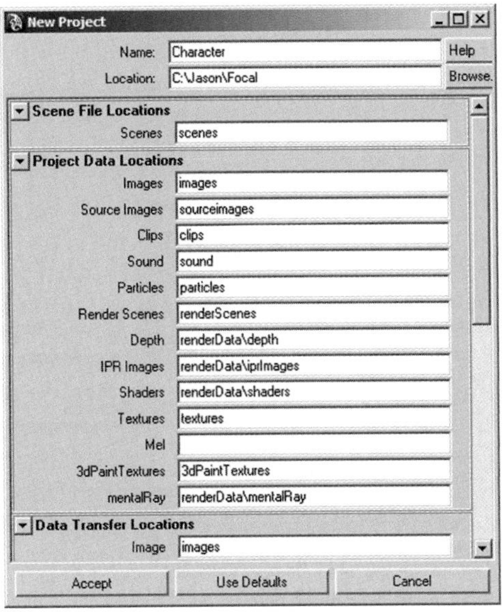

FIG. 9-5 Project settings.

FIG. 9-6 Polygon sphere (left) and
NURBS sphere (right).

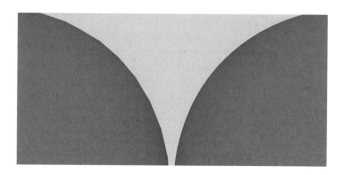

photorealism proved to be prohibitive for film work. Thus NURBS
(Non Uniform Rational B Spline) were used extensively at many film houses.
See **Figure 9-6**.

Notice that the polygonal sphere has blocky edges. In years past, the amount
of extra polygons needed to render polygon objects with smooth edges
similar to those of a NURBS object would have taken too many polygons to be
feasible and usable on high-resolution film projects. The render times would
have been too high. The nature of NURBS surfaces allowed for very organic
characters that would fit within the rendering budgets. With NURBS, though,
came the extra difficulty needed in working with the surfaces. Surface patches
could lose their stitching during rigging and animation. Surfaces also had to
be properly parametized for texturing, and surface trims had to be dealt with
if holes were needed in the model. Polygons, on the other hand, had none of
these drawbacks. Their one disadvantage was the incredibly high number of
polygons needed for organic characters. Polygons could be made of a single
mesh. UVs could be edited independently of the model, and polygons could
contain holes in the mesh as desired. Not only that, but polygons were usually
much easier for new artists to learn how to use for modeling.

That has all changed now. Within the last few years, more powerful computers
allow for the incredibly high amount of polygons needed for photorealistic
film projects. This was a huge turning point for polygonal modelers. Now they
could apply their work on film projects as well as videogames.

That being said, keep in mind that there are still plenty of times where other
modeling approaches will be useful. Though NURBS have fallen out of favor
for character modeling at most companies, they are still very useful for hard
surface modeling. Vehicles are a perfect example of the type of hard surface
model that many artists create using NURBS. The panel-type construction of
most vehicles lends itself very well to object creation using NURBS curves and
surfaces. Also, because the models are hard surfaces and won't deform, there
is no danger of gaps appearing where the different surfaces meet. If you need
a vase, simply create a curve outline and revolve it. Eyeballs are another good
use of NURBS; the surfaces are ready to accept textures, no UV editing required.

FIG. 9-7 A simple NURBS model.

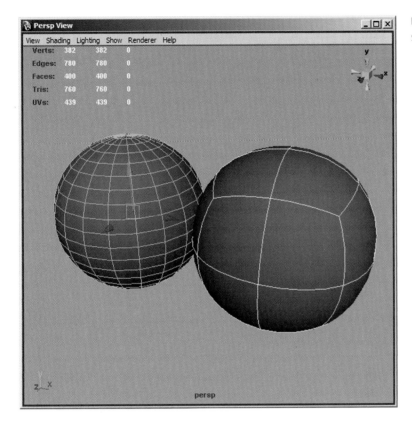

FIG. 9-8 Polygon sphere (left) and subdivision sphere (right).

Maya also comes with Subdivision (subD) Surfaces (see **Figure 9-8**). If a production pipeline includes displacement maps, then most likely subD surfaces will be included in the mix. SubD surfaces generally produce better results than polygons when using displacement maps. When working with displacement maps, most artists will generally create the model with polygons, because of the ease of working with them, and then convert the model to subD surfaces prior to rendering.

CHAPTER 10

Overview of Maya

Maya is at the forefront of 3D graphics. The newest version of Maya has a host of new features and improvements to help the modeler achieve amazing results.

Before we move into modeling, let's go over some guidelines that we want to stick with to ensure clean models. These are concepts to follow when dealing with all models, be it a low-polygon monster or a photorealistic human.

Use quad polygons. A quad is a four-sided polygon. Quad polygons are generally easier for everyone to work with. Quads subdivide in a predictable manner. It is easier for a character rigger to paint weights on quads. It is also easier for the texture artist to paint images with minimal stretching. If you need to terminate an edge loop, hide the triangle in a part of the mesh that is in an inconspicuous place that won't deform. Use of triangles should be kept to an absolute minimum. Polygons with more than four sides (*n*-gons) cannot be used.

Uniformly spaced topology. By uniformly spacing the polygons, you will be making everyone's job easier. Uniformly spaced models will subdivide in a predictable manner. Uniform topology has less texture stretching then unevenly spaced mesh, so it is easier for the texture artists to create images.

It's also easier for the character rigger to set up the model, because the weights are much easier to distribute evenly across the model.

Model your edge loops according to the muscles. An edge loop is a path of connected polygons. By having the edge loops follow the muscles, the character will deform much better when animated. Proper edge loops also allow you to add extra detail just to sections of the model where it is needed.

Although this chapter is intended for users with some experience using Maya, it should be noted that in this chapter I cover information that is important in setting up a proper workflow. Some of this may be old news for the more seasoned users. If it is, feel free to jump ahead to the information on the new tools available in Maya later in this chapter.

The Window menu is where you set the Maya scene preferences. It's very important that before you begin working on your model you have all of your preferences set correctly.

Go to Window > Settings/Preferences > Preferences to bring up the Preferences window (**Figure 10-1**).

FIG. 10-1 Settings/Preferences.

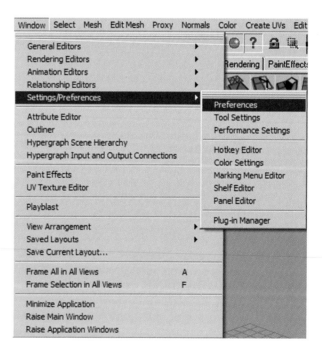

Click on Settings and set the World Coordinate System to Up Axis Y. Leave the other Settings options at their default. Maya uses centimeters for its internal measurements, so working in centimeters makes sense. Most people write scripts based on the default settings of Maya (**Figure 10-2**). It usually won't be an issue, but it's better to be safe. If you need to convert to inches, divide

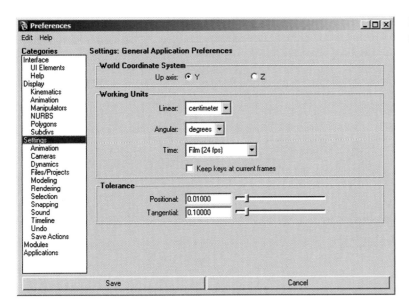

FIG. 10-2 The default Preferences window.

the number of centimeters by 2.5 to get the total in inches. Most production houses use Y up world coordinates, so you'll be making things much easier for yourself by setting your axes correctly to begin with.

Click on Cameras. I always uncheck Fit View and Fit View All under the Animated Camera Transitions section (**Figure 10-3**). Some people like this feature. Personally, I don't care for animated transitions. When I am cruising along modeling, the last I want to do is wait for the animated camera to finish its thing.

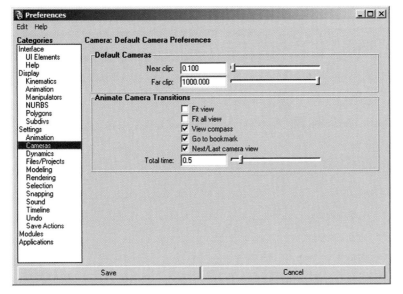

FIG. 10-3 Camera preferences.

Click on Selection (**Figure 10-4**). In the Polygon Selection section, select Whole Face. The default polygon face selection is Center, which is fine most of the time. But occasionally on very small faces, the center selection box is very difficult to click. By changing to whole face selection, this won't be a problem.

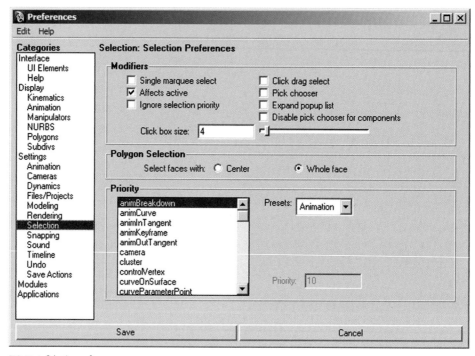

FIG. 10-4   Selection preferences.

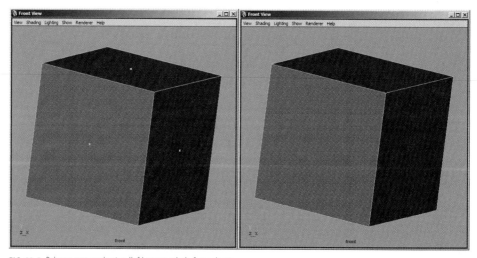

FIG. 10-5   Polygon center selection (left) versus whole face selection.

Next, uncheck Interactive Creation under the Create > Polygon Primitives window. Interactive Creation allows you to create a model anywhere you desire by clicking on the screen and dragging with your left mouse button. For creating a character, though, you need to have the model centered on the y-z-axis. You also need to make sure that Keep Faces Together is checked. This option keeps adjacent polygons that are extruded at same time welded together. To enable, click Edit Mesh > Keep Faces Together (**Figure 10-6**).

If Keep Faces Together is off (**Figures 10-7 and 10-8**), a new face is inserted between adjacent polygons during each extrude operation. Generally, this is undesirable with character creation.

Now that all of the preferences are set, let's look at the polygon modeling tools of choice and the new tools available in Maya.

You'll note that Maya has a revamped interface. Chief among the results for us is that all of the polygon tools have been moved to a new Polygons menu set

FIG. 10-6 Keep Faces Together.

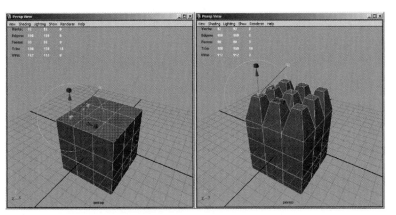

FIG. 10-7 A cube with Keep Faces Together turned off.

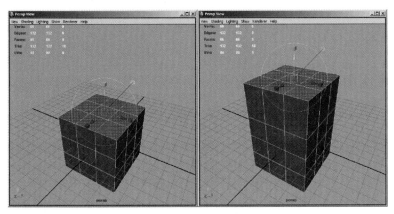

FIG. 10-8 The same cube with Keep Faces Together turned on.

239

(**Figure 10-9**). The Polygons menu is set up with more logic now. All of the tools are now very easy to find. This should help speed up productivity.

The Toolbox has a new permanent addition: the Paint Selection Tool (Edit > Paint Selection). This tool (**Figure 10-10**) allows you to pick components by painting your selection. This can save a huge time over manual section using the marquee tools.

When used in conjunction with Quick Select Sets, you have to select complex component groups only once (**Figure 10-11**).

FIG. 10-9 Polygons menu set.

FIG. 10-10 The Toolbox.

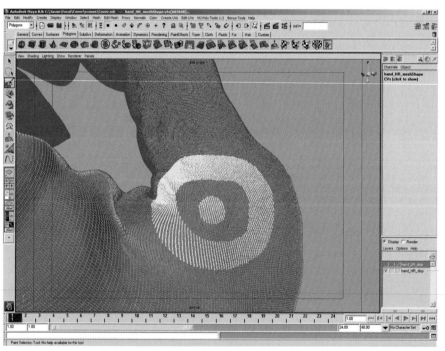

FIG. 10-11 Complex selection.

Right-click on an object and select the desired component (vertex, face, or edge) type. Click the Paint Selection icon in the toolbox. Paint the desired selection. This can be vertices for manipulation, faces for texturing, and so on. The paint selection tool paints only the visible side of the mesh.

With the components still selected, click Create > Sets > Quick Select Set (**Figure 10-12**). Keep in mind that quick select sets work with more than just

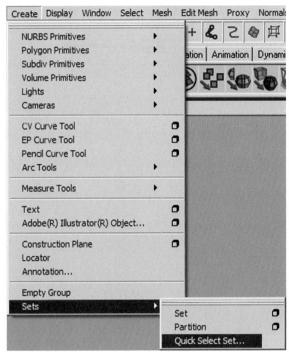

FIG. 10-12 Creating a quick select set.

FIG. 10-13 The quick select prompt.

components. They work with most nodes in Maya. This can really help organize your scenes.

At the prompt, type in a name for the quick select set (**Figure 10-13**).

Anytime you need to select the set, go to Edit > Quick Select Sets and select the desired set (**Figure 10-14**).

Still in the toolbox is the updated soft modification tool (**Figure 10-15**). The soft mod tool is an incredibly powerful tool for modeling. The soft mod tool now displays a color image of the falloff amount. No more guesswork. The brighter colors have a stronger deformation than the darker areas.

Click on the tool manipulator to switch to edit mode. Select and adjust the red manipulator to adjust the falloff amount. You can even move the modification position by translating the manipulator.

All of the component extrude operations now function under one command. Gone are extrude face, extrude edge, and extrude vertex from earlier versions of Maya. Now click Edit Mesh > Extrude to extrude the selected component type.

Most of the time, you'll extrude using the default settings. But don't forget about the options available in the extrude options (**Figure 10-16**). Taper and twist are very useful in creating things like horns.

FIG. 10-14 Using quick select sets.

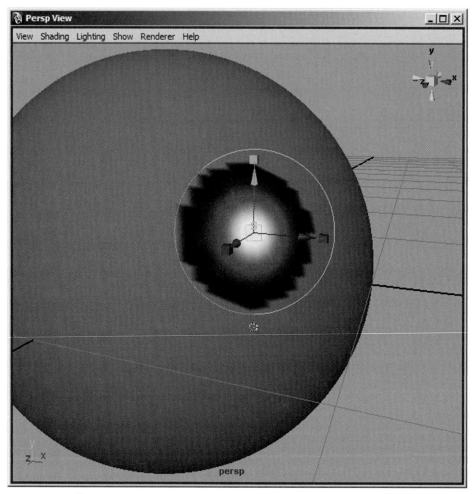

FIG. 10-15 Soft modification tool.

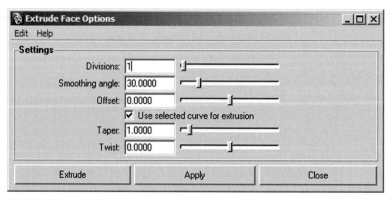

FIG. 10-16 Extrude options.

Click Create > Polygon Primitives > Cube to create a default cube.

In the front view, click Create > EP Curve Tool to create an edit point curve that begins at the center of the face and follows the shape of a horn (**Figure 10-17**).

Select the face and Shift-select the curve. By Shift-selecting the curve, you're telling Maya that the next extrusion will follow the curve (**Figure 10-18**).

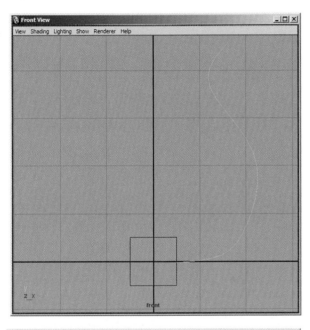

FIG. 10-17 Adding a curve to extrude along.

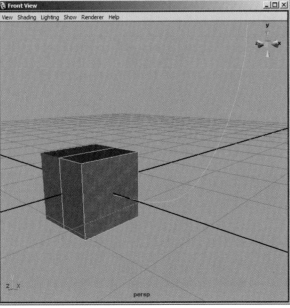

FIG. 10-18 Face and curve selected for extrude operation.

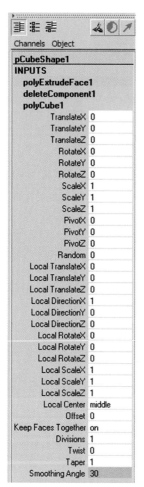

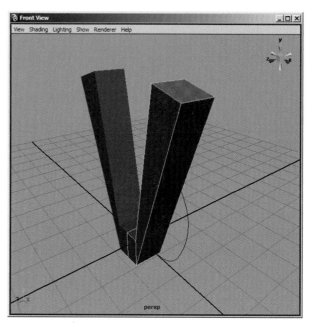

FIG. 10-19 Default extrusion along a curve. Notice how the face extrudes to the end of the curve.

FIG. 10-20 Extrude options viewed in the Channel Box.

FIG. 10-21 Scrubbing channels to interactively change the object.

Click Edit Mesh > Extrude. Usually I like to keep tool settings at the default and will change them later in the Channel Box or Attribute Editor (**Figure 10-19**). You can interactively change the settings this way, which makes it much easier to get the desired results.

Open the Channel Box to view the extrude operation (**Figure 10-20**). If you accidentally deselect the object, you can select the object and click the extrude node in the INPUTS section of the Channel Box.

Add some division levels to subdivide the horn. To change a channel's value, select it in the Channel Box with the left mouse button, then press the middle mouse button and scrub left and right in the modeling windows to interactively adjust the number (**Figure 10-21, 10-22**).

Adjust the Twist and Taper values until you get a nice spiraling horn. In **Figure 10-23**, I set the Twist value to −180 and the Taper to 0.

History is still intact on the horn, so you can still make adjustments to the shape by right-clicking on the curve and moving the edit points around (**Figure 10-24**).

If desired, you can smooth the horns by selecting the object and clicking Mesh > Smooth (**Figure 10-25**).

The edge loop tools have also been strengthened with the addition of the Offset Edge Loop Tool and Slide Edge Loop tools. The Offset Edge Loop Tool

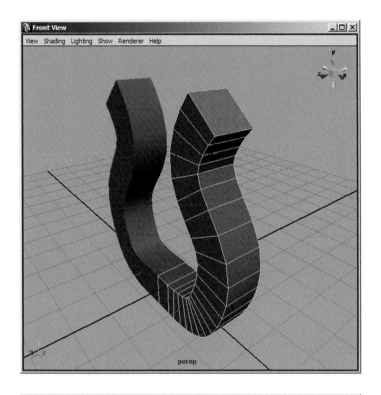

FIG. 10-22 Adding divisions to the horn.

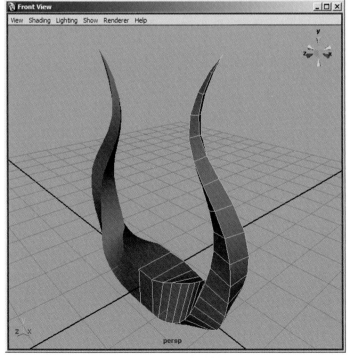

FIG. 10-23 Adding Twist and Taper to the horns.

FIG. 10-24 Manipulating the curve after creation.

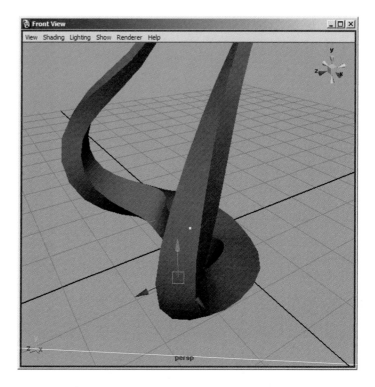

FIG. 10-25 Final smoothed horns.

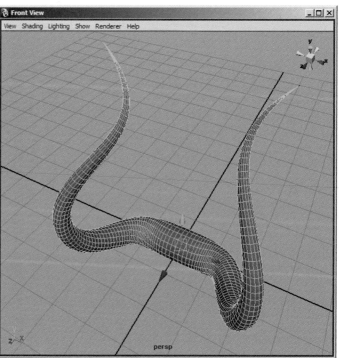

creates two new edges evenly spaced between the selected edge and the adjacent edge on either side (**Figure 10-26**). The Slide Edge Loop Tool allows you to adjust the position of edge loops by sliding them across the mesh. Proper edge loop modeling is vital for clean topology. Edge loops make it easier to layout the UVs. They also make it easier for the character TD to rig a model for proper deformation during animation. See also **Figure 10-27**.

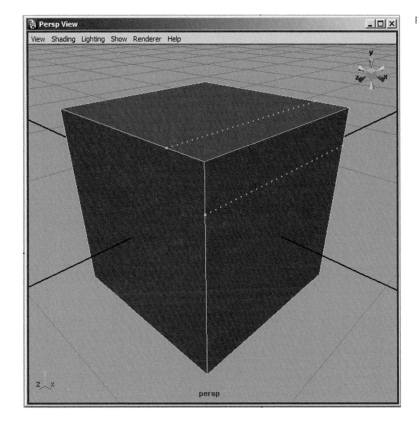

FIG. 10-26 Offset edge loops.

Although polygons have become the format of choice for organic modeling, don't overlook the value of subdivision and NURBS tools. Most pipelines are built around polygons these days, but there are still some instances where the other modeling formats are still useful.

Subdivision surfaces handle displacement maps better than polygons. Because of that, when using displacement maps, most artists convert polygons to subdivision surfaces at render time.

NURBS can also be used in a polygonal modeling pipeline. For instance, I almost always stick with a simple NURBS sphere when creating an eyeball. Because NURBS have imbedded texture coordinates there is little editing that

FIG. 10-27 Offset edge loops between different sized polygons. Notice how the tool evenly spaces the new edges between the adjacent edges on either side.

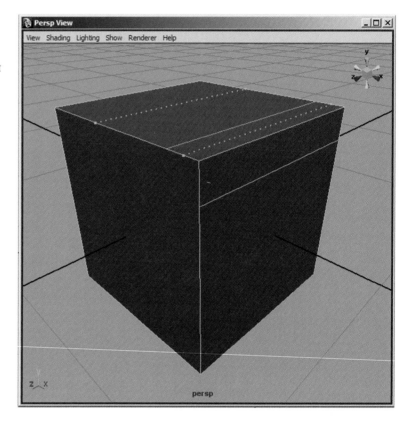

needs to be done when applying the pupil textures. By converting a NURBS object to polygons using the proper settings, an artist familiar with NURBS modeling can work with the tools they know and still deliver the required polygonal characters.

Create a NURBS sphere Create > NURBS Primitives > Sphere. Make sure that Interactive Placement is unchecked. The NURBS sphere will act as the eye (Figure 10-28).

Rotate the sphere 90 degrees on the x-axis. This will point the pole of the sphere forward on the z-axis. This can then be used as the pupil of the eyeball.

Click on Create > NURBS Primitives > Circle.

Name the circle eyeCurve1 and rotate it 90 degrees on the x-axis and place it in front of the sphere (Figure 10-29).

In the front viewport, right-click on the curve to go into component mode and adjust the control vertices into the desired shape of the eye (Figure 10-30).

In the side and perspective views, adjust the control vertices of the curve so that they conform to the shape of the eye (Figure 10-31). This will be the inside of the eyelid.

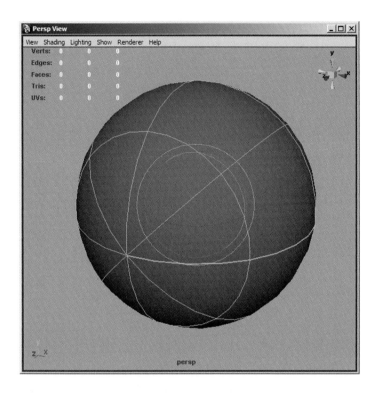

FIG. 10-28 Placing the eyeball.

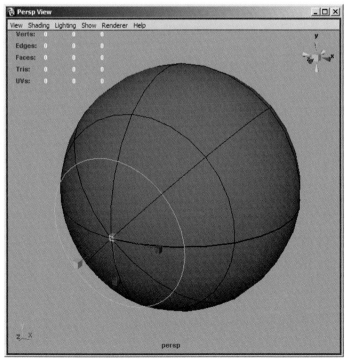

FIG. 10-29 Adding the first curve.

FIG. 10-30 Changing curve shape.

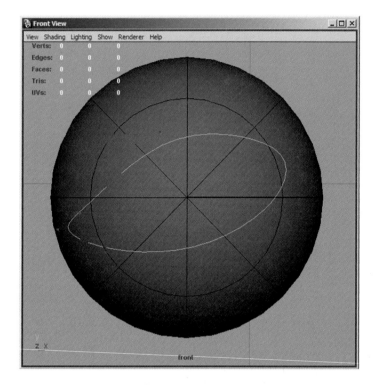

FIG. 10-31 Adjusting the shape of the curve.

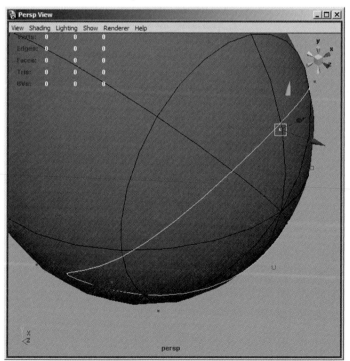

Duplicate the curve and scale it down slightly. Name the new curve eyeCurve2. To properly build the surface, all curves need to have the same number of control vertices. By duplicating the original curve, keeping the same CV (control vertex) count is very easy.

Move eyeCurve2 forward to help form the section of the eyelid where the lashes sit (**Figure 10-32**).

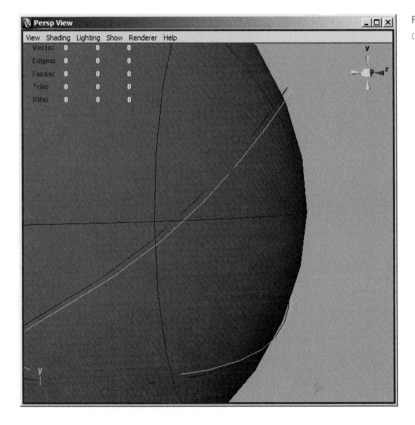

FIG. 10-32 Adjusting the second curve.

Duplicate eyeCurve2 and name it eyeCurve3 (**Figure 10-33**). Move the new curve forward a small amount, and scale it slightly up. By starting with these three curves, depth is given to the eyelids.

Duplicate eyeCurve3, name it eyeCurve4 and scale it up to start forming the surface around the eye (**Figure 10-34**). Use the CVs to start rounding out this curve.

Duplicate eyeCurve4 and name it eyeCurve5. Scale this curve up and continue shaping it to add to the shape around the eye.

Duplicate eyeCurve5 and name it eyeCurve6. Scale this up and continue shaping the curve. Your curves should be placed similar to **Figure 10-35**.

251

FIG. 10-33 The third curve of the lid.

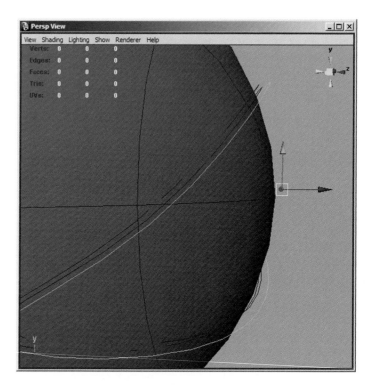

FIG. 10-34 The fourth curve of the lid.

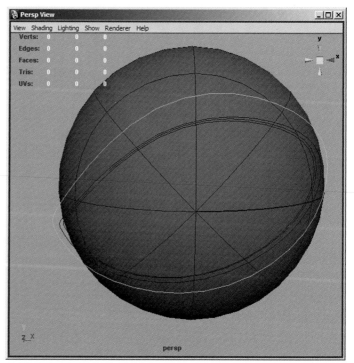

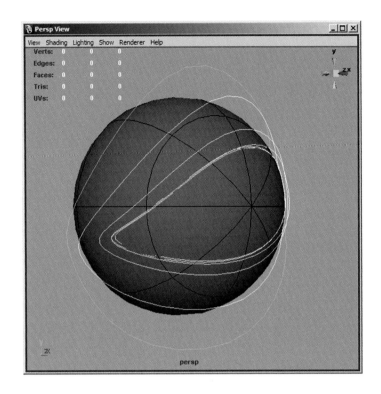

FIG. 10-35 Final curve placement around the eye.

Starting with eyeCurve1, select all of the curves in order. The curves must be selected in the right order, or the surface will not come out correct.

With the curves still highlighted, click Surfaces > Loft > □. Set the options according to **Figure 10-36** and press Loft. Chord length parameterization creates better curvature on new surfaces. Auto-reverse will help prevent twisting.

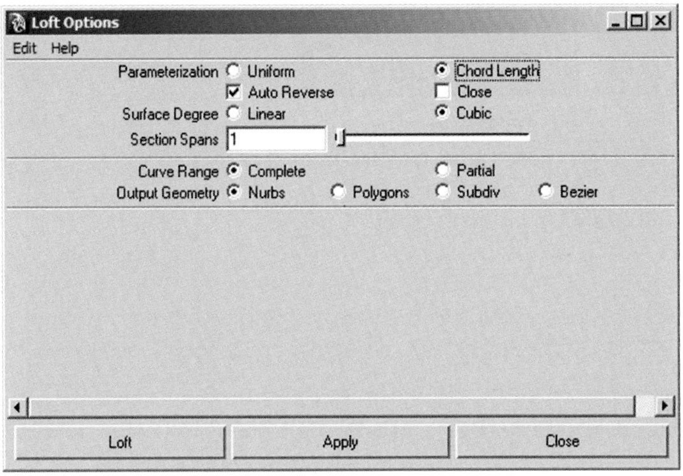

FIG. 10-36 Loft options.

253

FIG. 10-37 The resulting surface.

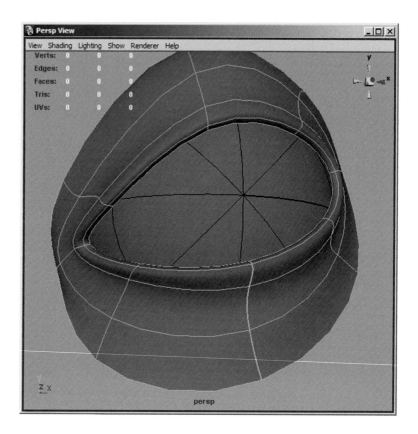

Cubic surface degree results in a smooth surface, whereas linear gives a faceted appearance. The section spans change the number of sections in each span of the surface (**Figure 10-37**). Keeping this set to 1 allows you to work with smaller amounts of detail. Always start small and work in the extra detail later.

Now to convert the surface to polygons. Click on Modify > Convert > NURBS to Polygons > □. Set the options according to **Figure 10-38** and press Tessellate. If you have multiple patches, you can check "Attach multiple output meshes." Our object is only one surface, so it can be left unchecked. Change the Type to Quads and the Tessellation method to General. This will allow us to better control the resulting polygonal mesh (**Figure 10-39**). Under Initial Tessellation Controls set both the U and V type to "Per span # of iso params" and the Number U to 2 and Number V to 1. This will allow us to control exactly how many polygons will be added to each span in the U and V directions of the surface. In this case, each span will have two polygons created in the U direction and one in the V. Leave the other options at the default.

Another very powerful modeling aid is the use of animation deformers. By applying deformers to a mesh, the object can quickly be changed in ways that would be too difficult or take too long using traditional methods.

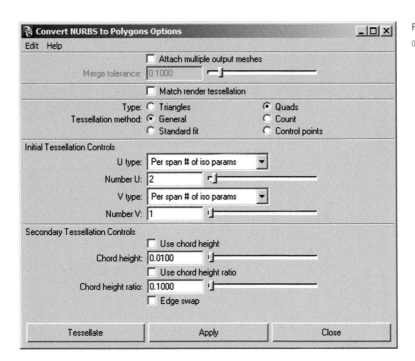

FIG. 10-38 NURBS to polygons options.

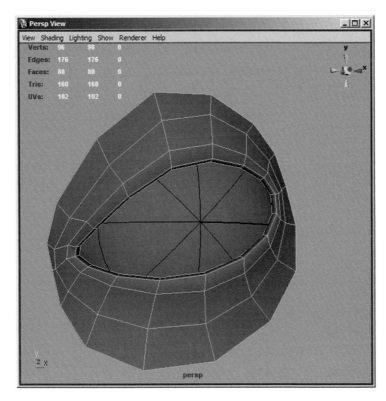

FIG. 10-39 Surface converted to polygons with good clean quad topology.

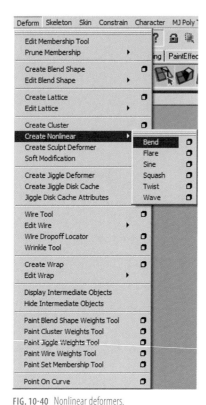

FIG. 10-40 Nonlinear deformers.

Create a polygon cylinder with a height of 6 and a subdivision height of 20. Select the cylinder and click on Deform > Create Nonlinear > Bend. This will add a deformer to the mesh (**Figures 10-40 and 10-41**).

If the deformer is oriented in the wrong direction, you can select it in the outliner and rotate to the correction position (**Figure 10-42**).

Adjust the bend deformer options in the channel box (**Figure 10-43**). Curvature will bend the cylinder in a way that would take forever using other methods. Low bound and high bound adjusts where the bend effect starts and stops affecting the mesh from the bottom and top, respectively.

Experiment with the other nonlinear deformers. Test the different channels for each type. As soon as the changes are acceptable, you need to select the mesh and delete its history by clicking Edit > Delete by Type > History. Deleting the history will remove the deformer while keeping the mesh in its bent state (**Figure 10-44**).

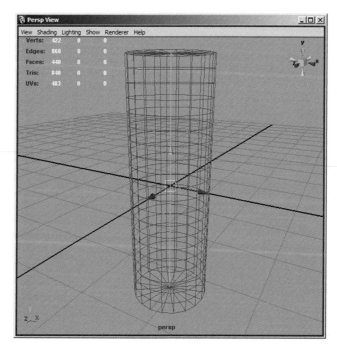

FIG. 10-41 Bend deformer.

FIG. 10-42 Locating the deformer in the outliner.

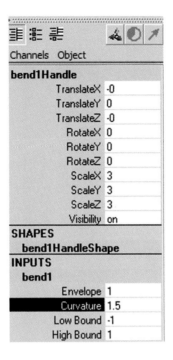

FIG. 10-43 Adjust the bend options. Here the curvature is set to 1.5.

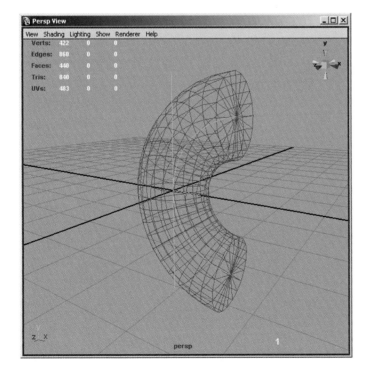

FIG. 10-44 The bent cylinder.

FIG. 10-45 Creating a lattice.

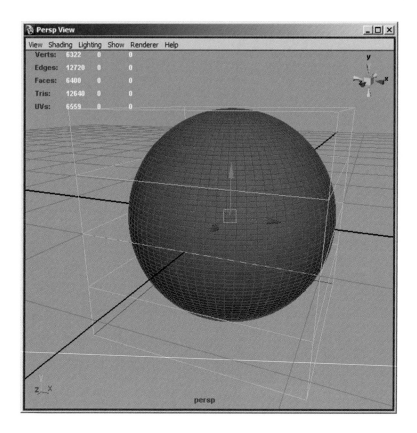

The other type of deformer useful for modeling is the lattice. Creating a lattice places a low-res cage that surrounds the selected object (**Figure 10-45**). You can then manipulate a high-res object using the lower number of points in the lattice.

Create a sphere with the subdivisions along the axis and height to 80.

With the sphere selected, click Deform > Create Lattice. This will place a low-res cage around the sphere.

Right-click on the lattice and select Lattice Point.

Select and move the lattice points until you get the desired shape (**Figure 10-46**). Notice how moving one lattice point adjusts a large number of vertices on the main object.

If you need more lattice points, click the lattice and adjust the S, T, and U divisions to the desired amount of the lattice shape node in the channel box. Remember that anytime you see S, T, and U, it is equivalent to X, Y, and Z.

If you've already changed the lattice, you will need to click Deform > Edit Lattice > Remove Lattice Tweaks before you can add extra divisions (**Figures 10-47 through 10-49**).

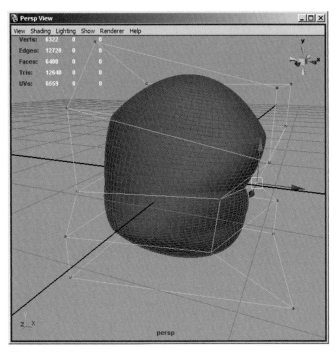

FIG. 10-46   Adjusting the lattice.

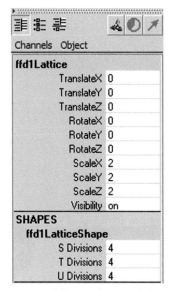

FIG. 10-47   Adding extra divisions to the lattice.

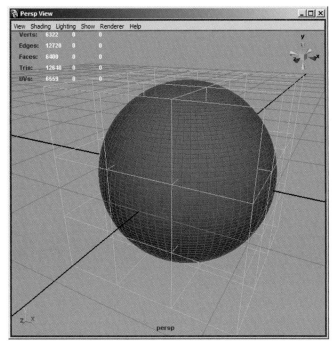

FIG. 10-48   The higher-resolution lattice.

FIG. 10-49 Adjustments to the high-res lattice.

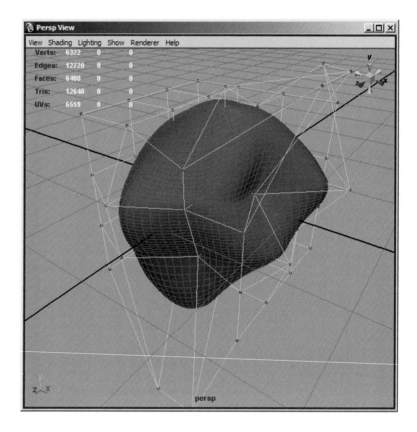

After you're finished using the lattice, you will need to select the mesh and delete its history.

Before you begin modeling, you'll want to have concept sketches and a minimum of front and side orthographic views of the character you plan on building (**Figure 10-50**). The concept sketches are for visual reference during model construction. The orthographic views, though, will be used directly in Maya to help you create your model. First, you will need to scan your orthographic drawings. Next, bring the scanned images into Maya for use as a template to build your model.

Create a new scene by clicking on File > New Scene. In the front viewport, select View > Image Plane > Import Image (**Figure 10-51**).

At the prompt, select the front view of the character to load it as a template image (**Figure 10-52**). In the side viewport, select View > Image Plane > Import Image. At the prompt, load the side view sketch of your character.

Go to Display > UI Elements > Channel Box/Layer Editor to bring up the Channel Box or click the show Channel Box/Layer Editor button on the Status Line (**Figure 10-53**).

FIG. 10-50 Front and side sketches of a character ready for construction.

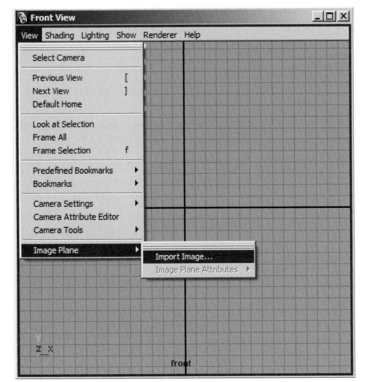

FIG. 10-51 Loading an Image Plane.

FIG. 10-52 Template geometry.

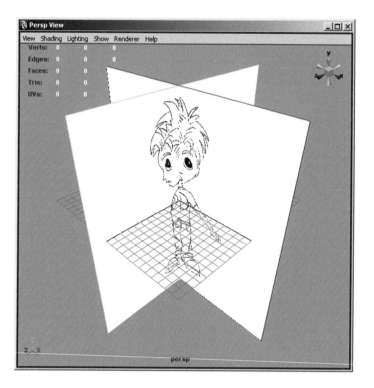

FIG. 10-53 Show the Channel Box and Layer
Editor.

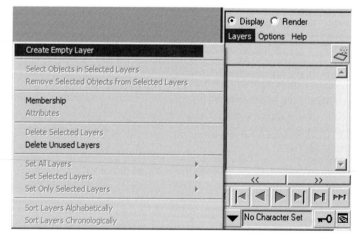

FIG. 10-54 Creating the display layer.

Press the Show the Channel Box and Layer Editor button near the top of
the Channel Box/Layer Editor window. Click on the Display radial. Select
Layers > Create Layer in the Layer Editor. Name the layer templateDisplay.
See **Figures 10-53 and 10-54.**

Select the newly created layer. Drag select the two planes in the Perspective view. In the Layer Editor, select Layers > Add Selected Objects to Current Layer.

Select the front image plane in the perspective viewport. By default, the image planes are created at the center of the world. This makes it very difficult to model. Fortunately this is fairly easy to correct (**Figure 10-55**).

Select the imagePlane input node in the INPUTS section of the Channel Box. Adjust the CenterZ channel so the image plane won't interfere with your modeling. Remember that in most cases, you should model with your character facing forward into the +z-axis so that would mean adjusting the CenterZ.

Select the side image plane in the perspective viewport. Select the imagePlane input node in the INPUTS section of the Channel Box.

Adjust the CenterX channel so the image plane won't interfere with your modeling. This time, the CenterX channel should be adjusted into the −x values.

Click the middle box of your Layer until it displays an R. Now the image planes can't be accidentally selected if you're working in the perspective view. If you need to open the layer for editing at a later time, click the middle box of the layer until it is empty.

Now you can go back to your scene and begin modeling. If you need to hide the template objects for any reason, click V in the first box of your layer until it is empty. This will turn off the layer visibility and hide any objects within it. See **Figure 10-56**.

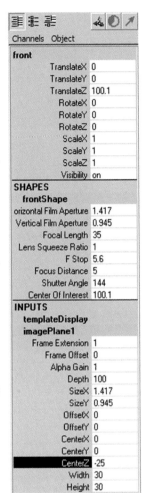

FIG. 10-55 Offsetting the image planes.

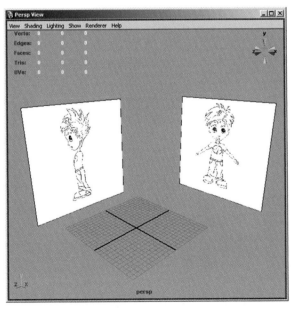

FIG. 10-56 Final template geometry.

It's time to begin modeling the character. The first stage is called "blocking." Blocking means creating a basic frame for your character. I can't stress enough how essential it is to start simple and add detail later. If you try to start with a dense mesh, editing the character later will become very difficult. Something very important to remember is that when you add vertical edge loops, they will travel through multiple sections of the character. The tutorials are presented in a step-by-step fashion so that it is hard to take that into account. As you become more familiar with modeling, you will probably want to shift around and do some basic shaping in all of the affected areas anytime new vertical edge loops are created.

Open your template. Make sure Edit Mesh > Keep Faces Together is checked. This option will keep extra polygons from being created in between adjacent polygons during extrude operations.

Click Create > Polygon Primitives > Interactive Placement to uncheck and turn off this feature. Remember, all modeling should be done on the +x-axis with the character facing forward into +z. Interactive placement creates objects wherever you click in the viewport, not in the center of the world like we need.

Click Create > Polygon Primitives > Cube □ (**Figure 10-57**). Set the Width divisions to 2 and click Create. Always start with a simple object and add detail as needed. I can't stress this enough. If you add detail too quickly, the mesh will become very hard to edit later. That makes a cube, which is one of the simplest of polygon meshes, the perfect primitive to begin modeling with.

Select the polygon faces in the −x axis and delete them (**Figures 10-58 and 10-59**).

FIG. 10-57 Cube settings.

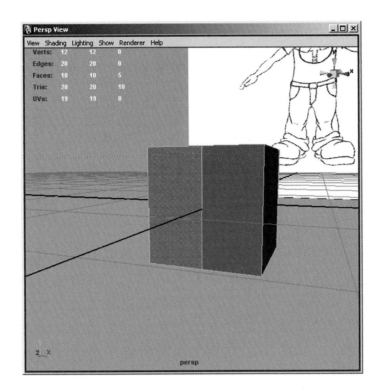

FIG. 10-58 Faces to delete.

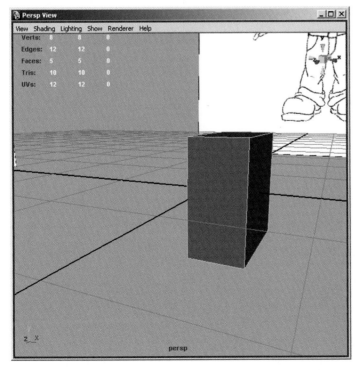

FIG. 10-59 Deleted faces.

Select the remaining half cube.

Click Edit > Duplicate Special □. Set the Geometry type to Instance (**Figure 10-60**). Change the x scale to −1. Press apply. Making a negative instance of the half cube creates a mirror of the object that will update with any changes made to the original half. By doing this, you work on half the object, but in the end get a full model. Half the work to get a complete model; always a good idea.

FIG. 10-60 Duplicate options.

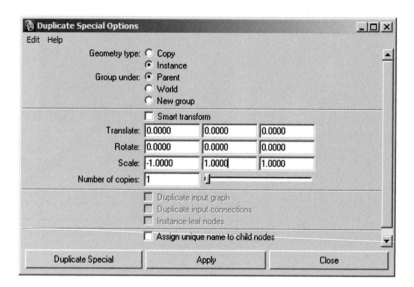

FIG. 10-61 Don't move these vertices on the x-axis.

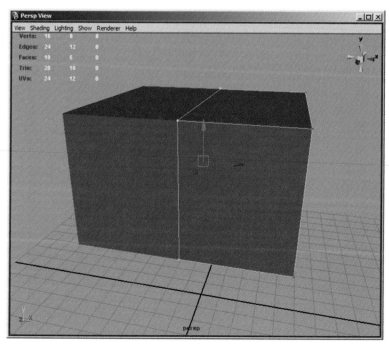

Note: Anytime you see columns in Maya, the first one represents x, the middle one is y, and the last one is z.

Using only component mode, position and scale the half cube so that it fits the character's chest area. By using component mode to adjust the model, the instanced half will update along with the changes to the original half. The center vertices can move on the y- and z-axes, but it's vital not to move them in the x direction. Doing this would cause holes to appear in the model. See **Figures 10-61 through 10-63.**

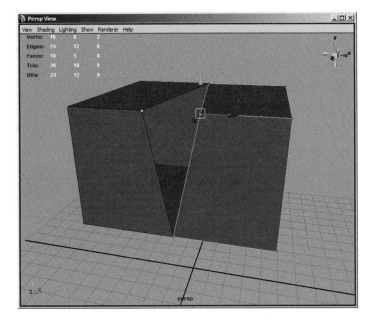

FIG. 10-62 Hole caused by moving center vertices on the x-axis.

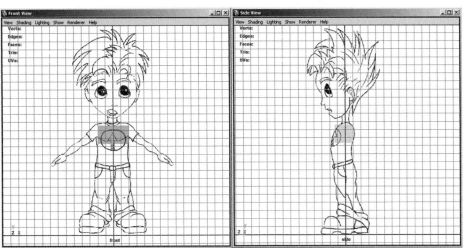

FIG. 10-63 Front and side views of positioned cube.

Select the bottom face (**Figure 10-64**).

Click Edit Mesh > Extrude, and the tool manipulator will appear (**Figure 10-65**). The extrude tool has two modes: local space and world space. The default, local space will extrude in the direction the polygon is currently facing. World space will extrude in the x-y-z direction of the main world coordinates.

Click the blue manipulator to switch the extrusion to world space.

Extrude this face down to the center of the belly (**Figure 10-66**). It's important to add detail in small amounts to keep the mesh easier to work with. The extrude modeling method that we use is really good for that.

You will notice that anytime you extrude along the center y-z-axes, a polygon is added. This needs to be deleted (**Figure 10-67**). Anytime a face is created in an area that lies hidden within the boundary of the mesh, it should be deleted or it can cause problems with the geometry later.

Again select the bottom face and extrude to the bottom of the crotch (**Figure 10-68**).

Select the new face that is created in the center on the y-z-axes and delete it.

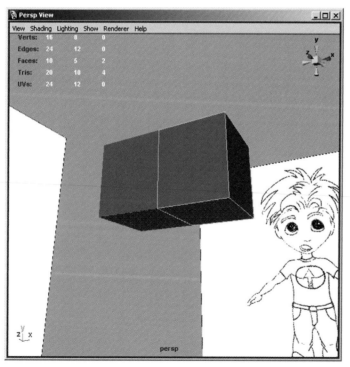

FIG. 10-64 Bottom face to be extruded.

FIG. 10-65 The extrude tool.

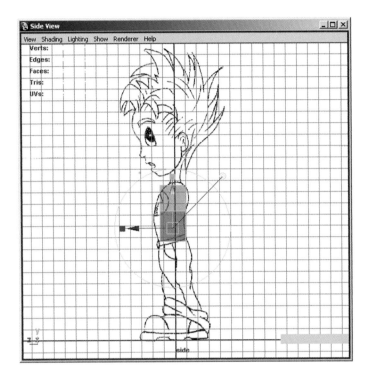

FIG. 10-66 Extrude to center of the belly.

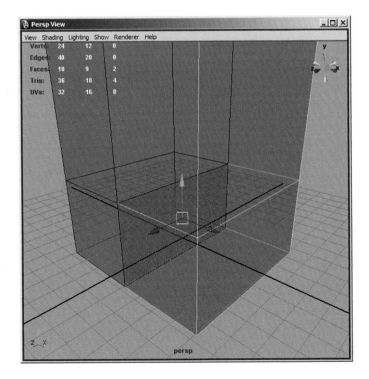

FIG. 10-67 Extra face to delete.

FIG. 10-68 Extrude to the bottom of the crotch.

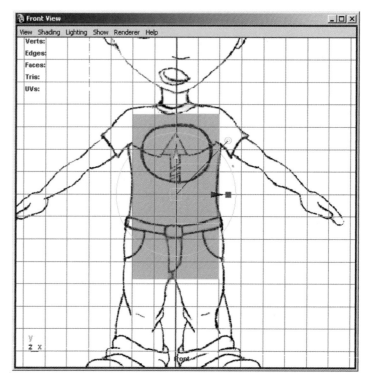

FIG. 10-69 Delete this face, too.

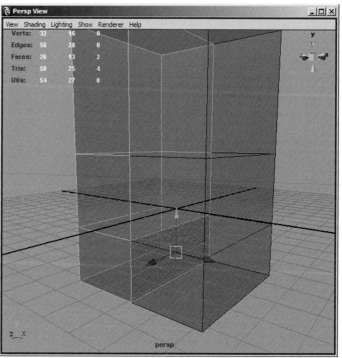

Begin shaping the torso by pushing and pulling the vertices and edges into place (**Figure 10-70**). It's very important to start shaping the mesh while it is still at low resolution.

Select the bottom outer edge and move it in to form the crotch. This is very important in allowing us to get proper edge loops in the legs (**Figure 10-71**).

Select the face that forms the hip (**Figure 10-72**).

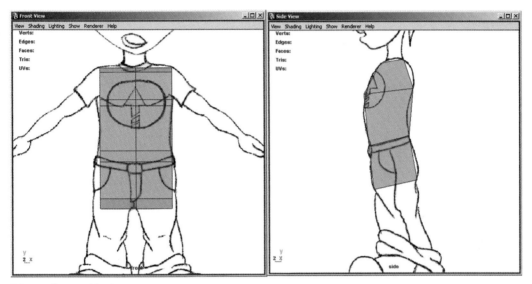

FIG. 10-70 The torso taking shape.

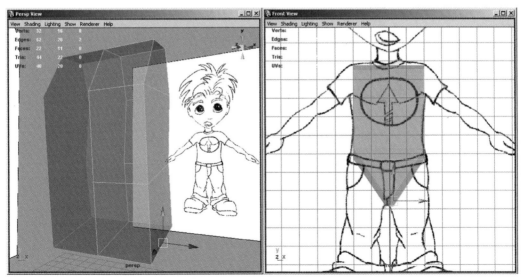

FIG. 10-71 Move this edge to form the crotch.

FIG. 10-72 The newly created hips.

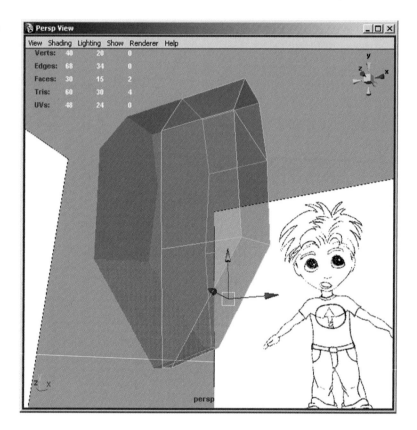

Extrude this face down in world space to form the beginning of the thigh. This is a crucial step in getting the edge loops to flow properly through the legs. Note that the inner thigh is formed in this step (**Figure 10-73**).

Now the outer thigh needs to be set. To do this, adjust the outer vertices of the newly created polygon so it matches the thigh of your template (**Figure 10-74**).

Next select the outer vertices of the thigh and pull them down in the front view (**Figure 10-75**). This is another step in forming the legs that will have proper edge loops.

Select the bottom face of the thigh and extrude to the top of the knee (**Figure 10-76**).

Extrude the new face to the bottom of the knee (**Figure 10-77**). It's very important to add extra edges around the joints so they will have enough polygons to deform correctly.

Extrude this new face to the ankle (**Figure 10-78**).

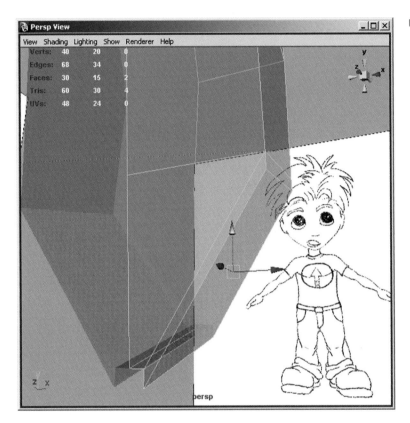

FIG. 10-73 Blocking out the thigh.

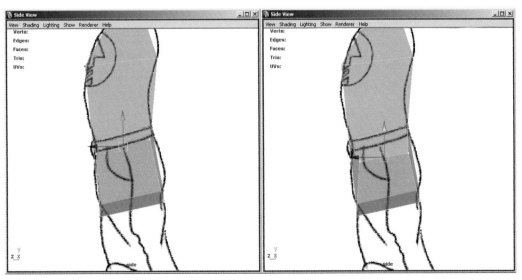

FIG. 10-74 Continuing to block out the thigh.

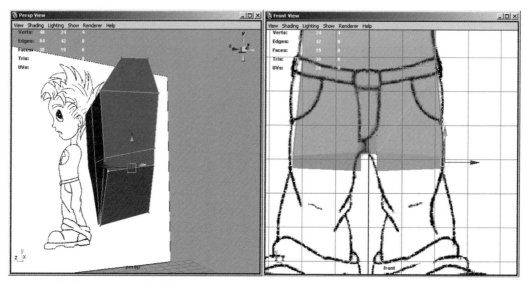

FIG. 10-75 Pulling down the vertices of the thigh.

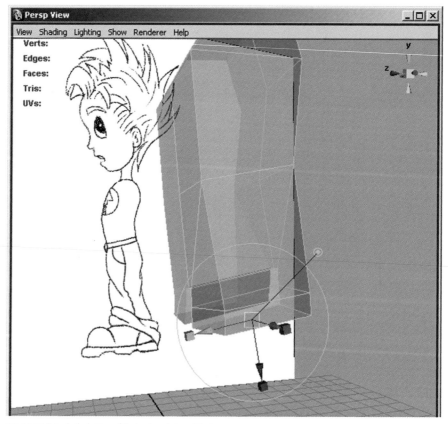

FIG. 10-76 Extrude the bottom of the leg faces to top of the knee.

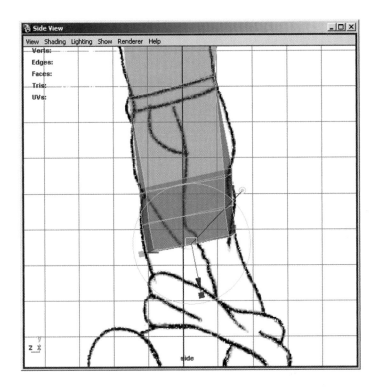

FIG. 10-77 Extrude the new face to bottom of the knee.

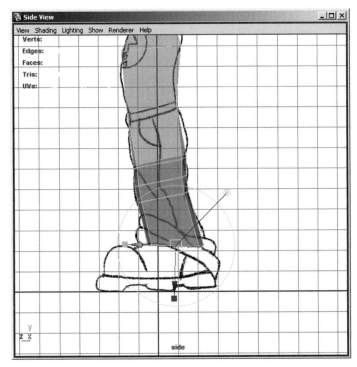

FIG. 10-78 Extrude to the ankle.

Next, you need to start forming the foot. Extrude the ankle to the bottom of the foot (**Figure 10-79**). Check the front and side viewports to make sure that the new foot is aligned correctly.

Now you need to move the back of the heel out (**Figure 10-80**). Select the rear bottom edge of the foot and slide it over. The heel is a bit on the outside when compared to the rest of the foot. This is one of those little steps that can add a ton of realism to your character.

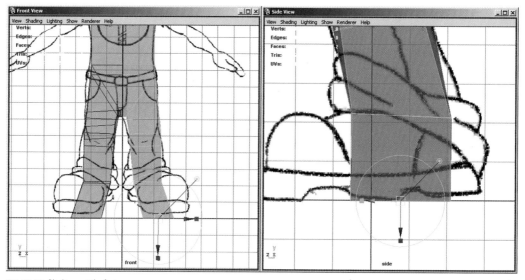

FIG. 10-79 Blocking out the foot.

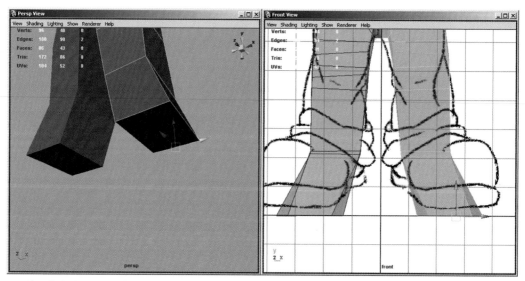

FIG. 10-80 The heel.

Select the front face below the ankle and extrude forward to the ball of the foot (**Figure 10-81**). Make sure it matches the foot from the reference image.

Extrude the front face of the ball forward to create the toe (**Figure 10-82**).

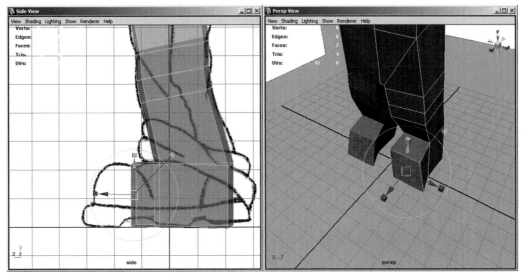

FIG. 10-81 The mid-section of the foot.

FIG. 10-82 Creating the toe.

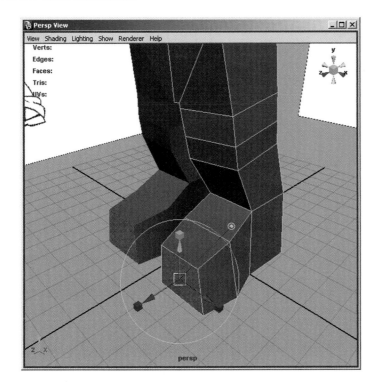

277

Use Edit Mesh > Insert Edge Loop Tool to create a new edge loop in the middle of the chest (**Figure 10-83**). Any time you add detail, make sure to keep shaping the form of the character. Remember if you wait to start shaping the form, you will have a much harder time. At this stage, we've moved on to other sections of the body. It's a good idea to work out the basic form for the entire character in the first pass. That way, when you begin adding more edge loops, they will travel correctly through the body.

Next, we need to start pulling out the arms. Select face on the side of the torso created from the newly added edge loop.

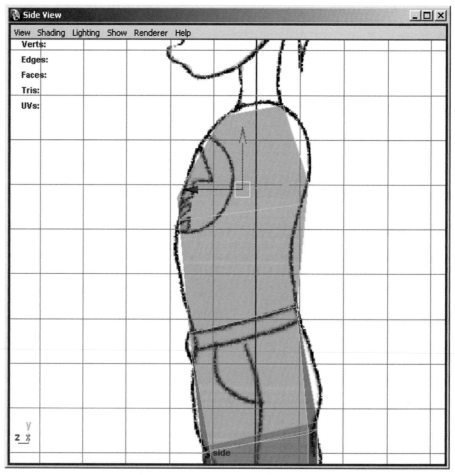

FIG. 10-83 Splitting the chest.

Extrude this face out and up to form the shoulder. Check the side and front views to help correctly shape the shoulder (**Figure 10-84**).

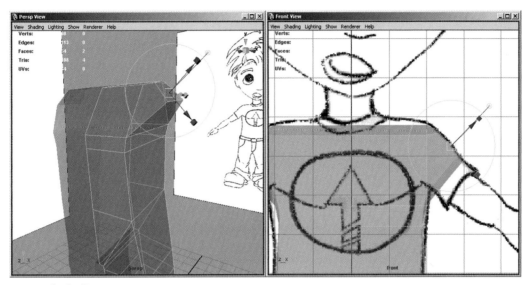

FIG. 10-84 The shoulders.

Next select the bottom face of the newly extruded shoulder and extrude down to the elbow to create the upper arm (**Figure 10-85**). The reason for extruding the bottom face of the shoulder is that it gives us nice edge loops from the chest, around the shoulders, and into the back.

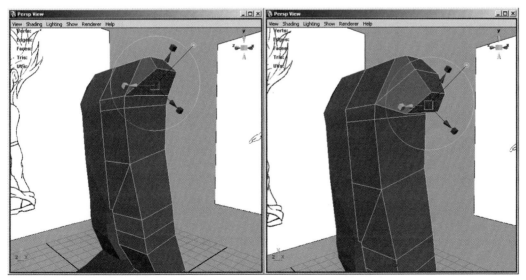

FIG. 10-85 The upper arm.

Use Edit Mesh > Insert Edge Loop Tool to add an edge loop across the top of the chest and through the shoulders. We want to add the loop now so you can use component mode to manipulate the vertices and edges to round off the shoulders (**Figure 10-86**).

Extrude the bottom face again to create the elbow (**Figure 10-87**). As you extrude the arm make sure to check all of the views to ensure it matches your reference images.

Make another extrude to the top of the wrist to create the forearm (**Figure 10-88**).

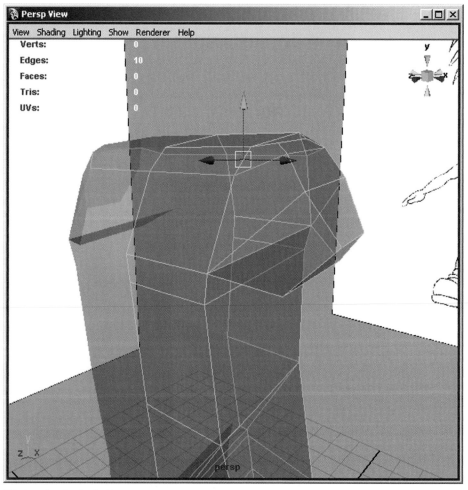

FIG. 10-86 Rounding the shoulder.

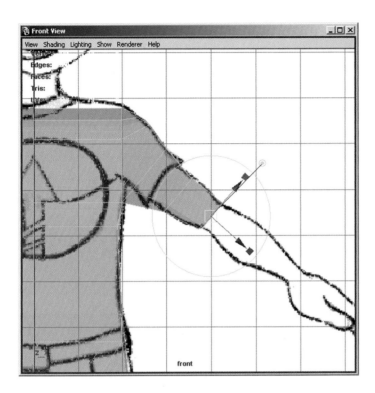

FIG. 10-87 The elbow.

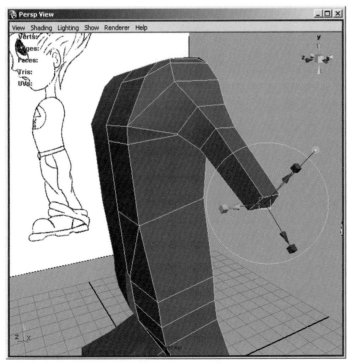

FIG. 10-88 Creating the forearm.

Rotate the bottom face of the arm 90 degrees to add the twist of the forearm created by the ulna and radius bones (**Figure 10-89**).

FIG. 10-89 Creating the forearm twist.

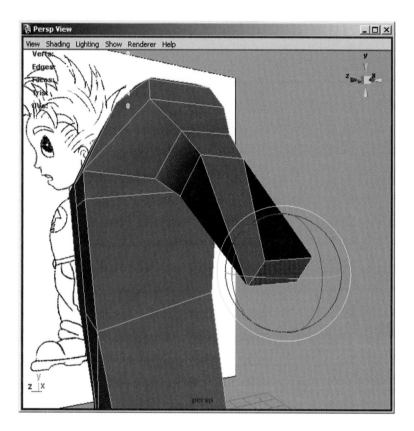

Next using the Insert Edge Loop Tool, add a loop in the middle of the forearm (**Figure 10-90**).

Select the polygon at the end of the arm and extrude it out to mid-palm for the beginning of the hand (**Figure 10-91**). Tilting the face up can help in shaping the rest of the hand.

Use the Insert Edge Loop Tool to a vertical edge loop through the new face. The new edge loop will travel around the length of the arm (**Figure 10-92**).

Add a second horizontal edge loop to the face (**Figure 10-93**). This edge loop will travel through the arm and down the side of the body. In this case that is good, because it gives us some more detail to help round out the body.

Remember to keep rounding out the form as you add detail.

Select and extrude the two faces on the thumb side to continue forming the hand (**Figure 10-94**). This is the metacarpal bone of the thumb and it forms the base.

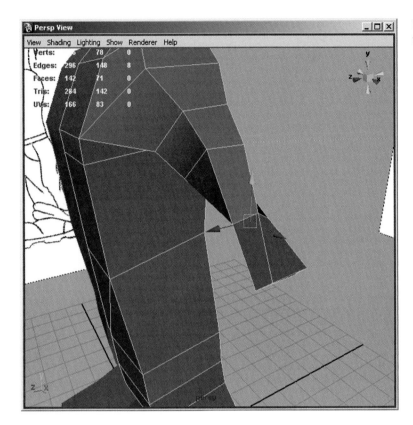

FIG. 10-90 Adding a loop to the forearm.

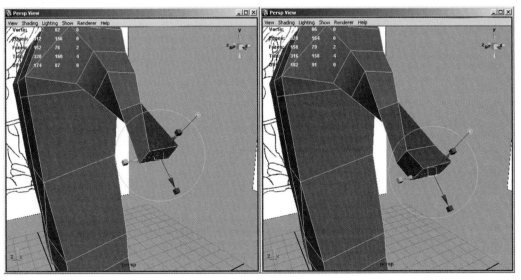

FIG. 10-91 Starting the hand.

FIG. 10-92 Adding a vertical edge loop through the arm.

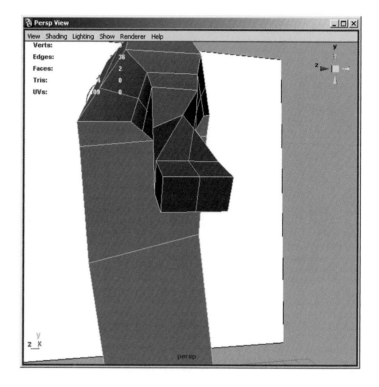

FIG. 10-93 Adding a horizontal edge loop through the arm.

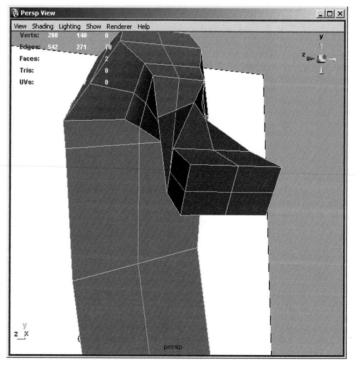

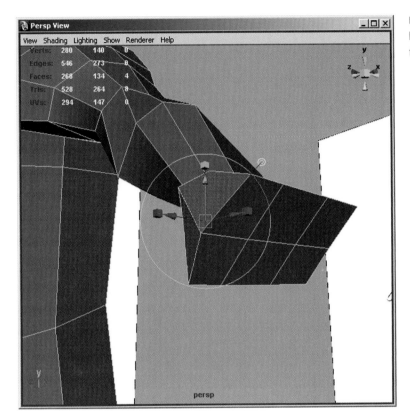

Select and extrude the two faces on the pinky side to continue forming the hand. This actually becomes the hypothenar muscles (the fleshy pad) on the pinky side of the hand (**Figure 10-95**).

Using component mode, adjust the newly added polygons to the proper shape of the hand. As always, you want to continue shaping the polygons as added (**Figure 10-96**).

Select the faces at the end of the hand and extrude them to the middle of the palm (**Figure 10-97**).

Continue shaping as you work. The hand has an indentation in the palm, so you should adjust the new faces to account for this. Don't add any extra detail though.

Select the end faces of the hand and extrude out to form the rest of the palm (**Figure 10-98**).

Using component mode, pull the vertices that form the base of the pinky finger back (**Figure 10-99**). If you look at your hand, you'll see that the base of the pinky is lower than the other fingers.

FIG. 10-95 Extrude to form the fleshy pad on the side of the hand.

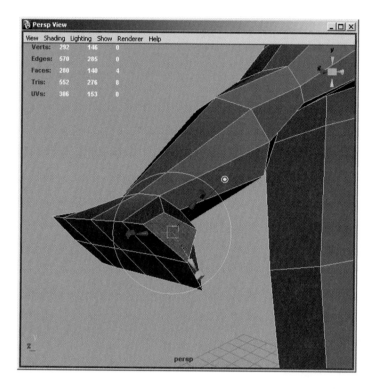

FIG. 10-96 Shaping the newly added polygons.

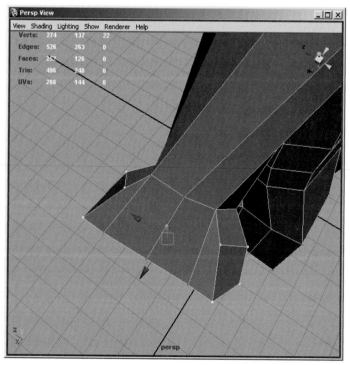

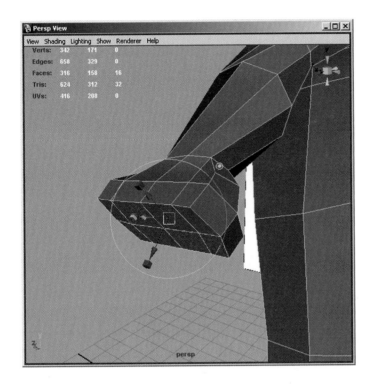

FIG. 10-97 Extrude to the middle of the palm.

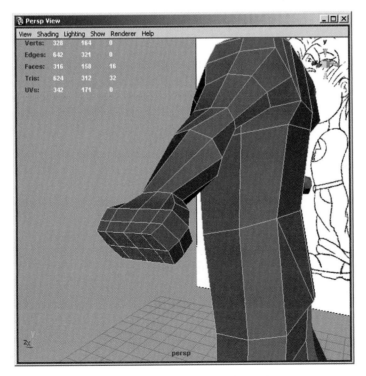

FIG. 10-98 Extrude to the end of the palm. Notice that the edges on the side have been pulled out to help round out the hand.

FIG. 10-99 Pulling the base of the pinky finger back.

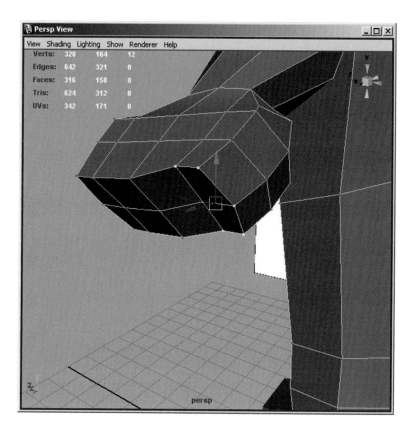

Click on Edit Mesh > Split Polygon Tool and create two new rows of edges that start at the top of the hand, loop around the inside edge of the index finger, and extend to mid-palm. We need to add this split because the fingers have a natural gap in between them (**Figure 10-100**). This is one of the easier ways to create fingers.

This will leave you with two triangles that you'll want to clean up. To do this, simply select the edge in between the two triangles and delete it (**Figures 10-101 and 10-102**).

Create the finger separation for the remaining fingers (**Figure 10-103**).

Now we can start extruding the fingers. The base of the finger forms the first, and largest, knuckle. Select the faces at the base of the index finger and extrude them out to the second knuckle (**Figure 10-104**). The finger tapers as it nears the tip, so be sure to resize the faces down as you extrude.

With the faces still selected, extrude out to the third knuckle (**Figure 10-105**).

Extrude the faces again out to the tip of the finger. At this point, don't worry about extruding the rest of the fingers. Once you've added extra detail, you'll actually duplicate the existing finger, thus saving yourself extra work (**Figure 10-106**).

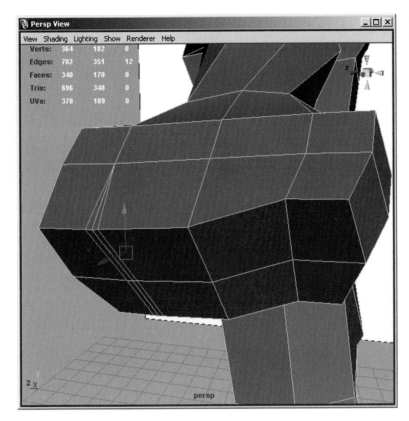

FIG. 10-100 Creating the finger separation.

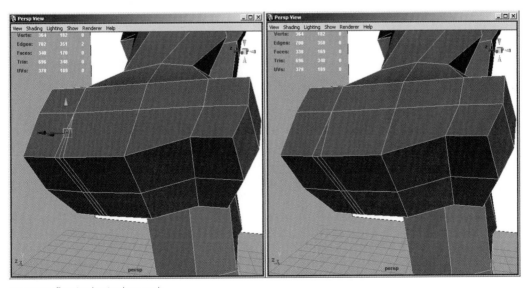

FIG. 10-101 Changing the triangles to quads.

FIG. 10-102 The split on the palm of the hand.

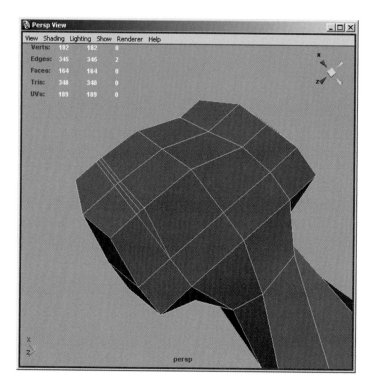

FIG. 10-103 Finishing the spacing of the fingers.

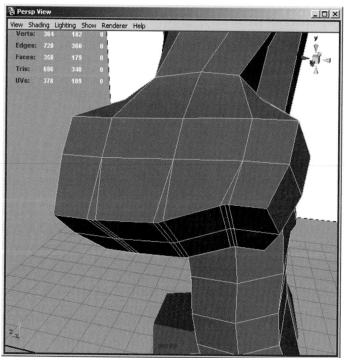

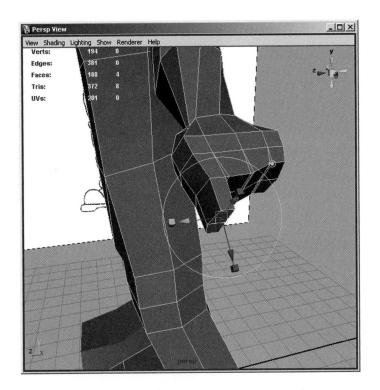

FIG. 10-104 Extruding the first part of the index finger.

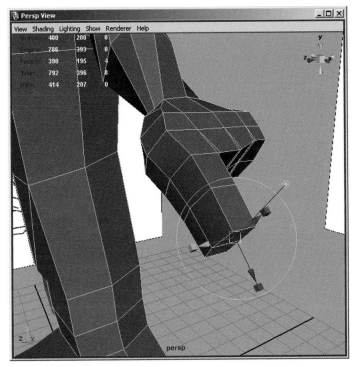

FIG. 10-105 Extruding the second part of the index finger.

FIG. 10-106 Extruding the tip of the index finger.

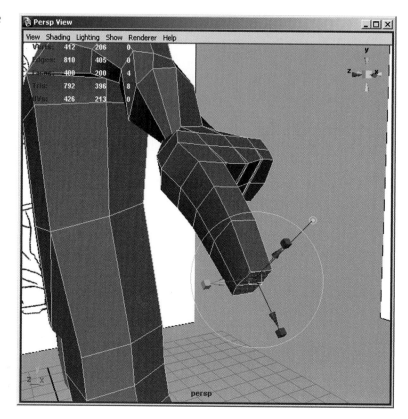

Using component mode, round out the form of the hand and index finger (**Figure 10-107**).

Now it's time to extrude the thumb. Select the faces that make up the base of the thumb. The outer face will form the first knuckle. The inside face extends onto the palm and forms the bulging muscles of the thumb. Extrude the faces down to the second knuckle and straighten the vertices (**Figure 10-108**).

With the faces still selected, extrude the faces again down to the tip of the thumb (**Figure 10-109**).

Pull down the indicated vertices and edge to help form the shape of the thumb (**Figure 10-110**). The vertices pulled down on the outside help define the first knuckle. The edge pulled down on the inside forms the large muscle at the base of the thumb that extends onto the palm. You also want to round out the shape of the thumb.

The final part needed to block out your character is the head. Select and extrude the faces at the top of the torso and shape them as indicated in **Figure 10-111**. These polygons form the trapezius muscle.

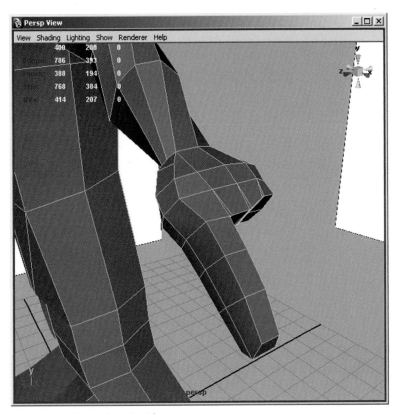

FIG. 10-107 Rounding out the hand and finger.

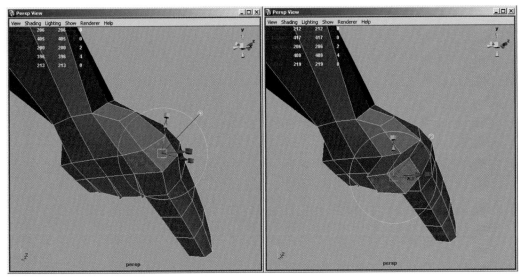

FIG. 10-108 Extruding the first part of the thumb.

FIG. 10-109 Creating the tip of the thumb.

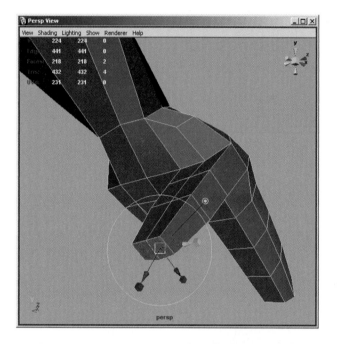

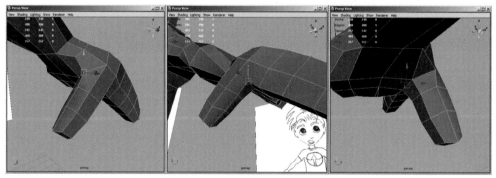

FIG. 10-110 Shaping the thumb.

FIG. 10-111 Extruding the trapezius.

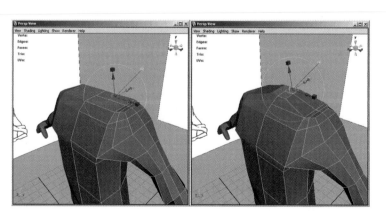

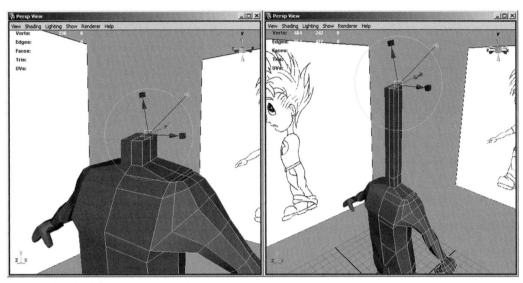

FIG. 10-112 Extruding the neck and start of the head.

FIG. 10-113 Creating the face.

Now select the faces of the top of the trapezius and extrude them up twice to form the neck and the start of the head (**Figure 10-112**).

Select the faces on the front of the head and extrude them forward to create the face (**Figure 10-113**). Remember to adjust the vertices to round out the face.

Insert an edge loop through the eye and round out the polygons to finish blocking the head (**Figures 10-114 and 10-115**).

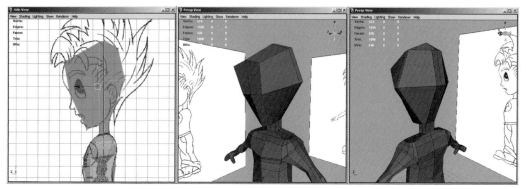

FIG. 10-114 Blocking out the rest of the head.

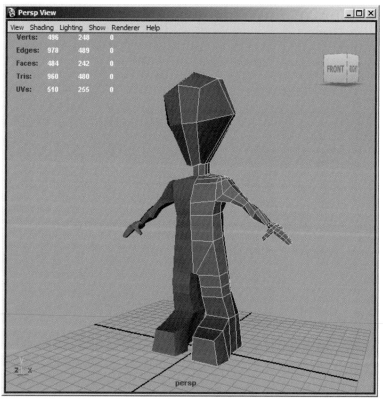

FIG. 10-115 Final blocking of character.

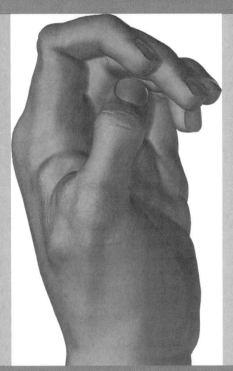

CHAPTER 11

Introduction to ZBrush Modeling

So what exactly is ZBrush? ZBrush is a 3D modeling and paint package from Pixologic, Inc. (**Figure 11-1**). ZBrush uses brush-based sculpting to allow the artist to add detail quickly to models. Highly detailed models with millions of polygons can quickly be created. ZBrush uses technology known as Pixols. Pixols are pixels that retain their depth and orientation information after they are created. That means you can change the lighting and it will affect the shading of the Pixols.

Many artists coming over from other packages might find the single-camera view a bit hard to get used to. But after spending a bit of time navigating the interface, you'll find that it really lends itself to modeling and texture creation.

Pixologic also has one of the best online communities for artists, called Pixolator (**Figure 11-2**). On this site, artists post work for critique or even a how-to.

Why is ZBrush in a game art modeling book? Simply put, amazingly detailed models can be created so easily in ZBrush that many artists and companies

FIG. 11-1 Pixologic Web site.

have incorporated the program into their modeling pipelines. Companies like Industrial Light & Magic, Luma Pictures, and id Software have all started using ZBrush for movie and game projects like *Pirates of the Caribbean 2: Dead Man's Chest*, *Underworld: Evolution*, and *Doom 3*.

As an artist, you have a tool at your disposal in ZBrush that allows you to create levels of detail in your models that were virtually unattainable before this program. And because models are created in an intuitive way using brushes, most artists can quickly create incredibly detailed models.

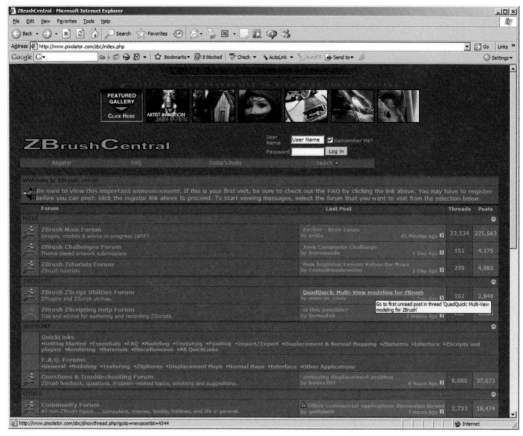

FIG. 11-2 Pixologic's forum site, Pixolator.

The first thing you will notice upon opening ZBrush is that it has a single viewport (**Figure 11-3**). This can take a bit of getting used to if you're coming from a standard 3D package with four views, like Maya.

Just like in Maya, hotkeys will also help speed up your work in ZBrush. The default hotkeys are:

T = Enter/exit edit mode
Q = Draw mode
W = Move
R = Rotate
E = Scale
G = Open the projection master
Ctrl+Z = Undo
Ctrl+Shift+Z = Redo
LMB = Click the left mouse button in a blank area of the viewport and drag to rotate model.

299

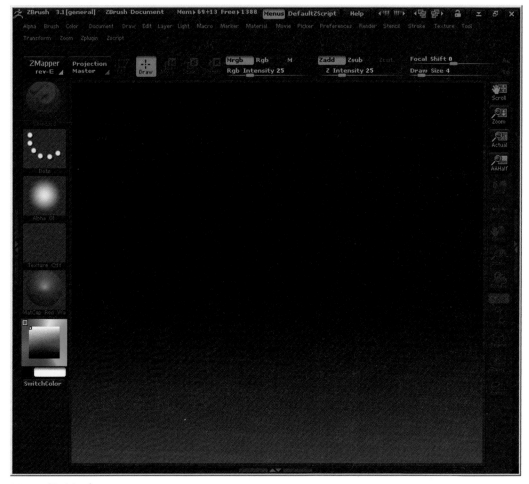

FIG. 11-3   ZBrush interface.

Alt+LMB = Click and drag model in the viewport.

Ctrl+LMB = Click in the viewport and drag onto a mesh to marquee select a mask on the object. Click and draw directly on the mesh to paint a custom mask. Clicking on a blank section of the viewport will inverse the masks. Dragging on a blank section of the viewport will clear the masks.

Alt+LMB = Inverse-paints the transform settings of the current tool. For instance, if you are currently inflating your model, this hotkey combo will instead deflate.

Shift+LMB = Switches the transform settings of the current tool to smooth.

Ctrl+Shift+ LMB= Drag marquee on mesh to hide polygons outside of the selection. Drag on a blank section of the viewport to invert the polygons that are hidden. Press the hotkey and click (no dragging) in a blank section of the canvas to unhide everything.

Along the top, you'll see the memory usage for your current scene (**Figure 11-4**). Keep close tabs on this as you work. If you begin dividing your model too much, the memory usage can become too high for your computer.

FIG. 11-4 Memory usage.

Below the memory usage are the menus. This is where you create new scenes, change the lighting, adjust tool settings, and so on (**Figure 11-5**). I'll go into more detail on the different menus that you will commonly use for modeling a bit later in this chapter after covering the main interface.

FIG. 11-5 Menus.

Below the menus are the tool options (**Figure 11-6**). Here, you can enter the Projection Master to add fine detail to your model. You can also enter Edit mode for your models and change your brush preferences as you work.

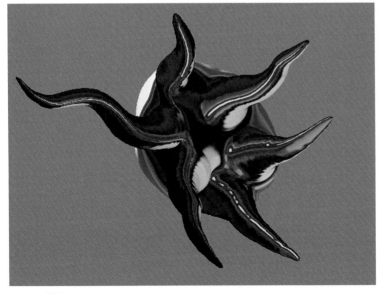

FIG. 11-6 Tool options.

Below the tool options is the viewport or work window (**Figure 11-7**). All of your painting and modeling takes place in this window. One of the things to keep

FIG. 11-7 Work window.

FIG. 11-9 Brush tools.

FIG. 11-8 The toolbox.

FIG. 11-10 Viewport control options.

in mind is that in the current version of ZBrush, you can't actually move the camera. You can spin and scale the mesh and zoom in on the canvas, but the camera does not actually rotate. This can take a bit of getting used to.

To the left of the viewport is the toolbox that allows you to change your brushes, alphas, stroke settings, materials, textures, and colors (**Figure 11-8 and Figure 11-9**). Clicking on one of the icons will bring up the different settings available to choose from.

To the right of the viewport are the options to adjust the viewport. Zoom, scale, pan, and so on are all found here (**Figure 11-10**).

Now let's go into some of the more commonly used menus. The Alpha menu is where you change your brush profile (**Figure 11-11**). By changing the brush alpha to a shape that you've created, you can paint detail in any way needed. Skin pores, wrinkles, and scales are types of things that can be created with different types of alphas.

The Color menu allows you to change the color of the current paint brush. This uses a color picker similar to what you'd find in most other paint programs. Click a color on the picker box and begin drawing.

The Document menu is for creating new scenes and changing the resolution. Note that import from the Document menu is for loading background images. Importing 3D objects is done from the Import menu in Tool.

Saving Custom Materials

Loading materials is very different with ZBrush than it is within Maya. There is, however, an easy way to reapply your textures and materials. Normally you work with 3D tools. After you spend time creating a custom material, save the document. This will store all of the material information. When you restart ZBrush, simply load the document before the ZTool and your custom materials will load as well.

The Draw menu is used to change the paint brush options. These options can also be changed using the tool options lines.

The Edit menu is for undo and redo. Each work area uses a different set of undos. For example, the work you do in Edit mode has a different undo buffer than the work you do in the Projection Master.

The Layer menu allows you to work in layers similar to those with Adobe Photoshop. Because ZBrush stores Pixol information, different objects behave differently when using layers. 3D objects interact with all layers, while brush strokes affect only the current layer.

With the Light menu, you can change the direction of the lights or even add more lights to the scene (**Figure 11-12**). By default, there are two lights active (designated by the orange boxes). To add more lights, click on a lightbulb to activate, then drag the orange box on the sphere to change the position of the light.

The Material menu is for creating new materials and editing existing ones (**Figure 11-13**).

FIG. 11-11 Alpha menu.

FIG. 11-12 Light menu.

FIG. 11-13 Material menu.

Using ZSpheres

ZSpheres can be thought of as a preview tool (**Figure 11-14**). Using ZSpheres you can quickly pose a model then apply the mesh on top.

To use ZSpheres, switch to the ZSphere brush and place one in the canvas window.

Press T to make it active.

Click and drag on the existing ZSphere in the spot where you need to place the next one (**Figure 11-15**). The size of the new ZSphere is defined by how long you click and drag. If needed, you can turn on the symmetry in the Transform palette to create mirrored ZSpheres.

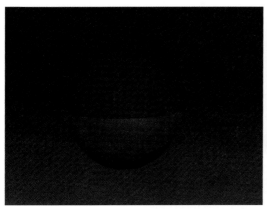

FIG. 11-14 ZSpheres.

FIG. 11-15 Placing more ZSpheres.

After you've created the ZSphere framework, you can see what the skinned version will look like by clicking Transform > Adaptive Skin > Preview. The higher the density slider, the more polygons will be included in the model.

If the adaptive skin is on, select Preview again to go back to ZSphere mode.

Rotate, move, and scale the ZSpheres to finish shaping the object. Periodically, you should switch to adaptive mode to see what the ZSpheres will look like skinned (**Figure 11-17**).

Once the ZSPheres are set and you are pleased with the preview, press Tool > Adaptive Skin > Make Adaptive Skin. This will create a new Z Tool called Skin_ZSphere#.

Click on the new Z Tool to switch over. You can now divide the mesh as needed and begin adding details.

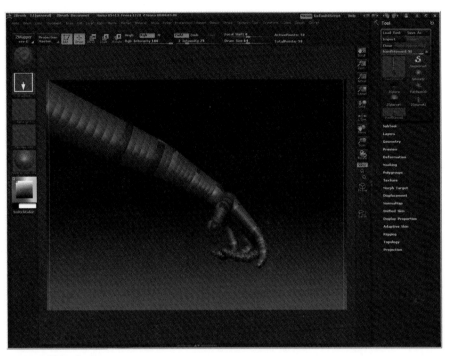

FIG. 11-16 ZSphere hand.

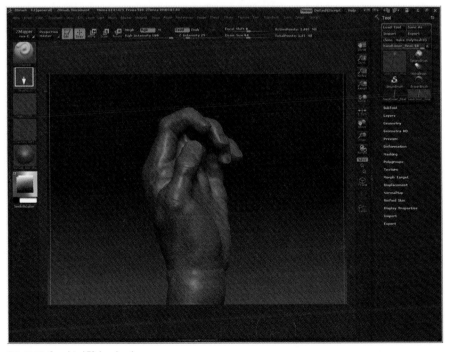

FIG. 11-17 Completed ZSphere hand.

Exporting a Model from Maya

Exporting from Maya to ZBrush is a fairly simple matter. Any model created in Maya for use in ZBrush needs to be exported as an OBJ file. The OBJ file format is a model format that is actually used by every 3D program.

Open your model in Maya. Select the mesh and click File > Export Selection. Don't forget that ZBrush's automatic UV creation method doesn't work very well with Maya. That being said, you should create your UVs in Maya before exporting. Also extra care should be given so that the UVs do not overlap.

Open ZBrush, click Tool > Import and navigate to the OBJ model. This will import the file as the current tool.

Click drag in the work area to place the model in the scene.

Immediately press the T shortcut key to enter edit mode. This is important. If you try to do anything else, the model will be dropped to the canvas and will no longer be a 3D object.

Exporting a Model from ZBrush to Maya

If you need to bring a model from ZBrush back into Maya for further editing or rendering, it is done as an OBJ.

In ZBrush select Tool > Export. Open Maya and select File > Import □. Set Create Multiple objects to False. This is very important. If the vertex order of the object changes in any way, the models will not work correctly when moving between the two programs.

Rebuilding Bad Topology

ZBrush has some great retopology tools. If you are working with a mesh that doesn't have well-laid-out edge loops, you can use the retopology tools in ZBrush to rebuild the mesh quickly (**Figure 11-18**).

Import your mesh and place it on the canvas. Remember to enter Edit mode.

Click Tools > Clone to make a copy of your mesh (**Figure 11-19**). I find that having this extra copy makes working with topology a bit easier.

Click on the ZSphere button in the Tools menu. The mesh will switch to a ZSphere. Don't worry—your mesh is still there, and you just need to switch over to a ZSphere in order to work with the retopology tools.

Click Tools > Rigging > Select Mesh. Select your original mesh in the pop-up. The ZSphere will now be drawn on top of your mesh.

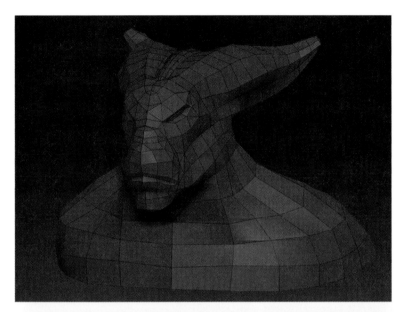

FIG. 11-18 Model with bad topology.

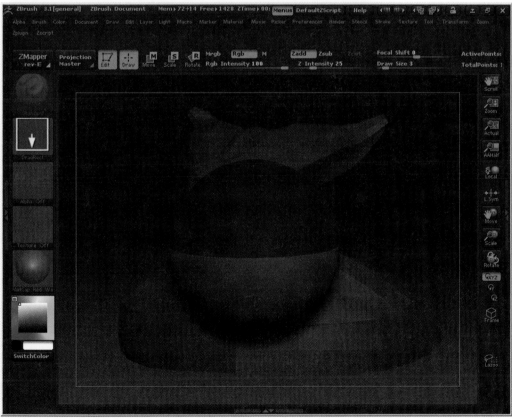

FIG. 11-19 Preparing for retopology.

Next click on Tools > Topology > Select Topo and pick the cloned mesh in the pop-up.

Click on Tools > Topology > Edit Topology to switch into Edit mode (**Figure 11-20**). A wireframe of your topology will wrap around the mesh. By erasing and recreating these lines, you can rebuild the entire topology of your character (**Figure 11-21**).

Press Transform > Activate Symmetry and turn on the X symmetry.

Shift-click while dragging across the faulty sections of the mesh to erase the current topology.

Shift-click and release on the mesh to designate where you want to begin creating the new topology. It can take a bit of practice to get the hang of this trick. Try not to drag when designating new build positions, as this will erase the topology.

Continue using the Shift-click technique to rebuild the character with proper edge loop topology (**Figure 11-22 and Figure 11-23**).

Press A to preview the new mesh (**Figure 11-24**).

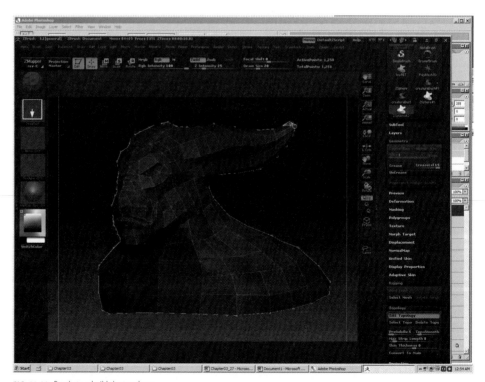

FIG. 11-20 Ready to rebuild the topology.

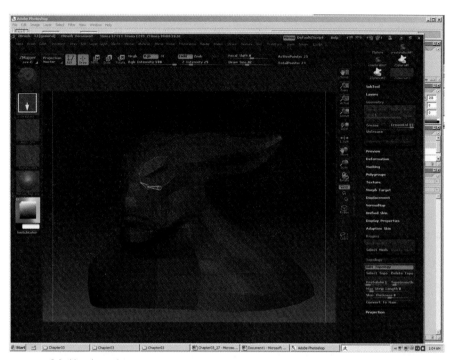

FIG. 11-21 Rebuilding the topology.

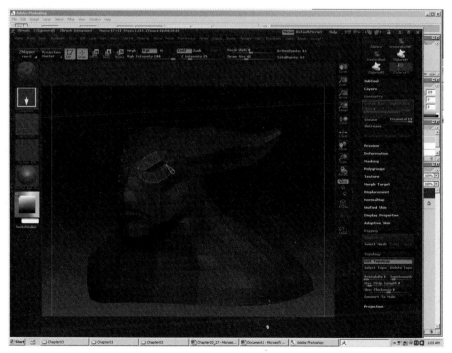

FIG. 11-22 Mesh in progress.

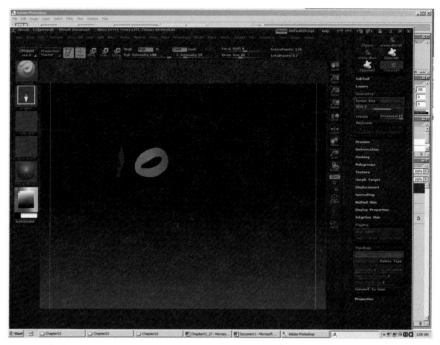

FIG. 11-23   Mesh in progress.

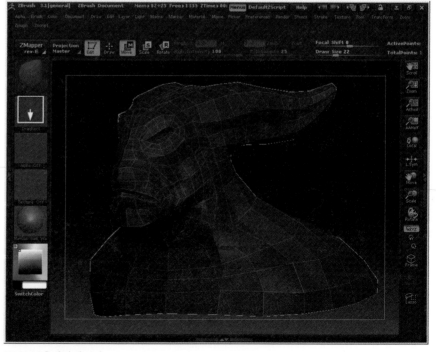

FIG. 11-24   Final rebuilt mesh.

Using HD Geometry

HD geometry allows you to work on models with higher polygon counts than your computer can normally handle.

Load your model into ZBrush (**Figure 11-25**). Divide the mesh as many times as your computer can work with. Click Tool > Geometry HD > DivideHD. Divide a few times to begin subdivide into HD geometry (**Figure 11-26**).

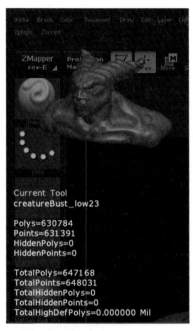

FIG. 11-25 Original mesh.

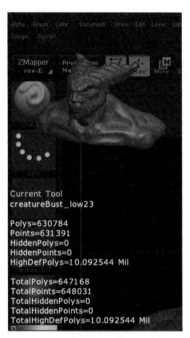

FIG. 11-26 Dividing the mesh into HD geometry.

Make sure that Click Tool > Geometry HD > RadialRGN is checked. Setting this option displays the safe radial region that you can work within.

Click Tool > Geometry > SculptHD. Hover the mouse cursor over a section of the model and press A to enable the radial region that you can sculpt in HD (**Figure 11-27**).

Sculpt the model using all of the normal tools.

When you need to work on a different section, press A to exit HD, hover the mouse of the new section, and press A again.

When rendering HD geometry, press the A hotkey when the mouse is not hovering over the model (**Figure 11-28**).

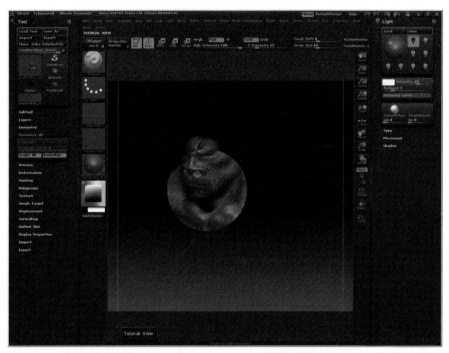

FIG. 11-27 HD radial sculpting region.

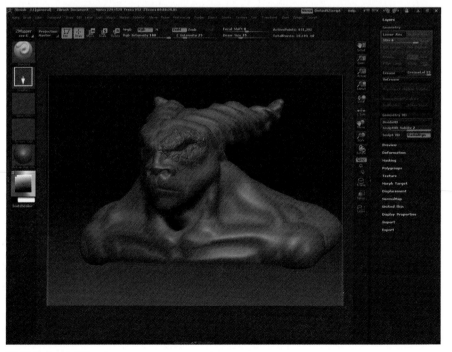

FIG. 11-28 Rendered HD mesh.

Using Smart Resym

If you lose symmetry on your model, you can use Smart Resym to regain it automatically. In the HD example, when modeling around one eye, the other half was hidden from view and thus did not get changed.

Ctrl+drag around the updated half of the model (**Figure 11-29**).

Click Tool > Deformation > Smart ReSym. Make sure it is set to resym across the x-axis. Smart ReSym can take a while, depending on the complexity of the mesh (**Figure 11-30**).

As you can see, ZBrush is an incredibly deep program. I recommend that as you are working with it, you always check out the great forum site http://www.pixolator.com. Here you can find tons of tutorials and critiques.

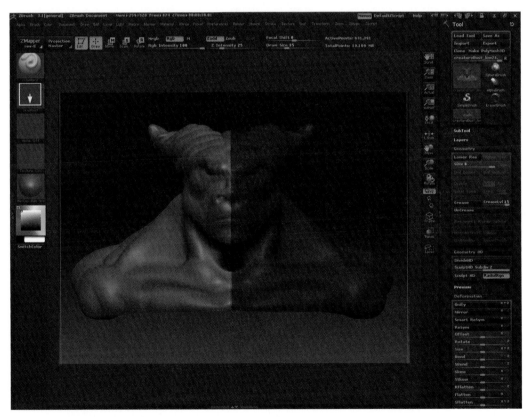

FIG. 11-29 Masking part of the mesh for Smart ReSym.

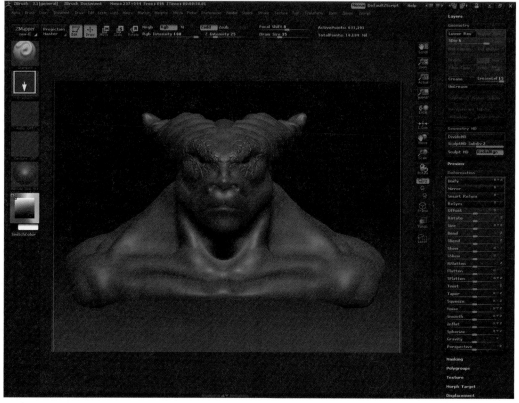

FIG. 11-30 The updated symmetrical model.

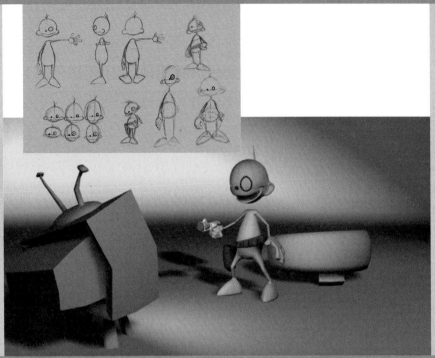

CHAPTER 12

Designing Your First Biped Character Using Photoshop and Maya

Former Student Spotlight: Zach Parrish

Rigging is the big step in creating a short film that most beginners completely underestimate. Many blossoming students or beginners are anxious to start making things move and do not give as much thought and foresight to the end result. The final outcome really begins the first time the character is sketched out. The concept for a character dictates its personality, which dictates how it moves, which dictates how it can be modeled and rigged. Give some thought to the whole picture as you work through your film and the result will be enhanced that much more.

The few problems I had on my short film were a direct result of not thinking ahead. I was too anxious to make things move and thus I didn't fully plan each step. My model's feet were big—almost as long as his leg. Consequently, I had to sort of swing his feet out to the side to make him walk semi-naturally. The problem was that I didn't think about this when I was modeling or rigging. So the rig was not as flexible as it could have been, which slowed and limited the animation process. The creation of that short film taught me more than I had anticipated. I think it's a big stepping stone in the maturation of a student film maker to do the whole process, even if it isn't for a whole film. It can be used to do a basic animation exercise. That way, you learn the pitfalls, the easier areas, and also the areas that you prefer to focus on. And finding your area of interest is the most important part.

Zach graduated with his Bachelor of Fine Arts degree in 3D animation from the Savannah College of Art and Design (SCAD). During his final quarter at SCAD, he began online courses through Animation Mentor. He was hired directly out of SCAD by Rhythm & Hues Studios in Marina Del Rey, CA. He is currently working at Rhythm & Hues, continuing his education with Animation Mentor and looking forward to his future endeavors in the world of Character Animation. You can see more of his work and what he is up to at his Web site: http://www.zapmyshorts.com.

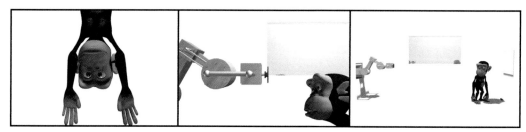

FIG. 12-1 "Bananas" by Zach Parrish (2006).

Workflow

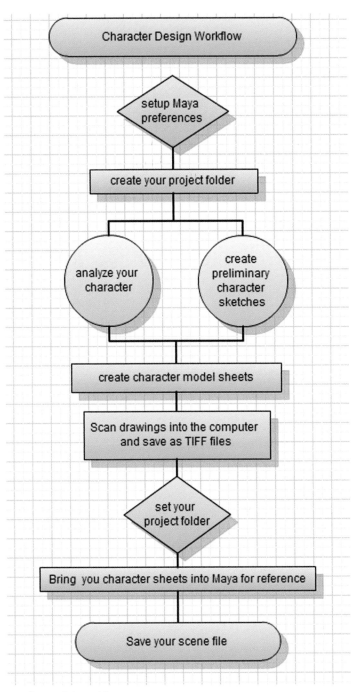

FIG. 12-2 Character design workflow.

Introduction

FIG. 12-3 "Bananas" by Zach Parrish (2006).

Creating a character can be an enormous task. Production studios invest months (and sometimes even years) simply to get the design of a character just right. Sometimes there is an entire team of artists with varied backgrounds (such as painters, sculptors, and concept artists) who work together to develop a single character.

When designing your first character to model, rig, and animate, it is important to remember the most important rule of all: *keep it simple*. Complexity will come later. A biped is a great character for beginners to start with, because of the varied problems that will be addressed during the process. It is also one of the easiest on which to gather research, as you are in fact bipedal. When you have a question about how something moves, you simply have to study your own mechanics. Many of the rigging solutions that are used for a biped can be reused with other types of creatures and props. However, it is important to stick to simple and stylized design ideas. The more realistic and detailed the character becomes, the more difficult it is to set up for animation.

Character Design

Analyzing Your Character

The first character that you design should be simple. Remember this general rule: the easier and the simpler you make the design, the easier and the simpler the entire process will be. This rule really applies to anything in life. You will encounter obstacles, so why complicate the situation—unless, of course, you thrive on challenges and have no problem tackling these obstacles on your own.

In addition to thinking about what your character looks like, you should consider other aspects that will help define their design. For a well-rounded character, you should base your design on a realistic character or story. Even though you may not be pursuing an animated story with the character for your first animation, in order to get a plausible character, there needs to be some type of background developed for personality, motivation, and purpose. If you do not have a concrete story idea, you can still answer questions that help create this background. This process is called "character analysis" and has been used by writers and actors for many years.

You should ask not only questions like color, gender, and height, but also questions that answer background information, such as whether the character has brothers, sisters, or is an only child. How old is the character? Is he a child? Is she a teenager? Is he a parent? Are they androgynous? Schizophrenic? All of these answers have a huge impact on how the character behaves and will actually help you come up with ideas for how they look. It is really not important that your audience knows the answer to these questions. As an animator, however, the more you understand your character, the more believable your character will become. As you answer these questions, try to visualize your character. Keep a sketchbook handy and begin preliminary sketches. As you sketch, think about the design considerations discussed in this chapter.

Design Considerations

For your first character design, there should be requirements as well as limitations. The first requirement is that your character is bipedal. You can design animal characters, as long as they move like a human. You can design tails, large ears, or antennae for added character. Stay away from birds, unless their wings will function like human arms, but realize that bird legs operate more like human arms than legs. Characters who use their arms to walk, such as monkeys, can be completed with this process, but I highly recommend that you feel comfortable with creating and animating bipedal characters before you attempt a character that walks on all fours. The reason for this is because it takes more time for research and development of creatures to which you do not have instant access. With a humanistic biped, you can refer to your own skeleton, muscle structure, and motion.

Others may tell you that designing and modeling your characters in a relaxed pose will bring you better deformations, especially in the shoulders, elbows, and knees. Although this may be true, this type of pose is definitely more difficult to rig for the first time. Your character should be designed, modeled, and rigged in the T-pose (arms parallel to the ground with the palms facing down (not forward) with fingers open) for a predictable and reliable process.

FIG. 12-4 Preliminary sketches in sketchbook.

FIG. 12-5 Character from "Trigger" by Ryan Yokley (2002). Adding big teeth, a tail, and antennae are great ways to give your character extra personality! This character's legs are drawn too close together. Make sure to leave some space between them.

FIG. 12-6 Character from "Sniff" by Dan Nichols (2004). This character's arms are not drawn parallel to the ground, and feet are too close together. This position can be more difficult to rig for the first time. Make sure that your arms are straight, not sloped.

Quite frankly, robots and aliens are overdone. In order for your design to stand out among the others, your design must be different. If you insist on designing a robot, make sure that all bendable areas (knees, ankles, toes, shoulders, elbows, wrists, fingers, neck, hips, and the torso) are designed for flexibility, like rubber hoses.

FIG. 12-7 Characters from "Botones" by Arturo deLaGuardia (2002). Robots and aliens can make great characters if your story and design are unique!

FIG. 12-8 Character by Neil Helm (2006). The man of many eyes!

Characters can also be made of primitive objects. Cylinders can be used for the limbs, a sphere for the head, and so on. The only real concern is to make sure that the objects have enough divisions for deformations later.

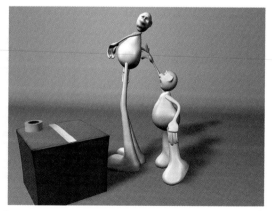

FIG. 12-9 Characters, storyboard, and frame from "Sticky" by Katie Folsom (2004). These characters are made from modified primitive objects. A simplified design can still convey emotion and tell great stories.

Proportions

FIG. 12-10 Character by Eric Urban (2006). Larger, exaggerated head and arms on this character create a focal point and require more work when animating. Extra arms means extra work. Fly wings are great; just stay away from bird wings as a beginner.

When you begin to draw a character design, you must consider proportions. The height proportion of a perfect human body is equal to eight heads high. The arm span from the shoulder to the fingertips is about three and a half heads long, and the opened hand is the same size as the face. However, this is animation: anything goes! We have the freedom to exaggerate anything that will make the character more interesting. For a simple approach and to ensure that your first experience rigging goes smoothly, I highly recommend a slender character with normal proportions, or perhaps one or two things exaggerated, such as longer arms or a larger head.

FIG. 12-11 "Libby" by Fay Helfer (2004). Longer, thinner character designs will ensure that your first experience in 3D character creation goes smoothly.

Anything that is exaggerated, especially larger, draws focus.

It takes greater effort to create plausible animation with an exaggerated body part, because it draws focus and the audience is paying more attention to that area. Larger heads are top-heavy, particularly if the body is smaller in proportions. Attention is brought to the head because of its size, and all movement is heightened. Because the head doesn't deform outside of facial features, it appears to be a floating boulder. Large feet are generally not a problem if the character has long legs. However, if the character has short or fat legs, the ankle movement is limited when flexing and pointing the foot. Large hands can be a huge problem and quickly die if the animator leaves them in a single position for too many frames. Much attention is drawn to the hands, because they serve a needed purpose, and we use them for so much of what we do, including expressing what we say. Therefore, an animator must keep them alive when animating.

Begin by figuring out how many heads high your character will be. The length of the arms, legs, and torso will need to be considered, because different challenges occur with different sizes. Short, fat characters are harder to set up and animate than tall and thin ones. Problems are encountered with shorter characters, because of a limited range of motion caused by their shorter limbs. If the character is overweight, that decreases the range of motion as well. A shorter character will waddle in lieu of walking or striding. For them to walk, they must take shorter, quicker steps. The arms have limited range of motion as well. If the character has to reach the top of his head, he probably won't be able to reach. This could introduce some funny animation. Imagine a character trying to scratch his head with short arms. If he can't reach his head, he might have to rub it on a wall or utilize a prop to satisfy this need. Another solution would be to design longer arms beyond normal proportions, or add some stretching ability in the controls for the arm, so that the character has the ability to extend his reach.

FIG. 12-12 "Bernie" by Fay Helfer (2004). Shorter, fatter character designs are more difficult. Longer arms can help with range of motion, but then become an exaggerated feature.

Clothing Considerations

If you design your character with clothing, make sure to stay away from rigid ornamentation and details in flexible areas of the body—particularly in the torso area. The torso is one of the most flexible areas of your body, so any rigid object will constantly intersect the deforming geometry of the clothing. Examples include buttons, belt buckles, and armor. There are more advanced ways of controlling these items (such as using hair follicles to rivet the button in place), but these techniques are outside the realm of this book. If the geometry of these items is treated as a flexible, rubbery object, be aware that the item will stretch and distort. Design your clothes with the idea that they are made of some kind of stretchable fabric or material, such as knit, Lycra, or rubber. If your detail objects are modeled separately and overlap other geometry, such as a necktie over a shirt, there are interpenetration issues that can be alleviated by setting up a control rig or by adding dynamics.

FIG. 12-13 Character by Nathan Englehardt (2005). Design your character's clothing to be simple and of stretchable fabric. It is fine to alter posture, but be careful not to distort the center of gravity too far.

Rigid objects can be placed in inflexible areas, such as eyeglasses on the face, a helmet on the head, a watch on the forearm, earrings on the ears, or rings on the fingers. Think about where the object will be positioned, and if the area has little or no need for bending, then the object should not cause a problem. Model these objects separately so that if they do become an issue, you can reevaluate their necessity and hide or delete them if necessary.

It is not necessary that your character be modeled as one seamless piece of geometry. Even if the character is designed without clothing, you can strategically place the seams so that they do not become a focal point.

325

FIG. 12-14   3D render and concept drawing for "Bernie" by David Leonard (2006).

FIG. 12-15   Concept drawings for "Eddie" by Adam Levine (2004).

Creating Character Sheets

Begin by creating some rough drawings of your character using lines, spheres, and cylinders. I prefer drawing the side views first, because I can think about the character's posture, draw a line to represent their spine, and then draw spheres or ovals where the shoulders and hips belong. Think about the shape of the head and torso. Some typical shapes include round, oval, pear, apple, and hourglass.

Once you have created preliminary sketches based on your character analysis and design considerations, you are ready to finalize the design into a "character sheet." In 2D animation, character model or turnaround sheets are typically used by the animation staff to ensure artistic consistency by all animators during a production. In 3D animation, these drawings are used as references during the modeling process.

For the most predictable motion achieved during setup later, the character's front pose should be drawn in the T-stance: arms parallel to the ground with the palms facing down (not forward) with fingers open. The thumbs can be in any position. The feet should be facing straight ahead and flat on the ground. The legs can be bent slightly and should be hip-distance apart with some space between them and the feet. Be careful not to make an inverted V shape with the legs. Having the legs spread too far will cause undesirable rotations. The head should also be facing forward. It is not necessary to draw the arms in the side view. You should also draw a top view of the arms with the hands and a separate top view of the feet. Additional drawings of the back and three-quarter views are not absolutely necessary, but can prove useful.

You should begin by drawing either the front or side view first. Once the first drawing is complete, you can draw horizontal guidelines to indicate the positions of the top of the head, the eyes, the chin, the top of the shoulder, the top of the pelvis, the top of the thighs, knees, and the feet to ensure that they line up in the other views.

When the drawings of the front, side, hand, and foot are complete, it is a good idea to photocopy the originals and ink the photocopies to clean up the lines. The inked images will make a cleaner scan than a pencil drawing. Ink your character outlines in black and the horizontal guidelines in blue. Scan the drawings and prepare them for use as a reference in Maya. You will then save these images into the source image folder in your project files, and bring these drawings into a Maya scene file to use as a reference when modeling.

Nick

Five spikes for hair

Right eye smaller left

three fingers

Hands reach mid thigh

one shoe, one sock

Summary

- When creating your character, *keep it simple*.
- The easier and the simpler you make the design, the easier and the simpler the entire process will be.
- The more you understand your character, the more believable your character will become.
- Creating a character analysis will help you achieve greater understanding of your character's background.
- Characteristics that you should include on a bipedal character for optimal learning:
  - Two legs.
  - Two arms.
  - Two hands and two fingers, which include a minimum of a thumb and middle finger or mitt.
- Characteristics that you should include for a more predictable outcome:
  - T-pose.
  - Feet should be planted on the ground, hip-distance apart.
  - Toes should be facing forward.
  - Geometry should be present in the crotch area.
  - Palms should face down.
  - Shoulders should be defined on top; arcs in the armpit.

- Characteristics that you should avoid until you have further experience:
  - Buttons and rigid objects.
  - Wings.
  - Four legs.
  - Poses other than a T-pose.
- Characteristics you can include to add personality:
  - Ears.
  - Tails.
  - Antennae.
  - Teeth.
- Design concerns:
  - Overweight characters decrease a character's range of motion, because geometry will collide, causing interpenetration.
  - Short legs equal a limited range of motion.
  - Large feet are awkward, especially with short legs.
  - Exaggerated proportions create a focal point.
  - Overlapping geometry creates interpenetrations when designing clothing.
- Creating a character sheet finalizes the design and aids in the modeling process.

Assignments: Designing a Character

Analyze Your Character

On a sheet of paper, answer the following questions about your character. Keep your sketchbook handy and draw any ideas that come to mind.

1. Where is your character from? Did your character grow up somewhere else or did he/she always live in the same place? Did he/she grow up in the city or in a log cabin on a mountain? Is he/she from this planet or another? Is he/she from a wealthy family or a poor one? Was he/she educated as a child? Is he/she an only child? Does he/she have siblings?
2. Where does your character live? What country, city, or planet does this character call home? Does he/she live in a city or the country? Alone or with a roommate? Still with his/her parents? Is he/she married? Does he/she have any children?
3. What is your character name and how old is your character? Is he/she a child? A teenager? An adult?
4. What does your character look like? Is the character male or female? What is your character's height? Is he/she small, or tall? Is your character thin or fat? Does he/she have an apple-shaped torso? Is it round? Is it square? What shape is the face? Does he/she have big ears? How about a tail? Does he/she have any physical abnormalities, such as large nose, big feet, and so on?
5. How does your character earn a living? What is his/her trade or career? Is he/she a student? A criminal?

Create Character Model Sheets

Materials Needed:
> pencil
> 8.5" × 11" paper or smaller, but no smaller than 5" × 7"
> black and blue markers or pen and ink
> access to a photocopier
> access to a scanner
> Adobe Photoshop or other image editing software

1. Draw front or side of character.
   a. First, determine proportions. Draw a circle for the size of the head. Then stack five to eight of these circles to establish your character's height. Draw horizontal guidelines across the page at the top and bottom of each sphere. Begin the drawing for your character to the right of this stack of circles. Proceed to *either* b or c.

FIG. 12-17 Proportional circles six heads high with horizontal guidelines.

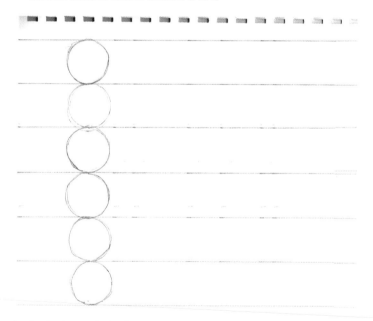

   b. Beginning with the front view: Draw a circle for your head. Don't worry about shape at this point; you can change that later. Think about how long the neck will be and then draw a smaller circle for the shoulder area and one for the hip area. Draw ovals to represent the feet.
   c. Draw lines for the neck, connecting the head to the shoulders. Draw lines for the torso, then lines for the legs. The arms and hands are 3.5 heads long. The hand alone should be three quarters of a head long—about the size of the face. Make sure that the character is drawn in the T-stance: arms parallel to ground, palms facing down, feet facing forward and hip-distance apart, space between legs and feet, head forward. Redefine the shape of the face if necessary.

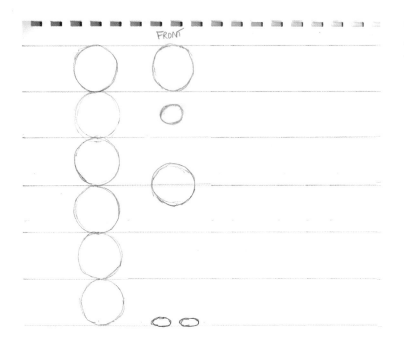

FIG. 12-18 Head, shoulder, torso, and feet roughed in for the front view.

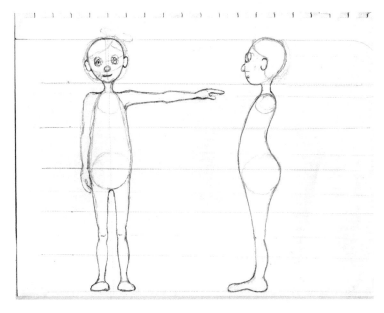

FIG. 12-19 Sketched character front and side drawings.

d. The side view should be drawn so that your character is facing to the left of your computer screen. Again, begin by drawing a circle for your head. Draw a curve that represents the spine and posture of your character. Draw a smaller circle for the shoulder area and one for the hip area. Draw an oval to represent the foot.

FIG. 12-20 Head, shoulder, torso, and feet roughed in for the side view.

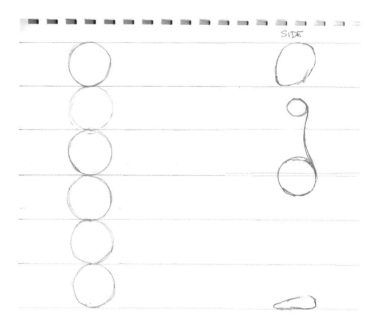

e. Draw lines for the neck, connecting the head to the shoulders. Draw lines for the torso, then lines for the legs; consider whether you want the legs to be bent or straight. Redefine the shape of the face if necessary.

2. Redraw horizontal guidelines. Once the front or side drawing is complete, redefine the horizontal guidelines to indicate the positions of the top of the head, the eyes, the chin, the top of the shoulder, the top of the pelvis, the top of the thighs, knees, and the feet to ensure that they line up in the other views. These lines are helpful to ensure that your proportions are consistent from one view to the next.

3. Draw the additional images, front or side, top of arm and hand, top of foot, and back (optional).

   a. Follow the same guidelines discussed already to complete the side or front drawing.

   b. On a separate sheet of paper, draw the arm and hand from the top view. Do not forget to use your proportion guidelines. The arms and hands are 3.5 heads long. The hand alone should be three-quarters of a head long—about the size of the face.

   c. On a separate sheet of paper, draw the foot from the top view.

FIG. 12-21 Arm and hand drawing, top view.

4. Photocopy the original drawings.
5. Ink the photocopy. Using a black marker or ink, trace the photocopy outline of your character. Using a blue marker or ink, trace the horizontal guidelines in blue.

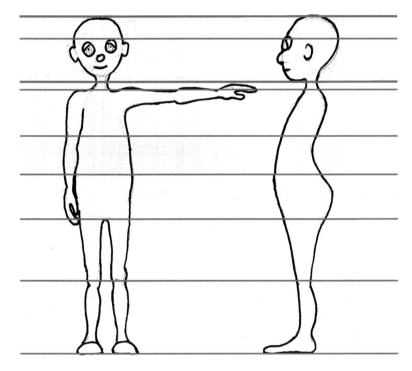

FIG. 12-22 Inked photocopy with blue guidelines.

Scan and Prepare

Materials Needed:
  access to a scanner
  Adobe Photoshop or other image editing software

1. Open Adobe Photoshop or your scanning software.
2. Scan your drawings with a resolution no lower than 200 (dpi, ppi).
   a. In Photoshop, go to File > Import and choose your scanner.
   b. In the scanner settings, choose the appropriate resolution.
3. Once scanned, you will need to clean up your image by doing the following:
   a. In Photoshop, go to Layer > Duplicate Layer … and click OK to create a copy of the background image. This is necessary in order to rotate in the next step.

FIG. 12-23 File > Import.

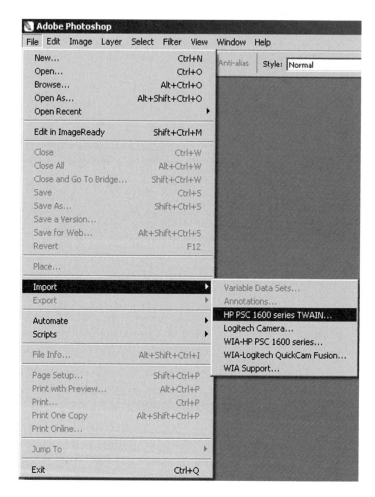

FIG. 12-24 Adjust your scanner
resolution to a minimum of 200 dpi.

b. Go to Edit >Free Transform or press Ctrl+T on the keyboard and rotate
the image so that the guidelines are perfectly horizontal across the
image. If your image was placed straight on the scanner, this will not be
necessary.

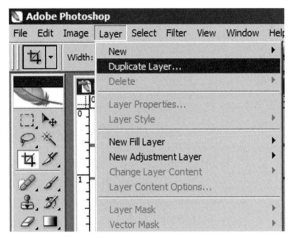

FIG. 12-25 Layer > Duplicate Layer . . .

FIG. 12-26 Edit > Free Transform.

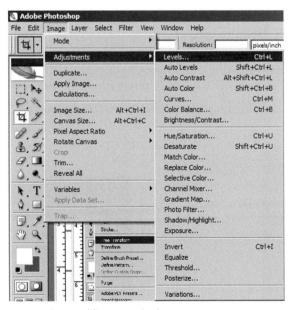

FIG. 12-27 Image > Adjustments > Levels.

c. Go to Image > Adjustments > Levels or press Ctrl+L on the keyboard. Beneath and to the right of the input level curve there is a white triangle, slide this to the left to set the highlights of the image.

d. Choose the paintbrush tool by pressing B on the keyboard. Erase any stray marks if necessary.

e. Choose the crop tool by pressing C on the keyboard. Drag-select around the front and side drawings to remove any unnecessary areas. Hit Enter on your keyboard to execute the crop.

FIG. 12-28 Clean up your image using a white paintbrush.

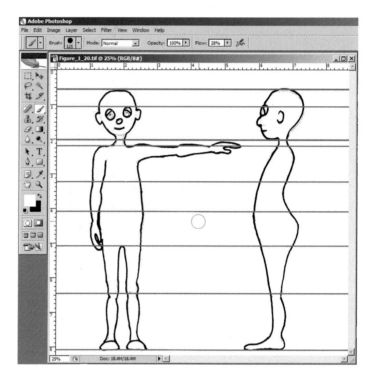

FIG. 12-29 Crop any unwanted area.

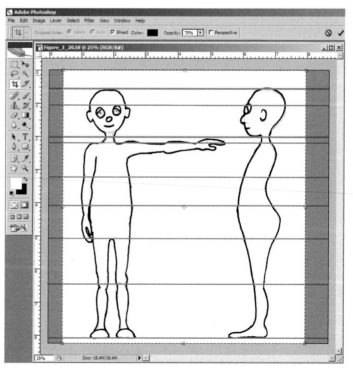

f. Go to Layer > Flatten Image. This step will remove the additional layer and prepare the file for saving.

g. Go to File > Save As and save the file in TIFF format. Type in the name of the file, something like the name of your character: name_characterSheet.tif. Save these files in your sourceimages folder in your Maya project file.

h. Repeat steps a–g for the arm and hand from the top view, the foot from the top view, and any additional drawings you may have.

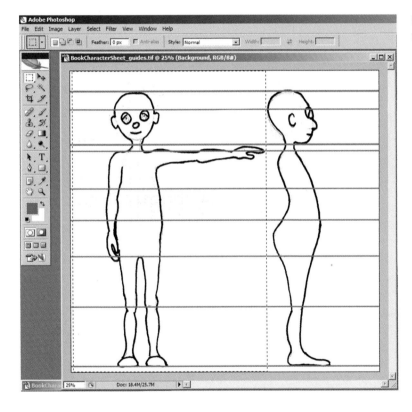

FIG. 12-30 Marquee-select the front view of your character.

4. Divide the front and side images into separate files.

a. In Photoshop, choose the Rectangular Marquee tool by pressing M. Drag around the front view to create a selection.

b. Go to Edit > Copy or press Ctrl+C on the keyboard to make a copy.

c. Go to Edit > New or press Ctrl+N to make a new file. Photoshop automatically creates the new file with image dimensions based on what was copied into the clipboard. Hit Enter.

d. Go to Edit > Paste or press Ctrl+V on the keyboard.

e. Go to Layer > Flatten Image.

f. Before closing the file, make a note of the image dimensions. Go to Image > Image Size …. Under Pixel Dimensions, make a note of the width and height of the image. You can include these numbers in the file name for accessible notation.

g. Go to File > Save As and save the file in TIFF format. Type in the name of the file: name_front_widthXheight.tif. Save these files in your sourceimages folder in your Maya project file.

h. Repeat steps a–g for the side view, naming the saved file name_side_widthXheight.tif.

i. Repeat steps a–g for the arm and hand from the top view, the foot from the top view, and any additional drawings you may have. Because I drew half a T-pose, I created a T-pose in Photoshop by duplicating and flipping the drawing horizontally.

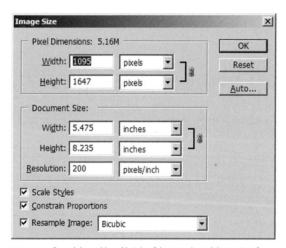

FIG. 12-31 Record the width and height of the image's pixel dimensions for use in Maya.

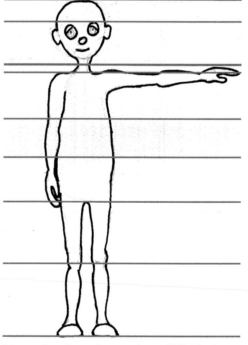

FIG. 12-32 Front view saved as name_front_widthXheight.tif.

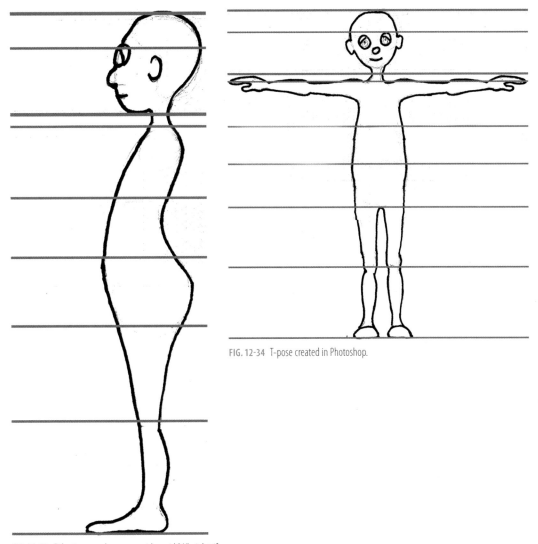

FIG. 12-34 T-pose created in Photoshop.

FIG. 12-33 Side view saved as name_side_widthXheight.tif

Bring Your Drawings into Maya

When bringing an image into Maya, I recommend the use of a NURBS plane and a file texture that is mapped onto that plane. I do not recommend the use of Maya's image plane, which is an option for the camera, because it is difficult to reposition camera image planes, which may be necessary during the modeling process.

1. If you haven't created a project folder already, make sure to do so now:
   a. Launch Maya.
   b. Once Maya is open, go to File > Project > New ... the New Project window will open.
   c. Enter the name of the new project in the Name text box a. For example, MayaCharacterRigging.
   d. In the Location text box, enter or browse to the directory that will contain the new project b (e.g., G:\ ).
   e. Click Use Defaults to let Maya assign the default folder names for your project.
   f. Click Accept.

2. Set your project.
   a. Go to File > Project > Set ..., browse to your project folder, and click OK.

FIG. 12-35 File > Project > Set . . .

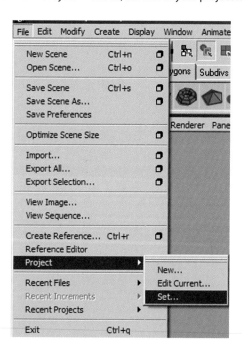

The proper way to start Maya is to set your project before you begin working for the day. You should never double-click directly on a scene file in order to open Maya, as this will change the relative paths to absolute paths when saving your files, which will cause problems, especially with larger scene files and in larger productions.

3. Create a plane for the front view and assign a shader to it. Go to Create > NURBS Primitives > and uncheck Interactive Creation.
   a. In the perspective window, go to Create > NURBS Primitives > Plane option box. Name the plane front_reference_plane.

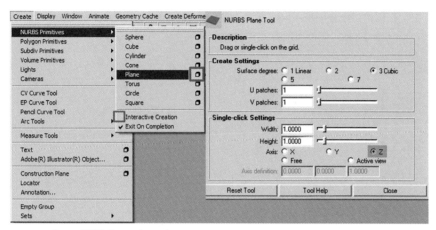

FIG. 12-36 Create a NURBS plane on the z-axis.

The Maya scene uses centimeters as the default proportions. You can change this option in the preferences.

   b. In the Channels box, rescale the plane according to your image dimensions from Photoshop, but at 1/100 of its original value. For example, my image is 1095 pixels × 1647 pixels. My width would be 10.95, the ScaleX value. The height would be 16.47, the ScaleY value. Otherwise, your image will be incredibly large for your scene.

   c. Go to Window > Rendering Editors > Hypershade.

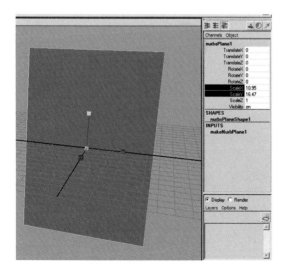

FIG. 12-37 Change the scale of the plane to match 1/100th of the pixel dimensions of the file.

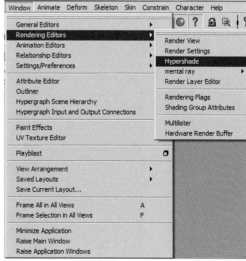

FIG. 12-38 Window > Rendering Editors > Hypershade.

d. In the hypershade, go to Create > Materials > Lambert (or click on the Lambert material on the left-hand side of the Hypershade window).

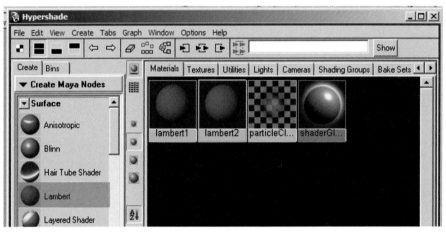

FIG. 12-39 Click on the Lambert material on the left in the Hypershade window.

Lambert material isn't shiny, so it's easy to see while you are working. You don't want to use the default Lambert1 material, because everything created in Maya has the Lambert1 material as a default. If you change that material, everything you create in Maya will have the changes as well.

e. MMB (middle mouse button)-click-drag the newly created Lambert material onto your NURBS plane, front_reference_plane.

f. Double-click on the newly created Lambert material to open the attribute editor. Rename the material front_reference_lambert. It is important to take the time to label everything in Maya to keep an organized scene file.

g. Click on the checkered box to the right of Color to open the Create Render Node window.

FIG. 12-40 Click on the checkered box to the right of the Color attribute in the Attribute Editor.

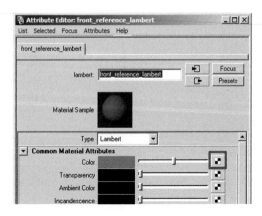

h. Under the 2D Textures section, make sure that Normal is selected. Then click on File to connect a File node to the color inputs of the shader.

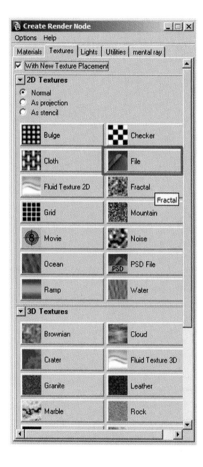

i. Click on the Folder icon to the right of "Image Name." This should open the sourceimages folder (assuming you set the project as this in step 1). Choose name_front_widthXheight.tif, which tells Maya where to find the file that you would like to display on your plane, then click Open. This file does *not* exist inside the Maya scene file. We have simply created a path to the file.
j. You should now see the image appear in your Maya view panel if you move your cursor over a view panel and press 6 on your keyboard, which turns on Hardware Texturing.

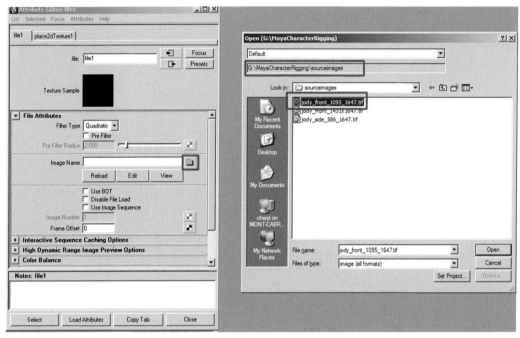

FIG. 12-42 Click on the folder icon in the Attribute Editor for file1.

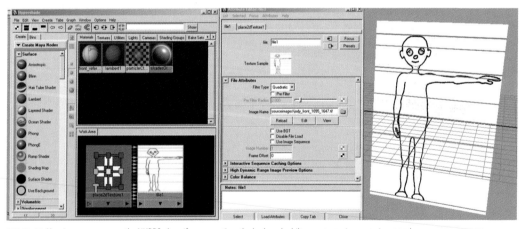

FIG. 12-43 Your image appears on the NURBS plane if you press 6 on the keyboard while your cursor is over a view panel.

4. Create a plane for the side view and assign a shader to it. These steps are similar to those for the front view, but changes have been made to the plane axis and the scale axis.

a. In the perspective window, go to Create > NURBS Primitives > Plane option box. Change the axis to the x-axis, then hold down the X key on the keyboard and click on the center of the grid. Name the plane side_reference_plane.

b. In the Channels box, rescale the plane according to your image dimensions from Photoshop. My image is 586 pixels × 1647 pixels. My width would be 5.86, the ScaleZ value. The height would be 16.47, the ScaleY value.

c. Go to Window > Rendering Editors > Hypershade. In the Hypershade, go to Create > Materials > Lambert. MMB-click-drag the newly created Lambert material onto your NURBS plane, front_reference_plane.

d. Double-click on the newly created Lambert material. Rename the material side_reference_lambert.

e. Click on the checkered box to the right of Color, and then click on File, listed under 2D Textures.

f. Click on the Folder icon to the right of Image Name.

g. Choose name_side_widthXheight.tif.

5. Repeat steps a–i for your top arm and hand view, top foot view, and any other views that you may have. Remember that you will have to change the axis that the plane is created on and that the scaling axis will be different for each view. Experiment to see which one will work.

6. Reposition the images and make them unselectable.

a. Your side image should be facing toward the left of your screen. If not, you can rotate it simply by clicking on the side_reference_ plane and in the channel box type 180 for rotateY.

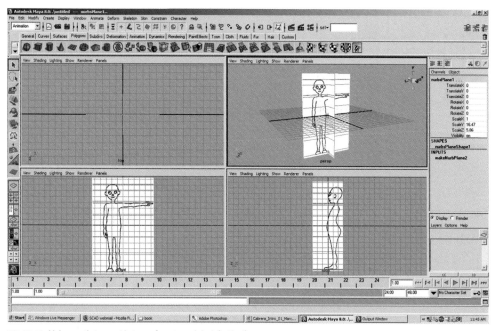

FIG. 12-44 Make sure that your side image faces toward the left side of your screen.

b. Click on your side image and using the Move tool. Press W click only on X (red arrow) and Z (blue arrow) to align the side_reference_ plane with the left edge of the front_reference_ plane.

345

FIG. 12-45 Reposition the side plane to line up with the left edge of your front plane.

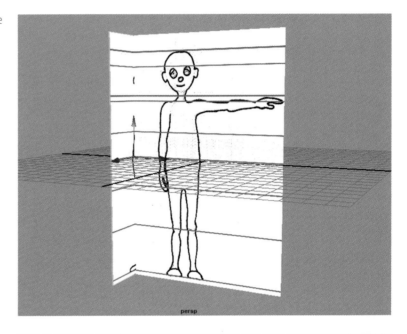

FIG. 12-46 Reposition your front and side planes to be centered on the grid.

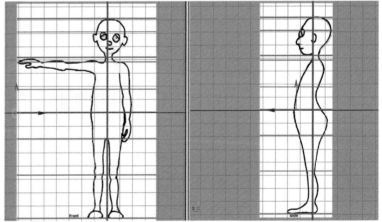

Shift-select both planes and then, using the grid as a guide and your move tool, make sure that the front_reference_plane is centered in the front view and the side_reference_ plane is centered in the side view.

c. The height of the planes should automatically line up. If not, use the move tool or press W and click only on the Y (green arrow) to adjust their positions. It is okay if your drawings do not line up exactly. These images are going to be used as a starting point when modeling, not the "be all and end all" of your design.

d. Reposition any other images as necessary.

e. In the Layer Editor of the Channel box, click the "Create a new layer" box. Double-click on the new layer (layer1) and rename this layer

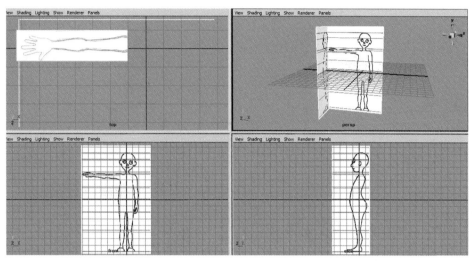

FIG. 12-47 Reposition other planes, such as the top arm view.

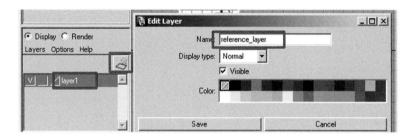

FIG. 12-48 Click on the "Create a new layer" button in the Layer Editor and rename it reference_layer.

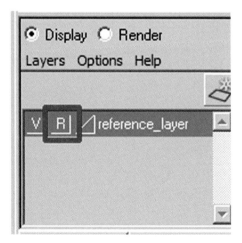

FIG. 12-49 Assign all of your planes to the layer and make it a referenced layer R.

reference_layer, then click Save. Shift-select all of the planes you have made, right-click and hold on top of the reference_layer, and choose Add Selected Objects. To make the objects unselectable, click two times in the empty box between the V (visibility) and the layer name.

An R (reference) should appear. This keeps any objects assigned to a layer visible but not selectable.

7. Save your scene file.
   a. Go to File > Save As, which should open the scenes folder of your project (assuming you set up the project as in step 1).
   b. Name your scene 01_referenceImages.ma.

FIG. 12-50 Name your scene 01_referenceImages.ma.

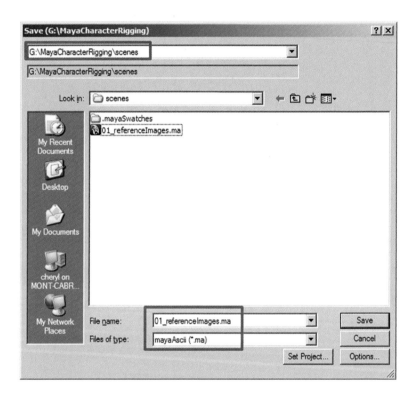

.mb or .ma?

Maya binary files (MB) are stored using binary code and are smaller in file size. Maya ASCII files (MA) are stored using text and can be opened for editing. It really does not matter which type you use; however, if you need to open a newer file in an older version of Maya, you can edit the ASCII file in WordPad, or another text editing program, to state the earlier version.

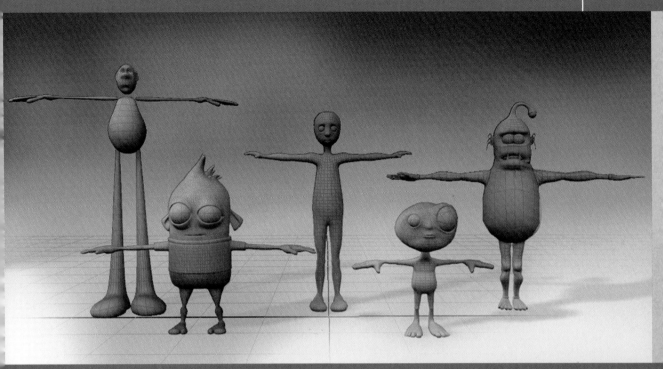

CHAPTER 13

Creating Your First Biped Character: Modeling Basics Using Maya

Former Student Spotlight: Jeff Gill

Once upon a time, I submitted a demo reel to a respectable animation studio, and was lucky enough to sit with them as they critiqued my work face to face. In one segment, I had animated a free rig from the Internet of a guy walking into a movie theater, eating popcorn, and reacting to what he saw on the screen. But rather than point out the flaws in my character's animation, the two recruiters focused purely on the character's design and the confusion it spawned over why anyone would enter a movie theater wearing nothing but a pair of underwear and some goggles. At the time, I had thought no one would look that deeply into the matter—after all, animations live in a world where anvils can fall from the sky without the slightest hint of reason.

However, when designing characters for animation, I've learned that it's truly important to consider your audience. The more simply you design your characters, the less your audience will be distracted from the storytelling of your animation, which will then result in a greater finished product. Simpler designs are not only easier to rig/animate/model/you-name-it, but actually help to show line of action, which is key to any successful character-driven piece.

So if it seems like a fun idea to model someone with an arrow jutting out the side of their head just because it looks cool, then go for it. But try to keep in mind how your characters will be animated and in what context they'll be shown. After all, the last thing you'd want to do is spend several weeks of your life toiling over a beautiful animation, only to leave your audience wondering "how on earth would that guy put on a shirt without stretching out the neck hole?"

Jeff Gill is a graduate from the Savannah College of Art and Design with a BFA in Animation. His work has been screened throughout the world, including the Black Mariah Film Festival as well as the San Francisco International Film Festival, and has received numerous awards for online competitions, such as mtvU's Best Animation on Campus and Firefox Flicks. For more information on Jeff or his work, visit http://www.jeffgill.net.

FIG. 13-1 "Snack attack" by Jeff Gill (2006).

Workflow

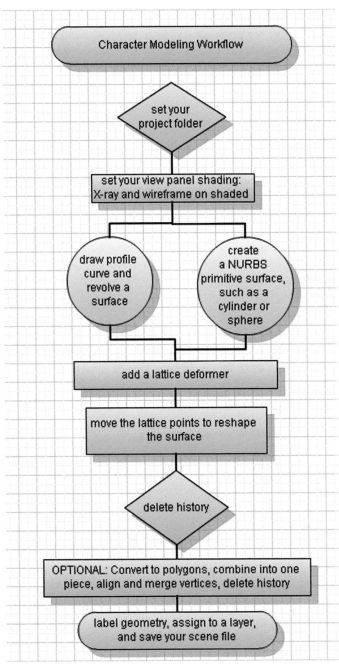

FIG. 13-2 Character modeling workflow.

Introduction

Modeling a character is an extensive process that can take many hours to complete. The modeling process will be easier and quicker to complete if you begin with a simple character design. When the design is more complicated, it will take longer to add the details. As with anything, the more you do something, the easier it becomes and the better you get at it. Practice makes perfect, right? So, don't expect your first character model to become the one you animate. Take this time to explore the tools and begin learning how to troubleshoot your approach and solve any problems in order to achieve the desired shapes. Problem solving, after all, is the true heart of working successfully in 3D. Understand that your first try at modeling a character should be for practice and that you shouldn't be afraid to scrap your experimentation and start again. You may discover that a second attempt leads to a more satisfying result.

Be aware that the method of modeling a character that is explained in this chapter is only one approach, and that as a student, you should be exploring and figuring out what works best for you. There is never "the best way" or "the only way" but rather techniques. Just as a fine artist develops his own style, you will find your own method. This approach analyzes the character's body and breaks it down into simpler shapes that make up the whole. Just as a stone or wood sculptor roughs out their proportions first and refines the details later, we will begin with basic shapes before we add the details.

Work in X-Ray Mode with Wireframe on Shaded

Because we are using NURBS planes to display our reference drawings, changing your display to wireframe mode by pressing 4 on the keyboard would cause the drawing to disappear. So, to resolve this, you can change your shaded mode by pressing 5 on the keyboard in your view panel under the Shading menu and set the display to X-ray (which allows you to see through your model) with wireframe on shaded (which allows you to see the lines on the geometry). This is important so that you can see what you are doing when modeling and still see your reference drawings.

Object Mode and Component Mode

All geometry in Maya can be manipulated on several levels. In Object mode, you can select the entire piece of geometry and translate (move), rotate, and scale the whole thing. If you right-click on top of the geometry, you will reveal a marking menu of component levels, which allows you to manipulate finer details, much like a sculptor would manipulate clay. You can also turn on the component level in the status line or by pressing F8.

NURBS, Polygons, or Subdivision Surfaces?

Which type of geometry should I use for my character? Many students ask me this question, and my advice is to work in either NURBS or Polygons or

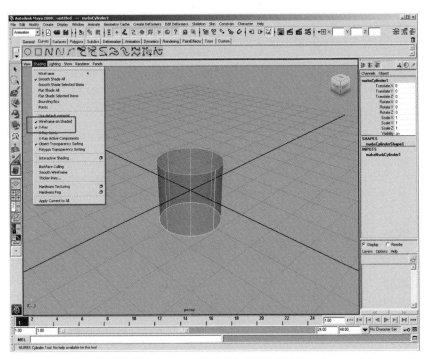

FIG. 13-3 Turning X-ray mode on with wireframe on shaded in each view panel makes it easier to see what you are doing when you are modeling in Maya.

object mode — ┌── component mode

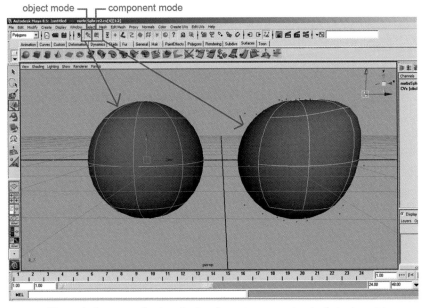

FIG. 13-4 Object mode allows you to affect the entire piece of geometry; component mode affects only a certain area.

FIG. 13-5 The status line mode options.

a combination of both, because subdivision surfaces can introduce other problems that lead to unpredictable results when bending and flexing during animation.

In the approach that I am going to show you, the character will be modeled first using NURBS. The geometry can remain as NURBS. I have also included optional assignments to show you how to convert the NURBS surfaces to Polygons if you want to create a single seamless piece of geometry. It is important to note that your geometry does not need to be a single piece. It is perfectly fine to have separate pieces of geometry for each part of the body. It is also perfectly fine to have some pieces as polygons and others as NURBS surfaces. Once the skeleton and rig is complete, they will move together in unison when you are animating them.

Modeling Tools in Maya

There are endless ways to approach modeling, and Maya has many tools that can be used during this process. This chapter covers only the tools that I feel give you the easiest finished product; these will be covered in the order that we will be using them. It is a good idea to read through this section first, then refer to the tool descriptions as you are working through the assignments.

Tools can be found in menu sets and shelves and will be indicated when each tool is discussed. Remember that the hotbox is a quick way of accessing your menu sets. To display the hotbox, place your cursor anywhere in Maya and hold down the spacebar. Be sure to select Hotbox Controls > Show All to display all of the menu sets at once.

Each tool usually has several optional settings. In order to prevent confusion and keep things simple, this chapter will explain only the options that will be used in the assignments. However, it is always a great idea to open the option boxes on all of these tools and explore the optional settings to see what they do.

Always work at the origin when modeling. The people who designed these tools assumed that modeling takes place at the origin.

Basic Toolbox

If you walk into a home improvement store and visit the tool section, you will notice a wide variety and range of equipment. Some tools are basic, but get the job done (like a hammer and nails). Other tools are much more complicated and expensive, but accomplish the same job (like a nail gun, which needs a compressor and special nails).

Equipping yourself with the fancier tools is truly unnecessary, because you can still hang a painting or build a house with a simple hammer and nail.

Maya is also full of tools. Just like the tools in the home improvement store, there are multiple tools that lead to the same goal. The first set of tools, which I have grouped into your basic toolbox, are sufficient to model your character.

The following tools are used in combination to create your character's head, neck and torso, arm, leg, eyes, hands, feet, hair, and other accessories. Here is a brief explanation of those tools and how to find them.

EP Curve Tool

The EP Curve Tool (Create > EP Curve Tool) creates curves by clicking a series of points (or vertices), much like a game of connect the dots. The line that is created between the points will be a curve when using the default settings. A reference drawing can be traced using this tool to create a profile, or silhouette, curve.

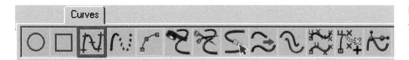

FIG. 13-6 The EP Curve Tool can be found on the Curves shelf.

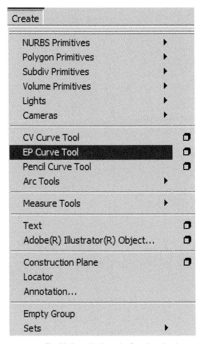

FIG. 13-7 The EP Curve Tool can be found under the Create menu.

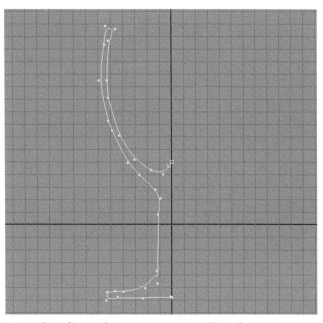

FIG. 13-8 The profile curve of a wine glass created with the EP Curve Tool.

355

Revolve Tool

The Revolve tool (Surfaces > Revolve) creates a surface around the chosen axis of a selected curve (such as the profile curve created with the EP Curve Tool). A NURBS surface is created by default around the y-axis, which works wonderfully for the head, neck, torso, and leg. The arm will need to be revolved around the x-axis, which can be chosen by opening the option settings window.

FIG. 13-9 The Revolve tool can be found on the Surfaces shelf.

FIG. 13-10 The Revolve tool can be found in the Surfaces menu set by pressing F4 on the keyboard under the Surfaces menu.

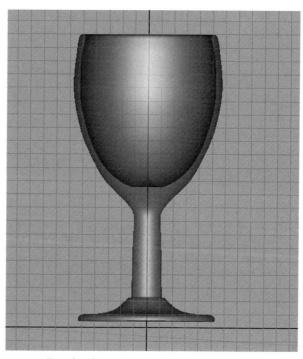

FIG. 13-11 The surface of a wine glass created from the profile curve with the Revolve tool.

NURBS Cylinder

A NURBS cylinder (Create > NURBS Primitives > Cylinder) is not a tool, but rather a menu item that creates a surface in the shape of a cylinder (one of several primitive, or prebuilt, pieces of geometry available in Maya). I list it here because it can be used to create your legs and arms, in lieu of using the EP Curve Tool and Revolve tool. The cylinder is defined in sections (vertical lines) and spans (horizontal lines). The default settings will create a cylinder with only one span, so you must increase the number of spans to about twelve to allow the geometry to bend in areas such as the knees and elbows. You can change the spans in the option settings or in the input section of the Channel box by clicking on makeNurbCylinder1, and changing the spans there. You can then scale and rotate the geometry into the place of the leg or arm.

FIG. 13-12 The NURBS cylinder can be found on the Surfaces shelf.

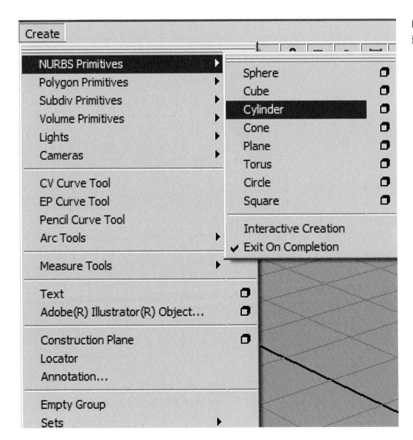

FIG. 13-13 The NURBS cylinder can be found under the Create menu.

Lattice Deformer

A deformer is a tool that is used to change the shape of an object and can be used during modeling to speed up the process on all types of geometry. Once created, a Lattice Deformer (Create Deformers > Lattice) surrounds the geometry to be deformed and looks almost like scaffolding around a building. When you move a point on the lattice, the geometry it surrounds moves as well.

357

FIG. 13-14 The Lattice Deformer can be found on the Deformation shelf.

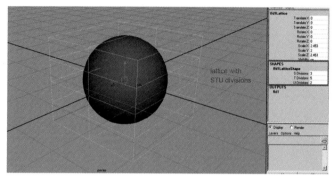

FIG. 13-16 The Lattice Deformer applied to a Sphere. Notice there are three S divisions (left to right), five T divisions (top to bottom), and only two U divisions (front to back).

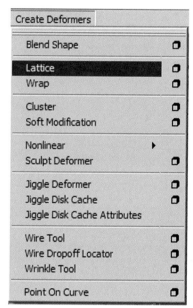

FIG. 13-15 The Lattice Deformer can be found in the Animation menu set by pressing F2 on the keyboard under the Create Deformers menu.

Much of the NURBS and polygonal modeling process relies on the ability to move points around to shape the geometry into the desired form. This can become a tedious procedure, so we want to minimize moving points as much as possible. The benefit of using a lattice (or any other deformer) is that it affects multiple points on the geometry at the same time, which speeds up your work.

The STU divisions of the lattice can be added to or changed in the Shapes section of the Channel box. STU is a special coordinate system for lattices (equivalent to X,Y,Z where S = X, T = Y, and U = Z).

NURBS Sphere

A NURBS sphere (Create > NURBS Primitives > Sphere) is another primitive geometry shape, like the cylinder discussed earlier, and is often used as the beginning shape when modeling things such as eyes, hair, ears, and fingers. In order to shape the sphere, the default sections and spans need to be increased, and should be evaluated on a case-by-case basis, depending on the detail needed for the object being modeled. Change the number of sections and spans in the option settings or in the input section of the Channel box, click on makeNurbSphere1, and change them there. There is also a start sweep and end sweep which opens the sphere and can be used to create eyelids that blink.

FIG. 13-17 The NURBS sphere can be found on the Surfaces shelf.

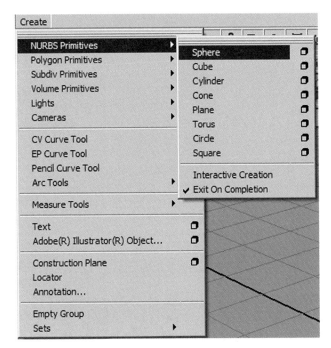

FIG. 13-18 The NURBS sphere can be found under the Create menu.

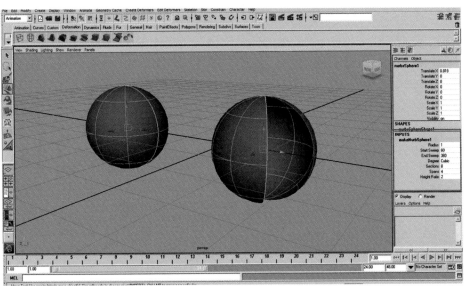

FIG. 13-19 These NURBS spheres have eight sections (vertical or longitude) and four spans (horizontal or latitude). The sphere on the right has a start sweep of 60 degrees, which opens the sphere.

Construction History and Deleting History

As you build geometry in Maya, most of what you do to that geometry is added to a list and remembered by Maya (Edit > Delete by Type > History), so that you can alter an earlier step in the phase if needed. For example, after the revolved surface is created, you can still move the original points along the curve and the surface will automatically update its shape based on the new shape of the curve.

This list is referred to as construction history, and it can be seen in the input section of the Channel box. Although this can be handy, sometimes the current tool affecting the geometry can be interfered with by something done earlier in the modeling process. Because of this, it is important to delete the history often, especially when completing a major phase of the entire character creation process, such as when you are finished modeling and after you are finished texturing. Another rule of thumb that I follow is to delete the history if the current tool is yielding undesirable results. However, be aware that there are times that you want to keep your history, such as when you are using a NURBS sphere to create an eyelid that blinks. Once it is deleted, there is no way to bring it back. It is wise to save a version of the scene file prior to deleting the history if you are unsure.

FIG. 13-20 The command to delete History can be found under the Edit menu.

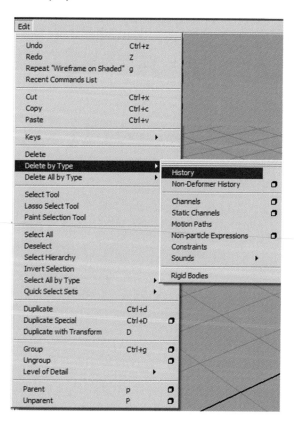

Inserting Isoparms

Isoparms are the lines that you see when a surface is selected. Additional isoparms can be added to the surface in order to create detail in the geometry, or to ensure adequate geometry in bend areas (such as elbows, knees, and the torso). When adding isoparms, be careful not to overdo it. Too many will result in heavy geometry, which will slow down animation and rendering. To insert a single isoparm, right-click and hold over a surface (which brings up the marking menu), choose Isoparms (which brings you into component level), click and drag on an isoparm on the surface near to where you want to add one, drag it into position, then select Edit NURBS > Insert Isoparms.

FIG. 13-21 The Insert Isoparms command can be found on the Surfaces shelf.

Sculpt Geometry Tool

The Sculpt Geometry tool (Edit NURBS > Sculpt Geometry Tool > option box) offers a much more artistic approach to modeling geometry. Using the artisan brush, you can paint on a surface wherever points exist to sculpt it by pushing, pulling, erasing, and smoothing. This tool is much more effective if using a pressure-sensitive tablet and pen. However, it is helpful for constructing noses and eye sockets, even with a mouse. This tool also affects polygonal and subdivision surfaces.

Moving Individual CVs

A control vertex, or CV, is the point where two isoparms intersect. For some details and shapes, adjusting an individual CV is the only way to reach the desired look. Right-click and hold over a surface (which brings up the marking menu), choose CVs (which brings you into component level), click on a CV, and use the Move tool by pressing W on the keyboard to click drag the CV into position.

Additional Tools for Your Toolbox

You can create an entire character from the tools discussed in this chapter, but if you would like to create a seamless character and have better control over texturing, you need to convert your character into polygonal surfaces. The next set of menu items and tools can be used to achieve this goal. You can see by the length of the following section that there are many more tools needed for this process, and it will take more time to achieve the look desired.

FIG. 13-22 The Insert Isoparms command can be found in Edit NURBS > Insert Isoparms.

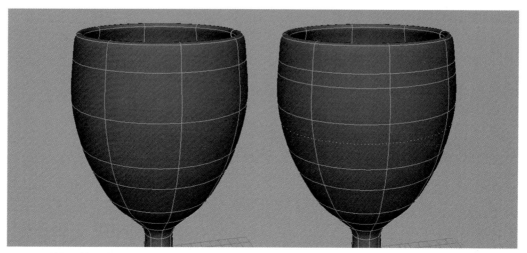

FIG. 13-23 Adding additional Isoparms.

FIG. 13-24 The Sculpt Geometry tool can be found on the Surfaces shelf. It can also be found on the Polygons shelf and the Subdivisions shelf.

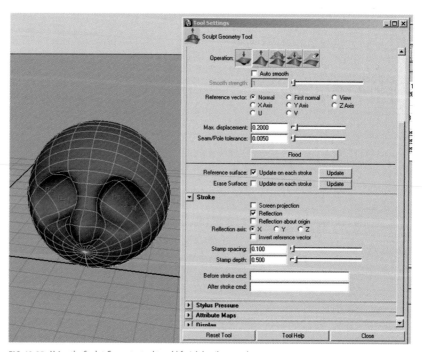

FIG. 13-25 Using the Sculpt Geometry tool to add facial details to a sphere.

FIG. 13-26 The Sculpt Geometry tool can be found in the Surfaces menu set by pressing F4 on the keyboard under the Edit NURBS menu.

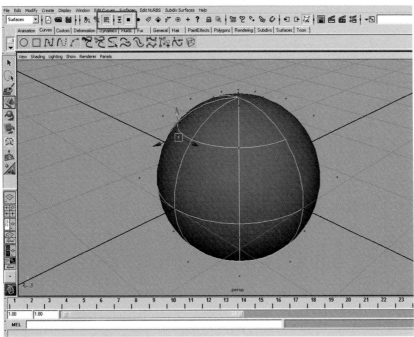

FIG. 13-27 You can also choose component mode and select points in the selection mask area in order to easily select and move CVs.

Make sure that your selection preferences are set to the whole face! Otherwise, you will always have to click on the little dot that appears in the center of the polygon. With this selected, you can click anywhere on the polygonal face to select it. (Go to Window > Settings/Preferences > Preferences > Selection. Set the following: Polygon selection—whole face.)

When blocking in your model, remember that your polygonal faces should be as close to square as possible. This will ensure that the geometry deforms better.

Polygonal Cube

Like the NURBS primitives, Maya has several polygonal primitives available. Many modelers begin with the polygonal cube (Create > Polygon Primitives > Cube) and create their entire seamless character from a single cube. This method is called box-modeling. This approach should be used to create the hands and feet if a single polygonal body is desired.

FIG. 13-28 The Polygonal cube can be found on the Polygons shelf.

FIG. 13-29 The Polygonal cube can be found under the Create menu.

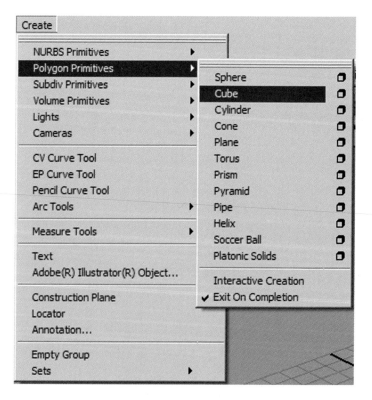

Split Polygons Tool

The Split Polygons tool (Edit Mesh > Split Polygon Tool) is great for dividing polygons to add more geometry when detail is needed. Be careful not to create *n*-gons in the process. Click on an edge (and drag with your mouse to position the first point) then click on another edge (and drag with your mouse to position the second point). Continue clicking on additional edges, if necessary, until you have made the split desired. Then hit Enter to complete the split.

FIG. 13-30 The Split Polygon tool can be found on the Polygons shelf.

FIG. 13-31 The Split Polygon tool can be found in the Polygons menu set by pressing F3 on the keyboard under the Edit Mesh menu.

```
Edit Mesh

  Keep Faces Together

  Extrude                      □
  Bridge                       □
  Append to Polygon Tool       □

  Cut Faces Tool               □
  Split Polygon Tool           □
  Insert Edge Loop Tool        □
  Offset Edge Loop Tool        □
  Add Divisions                □

  Transform Component          □
  Flip Triangle Edge

  Poke Face                    □
  Wedge Face                   □
  Duplicate Face               □

  Detach Component

  Merge                        □
  Merge To Center
  Merge Edge Tool              □
  Delete Edge/Vertex

  Chamfer Vertex               □
  Bevel                        □
```

FIG. 13-32 The Split Polygon tool.

Why quads?

When modeling in polygons, it is important to keep the faces as quadrilaterals (four-sided polygons) and stay away from tri's (three-sided polygons) or *n*-gons (more-than-four-sided polygons). There are several reasons for this. First, when texturing, you will have an easier time when unwrapping UVs (which is outside the scope of this book). Second, when smoothing your character, you will avoid pinching that occurs in the presence of tri's and *n*-gons. And third, if you are deforming your geometry, you will get nicer results.

Extrude Polygon

If faces or edges are selected in component mode, the Extrude Polygon tool (Edit Mesh > Extrude) allows you to pull those components out or push them in, while creating additional faces, which then builds the geometry into the desired shape.

If the faces are at an angle, the extrusion will be made at an angle. If you click on the little blue circle, you will change from local space to world space and your extrusion will then be made perpendicular to the graph.

Many modelers use the box modeling method and begin with a polygonal cube, then shape it roughly, and extrude the polygonal faces to form the torso and arms. I find that for a beginner, this is a difficult method to use when trying to achieve an organic shape. For some reason, beginners do not spend enough time shaping the form with this method, and the end result remains too angular and not smooth.

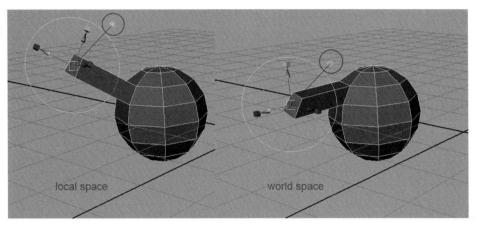

local space   world space

FIG. 13-33 The Extrude Polygon tool has a little blue circle which toggles between world space and local space, changing the direction of the extrusion.

Polygons

FIG. 13-34 The Extrude Polygon command can be found on the Polygons shelf.

Edit Mesh
Keep Faces Together
Extrude ▫
Bridge ▫
Append to Polygon Tool ▫
Cut Faces Tool ▫
Split Polygon Tool ▫
Insert Edge Loop Tool ▫
Offset Edge Loop Tool ▫
Add Divisions ▫
Transform Component ▫
Flip Triangle Edge
Poke Face ▫
Wedge Face ▫
Duplicate Face ▫
Detach Component
Merge ▫
Merge To Center
Merge Edge Tool ▫
Delete Edge/Vertex
Chamfer Vertex ▫
Bevel ▫

FIG. 13-35 The Extrude Polygon tool can be found in the Polygons menu set by pressing F3 on the keyboard under the Edit Mesh menu.

Keep Faces Together

If the Keep Faces Together option (Edit Mesh > Keep Faces Together) is unchecked, extruded faces will be separate pieces of geometry. This can be helpful, for example, when creating fingers from a palm. However, most of the time this option should be checked before extruding polygons or there will be interior faces as a result of polygonal faces that lie parallel to each other, which in turn causes nonmanifold geometry.

FIG. 13-36 The Keep Faces Together option can be found in the Polygons menu set by pressing F3 on the keyboard under the Edit Mesh menu.

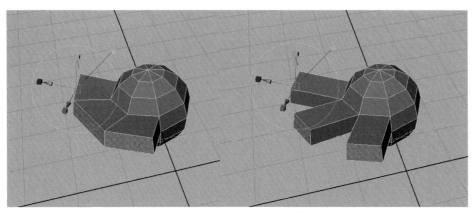

FIG. 13-37 Extruding polygonal faces with the Keep Faces Together option checked (left sphere) and extruding polygons with the Keep Faces Together option unchecked (right sphere).

Converting NURBS to Polys

This menu item (Modify > Convert > NURBS to Polygons) will change an existing selected NURBS surface into polygonal geometry. It is perfectly fine to leave your models as NURBS surfaces. However, sometimes it is necessary to use polygons (creating one seamless piece of geometry or finer control in the texturing process), so this is a simple way of making them. Once converted, you can use other tools to make separate polygonal pieces into one.

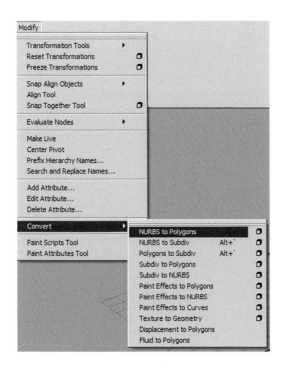

FIG. 13-38 The NURBS to polys command can be found under the Modify menu.

It is extremely important to open the option box and change the tessellation method to control points in order to create clean polygonal geometry, as the default settings do not provide a usable result. It may be necessary to add additional isoparms to the NURBS surface *before* converting to ensure that organic shape is maintained once polygonal. However, realize that the polygonal geometry will eventually be smoothed, and the addition of too many isoparms will result in an extremely heavy model. Any overlapping NURBS surfaces may result in polygonal geometry that may need additional cleanup (deleting of faces and rebuilding).

FIG. 13-39 The convert NURBS to polygons option.

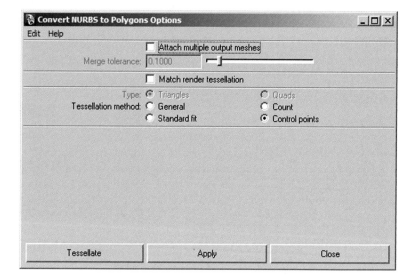

Delete Half of Your Model

In order to save time, delete half of the character and model just one side (right-click on geometry > Faces, select the faces and hit Delete). *Make sure* that the points in the center of the character stay lined up with the origin. This will make mirroring the geometry over to the other side predictable. Otherwise, your mirrored side will not be even and result in a character that is wider than expected, or overlapping.

Combining Separated Polygonal Pieces into One Mesh

Once the NURBS surfaces have been converted into polygons, the polygons need to be combined and overlapping or extra faces must be deleted. Combining polygons will make two or more polygonal surfaces act as one. However, they are truly not one piece and can be separated again. You must merge vertices in order for the two surfaces to become one. Make sure to delete any overlapping faces, as these are not needed.

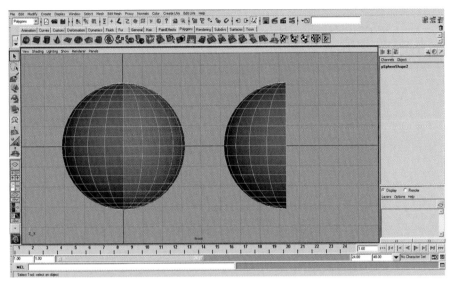

FIG. 13-40 Selecting polygonal faces and deleting them to leave half of the object (in this image, half of a sphere).

FIG. 13-41 The Combine command can be found on the Polygons shelf.

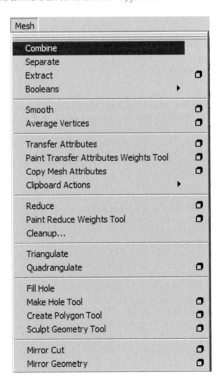

FIG. 13-42 The Combine command can be found in the Polygons menu set by pressing F3 on the keyboard under the Mesh menu.

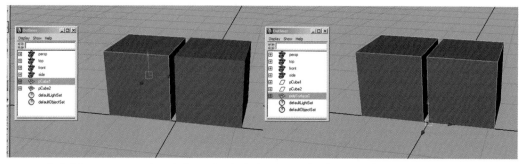

FIG. 13-43 On the left are two separate polygonal cubes; on the right they have been combined into polySurface1. Notice that the outliner still shows nodes pCube1 and pCube2, because of construction history.

Aligning Vertices with the Snap to Points Tool, Move Tool, and V Hotkey

After combining polygons and removing extraneous faces, the vertices should be snapped together to perfectly align the disjoined faces. Additional geometry may need to be added in order to have each face remain a quad and not become an *n*-gon. Right-click the surface and choose Vertex. Select a point with the Move tool, hold down the V key, and middle-click-drag over the point that you want to snap it to.

Closing Gaps or Holes

After selecting the Append Polygon tool (Edit Mesh > Append Polygon Tool), pink arrows will appear on the edges of polygons that surround a hole or gap.

FIG. 13-44 Snapping vertex points together using the Move tool and the V hotkey on the keyboard.

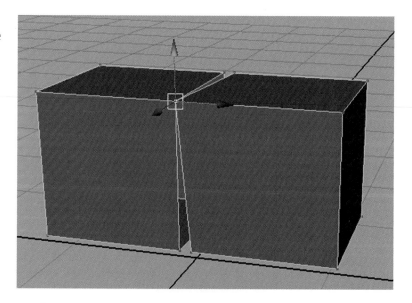

Click on one edge, then click on another edge, and hit the Enter key to finish the process.

Inserting Additional Edges

The Insert Edge Loop tool (Edit Mesh > Insert Edge Loop Tool) is used for dividing faces in order to create additional divisions in the geometry. It is

FIG. 13-45 The Append Polygon tool can be found in the Polygons menu set by pressing F3 on the keyboard under the Edit Mesh menu.

really helpful when ensuring enough geometry in areas that bend, such has ankles, knees, hips, wrists, forearms, elbows, shoulders, torso, and neck.

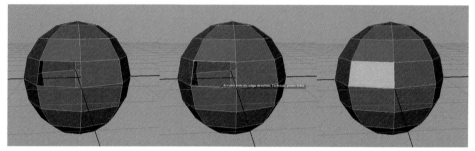

FIG. 13-46 Creating a new polygon to fill a hole using the append polygon tool.

Again, be careful not to add too much geometry. Generally, eight divisions around the length (such as vertical lines in the legs and torso and horizontal lines in the arms) are adequate. Five to seven cross-divisions around each bend point is usually sufficient.

FIG. 13-47 The Insert Edge Loop tool can be found in the Polygons menu set by pressing F3 on the keyboard under the Edit Mesh menu.

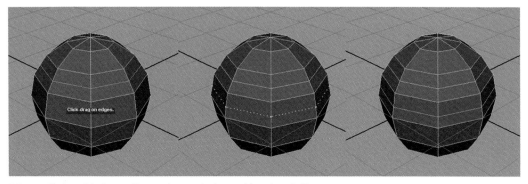

FIG. 13-48 The Insert Edge Loop tool inserts edges completely around the polygonal object.

Merging Vertices

To ensure the faces actually become connected, the overlapping vertices are selected and merged (Edit Mesh > Merge). Your polygons must have been combined before you can merge vertices; otherwise, it will not work. (There is no warning that this does not work. The only way to test it is to click on a single vertex and move it around. Just make sure to undo by pressing Z on the keyboard after testing.)

FIG. 13-49 The Merge command can be found on the Polygons shelf.

Mirror Geometry

Once you have half of the body modeled, you can simply mirror the geometry (Mesh > Mirror Geometry) to obtain a complete model. However, it is important to remember that all of the interior vertices must line up and be on the origin. If not, your mirrored geometry result will be undesirable. Make sure to open the option box and select the correct axis. If you have created your first half on the left side of the screen (your character's right side), you can use the default settings. If you have created the character's left side first, you would need to open the option box to change the axis appropriately; that is, to negative x.

Showing Your Polygonal Normals

During the process of modeling polygons, you may notice some areas that appear darker than others. This is because your normals have been probably flipped inward. To confirm this, with the object selected, you can display your face normals using Display > Polygons > Face Normals. To hide these again, repeat the command with the object selected: Display > Polygons > Face Normals.

FIG. 13-50 The Merge command can be found in the Polygons menu set by pressing F3 on the keyboard under the Edit Mesh menu.

FIG. 13-51 Clicking and moving a vertex that has been snapped on top of another shows that these two overlapping vertices are not merged together.

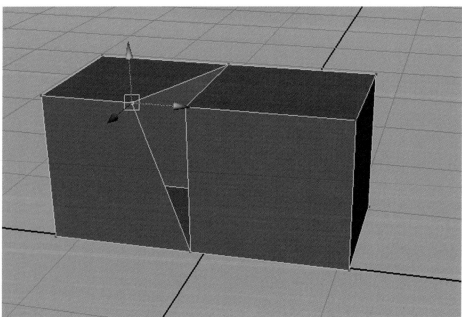

FIG. 13-52 The Mirror Geometry command can be found on the Polygons shelf.

Mesh

Combine
Separate
Extract   ☐
Booleans   ▶

Smooth   ☐
Average Vertices   ☐

Transfer Attributes   ☐
Paint Transfer Attributes Weights Tool   ☐
Copy Mesh Attributes   ☐
Clipboard Actions   ▶

Reduce   ☐
Paint Reduce Weights Tool   ☐
Cleanup...

Triangulate
Quadrangulate   ☐

Fill Hole
Make Hole Tool   ☐
Create Polygon Tool   ☐
Sculpt Geometry Tool   ☐

Mirror Cut   ☐
Mirror Geometry   ☐

FIG. 13-53 The Mirror Geometry command can be found in the Polygons menu set by pressing F3 on the keyboard under the Mesh menu.

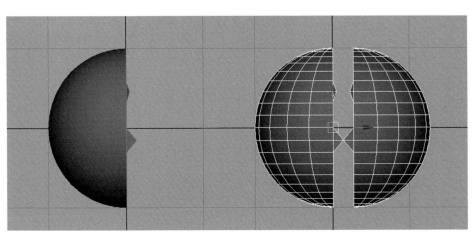

FIG. 13-54 If any vertex points are not lined up with the origin, you will not achieve the desired mirror.

Making Sure All Normals Face in the Same Direction

Once you can see the normals, you can select the entire object in object mode and use Normals > Conform to make all of the normals face in the same direction. The direction that they face depends on the current majority.

FIG. 13-55 The Face Normals can be displayed using the command found under the Display menu. The polygonal object must be selected before applying this command. The Face Normals can be hidden again by applying the same command.

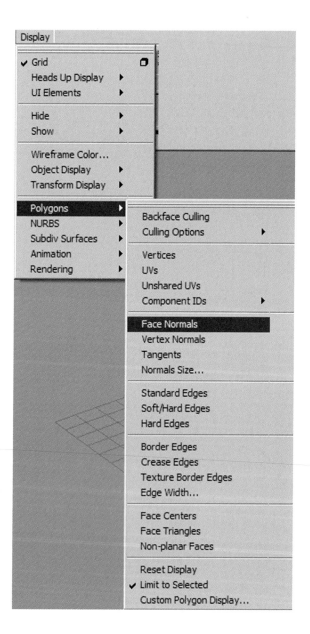

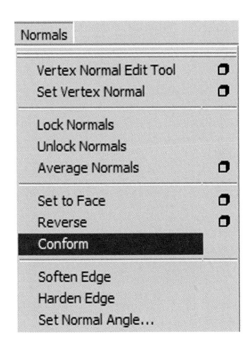

FIG. 13-56 The Conform command can be found in the Polygons menu set by pressing F3 on the keyboard under the Normals menu.

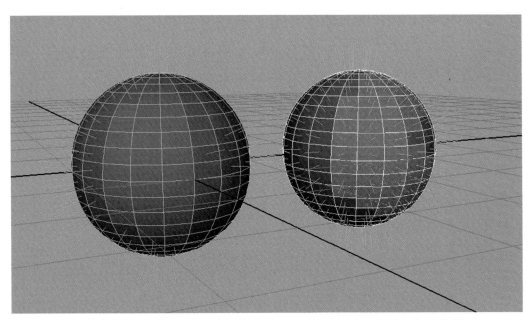

FIG. 13-57 The sphere on the left has some normals that are flipped inside; the sphere on the right is the same sphere after the Conform command has been applied. You can see that the selected faces have had their normals flipped back to the outside.

Making Sure that All Normals Face toward the Camera

Sometimes, the Conform command does not always work. If this happens, you can select individual faces pointing inward and use Normals > Reverse to make them point outward.

If the Conform command makes all of the normals point inward (remember, it depends on the direction that the majority already face), you can select the entire object in object mode and use this menu item to make all of the normals face outward.

Averaging the Distance Between the Normals

Once you have all of the normals facing outward, you can select the entire object in object mode and use Normals > Average Normals to average the distance between normals, which makes the geometry appear smoother without adding more physical geometry.

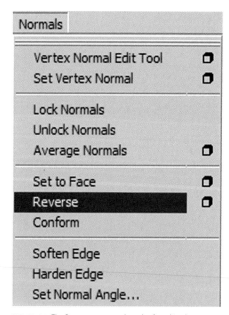

FIG. 13-58 The Reverse command can be found in the Polygons menu set by pressing F3 on the keyboard under the Normals menu.

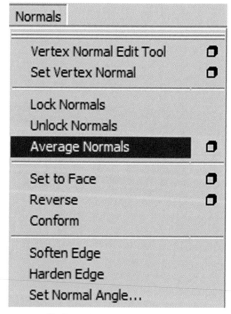

FIG. 13-59 The Average Normals command can be found in the Polygons menu set by pressing F3 on the keyboard under the Normals menu.

Smoothing

By smoothing your polygonal geometry (Mesh > Smooth), the geometry becomes more organic in shape. This procedure adds divisions and rounds out the surface. Note: This procedure should *not* be done to your character at this stage of the character creation process, because it adds too much

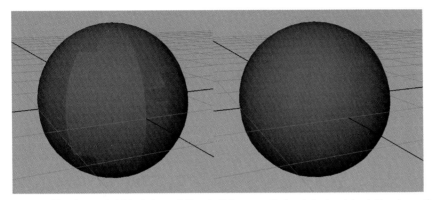

FIG. 13-60 The sphere on the left has had normals flipped, which can cause the faces to be viewed sharply. The sphere on the right is the same sphere after the Average Normals command has been applied. Notice how much smoother the sphere on the right appears.

geometry and causes the character model to become heavy and extremely difficult to work with when creating blend shapes and in the skinning process. If you want to see what your character will look like smoothed, make sure to undo this by pressing Z before moving on.

FIG. 13-61 The Smooth command can be found on the Polygons shelf.

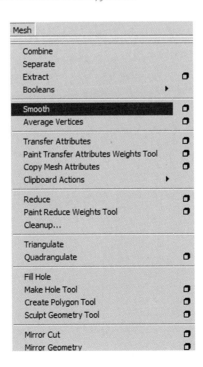

FIG. 13-62 The Smooth command can be found in the Polygons menu set by pressing F3 on the keyboard under the Mesh menu.

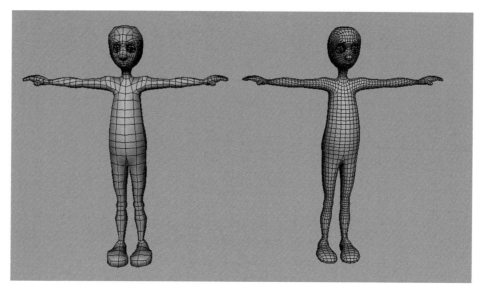

FIG. 13-63 The character on the left is the low-poly version, which doesn't look very polished. The character on the right has been smoothed. *Make sure* to undo the smooth at this point by pressing Z on the keyboard if you are testing to see your result.

You can preview what your model will look like when it is smoothed. With the polygonal object selected, press 2 on the keyboard to preview a smoothed polygonal object with a wireframe cage of the original. Press 3 on your keyboard to preview just the smooth polygonal object. Press 1 to turn off the preview and return to the actual polygonal object.

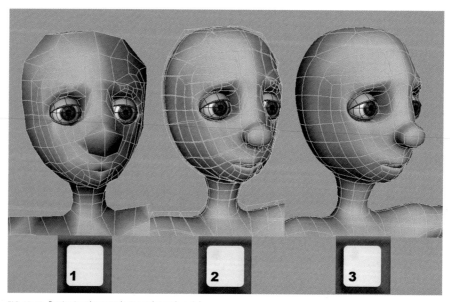

FIG. 13-64 Previewing the smooth on a polygonal model.

Remember: As you work, make sure to delete the history and label your geometry. Check your outliner and hypergraph after deleting the history to see what appears in the scene, and label your nodes appropriately.

Be sure to create a layer in the Layer Editor and add the character's geometry to that layer.

Make sure to freeze transformations on finished geometry to return the translation and rotation values to 0 and the scale values to 1.

Former Student Spotlight: Chris Grim

Character modeling is essentially the pedestal on which the animated short is built. Once the model is completed, it will be rigged, animated, and rendered out. A solid 3D short relies on one's ability to correctly model topology and understand the aesthetic look intended.

Producing a biped character from scratch can be a daunting task. The artist must create a visually appealing character that is "animatable" and that will correctly deform during the rigging stage. The balance between aesthetic form and function is a challenge in itself. In order to achieve a great model, the artist must successfully mesh form with function. If either overpowers the other, the 3D short will suffer.

During my work on character development, I noticed my skills improving at different rates. As my ability to create aesthetically pleasing characters improved, my knowledge of topology and deformation was only a step behind. It is important that you have a strong knowledge of both aspects in order to create a beautiful model that can be animated correctly.

Chris Grim received his BFA from Savannah College of Art and Design with honors and is currently finishing his MFA in animation. In 2006, he was awarded an honorable mention for modeling by Rhythm and Hues. He completed an internship at Gentle Giant Studios, and after graduating, started working for Blur Studios. His work can be viewed at http://www.chrisgrim.com.

Summary

- Once again, *keep it simple*. The simpler the character design, the easier it will be to model the character.
- Don't be afraid to explore tools and to experiment. Sometimes it is best to scrap your first attempt and start over.
- While working, it is suggested that you use X-ray mode and wireframe on shaded so that you can see what you're doing while modeling.
- Object mode and component mode are generally the two levels that are used during the character creation process. Object mode allows you to

FIG. 13-65 "Superman" by Chris Grim (2006).

affect the entire object, and component mode allows you to manipulate finer details, or pieces of the object.
- The type of geometry—NURBS, polygons, or subdivision surfaces—used for your character model truly does not matter. However, subdivision surfaces can still be unreliable when performing during animation.
- The EP Curve Tool creates curves by clicking a series of points, which then creates a line between the points.
- The Revolve tool creates a surface around the chosen axis of the selected curve, such as a profile curve created with the EP Curve Tool.
- A NURBS cylinder is a primitive object that can be used to create other shapes.

- A Lattice Deformer surrounds the object with a type of scaffolding, which can then be manipulated to change the shape of an object.
- A deformer is used to speed up the process of modeling, because it affects multiple points of geometry at the same time.
- A NURBS sphere is another primitive object that can be used as a base to create other shapes.
- Construction history is a list of processes used on an object during modeling. It is sometimes needed, but often it must be deleted. So that tools work predictably, construction history should be deleted often.
- The Sculpt Geometry tool provides an artistic approach to modeling and can be used on all types of geometry.
- Sometimes the only way to get the desired shape when modeling is to move individual CVs.
- To make polygons easy to select, change your selection preferences to whole face.
- When modeling with polygons, make sure that the faces are square. This provides deformation during the animation process.
- A polygonal cube is a primitive object that is generally the starting point for a method called box modeling.
- The Split Polygon tool can be used to divide the polygonal faces during the modeling process.
- When modeling in polygons, it is important to keep faces as quadrilaterals, or four-sided.
- During the box modeling process, Extrude Polygons is used often to create more faces.
- It is important to have the option for Keep Faces Together checked while extruding, except in cases when the faces need to be separate such as in the fingers.
- NURBS surfaces can be converted to polygonal surfaces in order to create one seamless piece of geometry. Make sure to convert using control points as the setting for the tessellation method.
- When working with polygonal geometry, it can be more efficient to model only half of the character and mirror the geometry for the other side.
- Separate pieces of polygonal geometry must be combined before the vertex points can be merged.
- Vertex points can be aligned easily by holding down the V hotkey on the keyboard while moving them.
- The Append Polygon tool is perfect for filling gaps or holes in polygonal geometry.
- The Insert Edge Loop tool divides polygonal faces completely around the entire piece of geometry.
- Two overlapping vertices can be combined into one by using the Merge command. Remember, if merging vertices on two separate pieces of geometry, they must first be combined.
- When mirroring geometry, it is important to make sure that none of the interior vertices have crossed the origin line.

- All polygonal normals should face outwards. Normals can be flipped during the modeling process. You can display them and then use some of the normal tools to flip them back out, if necessary.
- Although smoothing the polygonal geometry may be desired, it should not be done at this point in the workflow. Press 3 on the keyboard for a smooth preview.
- As you work, make sure to delete history and labeled geometry.
- When completing your geometry, create a layer in the Layer Editor and add the character geometry to that layer.
- Freeze transformations on finished geometry.

Assignments: Modeling a Character

When modeling a character in 3D space, it is important to make sure that your character faces front in the front view, side in the side view, and down in the top view, in order for all of the tools to work appropriately. The programmers created the character tools in Maya to work with your character facing in the positive Z direction.

Model a Head, Neck, and Torso

1. Open Maya and set your project. Go to File > Project > Set… and browse to your project folder, then click OK.
2. Open your last saved file in File > Open and select 01 > referenceImages.ma.
3. Set all four view panels to X-ray mode and wireframe on shaded.
   a. Turn on hardware texturing (press 6) so that you can see your reference images.
   b. In the top view panel, go to Shading > X-Ray, and then Shading > Wireframe on shaded.
   c. In the perspective view panel, go to Shading > X-Ray, and then Shading > Wireframe on shaded.
   d. In the front view panel, go to Shading > X-Ray, and then Shading > Wireframe on shaded.
   e. In the side view panel, go to Shading > X-Ray, and then Shading > Wireframe on shaded.
4. Draw a profile curve of your character's head, neck, and torso. If your character has clothing, it should be part of this profile curve. Clothing does not need to be separate, unless your character is going to change clothing in the animation.
   a. Go to Create > EP Curve Tool and open the option box, click Reset Tool, and close the option box.
   b. In the front window, trace your drawing by clicking points along the outline on the right side of your character (your left side), starting at the center of the head and ending in the crotch. Hit enter when finished. Ignore the arms for now.

c. You can adjust the positions of the points on the curve by right-click on top of the curve and choose Control Vertex. Use your move tool by pressing W to select points and move them around to refine the shape of your curve. You can also delete extra points by selecting them and hitting the delete key.

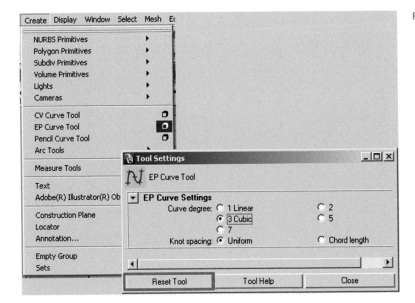

FIG. 13-66 Create > EP Curve Tool.

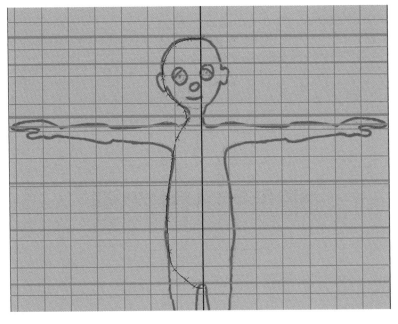

FIG. 13-67 Tracing your drawing with the EP Curve Tool. An X marks each click of the mouse and becomes a point on the curve.

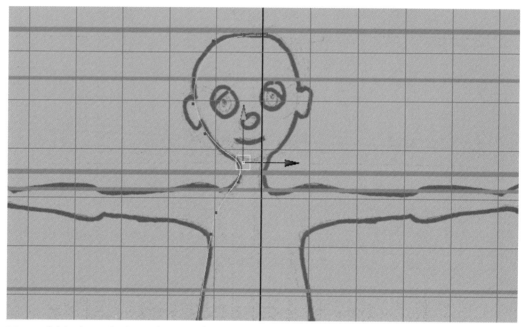

FIG. 13-68 Refining the curve by adjusting the positions of the points on the curve with the move tool.

5. Create the surface for your character's head, neck and torso.
   a. Select curve1, the curve you created, and go to Surfaces > Revolve. This process creates revolvedSurface1, a NURBS surface in the shape of the profile curve.
   b. Open the outliner Window > Outliner and select curve1, the curve you created. In the perspective view panel, right-click to the left of the curve (in a blank area of the window that does not touch the curve or the surface) and choose Control Vertex (this will show the CV points only on the curve). Use your Move tool by pressing W on the keyboard to select points and move them around to refine the shape of your surface. Because Maya has construction history, each operation you perform is connected to the preceding operation, and moving the points on the curve will automatically affect the surface and change its shape.
   c. Select revolvedSurface1, go to Create Deformers > Create Lattice, and with the lattice selected, in the Shapes section of the Channel box, increase the T divisions from 5 to about 10–14.
   d. In the side view panel, right-click on top of the lattice and choose Lattice Point. Use your Move tool by pressing W on the keyboard to click-drag (or marquee-drag) over points on the lattice (this ensures that you are selecting the points on both sides of the lattice) and move them around to refine the shape of your surface. In the perspective view panel, continue to move and scale (if adjusting 2 or 4 points on the same row) the points on the lattice to refine the shape of your

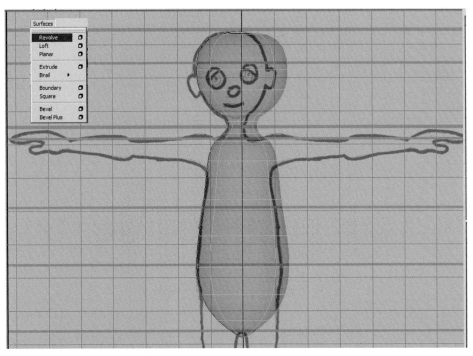

FIG. 13-69 Creating the surface for your character's head and torso using the Revolve command.

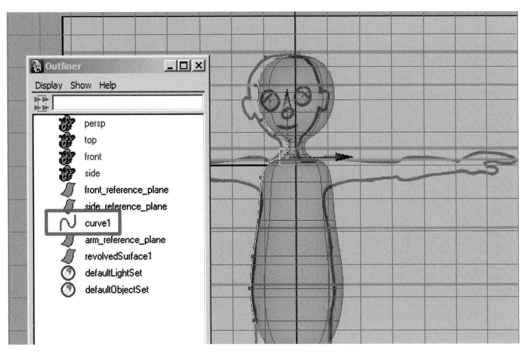

FIG. 13-70 Refining the surface by adjusting the positions of the points on the curve with the Move tool.

surface. Your reference drawings are just a reference. Feel free to make artistic changes while modeling in order to achieve the look you want.

e. Select revolvedSurface1, then go to Edit > Delete by Type > History. This will remove the lattice, but any changes that have been made are now permanent. This also removes the connection to curve1.

FIG. 13-71 Adding a Lattice Deformer to your head and torso shape. Using a lattice allows even distribution and the changes to affect the entire piece of geometry.

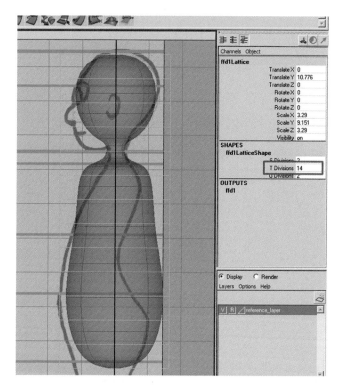

FIG. 13-72 Refining the surface by adjusting the positions of the lattice points with the move and scale tools.

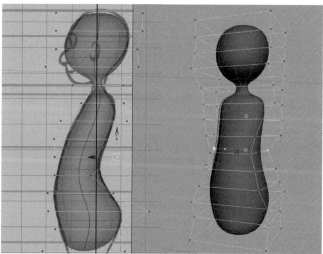

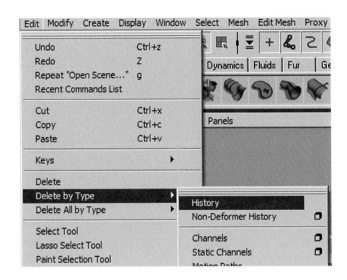

FIG. 13-73 Edit > Delete by type > History.

f. In the outliner, select curve1 and hit Delete.
g. Select revolvedSurface1 and rename to body_ geo by clicking on the name and typing in the Channel box.

FIG. 13-74 Renaming the torso and head shape in the Channel box.

h. In the Layer Editor of the Channel box, create a new layer. Double-click on the new layer (layer1) and rename this layer geometry_ layer, then click Save. Select body_ geo, right-click and hold on top of the geometry_ layer and choose Add Selected Objects. To make the objects unselectable, click in the empty box between the V (visibility) and the layer name. An R (reference) should appear. This keeps any objects assigned to a layer visible but not selectable.

6. Save your scene file.
   a. Go to File > Save as. This should open the scenes folder of your project (assuming that you set the project as in step 1).
   b. Name your scene 13_asgn01_body_geo.ma.

FIG. 13-75 Click on the "create a new layer" button in the Layer Editor and rename it geometry_layer.

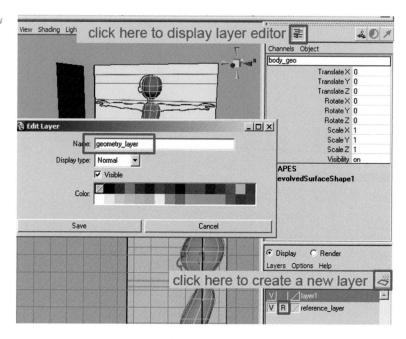

FIG. 13-76 Saving and naming your scene 13_asgn01_body_geo.ma.

Model a Leg

1. Open Maya and set your project. Go to File > Project > Set... browse to your project folder and click OK.
2. Open your last saved file. Go to File > Open and select 13_body_geo.ma.

3. Continue working in X-ray mode and wireframe on shaded.
4. Go to Create > NURBS Primitives > Interactive Creation to uncheck this
   option and turn it off. (Interactive creation allows you to click and drag on
   the grid to create the size and shape of a primitive.)

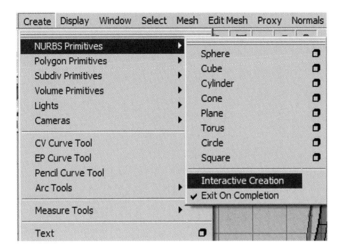

FIG. 13-77 Turning off interactive creation.

5. Create a NURBS cylinder (Create > NURBS Primitives > Cylinder).
   a. Move and scale the cylinder over the character's right leg.
   b. In the INPUTS section of the Channel box, click on makeNurbCylinder1
      and change Spans to 12.
6. With the NurbCylinder1 still selected, create a Lattice Deformer (Create
   Deformers > Lattice).
   a. With the lattice selected, in the Shapes section of the Channel box,
      increase the T Divisions from 5 to about 12.
   b. In the front view panel, right-click on top of the lattice and choose
      Lattice Point. (You may need to right-click in the perspective window, if
      your lattice is close to the geometry, in order to see the correct marking
      menu.) Starting at the hip area, in the front view panel, use your Move
      tool by pressing W on the keyboard to click-drag (or marquee-drag)
      over points on the lattice (this ensures that you are selecting the points
      on both sides of the lattice) and move them around to refine the shape
      of your surface. Then starting at the hip area, in the side view panel,
      continue to move the points on the lattice to refine the shape of your
      surface. Make sure to check the shape in the perspective window.
      Your reference drawings are just a reference. Feel free to make artistic
      changes while modeling in order to achieve the look you want.
   c. Select NurbCylinder1, then go to Edit > Delete by Type > History. This
      will remove the lattice, but any changes that have been made are now
      permanent.
   d. Rename NurbCylinder1 to rightLeg_geo by clicking on the name and
      typing in the Channel box.

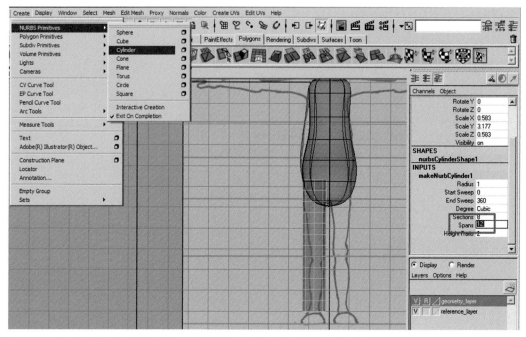

FIG. 13-78 Creating a NURBS cylinder, positioning it for the leg, and dividing it for adequate deformation later.

FIG. 13-79 Adjusting the lattice for additional divisions. Using a lattice allows even distribution and the changes to affect the entire piece of geometry.

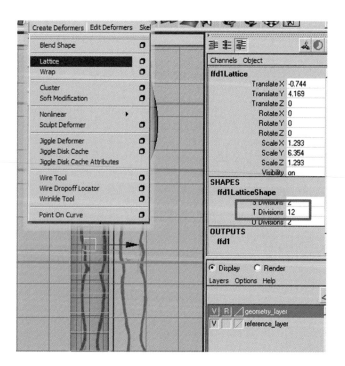

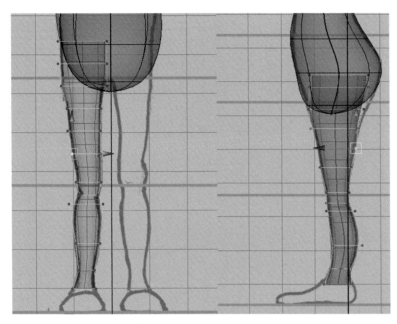

FIG. 13-80 Refining the shape of the leg by adjusting the positions of the lattice points with the Move and Scale tools.

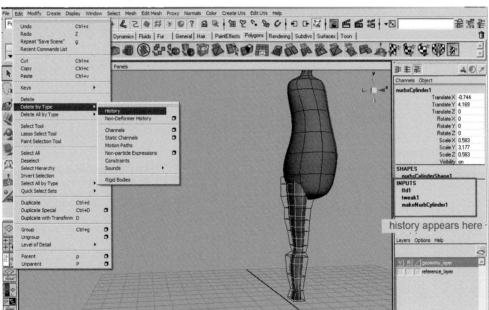

FIG. 13-81 Deleting history to remove the lattice and bake the changes to the shape of the cylinder.

    e. Duplicate rightLeg_geo (Edit > Duplicate or press Ctrl+D). In the Channel box, rename rightLeg_geo1 to leftLeg_geo, change the Translate X value to positive (which positions the leg onto the other side of the origin), and change the Scale X value to negative (which makes the leg invert).

FIG. 13-82 Keep your scene organized by labeling your geometry appropriately.

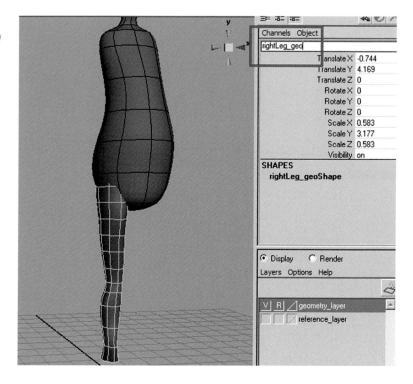

FIG. 13-83 Duplicating the geometry and changing the ScaleX value to the negative inverts the shape. Changing the TranslateX value to positive positions the leg evenly on the opposite side of the origin.

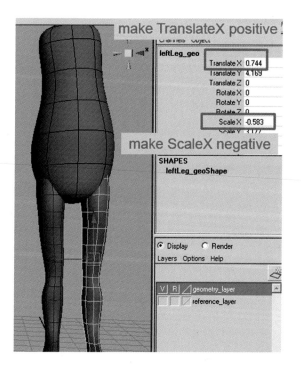

f. Select rightLeg_geo and leftLeg_geo (Modify > Freeze Transformations). Freezing transformations on finished geometry will return the translation and rotation values to 0 and the scale values to 1.

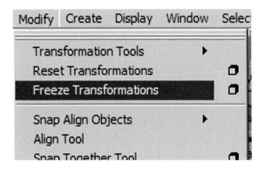

FIG. 13-84 Freezing transformations makes the geometry transformation values return to 0 for translations and rotations and 1 for scale.

g. In the Layer Editor of the Channel box, right-click and hold on top of the geometry_layer and choose "Add Selected Objects."

7. Save your scene file.
   a. Go to File > Save as. This should open the scenes folder of your project (assuming you set the project as in step 1).
   b. Name your scene 13_asgn02_leg_geo.ma.

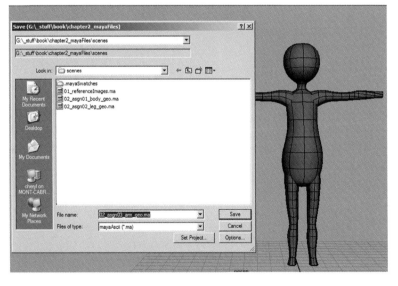

FIG. 13-85 Saving and naming your scene 13_asgn02_leg_geo.ma.

Model an Arm

1. Open Maya and set your project. Go to File > Project > Set… browse to your project folder and click OK.
2. Open your last saved file. Go to File > Open and select 13_asgn02_leg_geo.ma.
3. Continue working in X-ray mode and wireframe on shaded.

4. Continue working with Interactive Creation unchecked Create > NURBS Primitives > Interactive Creation.
5. Create a NURBS cylinder. Create > NURBS Primitives > Cylinder.
   a. In the Channel box, change RotateZ to 90.
   b. Move and scale the cylinder over the character's right arm.
   c. In the INPUTS section of the Channel box, click on makeNurbCylinder1 and change Spans to 10.

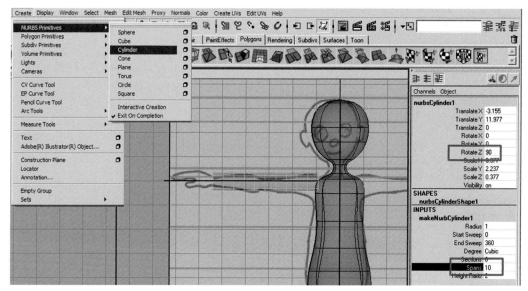

FIG. 13-86 Creating a NURBS cylinder, positioning it for the arm, and dividing it for adequate deformation later.

6. With the NurbCylinder1 still selected, create a Lattice Deformer (Create Deformers > Lattice).
   a. With the lattice selected, in the Shapes section of the Channel box, increase the T divisions from 5 to about 8.
   b. Starting at the shoulder area, in the front view panel, right-click on top of the lattice and choose Lattice Point. (You may need to right-click in the perspective window if your lattice is close to the geometry, in order to see the correct marking menu.) In the front view panel, use your Move tool by pressing W on the keyboard to click-drag (or marquee-drag) over points on the lattice (this ensures that you are selecting the points on both sides of the lattice), and move them around to refine the shape of your surface. Then starting at the shoulder area, in the top view panel, continue to move the points on the lattice to refine the shape of your surface. Make sure to check the shape in the perspective window. Your reference drawings are just a reference. Feel free to make artistic changes while modeling in order to achieve the look you want.

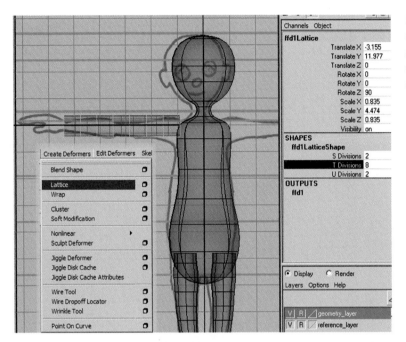

FIG. 13-87 Adjusting the lattice for additional divisions. Using a lattice allows even distribution and the changes to affect the entire piece of geometry.

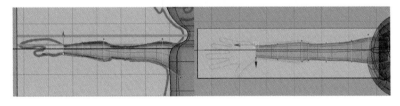

FIG. 13-88 Refining the shape of the arm by adjusting the positions of the lattice points with the Move and Scale tools.

c. *Optional:* For better deformation in the forearm later, you can rotate the last three rows of lattice points incrementally to total 45 degrees forward (starting with the row closest to the elbow, rotate slightly, then the next row, and the row at the wrist should have the points even again). To see what I am talking about, hold your arm out parallel to the floor and palm forward, then rotate your arm so that the palm is facing the floor, Notice how your skin moves with your forearm during this rotation.

d. Select NurbCylinder1, then go to Edit > Delete by Type > History. This will remove the lattice, but any changes that have been made are now permanent.

e. Rename NurbCylinder1 to rightArm_geo by clicking on the name and typing in the Channel box.

f. Duplicate rightArm_geo (Edit > Duplicate or press Ctrl+D). In the Channel box, rename rightArm_geo1 to leftArm_geo, change the TranslateX value to positive (which positions the arm onto the other side of the origin), and change the ScaleY value to negative (which makes the arm invert).

FIG. 13-89 Rotating the forearm for better deformation when the hand twists.

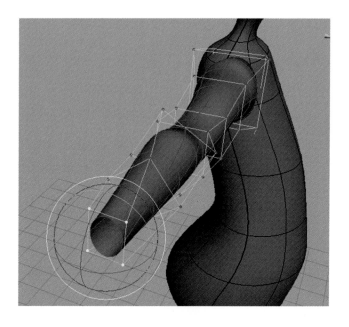

FIG. 13-90 Deleting history to remove the lattice and bake the changes to the shape of the cylinder, then renaming the geometry appropriately.

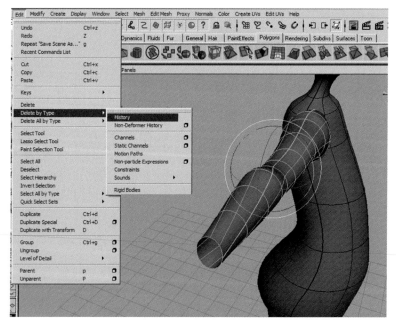

g. Select rightArm_geo and leftArm_geo Modify > Freeze Transformations. Freezing transformations on finished geometry will return the translation and rotation values to 0 and the scale values to 1.

h. In the Layer Editor of the Channel box, right-click and hold on top of the geometry_layer and choose Add Selected Objects.

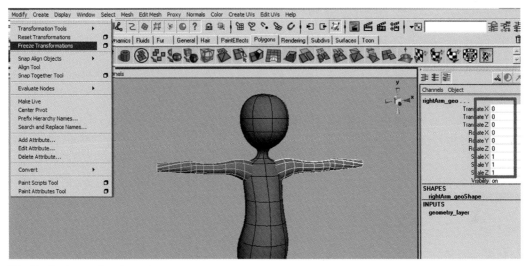

FIG. 13-91 Freezing transformations on the arm geometry.

7. Save your scene file.

    a. Go to File > Save as. This should open the scenes folder of your project (assuming that you set the project as in step 1).

    b. Name your scene 13_asgn03_arm_geo.ma.

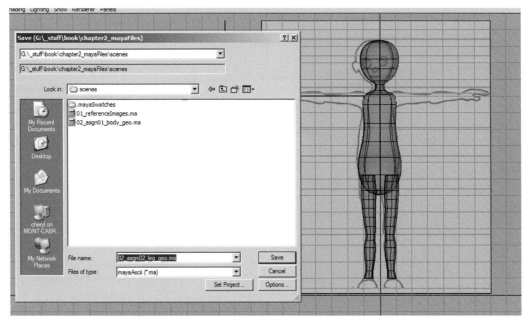

FIG. 13-92 Saving and naming your scene 13_asgn03_arm_geo.ma.

Model a Hand

1. Open Maya and set your project. Go to File > Project > Set… browse to your project folder and click OK.
2. Open your last saved file. Go to File > Open and select 13_asgn03_arm_geo.ma.
3. Continue working in X-ray mode and wireframe on shaded.
4. Continue working with Interactive Creation unchecked (Create > NURBS Primitives > Interactive Creation).
5. Create a NURBS sphere (Create > NURBS Primitives > Sphere).
    a. In the Channel box, change "RotateZ" to 90.
    b. Move and scale the sphere over the character's right palm.
    c. In the INPUTS section of the Channel box, click on makeNurbSphere1 and change Spans to 8.

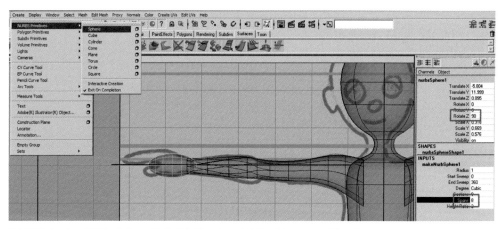

FIG. 13-93 Creating a NURBS cylinder, positioning it for the palm, and dividing it for adequate deformation.

6. With the NurbSphere1 still selected, create a Lattice Deformer (Create Deformers > Lattice).
    a. Starting at the wrist area, in the front view panel, right-click on top of the lattice and choose Lattice Point. (You may need to right-click in the perspective window if your lattice is close to the geometry, in order to see the correct marking menu.) In the front view panel, use your Move tool by pressing W on the keyboard to click-drag (or marquee-drag) over points on the lattice (this ensures that you are selecting the points on both sides of the lattice) and move them around to refine the shape of your surface. Then starting at the wrist area, in the top view panel, continue to move the points on the lattice to refine the shape of your surface. Make sure to check the shape in the perspective window. Your reference drawings are just a reference. Feel free to make artistic changes while modeling in order to achieve the look you want.

b. Select NurbSphere1, then go to Edit > Delete by Type > History. This will remove the lattice, but any changes that have been made are now permanent.

c. Rename NurbSphere1 to rightPalm_geo by clicking on the name and typing in the Channel box.

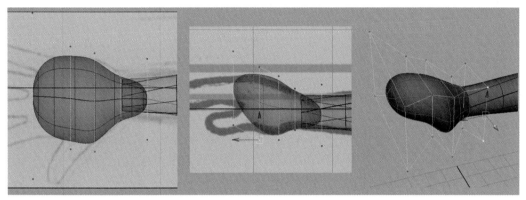

FIG. 13-94 Adjusting the lattice for additional divisions and reshaping the lattice to make the sphere into a palm.

7. Create another NURBS sphere (Create > NURBS Primitives > Sphere).
   a. In the Channel box, change "RotateZ" to 90.
   b. Move and scale the sphere over the character's right index finger.
   c. In the INPUTS section of the Channel box, click on makeNurbSphere1 and change Spans to 8.
8. With the NurbSphere1 still selected, create a Lattice Deformer Create Deformers > Lattice.
   a. Starting at the palm area, in the front view panel, right-click on top of the lattice and choose Lattice Point. (You may need to right-click in the perspective window if your lattice is close to the geometry, in order to see the correct marking menu.) In the front view panel, use your Move tool by pressing W on the keyboard to click-drag (or marquee-drag) over points on the lattice (this ensures that you are selecting the points on both sides of the lattice) and move them around to refine the shape of your surface. Then starting at the palm area, in the top view panel, continue to move the points on the lattice to refine the shape of your surface. Make sure to check the shape in the perspective window. Your reference drawings are just a reference. Feel free to make artistic changes while modeling in order to achieve the look you want.
   b. Select NurbSphere1, then go to Edit > Delete by Type > History. This will remove the lattice but any changes that have been made are now permanent.
   c. Rename NurbSphere1 to rightIndex_geo by clicking on the name and typing in the Channel box.

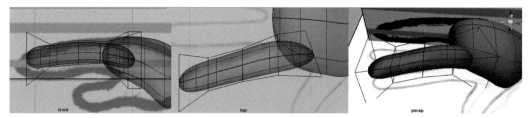

FIG. 13-95 Making the index finger.

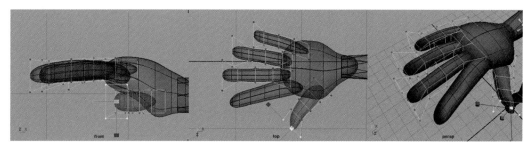

FIG. 13-96 Making the fingers and thumb.

9. Repeat steps 7 and 8 for each finger and the thumb, renaming them rightMiddle_geo, rightRing_geo, rightPinky_geo, and rightThumb_geo.
10. Duplicate the hand for the left side.
    a. Select rightPalm_geo and duplicate (Edit > Duplicate or press Ctrl+D). In the Channel box, rename rightPalm_geo1 to leftPalm_geo, change the TranslateX value to positive (which positions the arm onto the other side of the origin), and change the ScaleY value to negative (which makes the palm invert).
11. Repeat this process for each finger.
12. Select rightPalm_geo, rightIndex_geo, rightMiddle_geo, rightRing_geo, rightPinky_geo, rightThumb_geo, leftPalm_geo, leftIndex_geo, leftMiddle_geo, leftRing_geo, leftPinky_geo, and leftThumb_geo and apply Modify > Freeze Transformations. Freezing Transformations on finished geometry will return the translation and rotation values to 0 and the scale values to 1.
13. In the Layer Editor of the Channel box, right-click and hold on top of the geometry_layer and choose Add Selected Objects.
14. Save your scene file.
    a. Go to File . Save as.
    b. Name your scene 13_assgn04_hand_geo.ma.

Model a Foot

1. Open Maya and set your project. Go to File > Project > Set… browse to your project folder and click OK.
2. Open your last saved file. Go to File > Open and select 13_asgn04_hand_geo.ma.

3. Continue working in X-ray mode and wireframe on shaded.
4. Continue working with Interactive Creation unchecked (Create > NURBS Primitives > Interactive Creation).
5. Create a NURBS sphere (Create > NURBS Primitives > Sphere).
   a. Move and scale the sphere over the character's right foot.
   b. In the INPUTS section of the Channel box, click on makeNurbSphere1 and change Spans to 6.

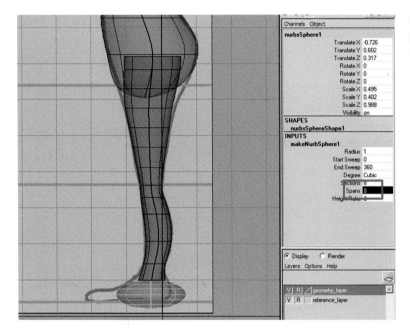

FIG. 13-97 Creating a NURBS sphere, positioning it for the foot, and dividing it for adequate deformation.

6. With the NurbSphere1 still selected, create a Lattice Deformer. Create > Deformers > Lattice.
   a. In the Shapes section of the Channel box, change the T divisions to 2 and the U divisions to 5. Starting at the ankle area, in the side view panel, right-click on top of the lattice and choose Lattice Point. (You may need to right-click in the perspective window if your lattice is close to the geometry, in order to see the correct marking menu.) In the front view panel, use your Move tool by pressing W on the keyboard to click-drag (or marquee-drag) over points on the lattice (this ensures that you are selecting the points on both sides of the lattice) and move them around to refine the shape of your surface. Check the shape in the perspective window. Reshape the front of the foot. Your reference drawings are just a reference. Feel free to make artistic changes while modeling in order to achieve the look you want.
   b. Select NurbSphere1, then go to Edit > Delete by Type > History. This will remove the lattice, but any changes that have been made are now permanent.

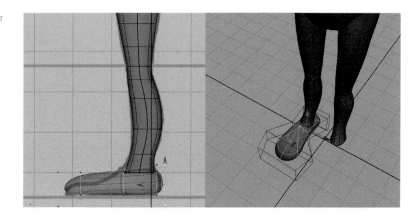

FIG. 13-98 Adjusting the lattice for additional divisions and reshaping the lattice to make the sphere into a foot.

c. Rename NurbSphere1 to rightFoot_geo by clicking on the name and typing in the Channel box.

d. Select rightFoot_geo and duplicate (Edit > Duplicate or press Ctrl+D). In the Channel box, rename rightFoot_geo1 to leftFoot_geo, change the TranslateX value to positive (which positions the foot onto the other side of the origin), and change the ScaleX value to negative (which makes the foot invert).

e. Select rightFoot_geo and leftFoot_geo (Modify > Freeze Transformations). Freezing transformations on finished geometry will return the translation and rotation values to 0 and the scale values to 1.

f. In the Layer Editor of the Channel box, right-click and hold on top of the geometry_layer and choose Add Selected Objects.

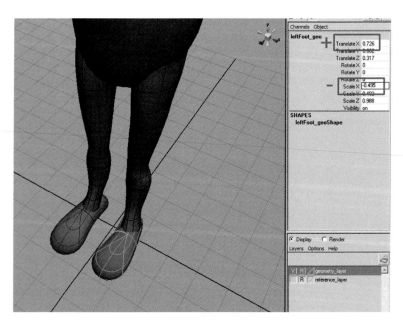

FIG. 13-99 Duplicating the right foot to create the left foot.

g. Save your scene file:
— Go to File > Save as.
h. Name your scene 13_asgn05_foot_geo.ma.

Model Eyes

1. Open Maya and set your project. Go to File > Project > Set... browse to your project folder and click OK.
2. Open your last saved file. Go to File > Open and select 13_asgn05_foot_geo.ma.
3. Continue working in X-ray mode and wireframe on shaded.
4. Continue working with Interactive Creation (Create > NURBS Primitives > Interactive Creation).
5. Turn your geometry_layer to invisible by clicking and hiding the V next to the layer.
6. Go to Create > NURBS Primitives > Sphere > option box. Change the Axis to Z and the Spans to 6. Click Create.
7. Rename NurbSphere1 to eyeball_geo by clicking on the name and typing in the Channel box.

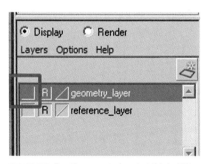

FIG. 13-100 Turn the geometry layer invisible by hiding the V in the Layer Editor.

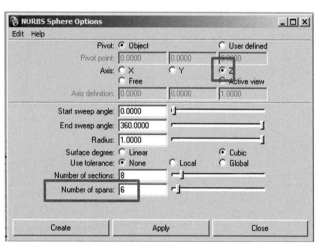

FIG. 13-101 The NURBS sphere option box.

8. Hold your cursor over the sphere and right-click and hold, and select Assign New Material > Phong. (Phong is a reflective material when rendered. You may want to try a different material to achieve your desired look.) The attribute editor will open. Rename the material eye_phong.
   a. In Attribute Material window, click on the checkered square next to the Color. Create Render Node will appear. Select 2D Textures—Ramp. Press 6 to see how the material looks on the sphere.
   b. Change the Ramp Attribute Type to a U Ramp.
   c. Click on the blue circle of color, then click on the blue box in the Selected Color section; this opens the color picker, where you can

change the color to a very dark blue, almost black. You really should never use black, as black is very flat and creates a visual death on the screen.

d. Click on the red circle of color, then click on the red box in the Selected Color section; this opens the color picker, where you can change the color to a very pale orange—almost white. For the same reasons as black, you really should never use white, either.

e. Click on the green circle of color, then click on the green box in the Selected Color section; this opens the color picker, where you can change the color to the color chosen for your character's eye color. You will also need to click inside of the ramp rectangle to create a fourth circle of color, which allows you to make your eyes two-toned for more interest.

f. Click and drag the circles up and down to adjust their position. The closer the circles are to each other, the sharper the edge of color.

FIG. 13-102 Adjusting the ramp attributes.

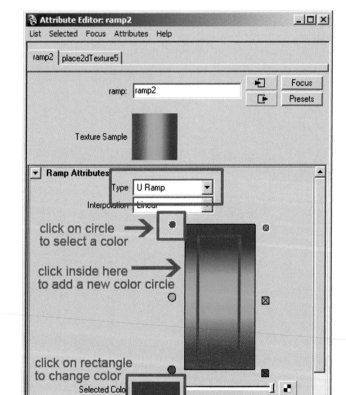

Don't be afraid to add more detail or your own ideas. For example, all eyes have a thin, dark ring around the outside of the iris called a limbus line. You could add this detail, because it also adds quite of bit of visual interest.

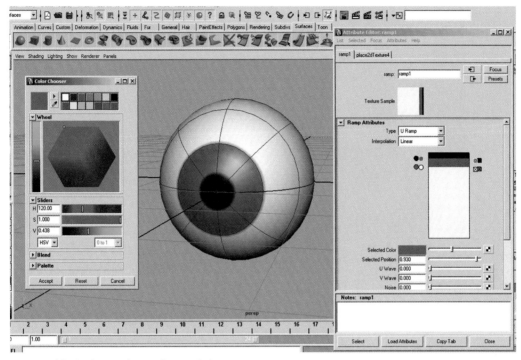

FIG. 13-103 Adjusting the ramp colors to make an eye shader.

9. Go to Create > NURBS primitives > Sphere > option box. Change the Axis to X, the Start sweep angle to 55, and the End sweep angle to 355. Click Create.

10. In the Channel box, in the INPUTS section, click on the makeNurbSphere, which reveals additional attributes, including Start Sweep and End Sweep, which will allow your character to blink. You can test this out by clicking on the WORD Start Sweep, then click and drag the middle mouse button in a view panel to see the eye blink. Make sure to undo this motion by pressing Z on the keyboard.

   a. Rename NurbSphere1 to eyelid_geo by clicking on the name and typing in the Channel box.

   b. In the Channel box, change RotateX to 206 (your value may be different), and ScaleX, ScaleY, ScaleZ to 1.02.

   c. Add dimension to the eyelid. Add a couple additional horizontal isoparms to the eyelid. To insert a single isoparm, right-click and hold over a surface (which brings up the marking menu), choose Isoparms (which brings you into component level), click and drag on an isoparm on the surface near to where you want to add one, drag it into position, then select Edit NURBS > Insert Isoparms.

   d. Right-click on top of the eyelid and choose HULLS.

   e. Select a hull near the edge of the upper eyelid, then Shift-select a hull near the edge of the lower eyelid.

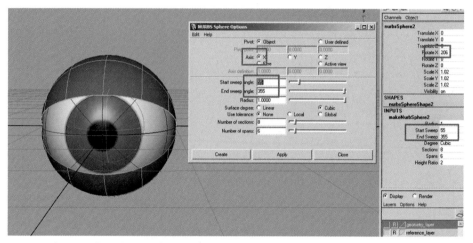

FIG. 13-104 Creating another NURBS sphere for the eyelid.

f. Right-click on top of the eyelid and choose Control Vertex.

g. Hold down the Ctrl key and drag-select each pole to deselect it.

h. Use the Scale tool to scale out a lip around the edge of the eyelid.

i. If you want to reshape your eye to something other than spherical, you can now add a lattice. Select both eyeball_geo and eyelid_geo, then Create Deformers > Lattice.

— Open the outliner and select both fftd1Lattice and fftd1Base. You will need to scale these up so that reshaping them doesn't cause intersection problems between the eyelid and eyeball when the eyelid closes.

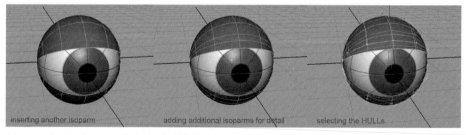

FIG. 13-105 Inserting isoparms and selecting the HULLS.

FIG. 13-106 Reshaping the eyelid to add dimension.

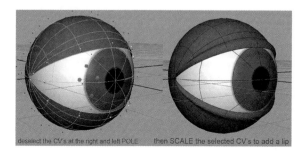

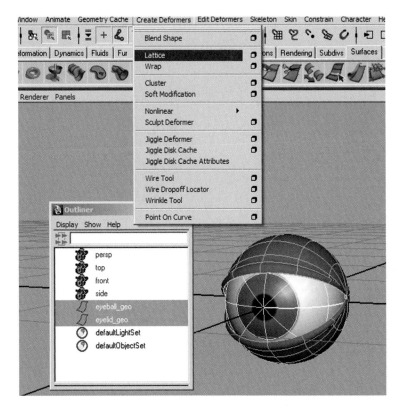

FIG. 13-107 Adding a Lattice Deformer to the eye and eyelid.

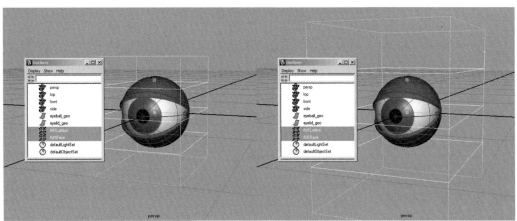

FIG. 13-108 Scaling both the lattice and the base larger.

— You can reshape the lattice by right-clicking on the lattice and moving the lattice points with the move tool by pressing W on the keyboard. If the eyeball starts to intersect the eyelid, scale the eyelid up slightly.

j. Open the outliner (Windows > Outliner). Select eyeball_geo, eyelid_geo, fftd1Lattice, and fftd1Base, and (if you have a Lattice and Base),

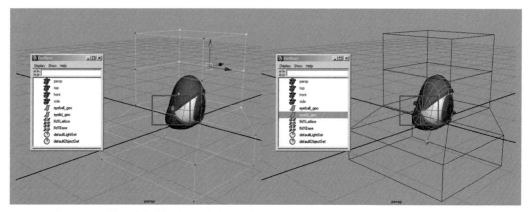

FIG. 13-109 Exposing part of the eyeball while reshaping the lattice (left) can be alleviated by scaling the eyelid slightly larger (right).

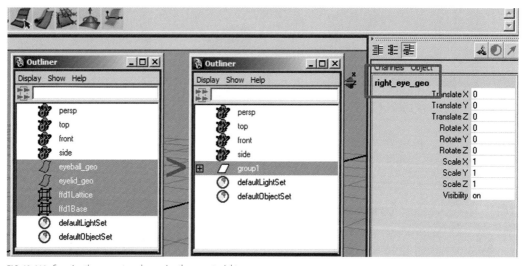

FIG. 13-110 Grouping the eye parts and renaming the group to right_eye_geo.

press Ctrl+G to group them together. Rename group1 to right_eye_geo by clicking on the name and typing in the Channel box.

k. Turn your geometry_layer to visible by clicking on the first empty box; V will appear next to the layer.

l. Select the right_eye_geo group in the outliner and move the eye into place. You can also scale this group if necessary. Adjust the lattice if needed as well, once the eye group is in position. Make sure that you do not move the individual pieces of the eye, as this will cause problems when the eye needs to rotate later.

m. Duplicate the eye (Edit > Duplicate Special > option box). Check "Duplicate input graph." Rename right_eye_geo1 to left_eye_geo. This keeps the input (makeNurbSphere), which is necessary for blinking.

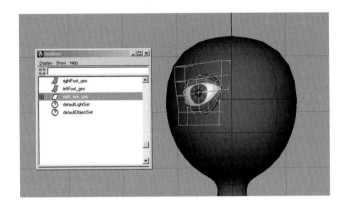

FIG. 13-111 Repositioning the right_eye_group.

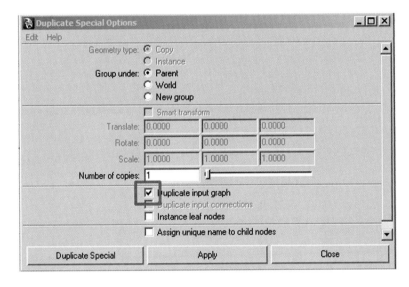

FIG. 13-112 The Duplicate Special option box with the "Duplicate input graph" option checked.

n. Change the TranslateX value of left_eye_geo to positive (which positions the eye onto the other side of the origin) and change the ScaleX value to negative (which makes the eye invert).

o. Select both lattice and hide them by pressing Ctrl+H.

p. Do *not* freeze tranformations or delete history on your eyes! Doing so will remove the shape changes and the lattice, as well as the INPUTS for makeNurbSphere, which is needed to create eye blinks.

q. Select right_eye_geo and left_eye_geo. In the Layer Editor of the Channel box, right-click and hold on top of the geometry_layer and choose Add Selected Objects.

11. Save your scene file.

   a. Go to File > Save as.

   b. Name your scene 13_asgn06_eye_geo.ma.

413

Adding Detail to the Face

You can continue to add additional spheres that are shaped by lattices to create the nose, mouth, and eyebrows. The technique that follows shows how to create those features and keep them as part of the head, instead of separate geometry.

1. Open Maya and set your project. Go to File > Project > Set… browse to your project folder and click OK.
2. Open your last saved file. Go to File > Open and select 13_asgn06_eye_geo.ma.
3. Continue working in X-ray mode and wireframe on shaded.
4. Continue working with Interactive Creation (Create > NURBS Primitives > Interactive Creation).
5. To add detail to the head:
   a. Add a couple additional vertical isoparms where the eyes would be. To insert a single isoparm, right-click and hold over a surface (which brings up the marking menu), choose Isoparms (which brings you into component level), click and drag on an isoparm on the surface near to where you want to add one, drag it into position, then select Edit NURBS > Insert Isoparms.

FIG. 13-113 Adding an isoparm.

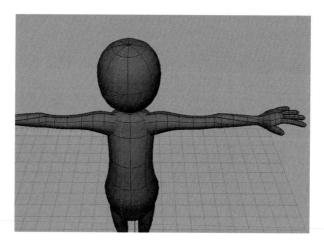

   b. Add additional horizontal isoparms as needed. You can add multiple isoparms at the same time by right-clicking and holding over a surface, choosing Isoparms, and Shift-selecting two isoparms. Open the Edit NURBS > Insert Isoparms > option box. Choose Between Selections and then type in the number of isoparms to insert.
   c. Use the Sculpt Geometry Tool (Edit NURBS > Sculpt Geometry Tool > option box) to pull out a nose for your character.
   d. With the view panel active, hold the mouse over the surface, hold down the B key, and middle-click and drag to interactively adjust the size of the brush.

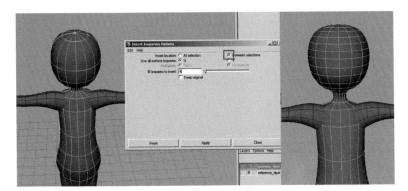

FIG. 13-114 Adding additional isoparms using the option for between selections.

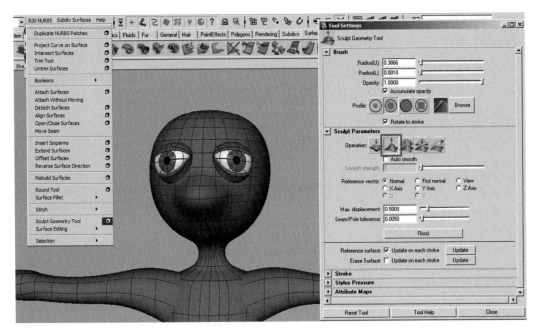

FIG. 13-115 Creating a nose shape.

    e. You can use the reflection option under the Stroke tab for creating the same changes on both sides of the face at once. This can be helpful for pulling out eyebrows. Also make sure that you reduce the maximum displacement from 1 to 2 so that the eyebrows are not pulled out as far.

    f. Continue to add isoparms to create the necessary detail. The more detail you want, the more isoparms are needed.

    g. Right-click over the geometry and choose Control Vertex in order to select CVs in the mouth area and pull them into make a mouth.

6. Save your scene file.

    a. Go to File > Save as. This should open the scenes folder of your project (assuming that you set the project as in step 1).

    b. Name your scene 13_asgn07_faceDetail_geo.ma.

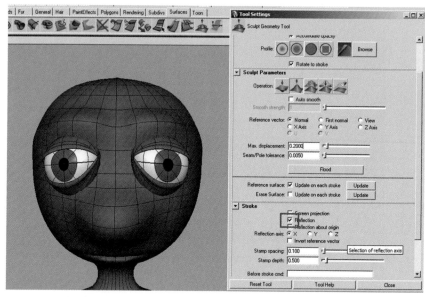

FIG. 13-116 Use the reflection option to create eyebrows.

Model Ears, Hair, and Accessories

This is an optional assignment, as not all characters have hair or ears. However, the ears a can change the appearance of your character and add an element that allows for character, personality, and a way of conveying expression.

This is not a step-by-step tutorial. Rather, you can use techniques learned so far to create ears and hair. A simple way of creating an ear is to begin with a sphere on the z-axis with eight spans, position it near the head, and scale it on the x-axis to create the proper thickness. Add a Lattice Deformer and reshape the lattice points to create an ear. Delete history and duplicate for the other side, changing the TranslateX value to positive, the ScaleX to negative, and rotate to position as needed.

FIG. 13-117 Creating an ear using a NURBS sphere.

A similar approach using a NURBS sphere and a lattice can be used to create the hair.

Try experimenting with a NURBS cone and nonlinear deformers, such as bend and twist. Make sure to add adequate spans to the cone before adding the deformer, so that the geometry will bend properly.

FIG. 13-118 Creating hair using a NURBS sphere.

FIG. 13-119 Curly hair using a NURBS cone.

Accessories, such as hats, ties, and other props can be modeled in similar ways. Hats, for example, can be created using a profile curve and revolving a surface, much like we did for the head and neck.

Combining Everything into a Single Polygonal Shape with Additional Approaches to Modeling Hands and Feet

1. Open Maya and set your project. Go to File > Project > Set... browse to your project folder and click OK.
2. Open your last saved file. Go to File > Open and select 13_asgn07_faceDetail_geo.ma.

417

3. Continue working in X-ray mode and wireframe on shaded.
4. Select all the body geometry. Use the outliner (Window > Outliner) or the Hypergraph (Window > Hypergraph > Hierarchy) to verify that all body geometry is selected. Do not select the eyes and eyelids. Select Modify > Convert > NURBS to Polygons except for the eyes and eyelids.
5. Delete the history on all converted polygons. Edit > Delete by Type > History.
6. Delete NURBS geometry, except for the eyes and eyelids.
7. Delete half of your model (right-click over geometry > FACES, select the faces and hit Delete): all except the eyes and hair, if any.
8. With the geometry still selected, combine separate polygonal pieces into one (Mesh > Combine).

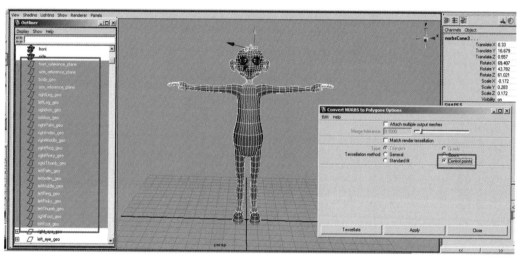

FIG. 13-120 Converting NURBS to polygons.

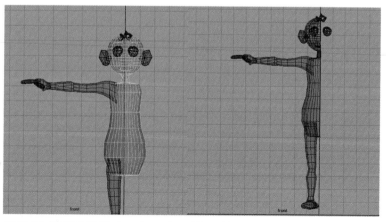

FIG. 13-121 Selecting half of the faces of your polygonal face and torso.

Note: You may want to review the box modeling section that follows for the hands and feet. It is easier to delete the NURBS geometry at this time, rather than deleting the polygonal faces after combining.

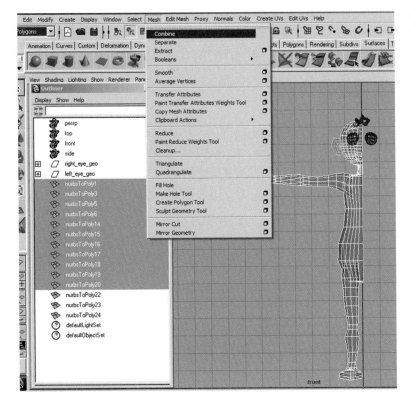

FIG. 13-122 Combining all polygonal surfaces into one.

9. Delete the history on polySurface1 and rename polySurface1 to body_geo.
10. Determine whether there are equal numbers of edges on the two areas that need to be attached, and add additional geometry where needed. Edit Mesh > Insert Edge Loop Tool. Click on an edge and drag the new edge into place.
11. Delete any overlapping geometry (right-click over the geometry, choose FACES, select the faces that you want to remove and hit the Delete key).
12. Using the Move tool by pressing W on the keyboard; hold down the V key and move-snap vertex points to line up with the other point nearby.
13. Select the row of overlapping vertices and merge vertices (Edit Mesh > Merge).
14. Save your scene file.
    a. Go to File > Save as.
15. Name your scene 13_asgn09_01_convert_to_polys_geo.ma.

FIG. 13-123 Add a new edge in order to align the torso with the leg.

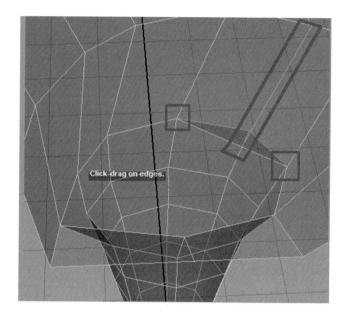

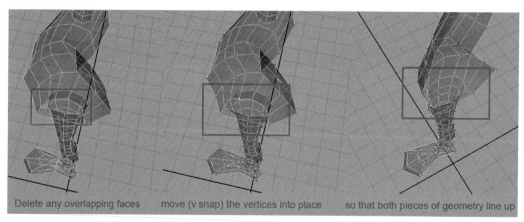

Delete any overlapping faces   move (v snap) the vertices into place   so that both pieces of geometry line up

FIG. 13-124 Aligning the torso vertices with the leg vertices.

You can repeat the process of deleting overlapping geometry, adding additional edges, V-snapping vertex points, and merging vertices for each separate body part. However, in the cases of the foot and the hand, it is easier to delete the existing parts and remodel them using the box modeling technique as shown in the following tutorials. Remember, deleting the foot and hand should be done before combining polygonal surfaces, as it is more difficult to select the overlapping geometry than it is to delete an entire uncombined object.

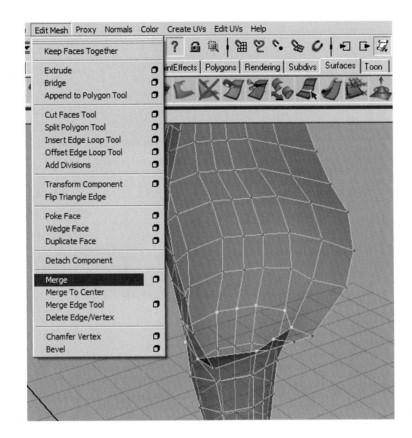

FIG. 13-125 Merging the overlapping vertices.

Box Modeling a Foot

1. If you have not deleted the foot as suggested earlier, remove the existing foot geometry if it was converted and combined: right-click over the foot geometry, choose FACES, select the faces that you want to remove, and hit the Delete key.
2. Create a polygonal cube (Create > Polygon Primitives > Cube > option box) and divide the width and depth to 2. Reposition it to where the foot should be, scaling as needed.
3. Right-click over the cube, choose FACES, select the top faces, and hit the Delete key.
4. Select the cube, Shift-select the body_geo, and combine them into one piece (Mesh > Combine).
5. Right-click over the cube and choose VERTEX. Using the Move tool by pressing W on the keyboard; hold down the V key and select a vertex to move-snap vertex points to line up with the other point nearby.
6. Delete the history on polySurface1 and rename polySurface1 to body_geo.
7. Select the row of overlapping vertices and merge vertices (Edit Mesh > Merge).

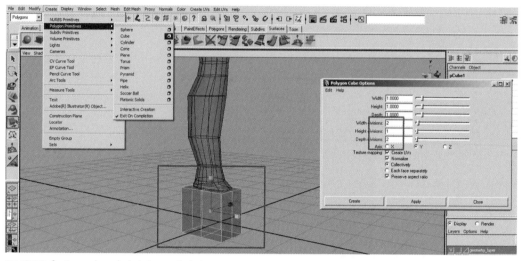

FIG. 13-126 Creating a polygonal cube to become the foot.

FIG. 13-127 Snapping the vertices of the cube to those of the leg.

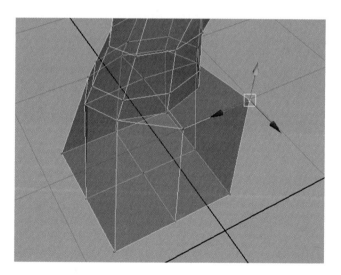

8. In the side view panel, right-click over the foot geometry, choose VERTEX, and select and move the bottom row of vertices to line up with your reference drawing.

9. Right-click over the foot geometry and choose FACES. In perspective view panel, select the two front faces and go to Edit Mesh > Extrude. Click on the little blue circle, and drag the arrow forward, which will extrude your polygons in world space, perpendicular to the graph. Do not extrude all the way to the tip of the foot; extrude only about a third of the way there.

10. Hit the G key to extrude again, and click on the blue circle before dragging the arrow forward, about halfway to the tip of the foot.

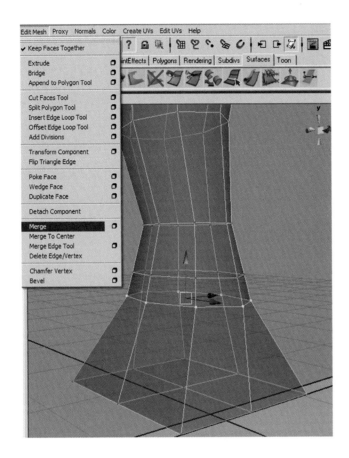

FIG. 13-128 Merging the overlapping vertices of the foot and leg.

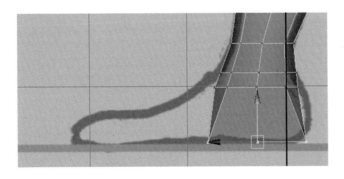

FIG. 13-129 Adjusting the bottom row of vertices.

11. Hit the G key to extrude again, and click on the blue circle before dragging the arrow forward, to the tip of the foot.
12. Right-click over the foot geometry, choose VERTEX, and use the Move tool to reshape the vertices into the shape of the foot. Be sure to not cross the origin line.

423

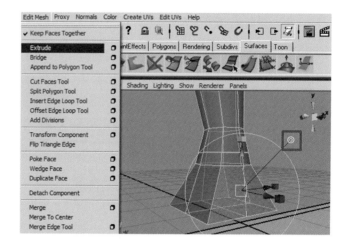

FIG. 13-130 Extruding the foot parallel by first clicking on the blue circle (shown yellow in this image, because it is already selected), then clicking on the arrow to drag the extrusion forward.

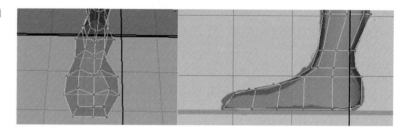

FIG. 13-131 Reshaping the extruded faces into a foot.

Box Modeling a Hand

1. If you have not deleted the hand as suggested earlier, remove the existing hand geometry if it was converted and combined. Right-click on the hand geometry, choose FACES, select the faces that you want to remove, and hit the Delete key.
2. Create a polygon cube and divide the width, height, and depth by 2 and reposition it to where the hand should be, scaling as appropriate.

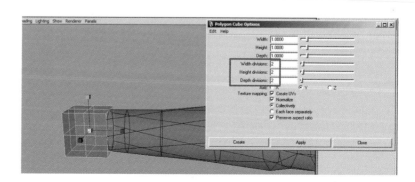

FIG. 13-132 Creating a polygonal cube to become the hand.

3. Right-click on the cube, choose FACES, select the side faces closest to the wrist, and hit the Delete key.
4. In the front and top view panel, right-click on the hand geometry, choose VERTEX, and select and move the vertices to line up with your reference drawing.

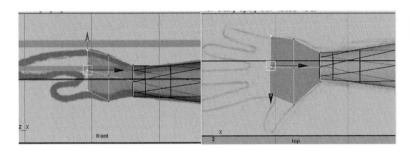

FIG. 13-133 Reshaping the cube into a palm.

5. Determine where the fingers will be and add additional geometry where needed Edit Mesh > Insert Edge Loop Tool. Click on an edge and drag the new edge into place. (It might be a great idea to limit your character's fingers to a thumb and two fingers for the first time you create one, as it takes additional time to create and control four fingers and a thumb.)

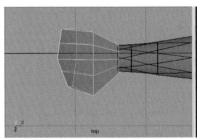
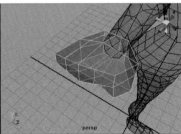

FIG. 13-134 Adding additional edges to divide the geometry for fingers.

6. Extrude the fingers:
   a. Before extruding, make sure that you'll get separate faces during the extrusion. Make sure to uncheck Edit Mesh > Keep Faces Together (right-click on the hand geometry and choose FACES). In the perspective view panel, select the faces where the fingers will be.
   b. Select Edit Mesh > Extrude. In the top view panel, drag the arrow forward, which will extrude your polygons. Do not extrude all the way to the tip of the fingers; rather, extrude only about a third of the way there (to the first knuckle). Then click on one of the scale boxes.
   c. Click on the center scale box, and middle-click and drag to scale the fingers slightly and separate the end faces. This will make it easier to reposition the vertices, because they will not be overlapping.

FIG. 13-135 Making sure that Keep Faces Together is unchecked.

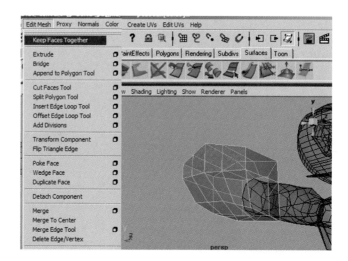

FIG. 13-136 Extruding the fingers to the first knuckle.

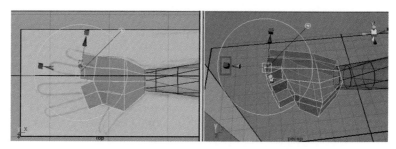

FIG. 13-137 Scaling the extrusion to separate the fingers.

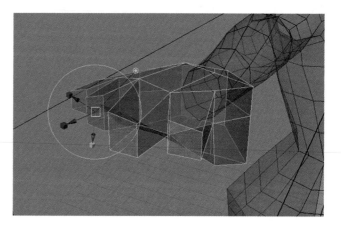

d. Using the Move tool by pressing W on the keyboard, in the top and front view panel, reposition the end row of vertices for each finger.

e. Right-click on the hand geometry, choose FACES. In the perspective view panel, select the end faces of each finger and go to Edit Mesh > Extrude. In the top view panel, drag the arrow forward, which will extrude your polygons. Do not extrude all the way to the tip of the

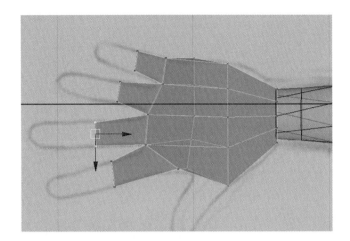

FIG. 13-138 Adjusting the positions of the finger geometry.

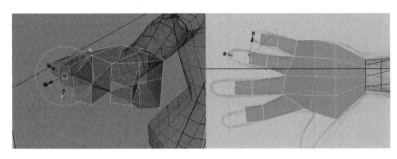

FIG. 13-139 Extruding the fingers to the second knuckle.

fingers; rather, extrude only about a half of the way there (to the second knuckle).

f. Using the Move tool by pressing W on the keyboard, in the top and front view panel, reposition the end row of vertices for each finger.

g. Right-click on the hand geometry and choose FACES. In the perspective view panel, select the end faces of each finger and go to Edit Mesh > Extrude.

h. In the top view panel, drag the arrow forward, which will extrude your polygons, all the way to the tip of the fingers.

i. Using the Move tool by pressing w on the keyboard, in the top and front view panel, reposition the end row of vertices for each finger.

7. Extrude the thumb:

a. Right-click on the hand geometry and choose FACES. In the perspective view panel, select the face where the thumb will be and go to Edit Mesh > Extrude.

b. In the top view panel, drag the arrow forward, which will extrude your polygons. Do not extrude all the way to the tip of the thumb; rather, extrude only about a half of the way there (to the first knuckle).

c. Using the Move tool by pressing W on the keyboard, in the top and perspective view panel, reposition the end row of vertices for the thumb.

FIG. 13-140 Extruding the fingers to the tip.

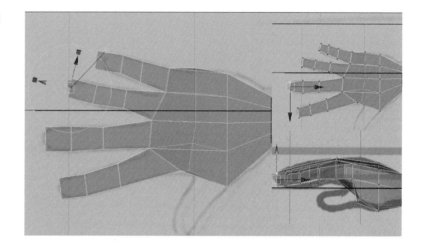

FIG. 13-141 Extruding the thumb to the first knuckle.

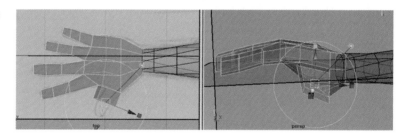

d. Right-click over the hand geometry and choose FACES. In the perspective view panel, select the end face of the thumb and go to Edit Mesh > Extrude.

e. In the top view panel, drag the arrow forward, which will extrude your polygons all the way to the tip of the thumb.

f. Using the Move tool by pressing W on the keyboard, in the top and perspective view panel, reposition the end row of vertices for the thumb.

FIG. 13-142 Extruding the thumb.

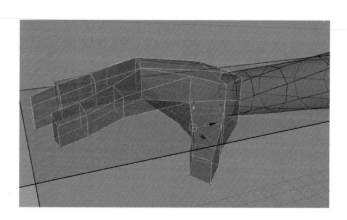

8. Combine the hand with the existing body_geo:
    a. Determine whether there are equal numbers of edges on the two areas that need to be attached, and add additional geometry where needed (Edit Mesh > Insert Edge Loop Tool). Click on an edge and drag the new edge into place.

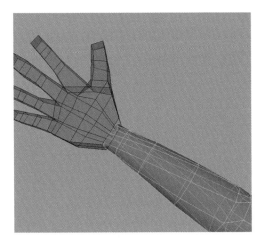

FIG. 13-143 Inserting a new edge in order to align the arm with the hand.

    b. In object mode (press F8 on the keyboard, with the selection tool), press Q, select the hand, Shift-select the body_geo, and combine them into one piece (Mesh > Combine).

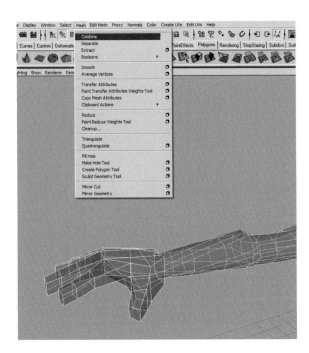

FIG. 13-144 Combining the hand and body geometry.

c. Right-click on the hand and choose VERTEX, then right-click over the arm and choose VERTEX. Using the Move tool by pressing W on the keyboard, hold down the V key and select a vertex to move-snap vertex points to line up with the other point nearby.

d. Select the row of overlapping vertices and merge vertices (Edit Mesh > Merge).

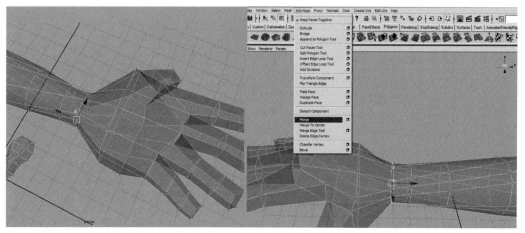

FIG. 13-145 Aligning the hand and arm vertices, then merging them.

e. Delete the history on polySurface1 and rename polySurface1 to body_geo.

9. Save your scene file.

a. Go to File > Save as.
   Name your scene 13_asgn09_02_convert_to_polys_geo.ma.

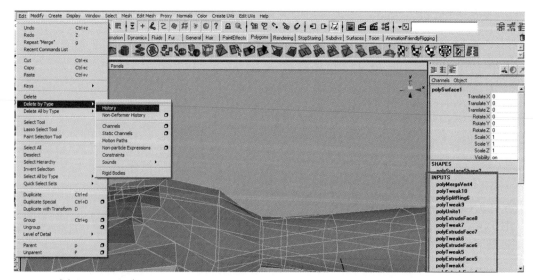

FIG. 13-146 Deleting construction history.

Ears and hair will also need to be deleted and remodeled using the box modeling approach, as this method is less tedious than trying to combine the spheres and cones originally used in the NURBS model with the polygonal topology of the head. It is perfectly fine to keep the hair separate. It really depends on how much time you want to dedicate to your model. Do not combine any accessories, such as ties or hats. These geometry pieces should remain separate so that they can be removed or controlled independently from the character's body.

Once you have combined everything into one half of your character, create the other side. Make sure that all of the interior vertices are lined up on the origin. When you mirror, you will know immediately whether there is a problem. You will probably need to delete the faces at the top of the head, near the pole, and then append them using Edit Mesh > Append Polygon Tool. Click on one edge, then click on another edge and hit the Enter key to finish the process. Remember to keep everything as quadrangles. In order to do this, you may also need to use the Edit Mesh _Split Polygon Tool.

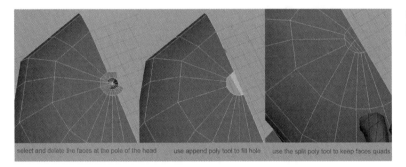

FIG. 13-147 Fixing the pole at the head into fewer quads.

select and delete the faces at the pole of the head   use append poly tool to fill hole   use the split poly tool to keep faces quads

1. Select body_geo and go to Mesh > Mirror Geometry.

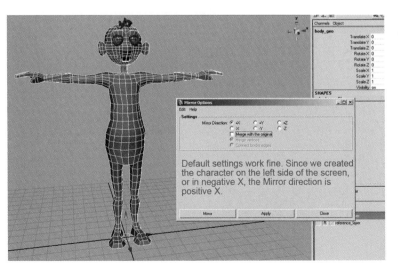

FIG. 13-148 Mirroring the right side to create the left side.

2. Pay close attention to the mouth area. You may need to separate the vertices (using the Move tool) before merging so that they do not merge the mouth shut in the center, then reposition them after the mirror is successful.

FIG. 13-149 Mirroring usually causes the mouth vertices to pinch.

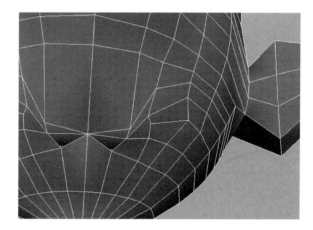

3. Once the mirroring is complete, check your normals to verify their position (Display > Polygons > Face Normals).

FIG. 13-150 Checking the position of the face normals.

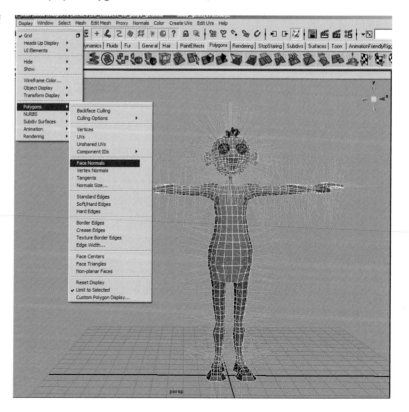

4. If any are flipped inward, change their direction by selecting the geometry and first going to Normals > Conform. This usually solves the problem; however, you may have to reverse them all if they now all face inward. If so, then Normals > Reverse will correct their direction. To hide the normals again, go to Display > Polygons > Face Normals.
5. Once you have all of the normals facing outward, you can select the entire object in object mode and go to Normals > Average Normals to make the geometry appear smoother without adding more physical geometry.
6. Delete the history on body_geo (Edit > Delete by Type > History).
7. Save your scene file:
   a. Go to File > Save as.
   b. Name your scene 13_asgn09_03_convert_to_polys_geo.ma.

As mentioned earlier in the chapter, a NURBS character is quick and easy with the approach covered in the assignments. However, if you would like to create a seamless character or to have better control over texturing, you must convert your character into polygonal surfaces.

Remember that the first time you model your character, you may not end up with the desired look. Do not be afraid to scrap the areas that are not working and start again.

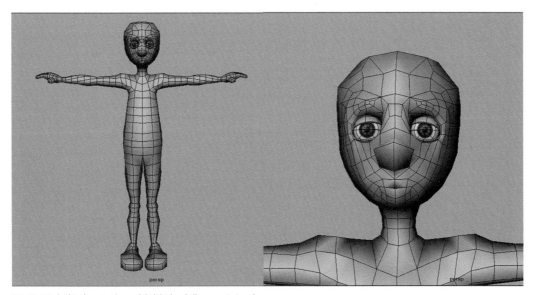

FIG. 13-151 In this character, I remodeled the head all over again in polygons.

CHAPTER 14

Creating Your First Biped Character: Facial Expressions Using Maya

Former Student Spotlight: Katie Folsom

The one thing that I'm still finding out—especially with rigging and animation—is that there will always be surprises, no matter how much you think you have things planned out. There is no way to avoid surprises, especially in the beginning. The good news is they do diminish over time. However, I feel that the best way to keep the number of surprises to a minimum is through consistency, organization, and plain old understanding. It sounds like a no-brainer, but you would be surprised at how easy it is to get lost in the process. Whether it's your naming conventions or the order in which you work, you will find that anything you might have avoided in an earlier stage will not leave you alone unless the problem is solved right away. In the end, it can really affect the quality of your work.

I think I had the most trouble with my blend shapes. I thought that I could just fix them when I got to that part of the animation, and I just really wanted to move on. Without going into too much detail, I ended up doing the second half of my project twice, spending time that I could have spent on fine-tuning and making my animation look better. Another thing I had to spend a lot of time getting right was rigging the hands. I had ten fingers and a lot of hand movement in my first short, so they had to be right. The orientation of the joints and the joint placement was something I had to keep going back and forth with. A lot of it is trial and error. With that being said, take the time to really understand what it is you're doing and whether it's the best way. Don't just go through the motions and think it's going to work to its full potential. Don't let the technical part of the process affect the artistic part. If you do breeze through it the first time, you got lucky.

From 1999 to 2001, Katie Folsom was a student at the University of Cincinnati in DAAP and graduated from Savannah College of Art and Design in 2004 with a BFA in computer art. Her professional experience includes the feature film Barnyard, *released in August 2006. You can see some of her work at http://www.katiefolsom.com.*

FIG. 14-1 "Sticky" by Katie Folsom (2003).

Workflow

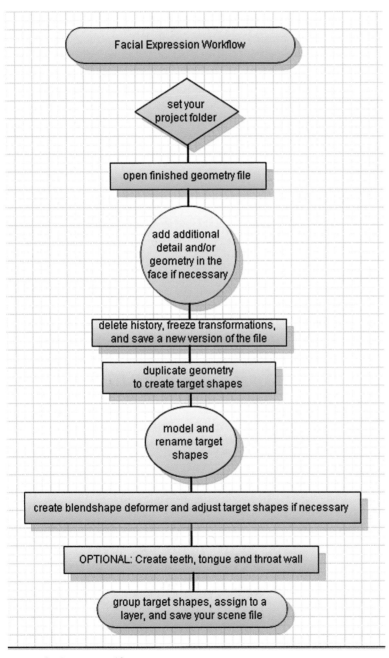

FIG. 14-2 Facial expression workflow.

Introduction

Facial expressions are a crucial part of your character's ability to communicate. Most of what your character feels will be articulated via facial expressions. Face language is universal. For example, we can instantly tell when someone is worried, happy, or sad based on the position of their eyebrows, cheeks, and mouth, no matter what language he or she speaks.

FIG. 14-3 The concept expressions for "Bernie," by David Leonard.

Depending on the amount of time allotted to preparing your character's facial expressions, you can create different levels of complexities. For example, you could create a worried face with eyebrows that are pinched together and lowered, and lips that are slightly pursed. Instead of creating a single worried expression, you could separate the eye and eyebrows as a separate shape from the mouth shape. For even further control, you could create asymmetrical poses for the left and right sides, ending up with four separate shapes that when combined create the worried expression.

You might be thinking to yourself, "Why spend time separating these single expressions into four or more partial shapes that need to be combined in order to achieve a single expression?" The answer is fairly simple. When you create independent pieces, you can assemble those pieces with others to create new facial expressions that were not necessarily planned.

The following facial expressions are the ones that I recommend you create. This is a list that I feel gives you the most possibilities with a minimum amount of work. I've divided them into eye, nose, and mouth areas. The eyebrows should be broken into left and right, for greater control.

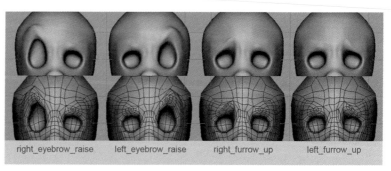

right_eyebrow_raise   left_eyebrow_raise   right_furrow_up   left_furrow_up

FIG. 14-4

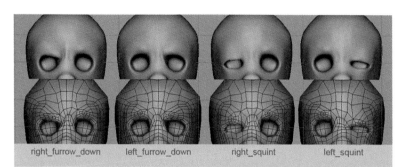

FIG. 14-5 Wireframe on shaded on the low-poly model prior to smoothing.

right_furrow_down   left_furrow_down   right_squint   left_squint

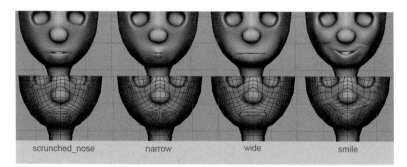

FIG. 14-6 The geometry smoothed.

scrunched_nose   narrow   wide   smile

Blend Shapes as an Approach to Creating Facial Expressions

There are two common approaches primarily used when creating facial expressions: blend shape–driven poses and joint-driven poses. In this chapter, we will be focusing on the former, as the joint-driven process assumes that you already have an understanding of joints and skin deformers. The joint-driven process is used for animation in the gaming field, because at this time, game engines do not support blend shapes.

A "blend shape" is a deformer that changes the shape of one piece of geometry to look like the shape of another. This deformer has also been referred to as a "morph," because its concept is based on a metamorphosis. Blend shapes can be used for pretty much any type of morphing. Although this chapter focuses on facial expressions, they can also be used in the rest of the body, such as muscle motion and making sure that the body geometry bends appropriately in areas such as elbows and knees, a process known as "corrective" blend shapes.

Once you do understand joints and the skinning process, you can actually use joints to create your blend shapes.

439

Before creating blend shapes, it is extremely important to finalize the geometry. Your finished geometry is considered your base shape. The base shape is duplicated into the target shapes (as many times as necessary), and each target shape is remodeled (with certain limitations) to reflect the desired facial expressions. Blend shapes work by comparing the positions based on the order of individual points in the surface (points such as vertices or CVs). Each point is numbered, so if you alter the geometry by adding or subtracting points, the blend shape will no longer work and an error message will be given. For this reason, you must finish the face model before creating blend shapes. The more refined and detailed the facial expression, the more geometry is needed in the area (more isoparms or edges are necessary to provide more CVs or vertices that can be pushed and pulled). However, you can get some basic facial expressions from very simple geometry.

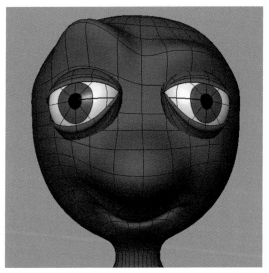

FIG. 14-7 A NURBS head with simple geometry can still be used to create a facial expression.

Never *freeze transformations* on blend shapes. You can freeze the base shape *before* creating your target shapes. However, once the target shapes are created, *do not* freeze transformations on the base or target shapes. If you do, the base shape will fly back to the origin when animating.

When modeling your face, it is always best to have geometry that is modeled along the muscle lines of the face. If you did not spend enough time on the modeling process, you may want to devote a little more time now to add adequate geometry before trying to make your facial expressions. It is also important to understand the movement of facial muscles and what effects they have on the face. Be sure to refer to anatomy books for images to study these patterns of muscle placement. The closer you can mimic these patterns, the more accurate your character's facial expressions will be, providing a level of believability even to the most stylized characters.

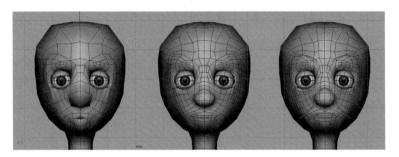

FIG. 14-8 This polygonal face needs more edges to create a more believable series of facial expressions. Understanding facial muscle structure will assist in making these expressions.

Tools Used for Modeling Blend Shapes

The most commonly used tool for modeling blend shapes is the Move tool (shortcut W) or the Scale tool (shortcut R). You can use the Move tool in component mode (right mouse button) over the surface or hit F8 for pushing and pulling points around just as you would when modeling to create the desired shape. Make sure to rename each target shape as they are created. This section focuses on three tools that can simplify much of this process.

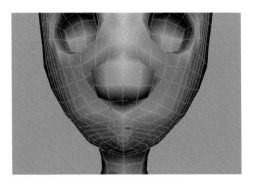

FIG. 14-9 Using the Move tool to create pursed lips for a target blend shape.

You cannot create a blend shape by scaling or moving on the object level. A change on the object level of the target shape does not affect the base shape.

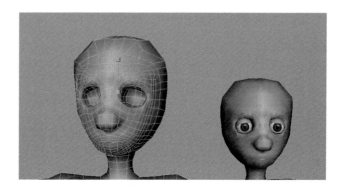

FIG. 14-10 Simply scaling your geometry does not make a deformable object. You must make changes on the component level by selecting the vertices or CVs first, then scale them.

Soft Modification Tool

The Soft Modification tool, under Create Deformers > Soft Modification and under the tool manipulators, is a deformer that allows you to click on an area and push and pull points, much like you do with the Move tool, but it affects the surrounding points as well as the point initially clicked. This tool is more intuitive for artists than the Move tool, as it simulates the pushing and pulling of clay. The greatest affect is on the area clicked, and the gradual drop-off can be adjusted for greater control. Color feedback is turned on by default, which is visually helpful when adjusting the drop-off rate. You can also select an area of points (vertices or CVs) and then apply the soft modification, which limits the deformers to only those points. Make sure to open the option box and turn on Preserve history, so that you can modify changes later if necessary.

FIG. 14-11 The Soft Modification tool can be found with the tool manipulators and in the Animation menu set (F2) under the Create Deformers menu.

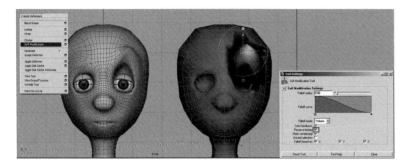

FIG. 14-12 Using the Soft Modification tool to create an eyebrow raise. Make sure to turn Preserve History on in the option box before using the tool so that you can adjust the position of the Soft Modification deformer later if necessary.

The Lattice Deformer, Create Deformers > Lattice, and the Sculpt Geometry tool, Edit NURBS > Sculpt Geometry Tool are also helpful for creating additional facial expressions.

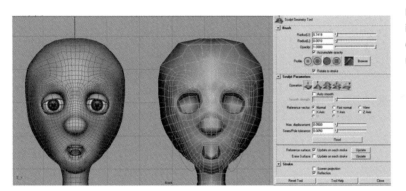

FIG. 14-13 After moving vertices in place, the Sculpt Geometry tool can be used to help shape the open mouth position.

Add Blend Shapes

Once the target shapes (facial expressions) have been created, you must apply them to your base shape (neutral pose) using the blend shape deformer (Create Deformer > Blend Shape). Holding down the Shift key, click on each target shape(s), then select your base shape. (Make sure that they have been renamed appropriately—that is, smile, frown, left_eyebrow_raise, and so on—*before* applying the deformer.) When defining a blend shape, the base shape must be selected last. To test your blend shapes, open the blend shape animation editor (Window > Animation Editors > Blend Shapes). This will open up the blend shape editor, which has a slider for controlling the movement between the shapes. You can also access the blend shape by clicking on the input node in the channel box and changing the value of the field. This attribute is accessible through the Attribute Editor (Ctrl+A) as well. It is also a really good idea to set up another control system for your blend shape sliders so that they can be animated more easily.

443

FIG. 14-14 The blend shape deformer can be found on the Deformation shelf.

FIG. 14-15 The blend shape deformer can be found in the Animation menu set (F2) on the keyboard under the Create Deformers menu.

FIG. 14-16 Creating the blend shape deformer.

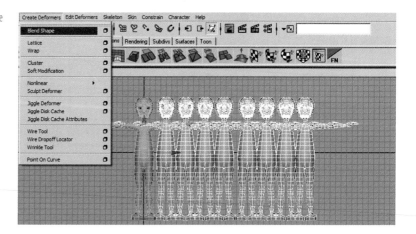

Make sure to rename each target shape *before* applying the deformer. If you relabeled them afterwards, Maya would not recognize them and your target shapes would not affect the base shape.

Do *not* delete history on the geometry after the blend shape deformer has been created. Doing so will delete the blend shape deformer. If this happens, you will have to recreate the deformer again.

Have I mentioned that you should *never* freeze transformations on blend shapes?

Update Topology on Blend Shapes

This tool (Edit Deformers > Bake Topology to Targets) is a relatively new one in Maya, as it was introduced to allow for topology changes to the base shape to be updated on the pre-existing target shapes. For example, if more edges needed to be added to create a particular expression, the existing target shapes would need to be applied to the base shape using Create Deformers > Blend Shape. Once the existing target shapes work, the base model can be modified (that is, more geometry added). This command will pass the modifications on to the target shapes.

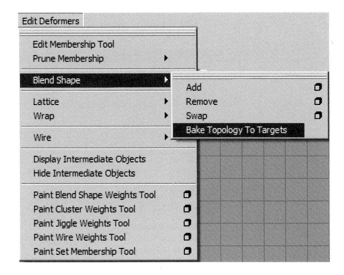

FIG. 14-17 Bake Topology to Targets can be found in the Animation menu set (F2) on the keyboard under the Edit Deformers menu.

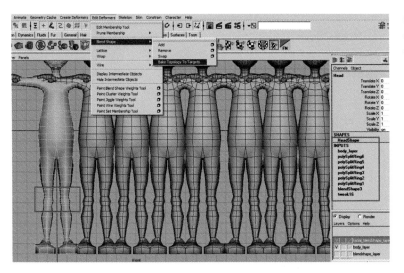

FIG. 14-18 Adding additional edge loops around the knees adds construction history.

445

FIG. 14-19 Bake Topology to Targets updates the target shapes and removes the associated construction history.

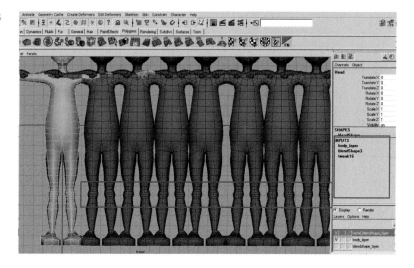

Not all changes to the geometry will work reliably. For example, you cannot delete faces. Therefore, make sure to incrementally save your work, in case of unpredictable results. Bake Topology to Targets works best with polygonal geometry.

Deformation Order

When working with deformers, especially for use with animation, it is important to know that history affects how a particular deformer affects the geometry. Multiple deformers can be applied to the same piece of geometry, and some deformers have to be applied before others to get the desired result. The order in which deformers are created makes up the deformation order for that object, and Maya evaluates them in that order. Creating deformers out of order is not a problem, as the deformation order can be changed.

When creating characters for animation using blend shapes, the blend shape deformer should be the first deformer created, as Maya must evaluate blend shapes before any other deformer. If not, bizarre things happen, like your character's geometry flying off of its skeleton. Remember, if you apply blend shapes after skinning, you must change the deformation order so that the blend shapes are evaluated first.

To change the deformation order, with the geometry selected, right-click the base shape geometry and from the pop-up marking menu, select Inputs > All Inputs. This opens up a List of Input Operations window that shows you a list of the deformers currently affecting this surface. Use the middle mouse button to click and drag the blend shape below any other deformers listed, or to the bottom of the list, which reorders the deformers. Maya evaluates the deformers on the list from the bottom up.

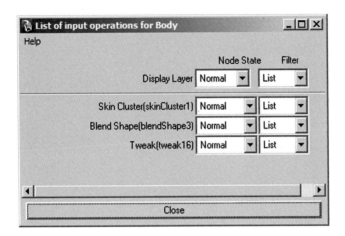

FIG. 14-20 The list of input operations that shows the correct order for the skin deformer and blend shape inputs.

Just in case you forget, *never freeze transformations* on blend shapes! Have you figured out how important this is yet?

Summary

- Facial expressions are crucial for your character's ability to communicate.
- It is best to divide each facial expression into parts that create the expression. Separating each expression into eyes, nose, and mouth areas provides a palette of options that can be combined while animating. The minimum suggested are the following:
- Eye target shapes:
  left_eyebrow_raise
  right_eyebrow_raise
  left_furrow_up
  right_furrow_up
  left_furrow_down
  right_furrow_down
  left_squint
  right_squint
- Nose target shapes:
  scrunched_nose
  nose_up (optional)
- Mouth target shapes:
  narrow_pucker
  wide
  smile (which includes raising the cheeks)
  open (which includes dropping the jaw)
  sad_frown
- There are two basic approaches for creating facial expressions: blend shape–driven and joint-driven.

- Blend shapes are a deformer that change geometry shapes using a morph process.
- Once you understand joints and skinning, you can use joints to create the blend shapes.
- Before creating blend shapes, it is extremely important to finalize the geometry.
- You can get basic facial expressions from very simple geometry.
- Never freeze transformations on blend shapes!
- Research muscle structure for facial expressions as an aid to creating believable motion.
- The same tools used for modeling your character can be used to model the blend shapes.
- All geometry changes must be on the component level when modeling blend shapes.
- The most common tools for modeling blend shapes are the following: the Move tool (to move components such as points), the Soft Modification tool, the Lattice Deformer, and the Sculpt Geometry tool.
- Be sure to label each target shape as it is created.
- Deleting history on target shapes is unnecessary.
- To create a blend shape, first select all target shapes, then Shift-select the base shape.
- Do not delete history on that base shape geometry after the blend shape deformer has been created. Doing so will delete the blend shape deformer.
- If there is a need for more geometry while creating the blend shapes, it is possible to add more divisions to the base shape and then update the topology to blend shapes that have already been applied. However, this process is not always reliable. Therefore, be sure to finalize your geometry before modeling your blend shapes.
- As always, there exists a certain workflow and order of operations. Blend shapes should be applied before the skinning deformer is applied. However, there is a list of input operations that allows the change of deformation order if necessary.

Assignments: Facial Expressions for a Character

Create Facial Expressions

1. Your finished geometry is your base shape. (This is the neutral pose for your face.) This can be one entire piece of geometry (the whole body) or a separate head. If your head is separated, do *not* combine it (if polygonal) after making your blend shapes, as this will make your blend shape targets not work any longer.
2. Duplicate your base shape fifteen times and create your target shapes. Move them above or below your base shape. Rename the target shapes appropriately, as follows.

- Eyebrow target shapes:
  - left_eyebrow_raise
  - right_eyebrow_raise
  - left_furrow_up
  - right_furrow_up
  - left_furrow_down
  - right_furrow_down
  - left_squint
  - right_squint
- Nose target shapes:
  - scrunched_nose
  - nose_up (optional)
- Mouth target shapes:
  - narrow_pucker
  - wide
  - smile (which includes raising the cheeks)
  - open (which includes dropping the jaw)
  - sad_frown

1. Use the following tools to reshape these into the facial expressions: Move tool, Scale tool, Soft Modification tool, Sculpt Geometry tool, Lattice Deformer.

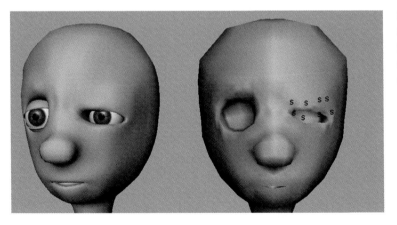

FIG. 14-21 Using the Soft Modification tool to create the left_squint eyebrow target shape. It may take several clicks of this tool to get the desired shape.

The Soft Modification tool can be used effectively to create all of the eyebrow target shapes, as well as the nose target shapes. To create the mouth shapes, you will probably need to start with the Move and Scale tools, then refine the shapes with the Sculpt Geometry tool.

Create the Blend Shape Deformer

1. Select your Target shapes, then Shift-select your base shape.
2. Select Create Deformer Create Deformers _ Blend Shape.
3. In the Layer Editor of the Channel Box, create a new layer. Double-click on the new layer (layer1) and rename this layer blend shape_layer, then click Save. Shift-select all of the target shapes you have made, right-click and hold on top of the blend shape_layer, and choose Add Selected Objects. To make the objects invisible, click V (visibility) to turn it off.

When defining a blend shape, the base shape must be selected last.

After creating the blend shape deformer, you should test the blend shape.

1. Select Windows > Animation Editors > Blend Shape to open up the blend shape editor, which has a slider for controlling the movement between the shapes.

FIG. 14-22 Opening the Blend Shape editor.

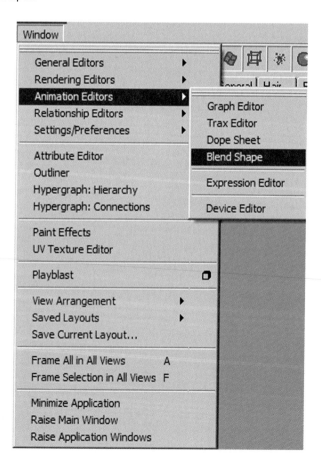

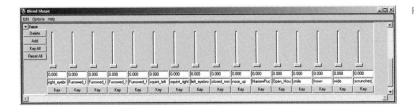

FIG. 14-23 The Blend Shape editor.

2. You can also access the blend shape by clicking on the input node in the Channel box and changing the value of the field. This attribute is accessible through the Attribute Editor as well.

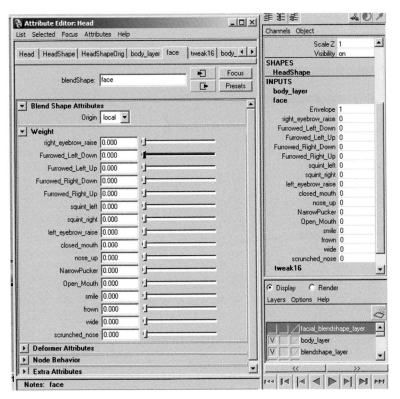

FIG. 14-24 The Attribute Editor and Channel box showing the blend shape attributes.

3. Make changes as necessary to the target shapes. You can update them as needed and they will automatically update the deformer. To make it easier to make changes, move the target shape right next to your base shape and make the changes with the slider turned on.

FIG. 14-25 If you push the slider up, you can make adjustments to the target shape and see the changes automatically on the base shape.

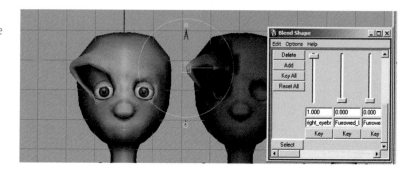

Create Teeth and Tongue (Optional)

If you plan on opening your character's mouth for any facial expressions or plan to have your character speak, you will need to model teeth and a tongue. This can be done without much detail.

FIG. 14-26 The teeth and tongue, front view and back view.

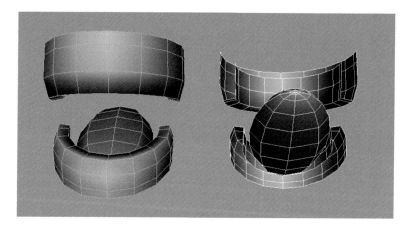

The tongue is simply a sphere created on the z-axis and reshaped using a lattice. The teeth can be made by creating a profile curve in the front view, performing a revolve, and changing the start sweep of the revolve to 180 in the Channel box.

FIG. 14-27 The profile curve of the teeth in the front view and the top view, showing the revolve start sweep be beginning at 180.

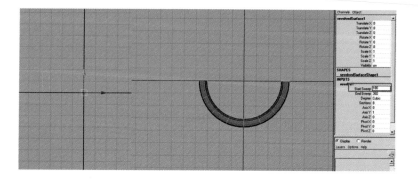

A Lattice Deformer can be used to create the narrower shape. The teeth can be duplicated and flipped to create the bottom row. Be sure to also add a shaped plane to act as the throat wall.

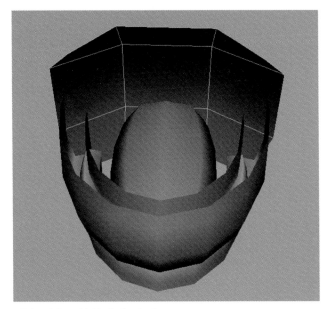

FIG. 14-28   A shaped plane added for the throat wall.

CHAPTER 15

Creating Your First Biped Character: Shading and Texturing Basics Using Maya

Former Student Spotlight: Nathan Engelhardt

Being a newcomer to intimidating 3D software packages like Maya, Max, Lightwave, and so on can be a frightening and frustrating experience. I remember the first day that I opened Maya on a school computer. I was so afraid that I'd melt my computer or something if a wrong button was pushed. To be honest, I think most people feel this way when first opening a major 3D package. First, it's important as a newbie to not get overwhelmed by the mass information that's infused in the software. Take your time, stumble, learn from your mistakes, and don't be afraid of pushing that wrong button over and over again. (I've pushed it many times with still no success of melting my computer, if that's what you also worry about.)

Second, and ironically more important than the first rule: be aware of what you are interested in. So often I hear about students who want to learn everything and anything about their preferred 3D software package—me included. They become a jack-of-all-trades (such as animation, rigging, texturing, lighting, effects, and so on), but master of none. Although being knowledgeable in many aspects of the package may be considered a valuable asset in smaller companies and productions, large animation and visual effects houses (Pixar, Dream Works, Blue Sky, ILM, Sony, and others) like a strict study in one category of interest: a focus! Becoming a generalist or a specialist is simply a matter of personal preference. The sooner you realize which you'd like to be, the better.

And last, and most important: understand that these software packages will come and go in time. Sounds easy enough, I know. Make sure you don't spend all your time learning Maya, its interface, its functionality, and so on, because when Maya is eventually bought out by The Melting Computers of America Association, Inc., and all the menus change and things that used to be familiar disappear…what then? A classically trained painter would easily side with the argument that knowing the process, techniques, and basic fundamental principles of lighting, composition, and so on are much more useful than knowing how to use a brush. Although the understanding of how to use a brush (Maya) helps an artist fully utilize a tool, it does not, however, make an artist out of anyone. Learn the principals of whatever it is you are interested in, and no matter what the newest and greatest tool is, *you* will never become outdated.

Nathan Engelhardt graduated from the Savannah College of Art and Design in Spring of 2007 with a BFA in Animation. His first position after graduation was as an animator at Blue Sky, working on Horton Hears a Who. *He recently enrolled in online classes to further his animation studies at Animation Mentor.com and expects to graduate from their program sometime in 2008 with an advanced study in animation. More of Nathan's work can be viewed at http://www. nathanengelhardt.com.*

FIG. 15-1 "Traffic Light" by Nathan Engelhardt (2007).

Workflow

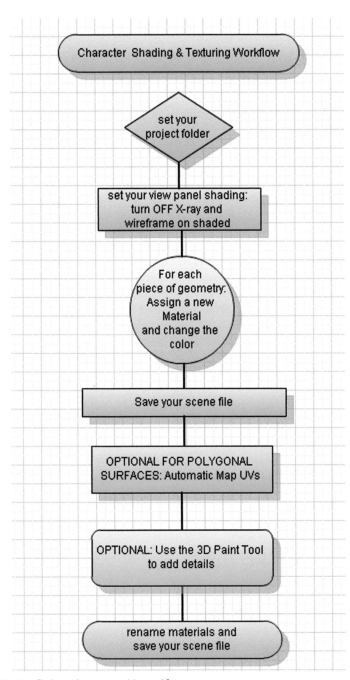

FIG. 15-2 Shading and texturing modeling workflow.

Introduction

With the theme of keeping things simple, this chapter is going to focus on an easy way to add color and a bit of artistic detail to your character. The topic of shading and texturing is a lengthy one, and it could easily be expanded to create an entire book (which has been done by several other authors).

The easiest solution for adding color to your character is by simply adding a material, or "shader," to your geometry. Maya has several surface materials available, and the chosen material depends on how much light is reflected or absorbed by the surface. The material applied to an object can also control its transparency.

Of course, there are many more qualities to a surface shader than color, transparency, and reflectivity. Additional detail can be added if textures are used. For this detail, we will be using the 3D Paint Tool, which allows an interactive level of painting directly on your 3D model. Other details, such as the consideration of how rough or smooth the surface is that you are trying to create, involves the use of bump or displacement maps, which is beyond the scope of this chapter. Once again, this chapter covers only the tools that I feel give you the easiest ability to add color and some detail.

The Hypershade

The Hypershade is a work area that allows you to create and edit the materials and textures necessary for your geometry. To create a material in the Hypershade, click on the desired surface and it will appear in the work area. To apply it to the geometry, you can middle-click and drag it onto your geometry in the view panel. Another option is to select the geometry first, then right-click over the shader in the Hypershade and choose "Assign material to selection" from the marking menu that appears. Although the Hypershade is a great place for organizing and keeping track of all of your materials needed in the Maya scene, the easiest way to add a material to an object is simply to right-click and hold over the object and choose "Assign new material" from the marking menu that appears. If working in polygons, a material can be applied to selected polygonal faces, allowing one surface to be defined into separate areas such as skin color or clothing. Once a material has been added to the geometry, it is a good idea to rename the material. With the material selected, the attribute editor can then be opened Ctrl+A and attributes such as color can be changed for the desired look.

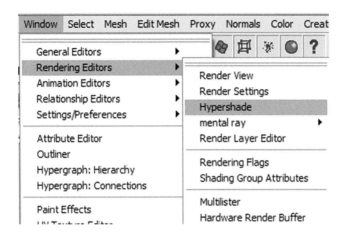

FIG. 15-3 The Hypershade can be found under the Windows menu in the Rendering Editors submenu.

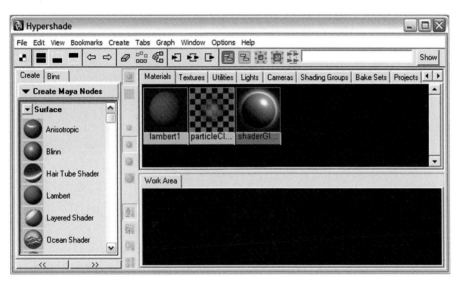

FIG. 15-4 The Hypershade window.

Materials

Each material defines itself by the amount of light that is reflected by the surface. The following materials are most commonly used as follows.

Lambert

This material does not have specular highlights and is perfect for matte surfaces, such as rubber or objects painted with matte paint. This material is the one I suggest for your character's skin and most cotton fabrics. This material is based on the Beer–Lambert law, which defines the relationship of how light is absorbed based on the properties of the material that the light is hitting.

Blinn

This material is great for simulating objects that are made of glass or metal. This material was developed by Jim Blinn.

Phong

This material is used mainly for glossy surfaces such as hard shiny plastic. It is a pretty good shader to use for eyeballs. This material, and the Phong E, was developed by Bui Tuong Phong.

Phong E

This material has a softer highlight than that of the Phong material. It's great for materials such as frosted glass, brushed metal, or any other material with complicated highlights.

FIG. 15-5 The different materials in the Hypershade.

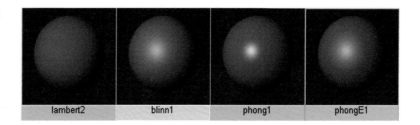

Automatic Mapping

Using the 3D Paint Tool allows the creation of the texture to fit the object. If you are working in polygons, before you can use the 3D Paint Tool to texture

FIG. 15-6 The Automatic Mapping command can be found in the Polygons menu set by pressing (F3) on the keyboard under Create UVs > Polygons.

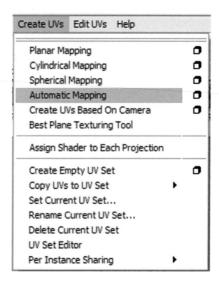

your model, you will have to lay out the UVs first. For most polygon models, the Automatic Mapping option serves quite nicely. NURBS models do not need to be mapped; NURBS utilize their CVs as UVs.

The 3D Paint Tool

The 3D Paint Tool is a relatively quick and simple means of adding a file texture (or marking areas for more detailed texturing in Photoshop or another painting program). This tool allows you to paint color (or transparency, or any channel available in the material attributes) directly onto your model using the artisan brush (the same brush used earlier for the Sculpt Geometry tool). The brush size, shape, feather, and opacity can be changed easily. Simple tasks such as erase, clone, smear, and blur can be applied directly onto your model. Maya's 3D Paint Tools encompass enough options to create a basic texture beyond simply applying single-color shaders to selected faces. As you are working, make sure hardware texturing is turned on **6** in order to see what and where you'll be painting later.

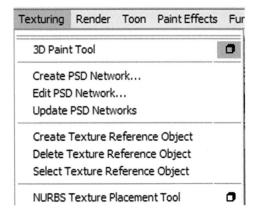

FIG. 15-7 The 3D Paint Tool can be found in the Rendering menu set by pressing F6 on the keyboard under the Texturing menu.

When working with the 3D Paint Tool, it is extremely important that you set your project so that Maya knows where to save the file textures. To do this, go to File > Project > Set and choose your project folder. This option will keep all of your project related assets in the same folder and keep your paths relative.

461

FIG. 15-8 The 3D Paint Tool options window.

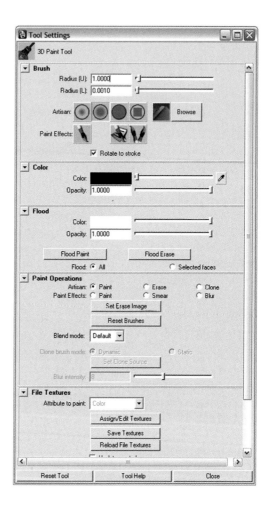

Summary

- Texturing and shading can be a lengthy topic, but it can also be approached in a simpler way.
- The Hypershade is the work area that allows you to create and edit materials and textures.
- A material defines how a surface is seen when the computer creates a rendered image.
- The most commonly used materials for character shading are: Lambert, Blinn, Phong, and Phong E.
- When texturing polygons, it is necessary to lay out the UVs for the geometry first.
- The 3D Paint Tool provides a quick and simple method for adding detail by an interactive creation of a file texture on your model.

Assignments: Shading and Texturing a Character

Apply a Colored Material to Your Character

1. Open Maya and set your project. Go to File > Project > Set…, browse to your project folder, and click OK.
2. Open your last saved file. Go to File > Open and select 03_asgn03.ma.
3. Set all four view panels to turn off X-ray Mode and wireframe on shaded.
4. Turn hardware texturing on by pressing 6 on the keyboard so that you can see your reference images.
5. Make sure that your geometry layer is set to Normal so that you are able to select the geometry.

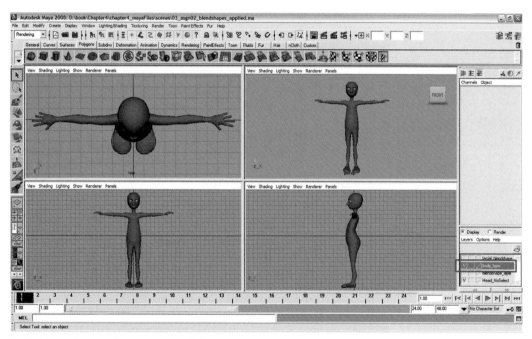

FIG. 15-9 The work area with the geometry layer set to Normal.

6. Select the piece of geometry you wish to color.
7. Right-click and hold over the object and choose "Assign new material" from the marking menu that appears. Once the material has been added to the geometry, the attribute editor is opened. Rename the material (something like body_lambert). Change the color by clicking on the color box, which opens the color chooser window and allows you to select any color desired.

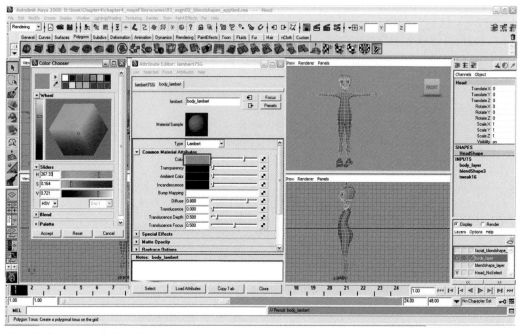

FIG. 15-10 Choosing a color for the body Lambert material.

8. Save your scene file.
    a. Go to File > Save as. This should open the scenes folder of your project (assuming that you set the project as in step 1).
    b. Name your scene 15_asgnOl.ma.

Add Details Using the 3D Paint Tool (Optional)

For best results, use a pressure-sensitive graphics pen and tablet for this process, instead of your mouse.

1. Open Maya and set your project. Go to File > Project > Set…, browse to your project folder, and click OK.
2. Open your last saved file. Go to File > Open and select 15_asgn01.ma.
3. Select the object you wish to texture. If your geometry is NURBS, skip to step 8.
4. Go to Polygons > Create UVs > Automatic Mapping. The default settings should work fine. If necessary, you can open the option box and reset the settings.
5. In the orthographic view panels, resize the projected planes to fit your geometry.
6. To view the layout of the map, look under Window > UV Texture Editor. The Automatic Mapping has created several sections of UVs. All of the shapes should be within the 0–1 texture space (the square colored by the material).

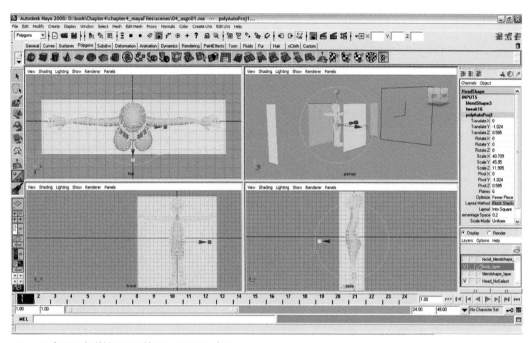

FIG. 15-11 Resizing the UV Automatic Mapping projection planes.

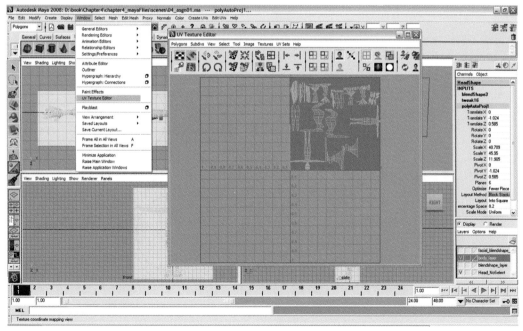

FIG. 15-12 The UV Texture Editor.

7. Go back into object mode (F8), because Automatic Mapping placed you into component mode.
8. Now we can paint directly on our model. Select the object you wish to texture. Go to Texturing > 3D Paint Tool, the tool settings window.
9. If you place your mouse cursor over your model, you will see a red X in the paintbrush circle. Before you can paint, you must first assign an image file texture to paint upon. Scroll down the tool settings window to the File Textures section. Choose which attribute you wish to paint (Color,

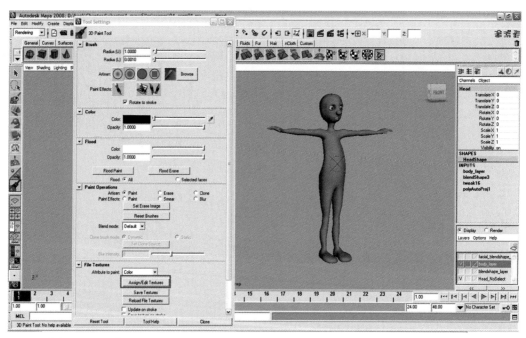

FIG. 15-13 Assigning a texture file.

Transparency, Bump, and so on), as well as which image format you want (default is set to Maya IFF, but if you want to edit the image outside of Maya, TGA would be better). Then click Assign/Edit Textures to open the Assign/Edit Textures window.

10. Decide how large your image needs to be. If painting an entire character's body, I suggest making the file size for X and Y 1024. This number represents the pixel dimension of the file that is applied to your model. Larger pixel dimensions will be necessary for larger models, so that the quality of the resulting texture is not pixilated. However, too large of an image will slow down the painting process and add expensive render time (a good rule of thumb is to keep the file size dimensions to 2048 or smaller). Keep Aspect Ratio should remain checked, as your map occupies a square; also, keep the size as a power of 2, because computer calculations are based on the binary system (128, 256, 512, 1024, 2048).

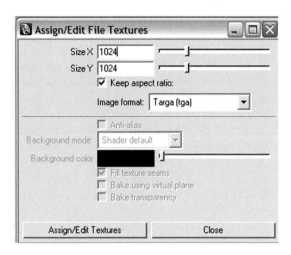

FIG. 15-14 Defining the file texture size.

11. Click Assign/Edit Textures.
12. Now you can paint! The base color of your model is the color you chose when you assigned the material in an earlier assignment; when you erase, you will actually be erasing back to this base color. If you want to change color from the color you chose when you first assigned the material, go to the Flood section and change the Color. Before doing any other painting, click Flood Paint. However, this does not change your base color. If you click Flood Erase, the area will return to the base color.
13. Under the Brush section, you can adjust the upper and lower brush radius; choose between a Gaussian brush, soft brush, hard brush, square

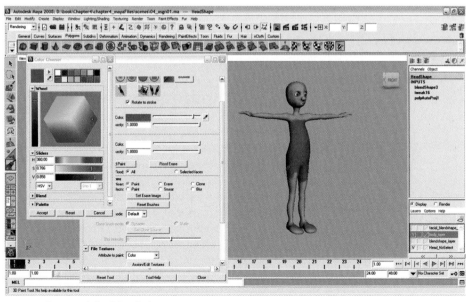

FIG. 15-15 Painting with the 3D Paint Tool.

brush; or load different brush shapes from the Artisan's Browse box (these include charcoal, hatched, marker, and even skin-bump brushes). You can even choose a paint effects brush and paint a 2D image of the paint effects brush. The hotkey to change the brush size interactively is B. Simply hold down the B key, place your brush over your model, and drag left to right to change the brush size smaller and larger.

14. Under the Color menu, you can change the color of the brush, as well as adjust the opacity.
15. Under the Paint Operations Menu, you will find both Artisan and Paint Effects operations, including Paint, Erase, Clone, and Blur. You can even change the blend mode, working with lighten, darken, multiply, screen, and overlay modes. (These work in a very similar manner to blend modes in Photoshop.)
16. Once you have painted your model, make sure to scroll down the tool settings window to the File Textures section. Click Save Textures. This should create and save the file into a 3DPaint Textures folder in your project folder (assuming that you set the project as in step 1).

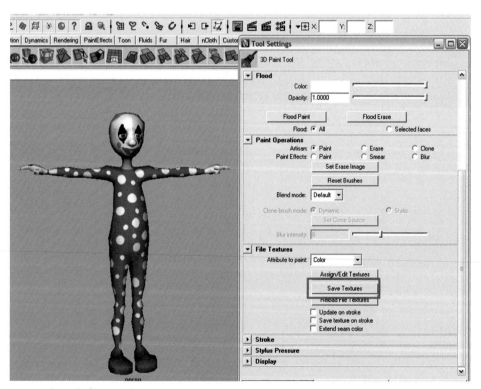

FIG. 15-16 Saving the file texture when painting is complete with the 3D Paint Tool.

17. Save your scene file. Name your scene 15_asg n02.ma.

CHAPTER 16

High Poly and Low Poly Character Modeling Using 3ds Max and Photoshop

Introduction

Being a 3D character artist is an incredibly rewarding job—it's great fun to turn your raw ideas into living, breathing beings, and there is always be a challenge around the corner. To create photorealistic and believable characters, you must balance your 3D technical expertise with a sound knowledge of human and animal anatomy. Without a doubt, your most important asset is your "eye": You must objectively scrutinize your creations at each stage of their development.

It is beyond the scope of this chapter to guide you through each and every one of the thousands of operations required to build this character. Instead, I would like to guide you through my working process, my way of thinking and the tools I use. You need a competent working knowledge of 3ds Max, and you need to solve your own problems from time to time. This tutorial starts off fairly basic and gets into some more advanced concepts as we move along. If you get stuck on a problem with any particular tool, your best friends are the help menu (press F1) and Internet search engines. This is how I advanced my knowledge of 3ds Max once I had absorbed everything that the entry level tutorials had to offer. As long as you make regular incremental saves (i.e., man01.max, man02.max, and so on), it's pretty hard to break anything—so press all the buttons to see what they do!

Our Pipeline

The way we work, the tools we use, and the order in which we do things are known as our "pipeline." I have refined my pipeline over many years to get things running as smoothly as possible.

Before we start the 3D work, let's first plan out exactly what we will do. Once we know precisely what we will be creating, we will make a rough, low-polygon "proxy mesh" that will capture all the basic proportions and main shapes of the character. From this mesh, we will develop a high-polygon mesh that has all the little details that bring the character to life. We will apply UV coordinates to the high-res mesh and create realistic surfaces by applying a number of different textures to the surfaces of the character. We can use this high-polygon mesh for portfolios, advertising materials, in game cut scenes, and any other prerendered media.

Next, we will return to our low-polygon proxy mesh and optimize his level of detail so that he is suitable for real-time videogames. After we bake down all the details from our original high-polygon mesh onto this new low-polygon game mesh, you might be surprised how similar it looks to the high-polygon mesh. This mesh will be suitable for inclusion in any modern Sony PlayStation 3, PC, or Microsoft Xbox 360 game, ready to be rigged and imported into the game engine.

Before You Start: The Concept

Perhaps the most common beginner's mistake is to rush headlong into modeling without sufficient planning. Modern video game characters can take more than five weeks of solid work to finish, so you don't want to get to the end only to find out that the basic design is flawed. The best approach is to have everything drawn out in color *before* you start. Most studios will have at least one concept artist for this job, often recruiting specialist character artists to do the job. If you draw out your idea and it doesn't work out, only hours or days are wasted—not weeks or months!

Often a good character starts with a simple thought, like "I'm going to make a tough-looking, futuristic commando," but it is the concept process that will prove whether your idea works visually. As you draw out a detailed character concept, you are visually solving problems that might not have been apparent when it was just a rough idea in your head.

It is usually much quicker to experiment with designs on paper than it is to make a series of changes to your 3D model. Early in the concept phase, many fast and loose pieces are produced to try out as many different ideas as possible in a short period of time. Once the concept artist is happy with a final look for the character he drafts up detailed blueprints to be scanned and colored on a computer. Using paint packages such as Photoshop makes it fast and easy to experiment with alternative colors, hairstyles, costumes, accessories, and so on. After the art director approves these concept designs, they are sent to the character artist for production.

Many character artists use a two-monitor setup: typically, one monitor is used for working in 3D applications and the other is used to display reference and concept images. This two-monitor setup works well; however, I recommend that you print out your most-used images and hang them on the wall near your desk. For the weeks that you will work on this character, you will save lots of time browsing folders looking for your reference, and you will free up your precious RAM and processor resources for those greedy multimillion-polygon meshes!

An Extensive Knowledge of Anatomy

If you're serious about specializing as a concept artist or 3D character artist, you need an extensive knowledge of human anatomy. Even the most weird and wonderful alien characters will most likely have some similarities to us, and your knowledge of human anatomy can add believability to your other-worldly creations.

The most intuitive way to learn anatomy is to spend a good amount of time in life-drawing classes studying direct from life, but it is essential to read up on your anatomy, too, unless you fancy cutting up some cadavers! Although there are many medical texts that will familiarize you with the inner workings of the human body, I've found it much easier to learn by reading artists' guides to anatomy. Artist-specific guides are more relevant, as they concern themselves only with representing the main forms and the surfaces of the body, without getting too bogged down in the details. You don't need to learn the names of each individual element, but it is essential to learn where all the major groups of muscles, tendons, bones, and areas of fat are on the body. It is quite common for beginners to focus on modeling all the muscles but forget about bony protrusions such as cheekbones, shoulder blades, and ankles. Your models will look formless and blobby without a good consideration of the bones that hold the body together.

The proportions of body parts in relationship to each other are of critical importance in character modeling; if you get the basic proportions wrong, your character will look terrible, even if you include loads of cool, small details. Small changes to proportions make a big different in how people perceive your character—especially in the face, where tiny adjustments to the eyes can have a massive effect on the personality and mood of the character.

I heartily recommend the classic series of books about drawing the human figure by Andrew Loomis. The first editions are now out-of-print collector's items, but you can find the books freely available for download on the Internet. *Drawing Comics the Marvel Way* by Stan Lee and John Buscema (Fireside, 1984) and the *How to Draw Anime & Game Characters* series by Tadashi Ozawa (Graphic-Sha) are also great, as they are very specific to the typical, idealized characters you often find in a contemporary game.

It may help to study classic artists such as Leonardo da Vinci. Leonardo shows in his art that there are many general proportional rules that loosely apply to almost everybody. Many of Leonardo's works (and those of many other artists) make extensive use of the "golden ratio," a number known in mathematics as *phi*, that can be observed in many instances in nature. This number (approximately 1.6180339887) can be measured in the proportions of spirals in seashells, the length of bones in animals and the distances between stems on plants. Look at the joints in your fingers; each successive joint is roughly 1.6 times longer than the last.

The ancient Greeks and Egyptians used the golden ratio in their classic architecture like the Parthenon and the pyramids. Modern studies have deemed these proportions to be aesthetically pleasing and closely linked with our perceptions of beauty. You could even apply your knowledge of it to your own fantasy creature creations; it would be fair to hypothesize that if aliens do exist they too might have evolved with the "golden" proportions.

Ask Questions

Upon receiving the "future commando" concept, our first job is to get to know him. As we want our character to be realistic and believable, let's start

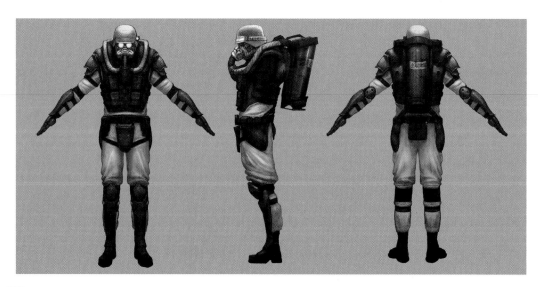

by assuming that he *is* alive. Usually I ask the team and myself a number of questions, such as the following:

Q. Where does he live?

A. *The scene is based in the United KingdomK; the reference was taken in an abandoned factory in the Northwest of England. It's not terribly important to tie the character to a location, but a Union Jack flag on his shoulder might be a nice detail.*

Q. What material is his suit made out of?

A. *He wears an NBC (Nuclear Biological Chemical) suit. The lightweight material is fairly tough, but flexible. The fabric has a charcoal layer in between the layers to protect him from nuclear fallout, gas, poison, or germ warfare. The fabric is unique; although it is flexible, it has a crisp quality and will hold creases. See if you can get your hands on an NBC suit in an army surplus store.*

Q. Has he had any previous battles, and have they left him with any damage to his suit?

A. *Being on his hands and knees in various combat situations has left him with many surface scuffs and areas of ingrained dirt on his suit, but there is no real damage. His suit is his lifeline; it is replaced every six months, and if its function is compromised in any way, it is replaced immediately.*

Q. What sort of soldier is he?

A. *He is part of a specialist fighting unit—a real bad-ass.*

Q. What kind of gloves is he wearing? It is unclear on the concept.

A. *They are slash-resistant Kevlar gloves with lead lining. Perhaps it would be a good idea to extend the gloves to half-gauntlet size, to give better protection from his flamethrower.*

Q. How old is he?

A. *To become this tough, he must have been in various branches of the military for a number of years—he is in his early 30s.*

Q. How old is his gun? What type of gun is it?

A. *It is a flamethrower, maybe with a small shell launcher or other weapon on the bottom.*

Collecting References

Before we get into the modeling, it's mandatory to gather a wealth of reference material. You might think you know what things should look like, but reference photos always help you add that extra touch of authenticity. Detailed reference materials show you things about your subject material that you might have overlooked: the way it fades in the sun, the wear from children scratching their names into it, or the bits of chewing gum that get stuck to it. These observed details put your object into a real-world context and prevent it from looking unrealistically new or featureless. When it comes to the texturing stage, your reference will help you to analyze the materials that make up your character—and you might be able to use a reference photo directly in your final textures.

For each object you research, it is advisable to get reference shots from as many different camera angles as possible. We need to know about every inch of the object's surfaces; within your range of images, there should be no blind spots where important details are hidden. Don't settle for just front, side, and back views. If you take the time to observe reference shots from the more obscure angles, such as the bottom, the back, and three-quarter views, it will add a professional level of depth to your models.

I use a Google image search for most of my research, set to "high-res images only" in the advanced settings. If this search is unsuccessful, I change the settings to medium- or small-size images. The Internet is a wealth of information, and there are many Web sites specific to whatever subjects you are researching. If you can't find what you are looking for, try using alternative keywords; use a thesaurus to come up with as many different names as possible for the thing that you are researching.

One of my favorite sites is http://www.3d.sk. For a subscription fee, you can download very high-res professional photographs of *real* humans—no airbrushed skin tones here! The library covers all shapes and sizes of humans: fat, thin, young, old, black, white, Asian, bearded, armored—pretty much whatever you might need as reference for your modeling. The images are all shot in scattered white studio light with no harsh shadows, which is perfect for use in your textures. The average subjects are normal everyday people, so you end up with lots of acne, spots, skin diseases, blemishes, moles and birthmarks—all the things that add character to your creations!

You should make sure to have folders full of images concerning every aspect of what you are about to model.

Getting Ready to Start: Setting Up Image Planes

Image planes are used so that you can trace over the concept artwork inside 3ds Max to ensure that your model remains true to the original vision. I strongly recommend that you do not trace photos directly in the viewport, but instead use your reference as a reference—not as the blueprint for your model.

All photos are distorted by the camera's lens, which exaggerates and warps the image. Wide-angle or "fish-eye" lenses like the one used on this page are an extreme example of lens distortion.

If you study some catwalk fashion photography you will notice that models are often shot from afar with a strong zoom lens to minimize the lens distortion effect. Ideally it is this type of photograph, if any, on which you should base your dimensions—but be warned that tracing warped images directly will lead to warped models. It's better that you study proportions from life instead of relying on tracing.

To get a photograph with truly zero perspective distortion, you would have to be an infinite distance away from the object, with an infinitely powerful zoom lens, just like the orthographic viewports in 3ds Max! Good concept artwork is drawn like this, with zero perspective, free from all lens distortion.

It is very important that the different views of the concept art are drawn out next to each other with ruled lines to ensure that the features match up accurately across the range of views. It can be very tricky to work from wonky and inaccurate concept art.

Let's open the concept art in Photoshop now to prepare it for use in 3ds Max as the blueprint for our character. We need three square images for front, side, and back that line up perfectly with each other.

Use the rectangle selection tool while holding down the Shift key to make a precise square selection around the front view, then copy and paste it into its own image file. Go back to the original concept art image again and use the

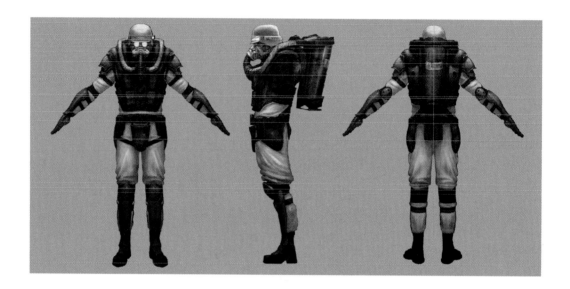

right arrow key to nudge your square selection over to the side view. Copy and paste the side view into its own image file, then repeat the process for the back view. Our use of a nudged selection to produce our three images ensures that they will line up perfectly in 3ds Max. Save each of these three views as a separate JPEG file.

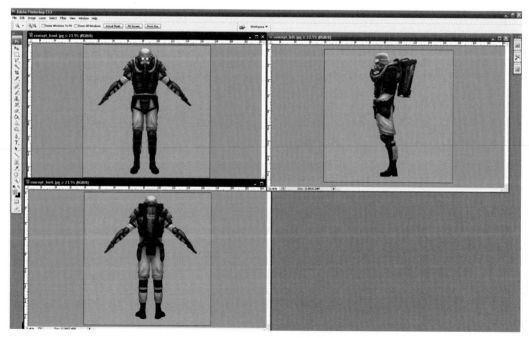

Rather than use 3ds Max's Viewport Background functionality, I prefer to create the image planes myself as geometry. I find it easier to manipulate the scale and position of the blueprints if I just map images onto planes. If I want to scale or transform the model, it's easy to include the image planes in the transformations and keep everything in sync.

Open up 3ds Max and create a square primitive plane (Create > Standard primitives > Plane). It is important to hold Shift as you drag out the dimensions of the plane to ensure accurate square proportions like the images we prepared in Photoshop. Be sure that Generate Mapping Coords is checked, to save yourself the trouble of manually creating UV coordinates. Apply a Blinn material to this plane object, with 100% self-illumination and the ambient color set to white, and load the front concept image into the diffuse slot of the material. Now position the plane so that the character is centered on the origin (the center of the world coordinate system) with his feet directly above the origin.

Select the "front image plane" object that you have just created and rotate it 90 degrees. My favorite way to do this is to hold Shift while rotating the object to copy and rotate the object in the same operation. Be sure to turn on the angle snap toggle button on the main toolbar to ensure an exact rotation of 90 degrees.

Apply a new material to this new copied object and map the side concept image onto it to create the "side image plane." Now copy/rotate the side image plane another 90 degrees and apply another new material to it to create the "back image plane," translating it back slightly to move it away from the front concept plane. The use of square images on square planes ensures undistorted and perfectly aligned features; no more messing around with translate, scale, and rotate trying to get everything to match up correctly.

Expert Mode, Hotkeys, and Scripting

Most modeling work involves a heavy amount of repetition, so it is more than worth your time to learn all the hotkeys for the major tools. If hotkeys are not assigned to your favorite tools by default, you can do it yourself using the Customize > Customize User Interface options. Sometimes I write a script that performs a series of commands that I repeat again and again—it's really not that hard to write basic scripts so don't be afraid to try it out yourself. Over the years, I have customized my workflow quite extensively to save me hours of repetition per day. Once you have made a couple of characters and want to save some time and energy, you should look at using scripting and hotkeys as a way of saving lots of time.

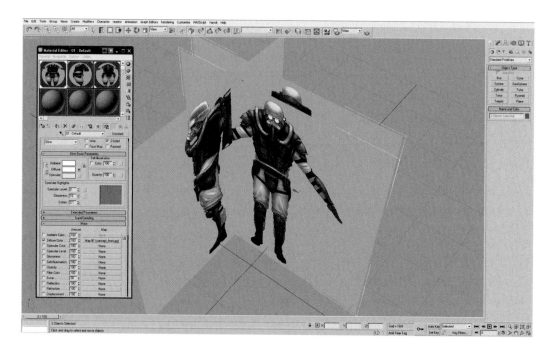

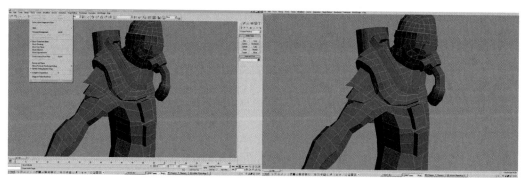

As I've been using 3ds Max for more than nine years, I'm very comfortable with the tools and my hotkeys for each modeling function that I use on a daily basis, so I don't often use the icons. I usually run Max in Expert mode (Views > Expert mode), which keeps my interface free of clutter, giving me more room for looking at my character. If you are just starting out you probably won't want this, as it is good to explore the interface and each tool that is available, but it is a great option once you know exactly what you are doing.

As we are concerned with modeling, not animating, you can definitely turn off the track bar to save some room on your interface (Show UI > Show Track Bar).

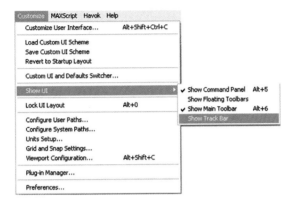

Viewport Preferences

By default, 3ds Max's viewports display rather low-res textures by today's standards. If you select Customize > Preferences > Configure Driver, you can increase the maximum texture size. Select 1024 and check "Match Bitmap Size as Closely as Possible" for both "Background Texture Size" and "Download Texture Size."

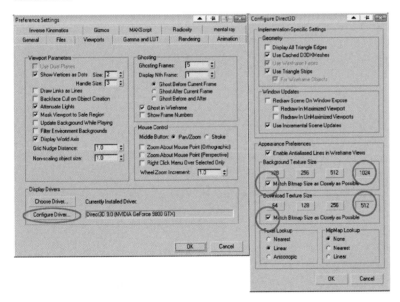

Getting the Basic Proportions Right

Let's start the modeling with the classic starting point, the "primitive cube," known in 3ds Max as the "box primitive." Right- click your cube to convert it into an editable poly. We will make half the character to start with. Press 4 to select polygon mode and the top polygon to select it. Now use the Extrude tool to extrude the polygon upwards to make a chest, select the top poly

on the left side of the shape and extrude out to make an arm, and select the
bottom poly and extrude out to make a leg.

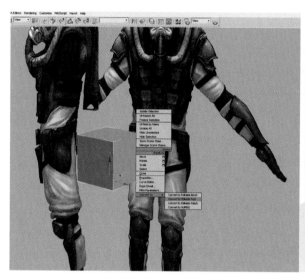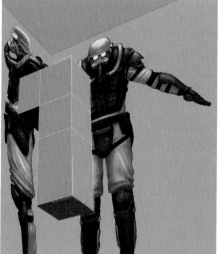

You might need to move the side image plane out of the way a little so that
you can see what you are doing as our character widens. Ensure that you
move it only by sliding the X transform handle: this way, we will not lose the
vertical "registration" with the front and back concepts. Press 1 for Vertex
mode and move all the object's vertices into better positions to match the
concept. It is easier to see what you're doing if you apply a new material to our
object, with 30% opacity and a strong red color.

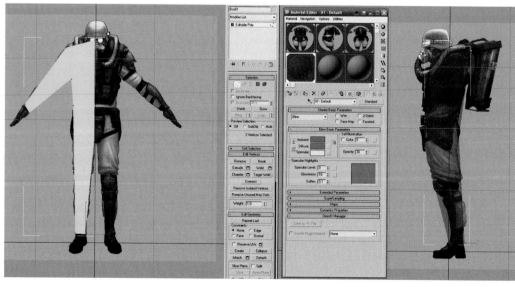

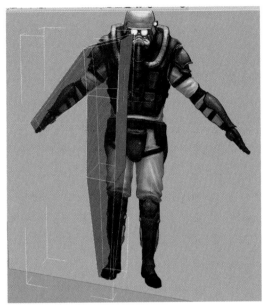

Next, select the polys on the inside of the mesh, where the line of symmetry will go, and delete them. Press F4 to show the edged faces clearly.

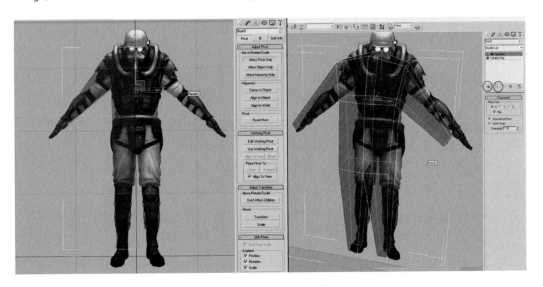

Let's mirror our mesh to make the full form—it would take twice as long to do everything if we didn't use symmetry to our advantage. Activate the Affect Pivot Only button in the Pivot panel and move the pivot to the origin: be sure to deactivate the button after you have finished. Next apply a Symmetry modifier; you might need to check the Flip box, and then adjust the threshold slider until the center vertices snap together. We now have a full figure.

If you click on Editable Poly on the stack, the symmetry will disappear. You must press the "Show end result On/Off toggle" button (the little test tube under the stack); this will switch on all items further up the stack, which is invaluable for modeling with most modifiers. As we work, you can also switch on and off the light bulb icon next to the Symmetry modifier to turn its effect on and off.

Let's add some more geometry to refine the shape. Select one of the horizontal edges running down the leg, and press the Ring button, which selects all the parallel edges running down the leg. When the mesh gets more complex, the Ring and Loop select functions become invaluable for making quick, accurate selections. Next, hit the rollout box to the side of the Connect button in Edit Poly to connect these edges with new polys and select two segments.

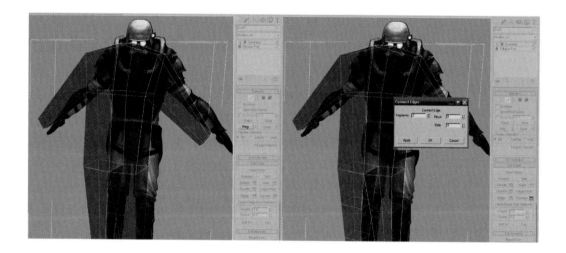

Repeat the select Edge, select Ring, and Connect process for the vertical edges running across the arm and the torso to increase the detail level further. Now spend some time moving these verts around to fit the concept sketches. The key to modeling fast is to add new geometry only as you need it. Before you add any new polys, make sure that the ones that are there already are well-placed. This reduces the amount of translating work you do substantially, as any new geometry you make will already be somewhat in the correct area. Create, refine, create, refine: our basic workflow.

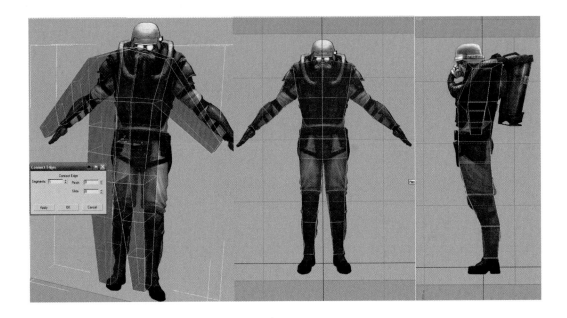

Click the poly at the end of the arm and extrude it out to make a hand; do the
same at the end of the leg to make a foot.

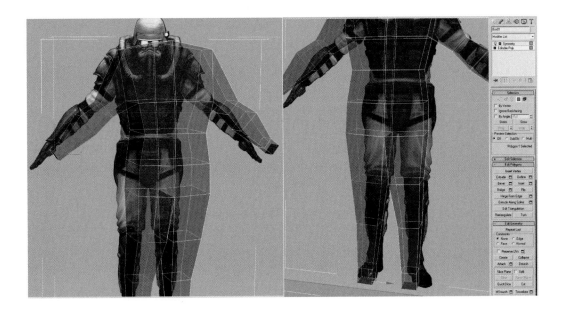

Extrude out the poly at the front of the foot to make it more natural-looking, and refine all the verts of the hand and foot into better positions.

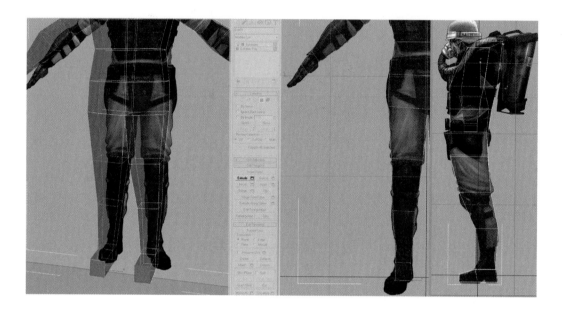

Now let's add more geometry so that we can match the concept more closely. Select Poly mode by pressing the 4 key, then press Ctrl + A to select every poly on the model. We will turn every poly into four polys by pressing the Dialog Box button next to the Tessellate button in the Edit Poly rollout.

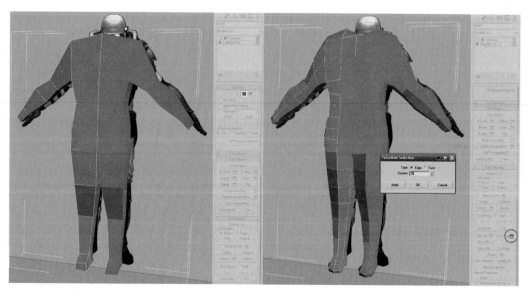

Now refine the verts to match the concept shape better. If you like, you can change the opacity of the material a little to make it easier to see the concept underneath.

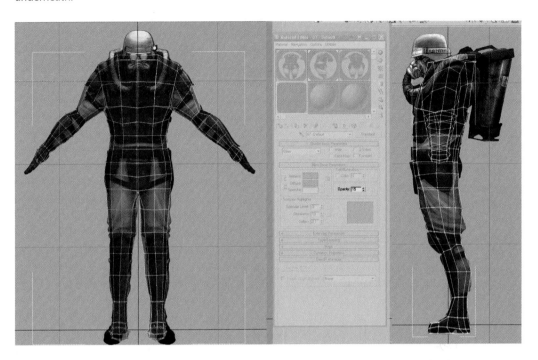

To make the fingers, connect the edges at the end of the hand to make four columns of polys.

One by one, extrude each column of two polys to form each finger.

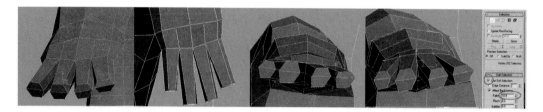

Refine the new vertices to make more natural finger shapes. I used Soft Selection with a larger Falloff setting to put a natural bend into the hand without having to move each point separately.

When moving verts in the Perspective view, I find it useful to switch the coordinate system from View to Screen. Screen coordinates aren't locked to the world x,y,z-axes like the View coordinates are, making fine adjustments in a perspective view much quicker and more intuitive.

It's important with nearly all models to keep a clean, quad-based topology. A pure quad mesh is much easier to "read," and you can work faster using the Loop and Ring functions. It's hard to see what's going on if you use a lot of triangles in your mesh, and they subdivide very unpredictably.

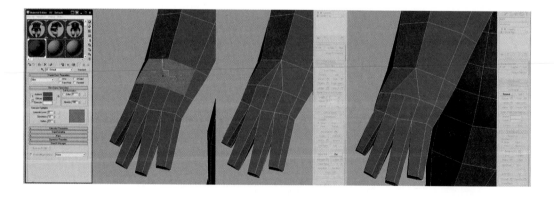

If you study the previous figure, you will notice that the two selected polygons have five vertices each. These faces with more than four verts are called *n*-gons. *N*-gons are just as bad as triangles when subdividing; during rendering they are triangulated unpredictably, so it's better that we turn them into quads. Use the Cut tool to cut some new edges as shown previously, then select the center edge and use the Remove button to eradicate it. Do the same on the bottom of the hand, too, to rid our mesh of all the evil *n*-gons.

Let's add more detail to the upper arms. Select and connect the top two rings of edges.

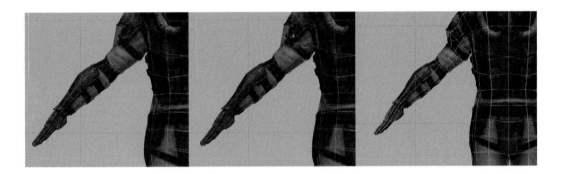

Work the forms into the mesh, adding new edge loops wherever you need more detail.

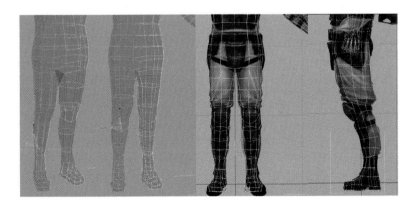

Add more edge loops to the legs and then shape the details. Try to model the edge loops along the main creases. Notice where I have angled the edge loops down to fit the shape of the kneepads.

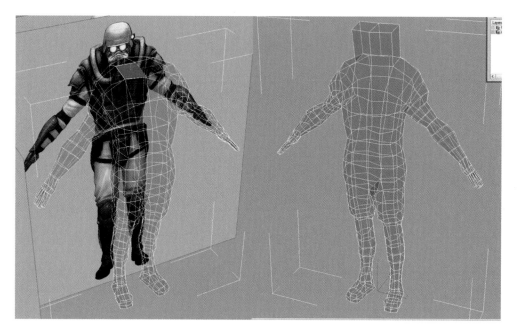

Extrude out a head from the top center polygon, make sure to delete the polygon that the extrusion creates on the line of symmetry then Tessellate the head to add more detail.

Cutting in More Detail

Now that we have the basic character shapes, let's cut in the medium-frequency details. These are the sub-shapes within each major shape, such as the main shape of each piece of armor, each strap, and the main flow of the fabrics. Add more geometry to the head, taking care to preserve a clean quad-based surface as you go. Take care not to make tiny details in one area before you have cut in all the main shapes—keep the level of detail consistent across the mesh.

The flow of the edges is very important; our aim is to try to make all the edge loops join together in flowing and continuous lines. Good edge flow makes much smoother and more natural surfaces.

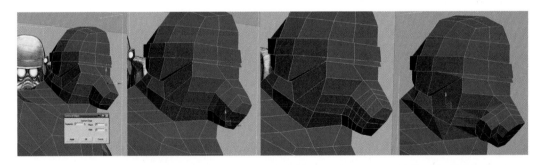

Notice the bad edge flow on the selected polygons in the previous image. There is a triangle in there, too, which isn't ideal. If we add edges and rework the topology, we can create a more organized surface. Don't expect the art of a perfect quad-based surface to come to you overnight, but with lots of practice, you will prevail. If you need some inspiration, visit some Internet forums and study other people's meshes to see how they are arranging their edge flows.

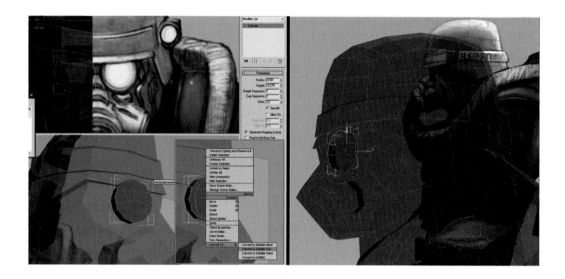

A primitive cylinder makes a great starting point for the eye, as it is perfectly round. We must make efficient use of our polygons so play with the parameters until you get a good balance between a nice model and a reasonable amount of geometry. I chose twelve sides and only one height segment. Convert the primitive into an Editable Poly when you are done, and remember to delete the back facing polygons. A classic beginner's mistake is to have loads of unnecessary polygons that are never seen because they are inside the mesh hidden by other polygons—don't do it!

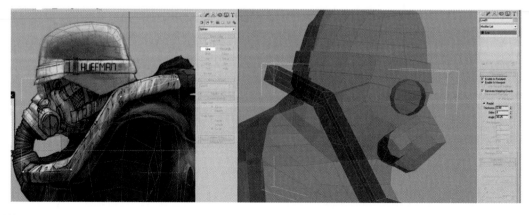

Another great starting point for your pipes, legs, and other twisty cylinders is the Line primitive in the Shapes section of the Create panel. First, draw out your line with a few simple vertices, then in the Modify panel, enable the line in the renderer and viewport, generate Automatic Mapping Coords (saving you UVing time later) and play with many aspects of the topology on the fly. It's easy, fast, and versatile, but best of all is that it creates very accurate meshes.

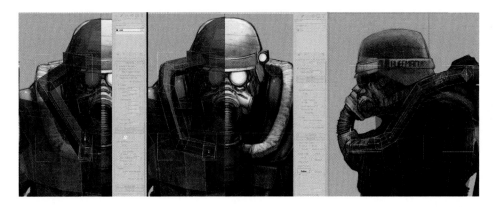

You can select and move the vertices in the Line, similar to how you would in Edit Poly, by using the stack in the Modify panel. Once you get the verts in the right place in each viewport, you can use the Refine tool to add more points to get the correct shape. Change the Sides parameter to give your line four sides and perhaps adjust the Angle setting, too. If you are happy with the shape, you can convert it into an Editable Poly. Before you do so, make a copy of the line and hide it—you can return to this hidden line if you want to make quick changes to the pipe topology later on.

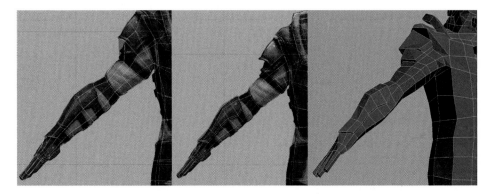

Once you have the main shapes and the edge flow working well on the arms, it's time to start extruding the pads and the straps to block out the detail. Be careful that your extrusions do not create hidden polygons inside the main geometry. The Hide/Unhide Polygon tools in Edit Poly are your best friends when things start to get a little more complex.

491

Remember to work on your model from as many angles as possible as you develop it. It will start to look flat if you only use the front and left views.

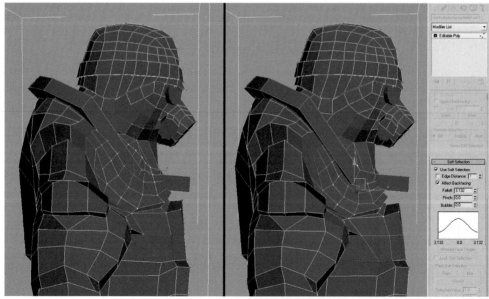

When meshes get more complex, it can be time-consuming to make changes to the overall shape, so remember to use Soft Selection. Why move one vertex at a time when you can move hundreds together? Adjust the falloff and away you go.

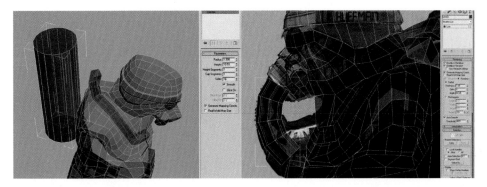

A primitive cylinder makes a good start for the oxygen tank; another line primitive does a great job for the central pipe on the mask.

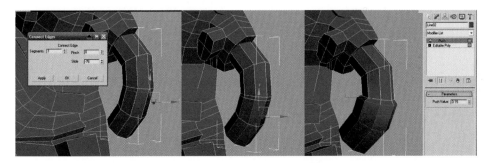

Select the line that makes the central pipe on the mask and select Convert to Editable Poly. Select the ring of edges where we want to increase the diameter of the pipe and connect the edges; use the Slide parameter to move it higher. Select the two lowest rings of edges below and apply a push modifier to flare out the pipe a little, then collapse the stack back down to an Editable Poly.

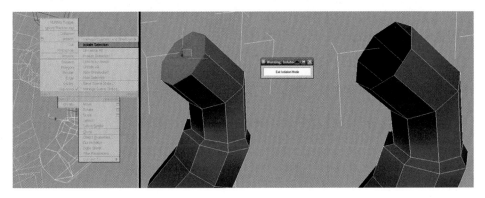

Right-click on your pipe object and choose Isolate Selection. This command is very useful when you want to see all sides of the object without other objects getting in the way. Delete the hidden faces at the top, and click the Exit Isolation Mode button.

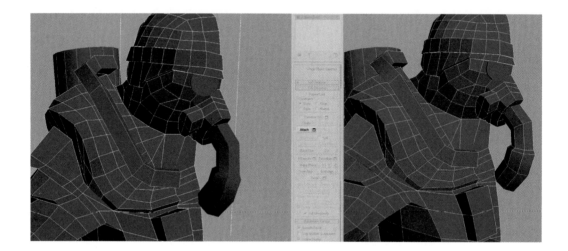

To add this pipe geometry to the main mesh, first delete the left-hand side of it so that it can be mirrored like the rest of the model. Select the main mesh, click the Attach button, and click the pipe.

Add some more geometry around the torso and under the arms. It's important to visualize the body underneath the clothes as you mold your character. Imagine where the major muscles are sitting, and how they are pushing on the clothes. It's a good idea to look at the model from underneath quite often; if you make your model look correct from this often-overlooked view, it helps make your model more accurate.

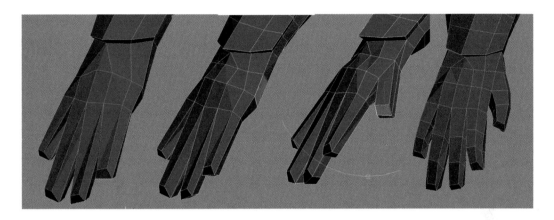

Start on the hands by extruding out a thumb, and cut in some more loops on the fingers to add a slight curve to each finger.

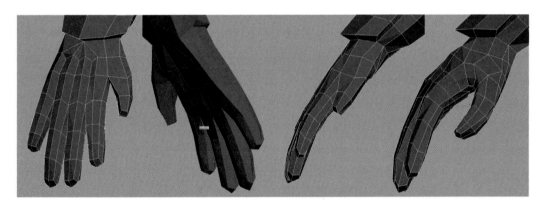

As you develop the hand/glove, it's useful to have your reference by your side, so that you can copy the real-life hands/gloves as closely as possible. If you're having trouble making your hand look correct, study your own hand. One of the most common beginner's mistakes is to make the thumb bend like the fingers. The thumb should bend at 90 degrees to the bend of the fingers. It's also very important to build curvature into the palm.

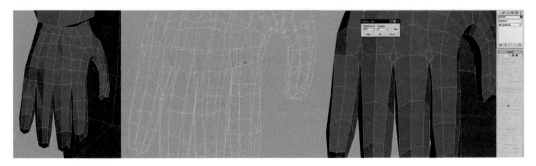

Let's make the gaps between the fingers less angular and more natural; select the edges between each finger and chamfer them.

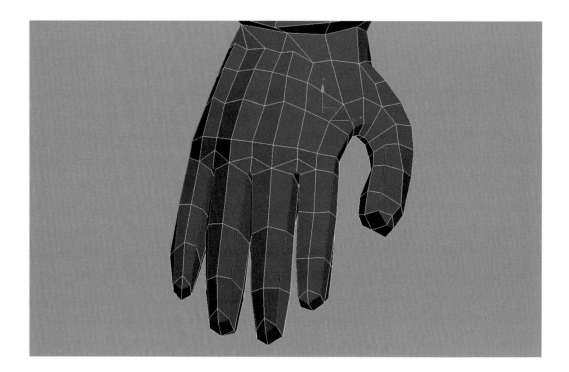

Cut some edges and weld (I like to use TargetWeld) the rogue points together so that you get a topology something like the following figure. The aim is to get a smooth loop that flows around the rim of the glove. The glove isn't perfect yet, but let's move up the arm so that we keep an even amount of detail across the body.

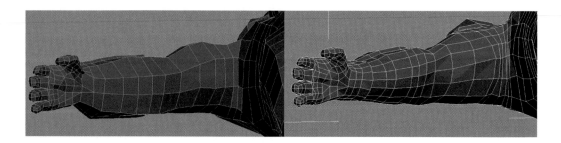

Try to improve the look of the arm as much as you can without adding any more geometry. Once everything is in place, cut in more loops to define the straps and pads on his arms. Pay attention to the direction of the loops: they must follow the contours of the outfit.

When modeling hard-to-reach places such as the cavity near the shoulder pads, you have a few secret weapons in your arsenal. It will be much easier to rotate around your selections if you activate Arc Rotate SubObject near the bottom right of the interface. You can flatten areas by selecting the relevant polygons and pressing the Make Planar button; if you wish to smooth out a selection of polys, press the Relax button. Another top tip for being able to see what you are doing in difficult places is to hide some polygons. Press the Hide button to hide your selection of polys; Unhide All brings them back when you have finished.

Continue going around the body, looking at it from different angles and tightening things up. Be sure to study some reference material of a suitably tough-looking male shot from as many different angles as possible. Good anatomical references help you build up the volumes of muscle, bone, flesh, and fat that lie underneath our characters clothing. Again, working from the obscure top and bottom angles that really helps give an extra "punch" to the forms.

At this point, you should have all the major shapes modeled as in the following images. The total character at this point contains approximately 5,000 triangles.

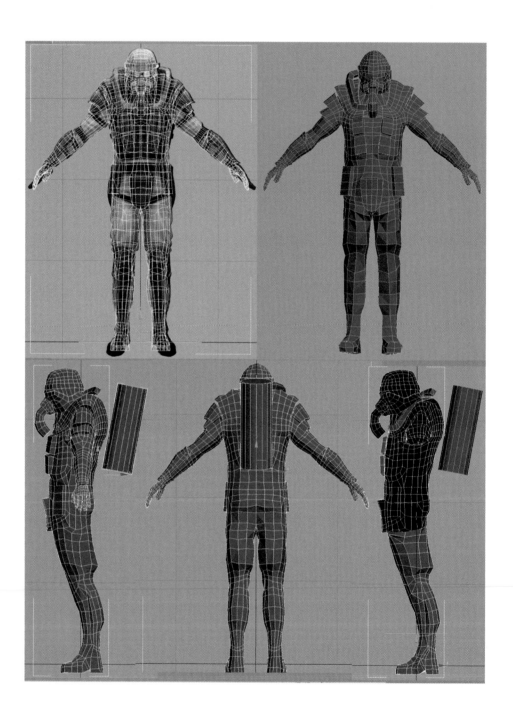

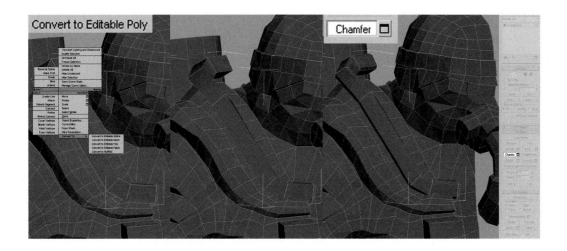

Once you are happy with the air pipes that you made with the Line primitive, you can convert them to an Editable Poly. The edges are a little sharp, so use the Chamfer function to round them out a little.

Continue to work more detail into the main lines of the mesh, using all our old favorites, such as Cut, Move, Loop, Ring, Connect, Extrude, Relax, and so on.

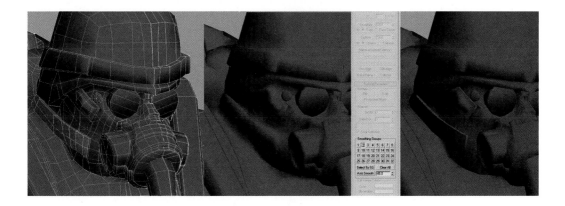

I find it easier to work with the mesh if I give each major group of polygons (kneepads, soles, gloves, and so on) a different smoothing group; this allows us to better see the boundaries between different areas as we work. A fast way to do this is to use the Auto Smooth button, but you might need to refine its work in places.

Keep adding details until your mesh is about 13,500 triangles, you can use the following images for rough reference. Don't go crazy trying to match my model exactly, but the detail should be evenly spread throughout the body, with a slight emphasis on the face.

Make sure to save your mesh around this point. Although it isn't detailed enough for our high-res mesh, it is certainly a good starting point for additional detail. Also, with a little tweaking, it will make an excellent game mesh when we load it back up later on. I call this mesh the "proxy mesh," because it is approximately the same form as both the game mesh and the high-res mesh.

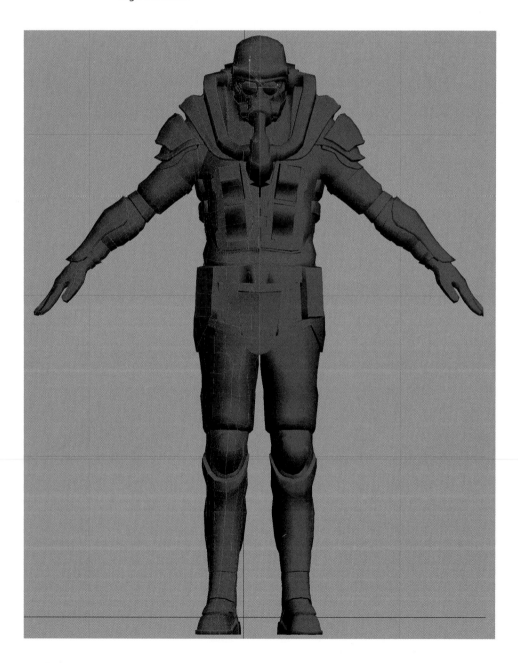

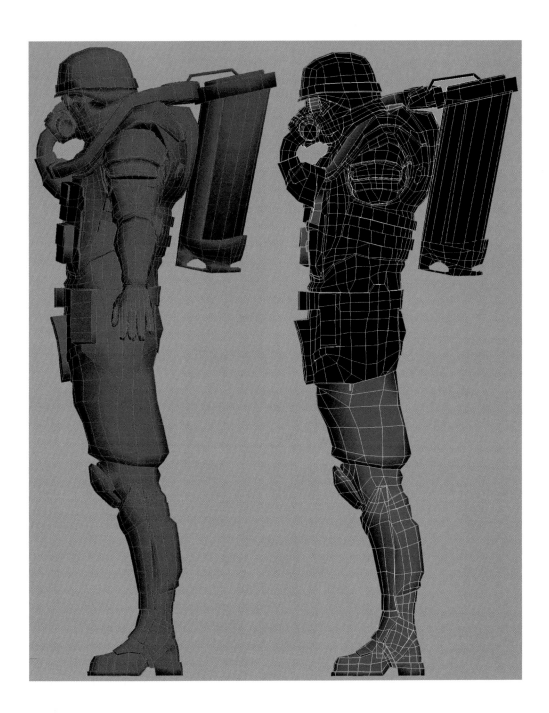

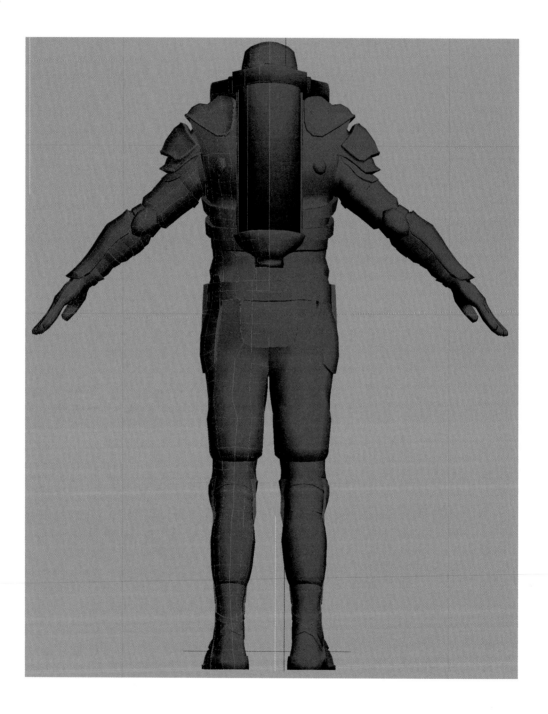

The High-Resolution Mesh: Breaking Up the Shapes

Now it is time to start the high-res modeling. As the level of detail increases, I find it much easier to work if we break up the mesh into each individual component. Select the polygons for each distinct part of the body, and break them into separate meshes using the Detach button. Each mesh can then be isolated if you need to work on the hard-to-see areas.

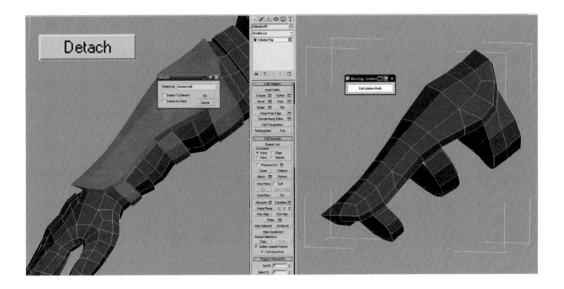

If the separate parts of the mesh aren't actually welded together, you can easily select them for detaching using the Element selection.

The Shell Modifier

It's very important to give even the thinnest shapes some amount of thickness. The quickest and also the most accurate way to do this is to apply the shell modifier and increase either the Inner Amount or Outer Amount parameter. You might want to delete some of the polygons on the inside, as they won't be seen.

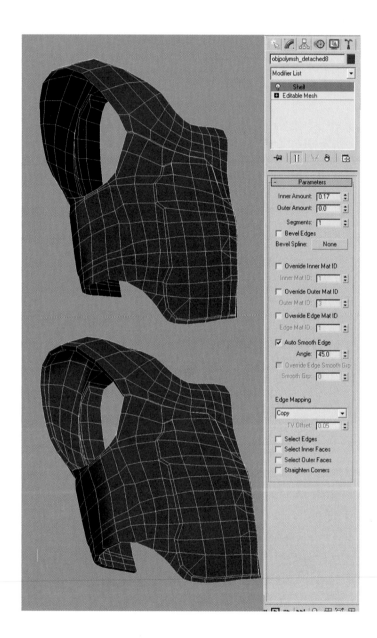

The High-Resolution Mesh: Adding More Detail

As you add all the sub-shapes that make up each piece of the character, you should not need any other tools than the ones we've used already. Just study the concept and the reference material very carefully as you work. Be careful not to get into too much detail in any one area of the character. The aim is to roughly mark in all the shapes until you get to about the level of detail in the following images:

Helmet

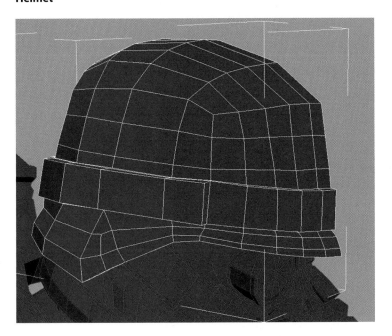

Mask

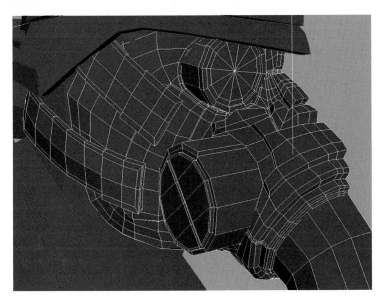

Vest

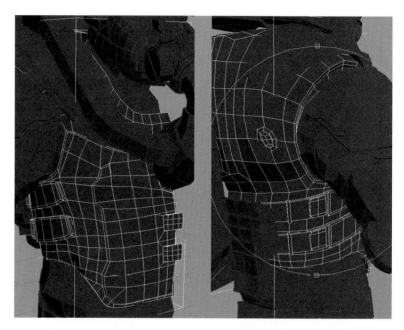

Shoulder pads

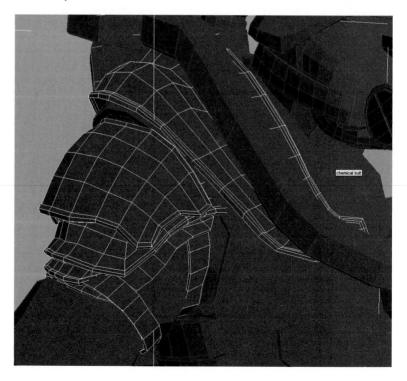

Forearm pad and kneepad

Gas tank

Glove

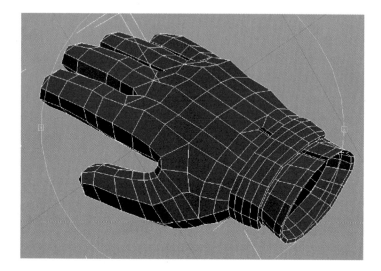

Belt and details

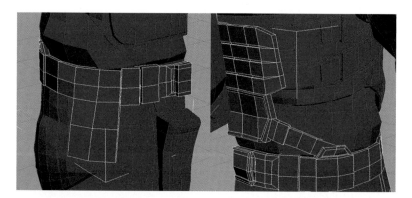

Codpiece and other details

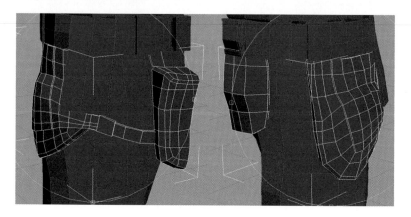

Shin pads

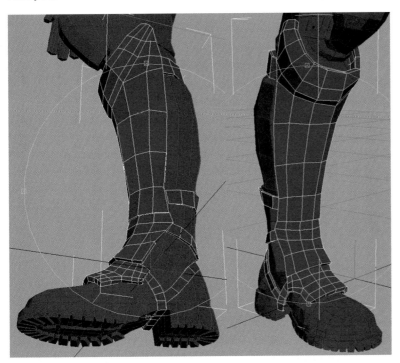

Kneepad and shoe

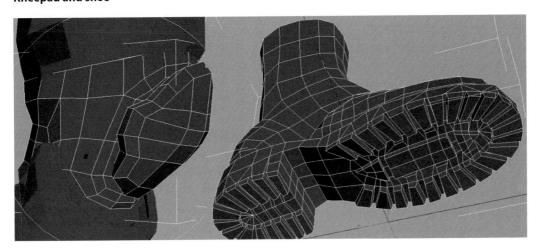

Chemical Suit

Most importantly, the chemical suit is modeled underneath everything. This will make sure that there are no gaps left in our mesh. A common beginner's mesh will have lots of holes in it where the various meshes meet, and this is a great way to avoid that. Don't model in any creases or folds yet; we will tackle that later.

Breathing Pipe

An accurate and superfast way to make the breathing pipe is to use the Loft compound object. Delete the old breathing pipe, and in the side view, draw out a rough spline using the Line primitive. I've indicated on the following image the three clicks that I made to draw the line. Be sure to hold the left mouse button down as you drag out each point, so you can control the shape of the line as you create it.

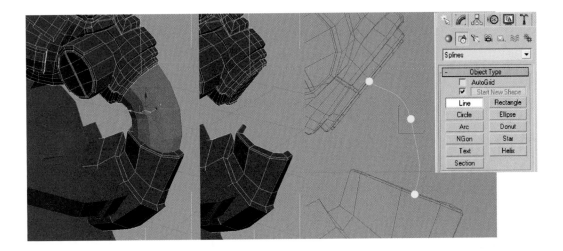

If your line is anything like mine it still looks a little wonky! Go into the Modify panel, select Vertex, and then click on each point and adjust the handles to get a good, smooth line. Also check that your line is correctly positioned in 3D space; it should be centered on the symmetry line of the model. We will call this line the Path of our loft, and it gives the shape to the length of the object.

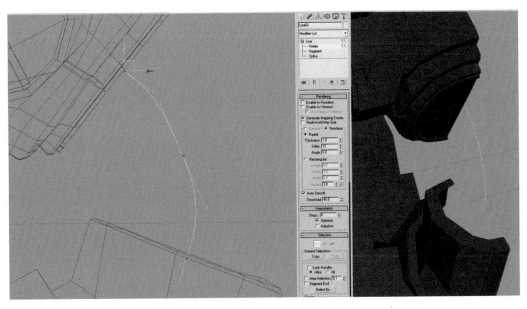

Let's draw the shape of the Profile curve that will give the volume to our Path line. For this we will use a circle primitive from the Splines rollout. Drag out the circle from the top view and scale and position it at the top of the Path curve. Take care to *not* rotate it.

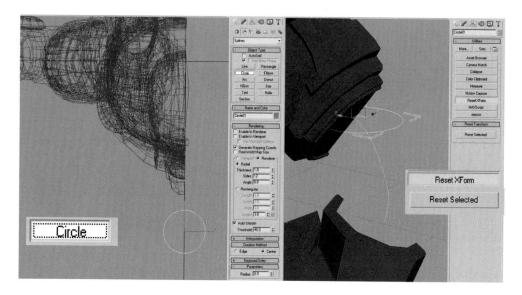

The next step is to reset the Xform of these two splines, Reset Xform resets the translation, scale, and rotation information back to how they were when the object was created. Having "zeroed out" transform values is critical for operations such as lofting that rely on this information. Reset Xform can be found in the Utility panel; with each of the two loft curves selected, press the Reset Selected button.

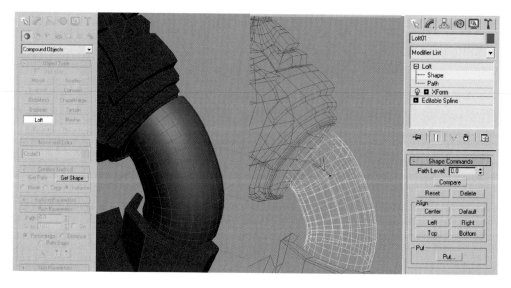

Select the Path shape and execute the Loft command, which is hidden in the Create Panels Geometry section (select Compound Objects from the drop-down menu). Click on the Get Shape button, then in the viewport, select the Profile circle, and 3ds Max should create a basic Loft shape.

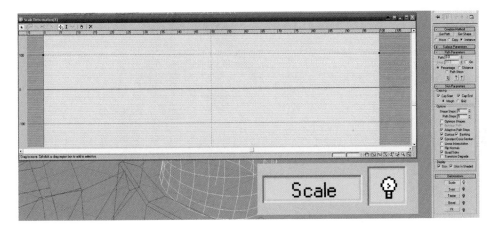

We have the basic shape looking pretty good now, but the real power of Loft shapes comes with the Deformation controls. Let's use the Scale deformer to add the ribbed details to the surface. At the bottom of your new Loft object's modifier panel, click on the Scale deformation button. Adjust the graph that pops up so it is long and thin as shown in the previous image. You might find that the zoom extends the horizontal button—useful for framing the graph correctly in the window.

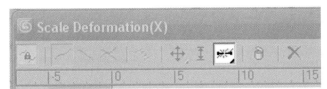

Select the Insert Bezier Point button from the Scale Deformation interface.

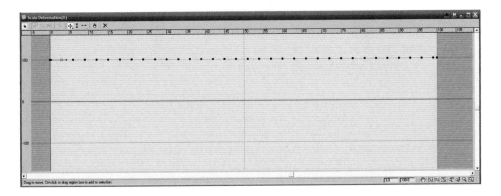

With the Insert Bezier Point tool active, click on the red line to add a Bezier point at roughly every four units along the x-axis across the line, your line should look something like the image shown previously.

With the Move Control Point tool active, select any one point on the graph. You can see the x-y coordinate of the selected point in the bottom right-hand area of the Scale Deformation window.

The "x" represents how far along the Path we are, and "y" represents the scale (which is constant at 1 the whole way across, at the moment). To get our ribbed details spaced apart with precision, let's type in an exact number into the left-hand x coordinate box for each point. Here, your knowledge of your "3" multiplication tables will pay dividends! Repeat after me: 3, 6, 9, 12, 15, 18, 21, 24…96, 99.

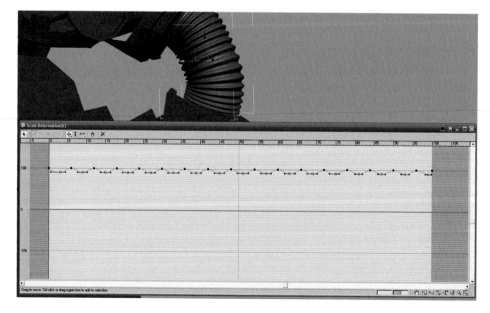

To create the bumps in the ribbed surface, select every other vertex (that is, the ones at 3, 9, 12, 18, and so on), and in the "y" coordinate box, type in 90. Boom! The details appear. Open up the Modifier panel and check the Generate Mapping Coords option, which will save us time when generating UVs later.

Subdividing Your Model with TurboSmooth

The mesh is getting pretty detailed now, but it would take an eternity to keep adding geometry until we lose the harsh, angular look. This is where the TurboSmooth modifier comes in very handy.

Each iteration of TurboSmooth subdivides each polygon into four smaller polygons, relaxing them at the same time. Similar technologies exist in all major 3D applications. These types of surfaces are generally known as "subdivisional surfaces," or SUBDs for short.

The key advantage to using TurboSmooth is that we can make fast changes to a simple poly mesh and not get bogged down tweaking millions of vertices to make a smooth curve. This smoothness is also the biggest drawback; at times it can be very tricky to preserve areas of the model that require sharp edges.

515

Micro-Bevelling

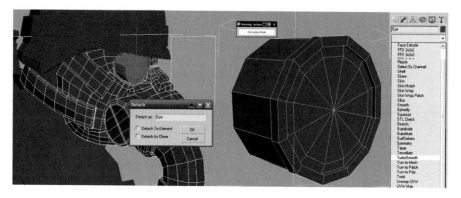

Let's start our smoothing process with one of the simplest objects: the lens of the goggle in the mask. Select just your eye geometry, and detach it to create a separate mesh.

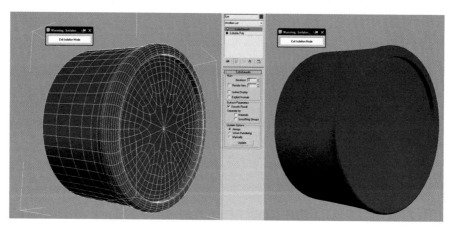

Apply a TurboSmooth modifier and push the iterations up to 2. As you dial up the iterations, the circular form of the eye gets rounded nicely, but we lose the crisp edges on the corners.

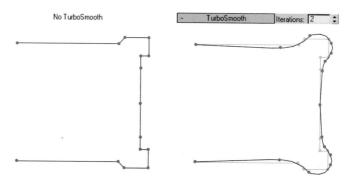

We can see the TurboSmooth effect most clearly by studying the side profile. TurboSmooth works by averaging out the positions of the vertices; those that are far apart from each other get moved quite substantially, and not always to your advantage. If you build your models with vertices closer together in areas with drastic changes of shape (sharp edges), they will be less dramatically affected when TurboSmoothed.

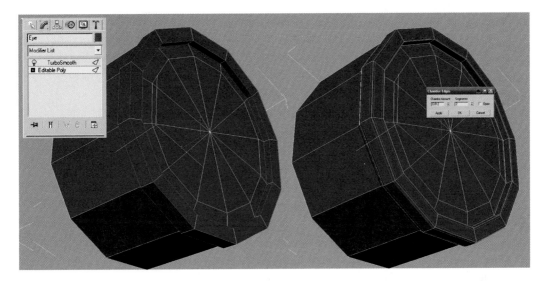

Go down the object stack and select Editable Poly. Select all the corner edges that you would like to sharpen up using the Loop tool. Chamfer these edges so that you get a nice corner bevel on each edge; I used the setting 0.012 for the chamfer amount, but this will change depending on the scale of your scene. Select two segments for each chamfer.

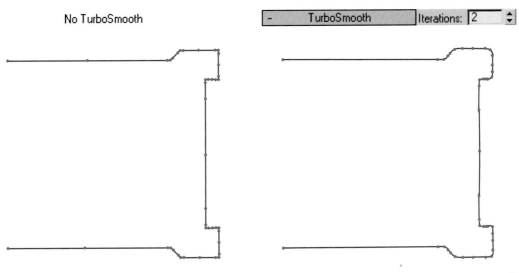

Your cylinder should look something similar to this figure from the side profile; the extra geometry locks into place the effect of the smoothing.

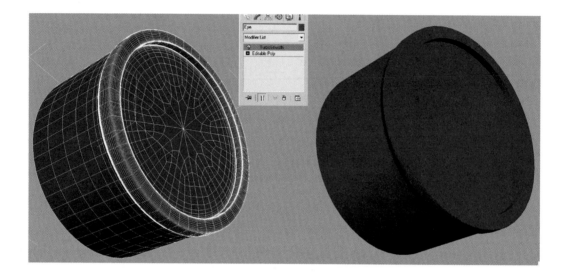

The results should be like the previous image: a perfectly round cylinder with hard edges at the corners. This technique is dubbed "micro-bevelling" in the industry, because sometimes the detail you must put in on an awkward corner area gets pretty tiny.

If you build your models with nice, orderly quads it is very fast and easy to add micro-bevels by selecting loops and chamfering them. Another advantage of doing your modeling operations on loop selections is that it keeps everything uniform across the edge. Most machined, inorganic forms like this goggle lens are made on a production line in a factory, and as such are very regular shapes. Unless you want this type of shape to look worn or old, you should try to avoid going in and hand tweaking individual vertices; it will lead to irregularities that will make them look handmade. Instead, do your inorganic modeling using modifiers and operations on loop-based selections.

Micro-Bevelling the Shoe Edges

The really tricky SUBD stuff comes when we have edges on more than one axis coming together. For example, take the edges of the sole of the shoe where the tread pattern might involve bevelled edges meeting on all three axes at many corner points. The simple solution is to do all your chamfering at the same time.

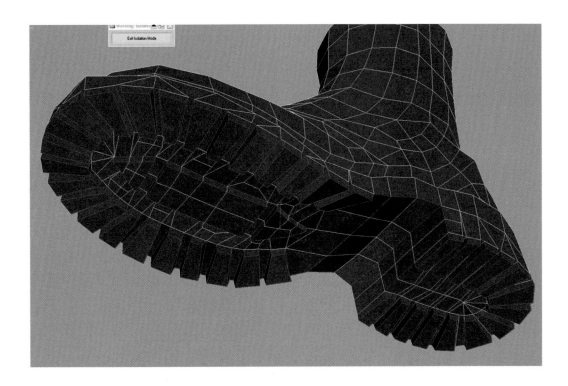

First, select all the edges that you would like to perform the chamfer on.

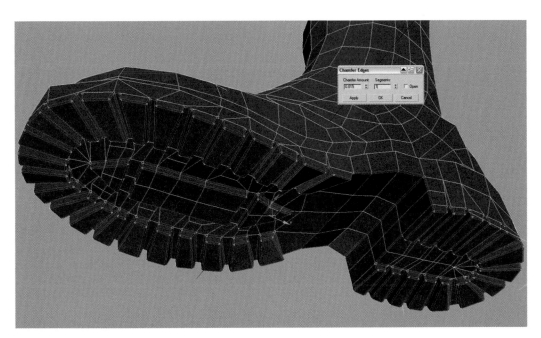

Then use the Chamfer button and tweak the amount to control the roundness of the edges.

This way is much faster and cleaner than doing your bevelling one piece at a time. If you select some edges, chamfer them, and repeat the process for other nearby edges, things quickly get messy. If we perform the chamfer operation to all the edges at the same time, we create a relatively orderly and even topology.

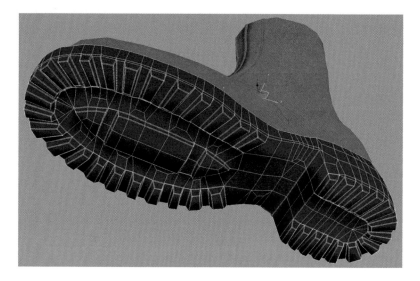

The last thing to do is to go through the mesh and reorder the topology to get the nice and clean square-quads look that characterizes a high-quality SUBD mesh. I've detached the sole from the shoe to help keep things simple.

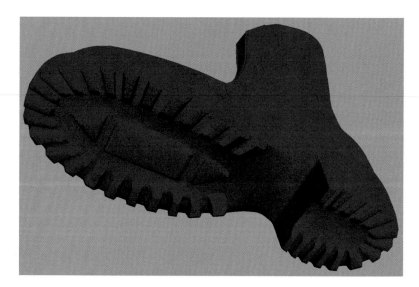

Finishing the Symmetrical Details

One by one, work through your objects, adding TurboSmoothing, refining the details, and taking special care with the details of sharp and bevelled edges. Avoid creating any asymmetrical details (such as the creases and folds of the trousers); we will tackle these details later on.

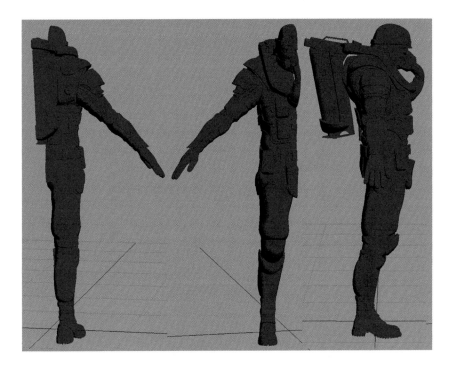

Your mesh should now look something like the previous image, with everything apart from the asymmetrical folds and creases of the clothing modeled in fine detail. Once you are happy with your half-character, give it another quick check for holes and other defects. It's going to be much quicker to fix things now, before we copy the mesh across the central line of symmetry and create a right side and a left side that both need identical repair work.

In 3D modeling, it is always beneficial to use symmetry to your advantage. If you take care to get things as good as you can before you mirror them, it will make your modeling almost twice as fast.

Making the UVs in UVlayout

In order to get a texture onto our high-res model, we need to give it UV coordinates. This procedure can be time-consuming and, dare I say it, tedious and boring! Typical high-res meshes have polygon counts measured in the millions, so we need every trick in the book to get these UVs done well and in a reasonable amount of time. 3ds Max has some fairly good UVing tools for production, like the Pelt Mapper and the Relax function, but I've found a small program called UVlayout to be far superior when generating UVs for complex high-res shapes. UVlayout optimizes your UVs for subdivision, taking into account how the UVs will be stretched when subdivided.

The UVlayout interface is not very pretty or intuitive, but if you watch the tutorial videos available for download from http://www.uvlayout.com, you will see just how amazing the program is. So don't judge that book by its cover! In my experience, unwrapping in UVlayout is more than twice as fast as unwrapping in Max, Maya, or XSI. The quality of UVs that UVlayout produces is also much higher. The distortion-free UVs generated by UVlayout will save us lots of time and prevent frustration later when we texture this object. A trial version of this software is available on this book's DVD under \UVlayout\.

To keep things simple, we will import and unwrap each part of the character one piece at a time in UVlayout, so export each part as a separate Wavefront (OBJ) file from 3ds Max (File > Export Selected). You should now have a list of objects organized in a UVing folder (such as belt.obj, boots.obj, vest.obj, and so on).

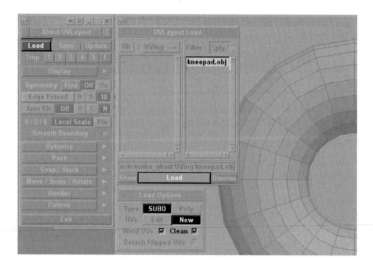

In UVlayout, click the blue Load button and browse to your UVing folder where you saved all the OBJ files. Load up kneepad.obj first; it's a simple object that will make a nice introduction to UVlayout. Remember to check your Load Options before you load the mesh; UVlayout will take the effect of the TurboSmooth SUBDs into account if you select Type SUBD. Be sure to select the UVs New button too, which deletes any old UVs that might be already applied to your object. Check the Weld UVs and Clean boxes to ensure a tidy mesh, and then, with the correct object highlighted in blue, click the green Load button.

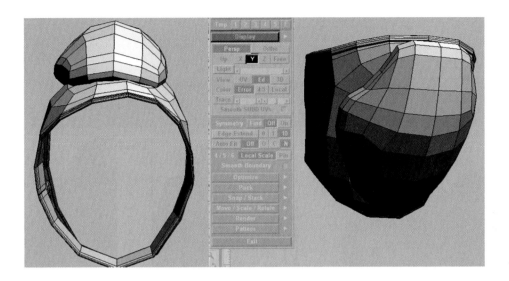

The first thing you might notice is that your kneepads are being viewed from below. Open up the Display panel and select "Y" to change UVlayout's coordinate system. If you hold Alt, you can navigate in the 3D scene using the left mouse button to orbit, the middle mouse button to pan, and the right mouse button to zoom in and out. In the Display section of the interface, there are three different types of views, which you can select quickly using the 1, 2, and 3 keys:

- UV view shows in 2D your unwrapped UV coordinates.
- Ed or Edit view shows in 3D only your objects that currently have no UVs assigned yet.
- 3D view shows the original 3D object intact.

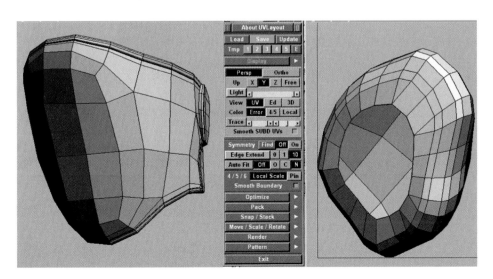

When you load the kneecap object into UVlayout, the default view is the Edit view. As you selected NEW when loading the object, it will have no UVs, and therefore its surface should be gray. If you move the mouse cursor over the main plastic kneecap shape at the front of the object and press D, the kneecap will disappear. The shape has not been deleted; instead, UVs have been assigned to it, so it is not shown in the Ed view anymore. Press 1 to jump to UV view and locate your kneecap UVs, which should still be a gray color, as they are not flattened out yet.

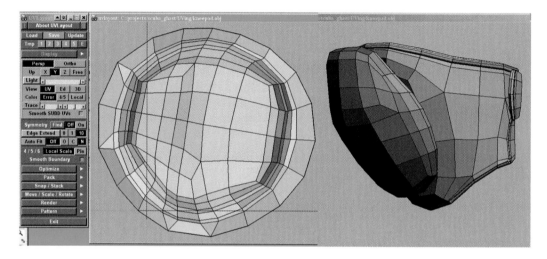

While you are still in the UV view, hold your mouse cursor over the kneecap UVs, hold the spacebar, and press F. Watch with joy as the UVs unfold themselves in a weird and wonderful way. Colors appear on the UVs now; red represents areas that do not have their fair share of UV space and blue represents areas that have too much UVspace. Both red and blue areas show distortion, and we must seek to minimize that. If you press 3 to jump to the 3D view, you can see the colors now applied to the kneecap, showing in 3D space where the distortion is occurring.

Let's help the UVshell to relax a little more by making some cuts; cuts in the correct places will help our geometry unwrap. For most "closed" objects, cuts are mandatory—anything circular like a cylinder or sphere needs at least one major cut in order to be able to unwrap at all. I like to think about unwrapping similar to how a primitive stone age hunter might skin an animal to make a cave jacket. A less gory analogy is to compare your final layout of UVs to how a tailor cuts shapes from a blank piece of fabric to make a garment.

Like the seams that a tailor deals with, cutting up your shell generates UV seams in the UVlayout. The UV seams are a necessary evil that you must minimize. These could cause problems later if you want to paint your textures quickly and easily in Photoshop. You will need a 3D paint program such as ZBrush or Bodypaint in order to be able to paint continuous textures over seam areas. Furthermore each UV seam can cause problems further down the line with normal mapping.

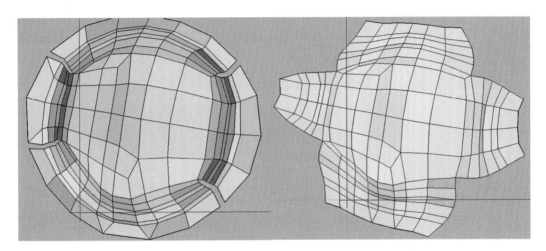

Press 1 to jump back to the UV view and then zoom into the top half of the kneecap UVs so that you can clearly see the details of each edge. With the mouse hovering over the relevant edges, press the C key a number of times to make cuts as shown above. Remember that the first cut you make must start from an open edge on the outside boundary of the shell, you cannot start your cuts from the middle of the shell. If you make a mistake, you can weld your cut edges back together by hovering over them and pressing the W key. With the mouse cursor hovering over the object, hold the spacebar again and press F to unfold the object once more. It should be able to relax much better now with the new cuts, giving you a new relatively distortion-free unwrap.

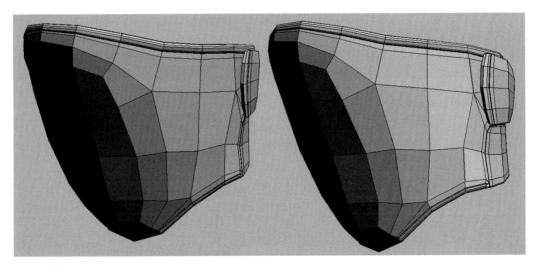

In Edit mode, the C and W keys have extended powers in that they work well with Loop-based topology—another great reason to model in clean quads as much as you can. As UV seams hinder our texturing, we must hide them away, thinking carefully about their placement before we draw them.

On character legs, the most unseen areas are the inside surfaces, as they are normally hidden by the opposite leg. Go to the inside leg side of the "kneepad elastic" shape and press the C key on one of the vertical edges. Your "cut" edge is marked in red. UVlayout will try to predict how you would like to continue the cuts along the loop with lines marked in yellow; if you disagree with any of these yellow lines, you can weld them back together with W. It takes only two or three clicks with C for you to have made enough cuts to unfold this area successfully.

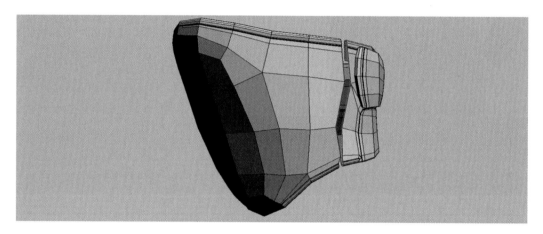

As we are dealing with a closed shape, before we drop the shell into UV space, we need to "split" the cut edges. Hold your mouse over the red and yellow edges that you wish to split and press Shift+S to use the Split Seams command. The edges should split apart like in the previous example.

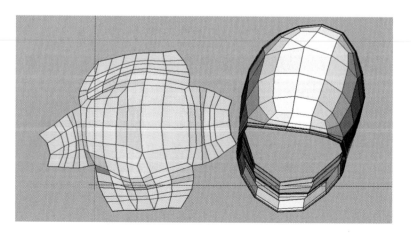

Now you can press D on this mesh to drop it into UV space, press 1 to go back to the UV view, and then unflatten it as shown below.

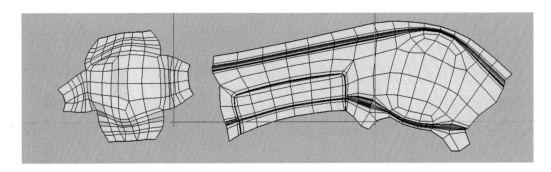

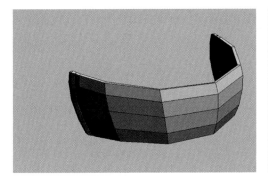

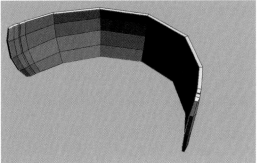

Press 2 to jump to Edit view, and you will see that there is now just the strap, which doesn't have UVs. Use the C key to make cuts until you have a closed loop of cuts going around in a circle. As always, it is best to hide the seam on the inside surface of the strap where it won't be seen clearly; you will get an intuitive feel for where to place seams after spending plenty of time unwrapping various objects.

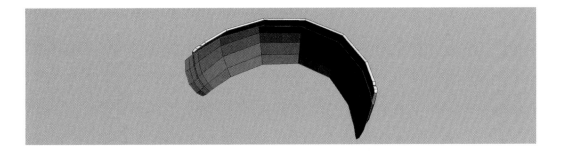

Press Shift+S again to split the seams, then press D to drop each piece into the UV mode. Press 1 to go back to UV view and unflatten each piece.

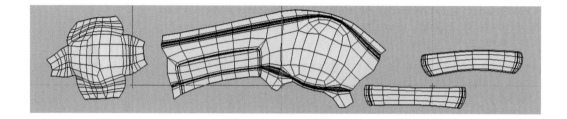

If you press W on a few of the shared edges of these two straps, you can see the matching edges turn red to indicate that it is possible to weld them back together. Press Return on one of these shells once you've marked some red weld lines, and UVlayout will join them back together. Unflatten the shells again to finish, and save your work.

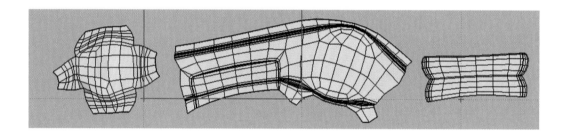

For anyone from the old school of UV unwrapping, UVlayout is nothing short of a revolution. It would take me days to unwrap a simple 1,000-poly character in 3ds Max 3 with the Unwrap modifier; the same job now takes less than an hour and I get much better results. UVlayout is incredibly powerful software, but I can't hope to cover all the cool features like pinning UVs, straightening UVs, and auto-packing UVs in this chapter. If you want an easy life with UVs, you would be wise to watch all the tutorial videos posted on the UVlayout Web site (http://www.uvlayout.com).

It's essential to unwrap our half-character *before* we mirror over our character; this precaution will make things go almost twice as fast. Once you are happy with your half-character unwrapped, you can add a Symmetry modifier to the mesh, collapse the stack, and then select and flip the UVs from one side to the other. It is then a simple job to weld the left and right halves together to get rid of any unnecessary seams. When arranging my UVs, I start with the largest shapes first; the smaller shapes will fit in the gaps once you have the main shapes in place. Try not to waste big areas of space in your UVlayout, because in video games memory is critical and shouldn't be frittered away on half-empty maps.

I like to lay out my UVs in a meaningful arrangement, with the head at the top and the feet at the bottom arranged as if the character is looking straight at you. If you pass your work through a production pipeline, anyone who has to pick up your work and make some tweaks to the texture will thank you for making the texture layout as readable as possible.

The Asymmetrical Details: Making the Folds and Creases

It is now very common in professional modeling production pipelines for two or more apps to be used as each application offers its unique advantages. More and more studios are turning to ZBrush to make the organic shapes that characterize the folds and creases that occur on clothing and anatomy. ZBrush can make the process of organic detailing quick and easy, but as this book focuses on 3ds Max, we are going to make the folds the old way: with SUBD surfaces. Traditional SUBDs take longer to produce, but one benefit will be the efficient use of polygons and system resources. Our Max clothing will be perhaps ten times lighter (very high-poly assets are described as "heavy" in industry jargon) than a typical garment detailed in ZBrush, and it is good practice for making flowing SUBD geometry.

On the concept that I have been given, the creases are symmetrical— probably a measure taken by the concept artist to shave some hours off his busy schedule. Copying this symmetry into the 3D model is not good for realism, as the creases in all clothing are asymmetrical. Knowing when to follow the concept and when to correct it is very important. Keep a sharp, critical eye on your work so that the mistakes of the concept artist don't get transferred to your models.

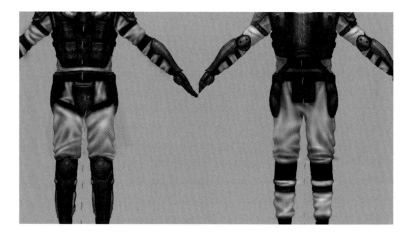

As the creases and folds of the fabrics can take a couple of days to model in SUBDs, I've sketched out a quick plan for my creases first. This way, if I don't like the flow of the creases, I can quickly amend them in minutes, not hours.

Flow, Flow, Flow!

When modeling organic shapes like the creases, it is critical that each curve flows smoothly into the next; look for unnaturally straight lines and eliminate them. Use Relax to melt the polygons into each other. It makes sense to assign a hotkey to the Relax button, as you should constantly use it. Take care that your creases don't all point in one direction; study some photos of people in clothing and you will see the multilateral qualities that creases take on as they try to conform to the shape of the body.

If you use Relax multiple times and the geometry still looks jagged and awkward, the problem is probably your edge flow. Put your mesh in wireframe and adjust any areas where the edges don't run together in nice smooth lines.

Gravity, Tension, and the Feel of the Fabric

Be aware of gravity and how it affects your garments; baggy areas sag, but areas supported by the body remain firm. Imagining the body underneath the clothing is very important. Be aware that protruding parts of the body, belts, and straps pull on the fabric, creating areas of tension. I keep lots of references of the material that I'm modeling handy as I work to make sure that my model has the same look and feel as the fabric that I'm trying to mimic.

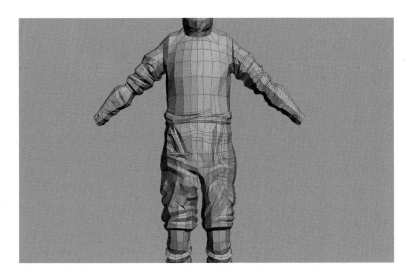

To start, just model in all the major creases of the body without too much care for the topology. Just try to get the edge loops pointing in the same direction as the flow of the fabric for now—it should look something like the following figure, in which I have isolated the mesh for better system performance, but for many areas, it's important to view the rest of the character as you create an NBC suit, so that you can really get the feeling of the suit material bunching up in areas where it is restricted by the pads and elastics straps on top of it.

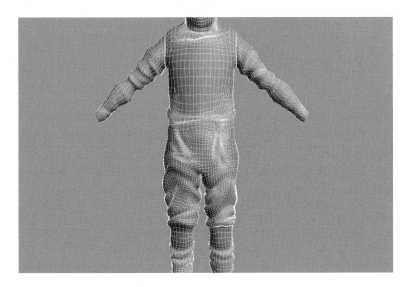

Once you have cut in the basic shape of each and every crease and fold, you can add additional details to refine each part. When all the details have been modeled in, it is just a matter of reflowing the topology to eliminate any awkward areas that don't look so smooth and natural. It is good to preview your suit all smoothed out with the TurboSmooth modifier at regular intervals so that you can see how it will look when it is finished.

Bear in mind that although it is possible to model on the Editable Poly with the TurboSmooth showing further up the stack (using the Show End Result toggle), in the industry, it is generally considered bad practice. Meshes created in SUBD mode like this quickly get messy and tangled up, and are very confusing to work with if you have to drop back down to the Edit Poly level to make a change. With SUBDs, experience is the best teacher; a few projects down the line, you will be able to accurately predict how your meshes will subdivide. Don't rely on TurboSmooth to create a smooth mesh for you—it's only as good as the base mesh that you feed into it.

Once you've finished adding all the creases, reflatten your NBC suit UVs in UVlayout and make any final tweaks to the layout. It's important to get the UVs as distortion-free as possible to make life easier when texturing.

The Ambient Occlusion Bake

Ambient occlusion (AO) maps are an industry-standard method of baking subtle lighting information into models. AO maps describe how exposed each part of the surface is: the cracks and gaps hidden away in cavities receive very little light and render in dark tones, and the flat, exposed surfaces render in light tones. An AO's soft, scattered light adds a great feeling of depth to your creations. I find it very useful when finishing off my model to render an AO map and apply it to the model. Rendering AO maps in 3ds Max is very simple:

• Apply a white Phong material to your character.

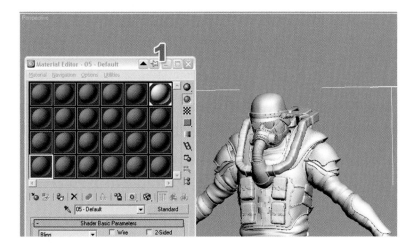

• Go to the Lights creation panel and select Skylight. Click to create a Skylight anywhere in the scene. The placement is not important; anywhere will do.

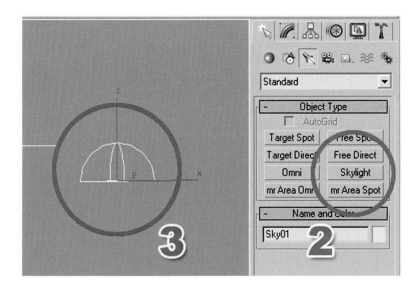

- Select Render > Advanced Lighting > Light Tracer. Be sure that the "Light tracer active" tick box is checked.
- With the character object selected, select Rendering > Render To Texture.

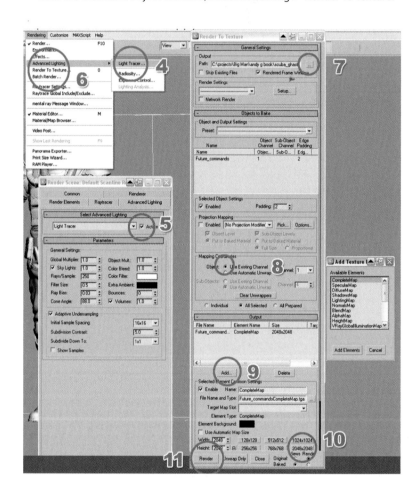

- Choose an output path for the AO map. Be sure that this render will use the Existing (UV) channel.
- Add a CompleteMap render element. Choose a map size of 2048 × 2048.
- Hit Render and watch as 3ds Max calculates the AO and renders it to a texture.

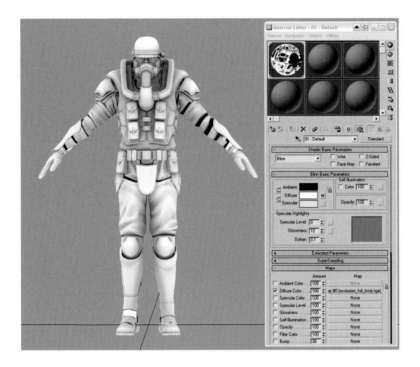

- Apply the newly created AO map to the diffuse map slot in the character's material, and set the diffuse color to white.

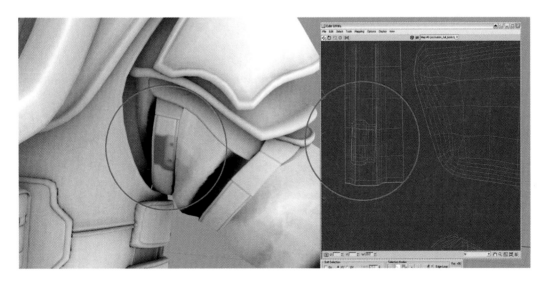

With AO applied to the model, it is a lot easier to see where all the overlapping geometry, holes, and other UV errors are occurring.

If you get areas that have been rendered with weird-looking patterns on them, the chances are that you have overlapping UVs. Apply the UnwrapUVW modifier and make sure that all the UVs have their own space; get rid of all the overlapping UVs.

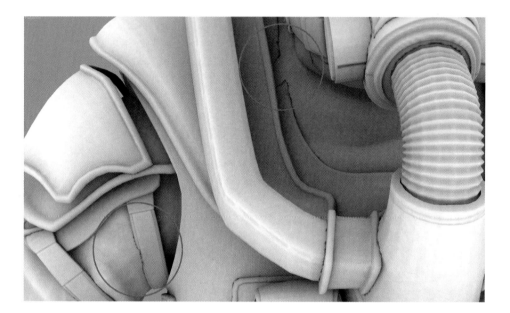

AO helps me a lot when fixing overlapping areas as it really highlights anything that's not right. Have a quick look over your model to see if you have any problems with intersecting geometry. Once you've fixed all these problems, you can render the ambient occlusion map again; if there are still problems, repeat the process until you are entirely happy with the model and the UVs.

Final Tweaks

So you think you've finished the modeling? I ask you to take another detailed look over your model—you will probably find some mistakes. Perhaps wait a day and come back to your work with fresh eyes. I know some artists who like to flip their work upside down or mirror it horizontally when reviewing their work, as this can give you a different perspective on that model you've been staring at nonstop for upwards of three weeks! I like to squint my eyes when looking at the overall proportions, which blurs out the details and allows me to focus on analyzing just the basic colors and shapes.

Art is subjective, and it is important to note that no artist is perfect; this is why getting other people's opinions of your work is very important. If you have no immediate group of peers, Internet forums can be an important place to get constructive criticism of your work. Good constructive criticism offers ideas for improvement of your work, and does not dwell on the mistakes, apart from a positive way of improving your work.

People make mistakes. This is why the work of companies is often (but not always) superior to the work of individuals, more eyes checking for mistakes—too many cooks don't always spoil the broth! Get opinions from your friends: maybe even your family can help you spot weak areas that need improvement. Everyone is an expert when it comes to looking at people, and even your little sister might be able to spot something that you overlooked, like a nose that is too big or legs that are too small.

On my first check of the model, I noticed and fixed lots of little gaps between the objects and added the bumpy creases to the two breathing pipes leading to the mask. I also tweaked a few of the folds on the NBC suit to make them look more natural. On my second pass around the character, I moved the head back and the shoulders forward a little, as his head looked too far forward on the concept. To make the gloves look used, I added some creases and bumps to the gloves. On my third check of the character, I noticed a big gap under the shoulder pads, so I built some geometry to act as the inner padding.

The following figure shows the final high-res model.

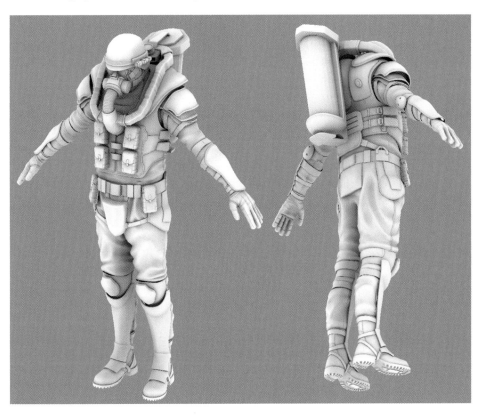

Texturing Eats Your RAM!

The texturing process can really put strains on your system, and in particular your RAM, which holds all the texture information in temporary memory. During the texturing process, I sometimes need to use from two to five applications at the same time, which can really stretch the multitasking capabilities of your machine to the limit. If you encounter long periods of down time as you swap applications or perform operations, you probably don't have enough RAM.

To compound the RAM problems during the texturing process, I will be working with a rather large 4 K (4096 $\times$ 4096 pixel) PSD file, even thought the final textures will only be 2 K (2048 $\times$ 2048 pixels). Working like this with a higher-resolution PSD file ensures that your final textures won't lose clarity after you have resized, warped, and liquefied them several times. Another advantage is that you can use the full 4 K maps for detailed close-up renders of your character—this will win you the dream job for sure!

I recommend a bare minimum of 2048 MB (2 K) of RAM in your system, especially on the RAM-greedy Microsoft Windows Vista. There is really no such thing as too much RAM when working in the CGI industry. If you have problems, you could consider networking your desktop to another computer like a laptop, which you could use beside your desktop computer to run Photoshop and create the textures, freeing up your main system's RAM for the demands of 3ds Max. If you really have problems with texturing on your system, you might want to halve the dimensions of all the textures I use during this chapter; this will make the texture size four times smaller. Instead of previewing my textures in large, uncompressed TIF format, as some people recommend, I prefer to use high-quality JPEGs to save on RAM.

Today's 32-bit operating systems like Windows XP Home Edition register a maximum of only 3.2 GB of RAM; any more than this is wasted, as the 32-bit OS will just ignore it. An emerging solution to your RAM woes is to use one of the new 64-bit operating systems like Vista 64 or XP 64, which will theoretically work with up to 16 exbibytes of RAM! That's more than enough for your needs.

Baking the Basic Colors

Let's get some colors on the model now. We could paint them in Photoshop, but I prefer to apply the colors in 3ds Max and bake them onto the texture. Baking the colors is much faster and usually offers better quality, as you don't have to do any fiddly paintwork in Photoshop. Painting the color texture by hand in Photoshop can be time-consuming and problematic, as it can be hard to work out what's what in the confusing sprawl of UV shells. I find it much easier to apply the base colors if I assign them to different selections of polygons in 3D, where I can preview the results in real time. What really makes the baking method a winner is that each baked color will generate a coverage alpha channel, which we can use to quickly select and tweak different materials inside Photoshop.

I have identified thirteen different materials on the character: gray steel, self-illuminated lights, black leather, dark gray Kevlar, elasticized straps, painted steel on the oxygen tank, black plastic, dark cloth, fire retardant piping, rubber-soled shoes, gray plastic mask, black rubber, and NBC suit.

Break up your model into thirteen corresponding pieces using the Detach and Attach buttons in Edit Poly. Each object that you create should be assigned a different colored material. The colors are not important; we will throw them away later. I've used crazy colors just to help myself differentiate between the various types of surface.

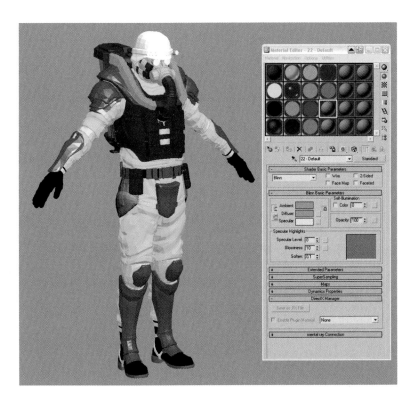

Once you are happy with the material groups, bake these different surfaces onto the texture using the Rendering > Render to Texture dialog. For each object, repeat this process:

- Choose the output path and give each file a descriptive name, such as Gray Steel.

- Be sure that "Use existing (UV) channel" is selected, as it would be a shame to waste those lovingly crafted UVs!
- Add a DiffuseMap output.
- Choose a 4096 × 4096 texture size (4 K).
- Hit render.

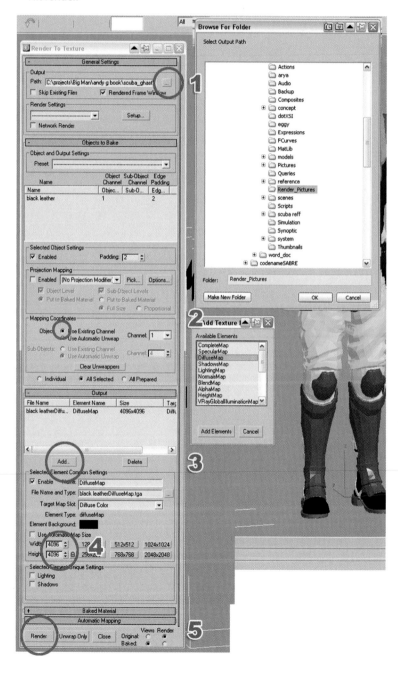

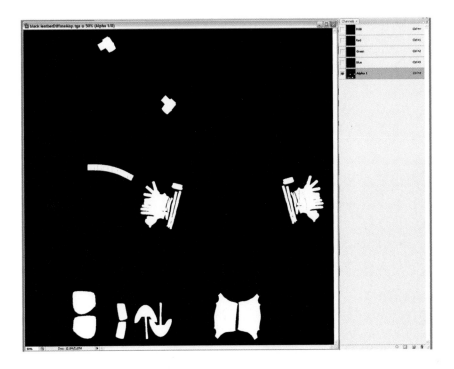

If you open up the black leather texture, it's just a black square, because we rendered a black material onto a black background! Open up the Channels window, though, and go to the alpha channel to see that we have a map that describes perfectly which areas on our UV sheet are black leather.

Let's make a new 4096 × 4096-pixel (4 K) document to collect all these alpha channels together. Save the new document as Future_Commando_01.psd.

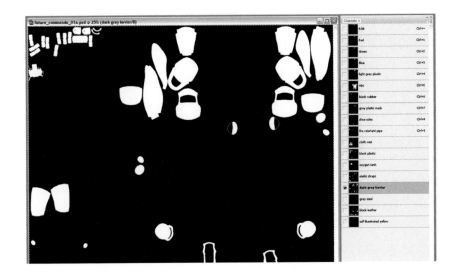

One by one, click on the alpha channel of each of your fourteen material renders, copy it (Ctrl+C), and paste the channel (Ctrl+V) into a new channel in the Future_Commando_01.psd file. Once you have named each channel accordingly, you will have a collection of channels like the previous figure.

Click on the RGB channel at the top of the Channels window and open up the Layers window again. Let's make a new layer for the NBC suit. Select an off-white color and fill your new layer with this color.

Masking Each Layer

Now comes the cool bit: go back to Channels and hold Ctrl as you click on the NBC suit channel to select all the white areas of the channel. Now go back to the Layers window and click Create Mask.

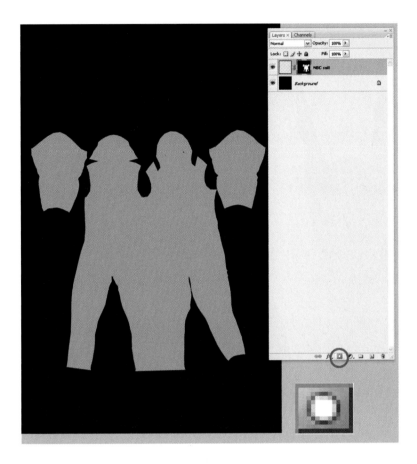

If you have done this correctly, the mask will hide the areas outside of the
NBC suit UVs. The gray color of the NBC suit layer shows only where the mask
is white; areas where the mask is black are transparent, so we can see the
Background layer underneath.

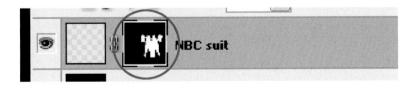

A black-and-white mask icon should have appeared in the NBC suit layer.
If you hold Alt when you click this mask, it will be isolated so that you can
see the mask clearly in black and white. To de-isolate the mask, click on the
eyeball icon (Layer visibility) of the NBC suit layer.

Masks and channels are the professional way to edit images in a nondestructive manner, if you want to make changes to something, it often makes more sense to do this with masks. If you don't like your mask, you can throw it away, keeping the original image intact.

As an advanced Photoshop user, it is imperative that you learn all the ins and outs of layers and masks. Masked layers have two thumbnail images instead of the usual one thumbnail. Click the thumbnail on the right to edit the mask; click the thumbnail on the left to return to editing the color layer. You can Ctrl+click on the mask to select all the areas that are white, which can be incredibly useful for making selections. Shift+click on the layer to toggle its effect on or off.

One by one, you can repeat the "fill new layer" command with color and then apply the relevant mask process to each of the thirteen different materials that we have a channel for. Try to avoid coloring things black or white, as there aren't many things that are truly black or truly white. It's better to settle for off-tones that are more realistic.

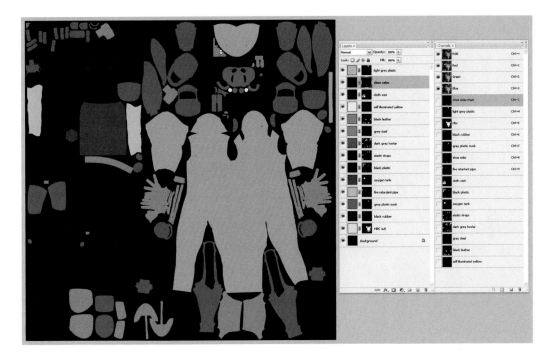

When all thirteen materials have their own color layer and mask, the texture will look something like the previous figure. I don't like the color of the suit I've applied—it's too dark—so let's tweak it with levels. Click on the NBC suit RGB color icon (the one to the left of the black and white icon) and press Ctrl + L to bring up the Levels command. Move the little triangles in the levels around to adjust the colors. This is a powerful way to make sweeping changes to your layers or selections.

Open up the old AO map that we rendered earlier, go to Image > Image size, and convert it into a 4 K map, then press Ctrl+A to select all, Ctrl+C to copy it into memory, and Ctrl+W to close it. We now have the AO map at 4 K in our clipboard.

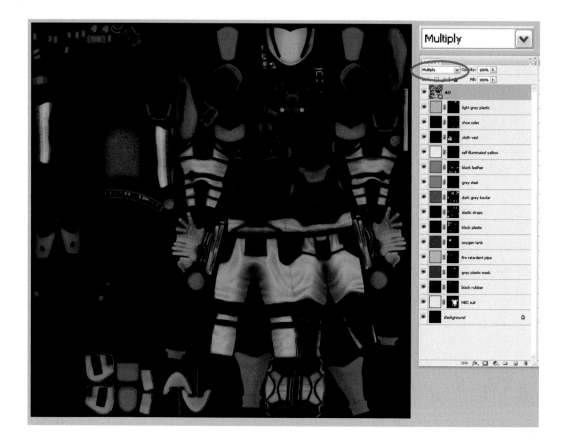

Select the top layer in your PSD, and press Ctrl+V to paste in the AO map from the clipboard. Name the layer AO. With the AO layer selected, select the Multiply layer mode from the drop-down menu. The Multiply command takes the dark parts of an image and multiplies them with all the colors in the layers below, darkening them. Anything that is white in the Multiply layer is invisible, and lighter shades have little effect.

To preview the work-in-progress (WIP) in Max, save a copy of the PSD as a JPG. Apply a new Standard material to your model in Max and load the WIP JPG into the Diffuse color slot. I like to give the material 100% self-illumination so that I can see clearly every surface on the model—there is plenty of time for gloomy, atmospheric lighting later on. It's also good to raise the specular levels to about 50; the specular highlights will help us to see some of the details of the surface.

If your colors are anything like mine, you probably made them all too dark, so go back to Photoshop and sort them out with the levels. Keep tweaking until you get something that you are happy with. I've put the "Self-illuminated lights" layer above the AO to get the effect that it is lit from within.

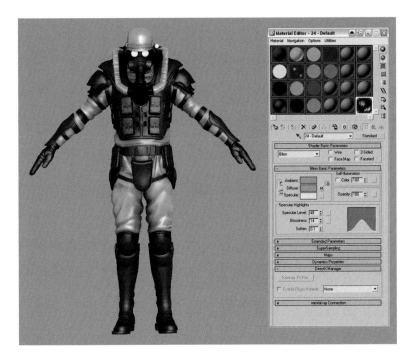

Once you are happy with the basic color layers that you just made, it is a good idea to merge them. We still have the channels if we want to make specific selections quickly, and merging all the layers will save us lots of RAM. Select all the layers apart from the AO and the self-illuminated yellow layer (for the eyes and torch), and press Ctrl+E to merge them together. When you have finished, it is a good idea to rename the Background layer: double-click the Background layer and type in the name Base Colors.

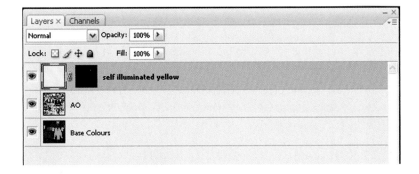

3D Paint Applications

When painting textures by hand, it is much more intuitive to use a 3D paint application, as you are not faced with the problem of working out which areas in the UVs correspond to which areas in 3D space. 3D paint applications allow us to paint seamlessly across multiple seams, something that is nearly impossible when painting in 2D in Photoshop. Painting in 3D has another advantage in that if you have any distortion in your UVs (sometimes a little distortion is hard to avoid), the 3D paint app will automatically make predistortion adjustments to your 2D texture to compensate for the distortion. The results will look distorted in Photoshop but perfect in 3D—something that you could never do without the 3D paint app.

Bodypaint 3D is a good standalone 3D paint application, but I recommend the use of ZBrush for your 3D painting. ZBrush's ZAppLink feature allows it to plug straight into Photoshop for an unrivalled texturing workflow. Why learn the inferior painting tools of another app when we can use the already familiar and industry-standard Photoshop tools?

Graphics Tablets

Trying to draw with a mouse is a bit like brushing your teeth with a toilet brush—it's not the ideal solution! Professional texture artists use graphics tablets (digital pens) for any demanding hand-drawn texturing. I recommend the use of the Intuos 3 tablet by Wacom; the pressure sensitivity of pen is excellent.

Rendering the UV Template

If you do not have access to a good 3D painting package, you can render a UV template to help you with your painting in 2D in Photoshop.

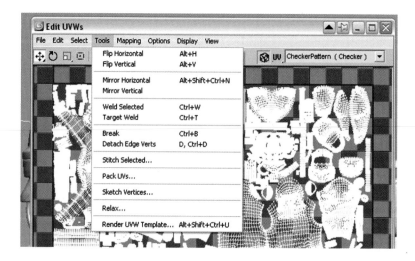

Add an UnwrapUVW modifier to your model and click Edit to open up the Edit UVWs window. Select Tools > Render UVW Template.

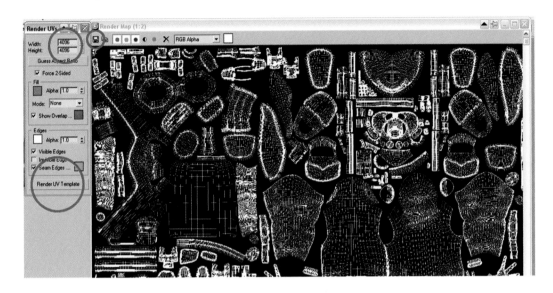

Select 4096 for the width and height and click Render UV Template. A Render Map window should appear with your UV coordinates nicely rendered; press the Save button (the disk icon) to save the image to a file. Open up this image in Photoshop, select all (Ctrl+A), copy it (Ctrl+C), and close it (Ctrl+W).

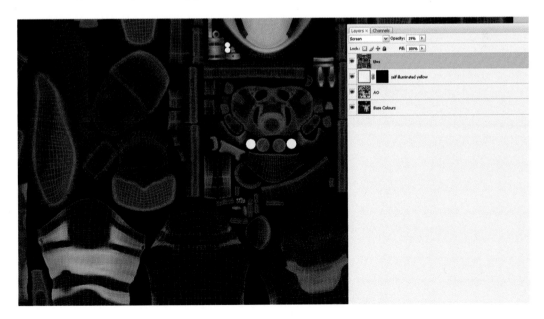

Click the top layer in your PSD and paste this image (Ctrl+V) at the top, renaming it "UVs." Put the layer into Screen mode to ignore the black areas. Now only the white areas should show through to lighten the layers below. You can turn on and off this layer as necessary while painting your texture;

sometimes it is really useful for seeing the boundaries of the UVs. I often reduce the opacity of this "UVs" layer to something like 20%.

Painting the Dirt Map

Our character is looking pretty good now, but he lacks the small, real-world details that will really bring him to life. I almost always paint some kind of dirt map to give a more realistic look to my characters. If you study anything in the world around you, you will notice dirt and small imperfections on the surfaces of objects.

When creating a texture for a character, I try to imagine their history and lifestyle. What does the character do on an average day? Where has he/she been? Has your character been relaxing in a pristine palace all his/her life? Or bathing in mud? When treated with subtlety, the incidental effects will really bring your character to life—the eye of the viewer will pick up on these small details that give credibility to your digital creations.

Many companies specialize in producing photo libraries of dirty surfaces, available for royalty-free use in your textures, but they can be quite expensive. A cheaper solution is to take photos of dirty surfaces yourself. Go to your local industrial area and you will find an area rich with grime. No one appreciates a good dirty surface quite like the 3D artist does!

The previous figure is an example of detail from one of the dirt images that I've collected, before I cleaned it up and adjusted the levels. I like to photograph smooth white surfaces, as it makes it very easy to get just the dirt without any other surface features that will need to be removed to isolate the dirt. Get as many different types of mud, grease, and dust as you can; the more images you have in your library, the more variation you will be able to include on your characters' dirt maps.

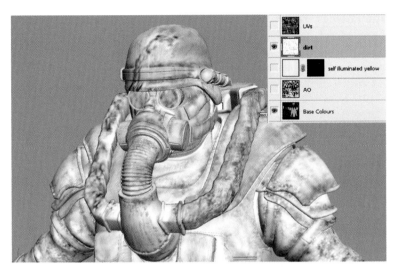

I like to paint on the dirt generously to start with, working fast and rough and not caring too much about any specific details. I mix manipulated dirt images from my photo library with hand-painted dirt using the Paint Brush and Burn tools. Next, I go around the model and clean off the dirt with a white paintbrush in the most exposed areas. If an area looks unrealistic I will give it a heavy blur, paint in more detail, blur a little more, then add more detail again. It is this iterative process that helps me to build up a history of past incidents on the surface of the character.

Painting your dirt in a 3D app will really make it come alive, as you can see very clearly which parts might not get cleaned as easily, and which areas might get cleaned on a more regular basis. Remember that weathering, friction, and collisions will remove the dirt from the most exposed areas, leaving behind the dirt that is protected in the cavities.

If you change the dirt layer to Multiply mode you will see the dirt on top of the Base Colors and AO layers. If you want a quick and dirty effect, sometimes this is enough, but this technique produces dirt that is only monochrome, because of the limitations of Multiply mode. The multiplied dirt layer does not show up very well on any of the darker fabrics, as dark × dark = very, very dark. Dirt usually makes dark objects lighter, so it's a better idea to use another image to create a muddy color, and use our dirt map to mask it.

Here is a photo that I took of a muddy area of a field. I've used the Rubber Stamp tool to repeat the texture across the surface. This will make a good color for our dirt.

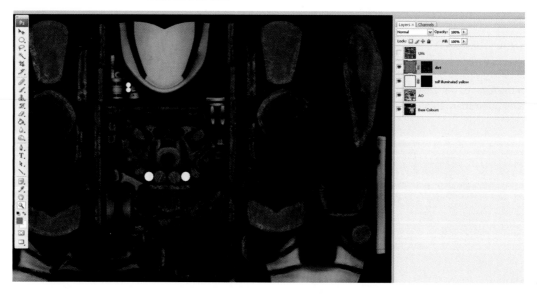

To apply our black-and-white dirt map as a mask to this muddy layer, select the original black-and-white dirt layer, select it all (Ctrl+A), copy it to the clipboard (Ctrl+C), and then delete the layer. Create a new mask on the color muddy field layer, Alt+click the mask to isolate it, and paste it (Ctrl+V) in the black-and-white image from the clipboard. With the mask still selected, invert it (Ctrl+I), because it is the wrong way around.

Here I've reduced the opacity of this layer to 40%. Subtlety is the key to getting it right, as we don't want the guy caked in mud, but his costume must look like it has been used in a real-life combat situation. We can make certain parts more or less muddy by selecting those areas of the mask with our channels and applying a levels adjustment. I've deliberately understated the dirt here a little, because later we will apply the dirt to the specular map, too, to strengthen the dirt effect. In some areas, I have blurred the muddy colors of the layer to get an ingrained, old dirt look, and I have left other areas of the layer quite sharp to get a new mud feel.

Painting the Scratch Map

In the real world, things get scratched in everyday use—especially on the battlefield! On a new white layer, I've painted black scratches, again I've used a 3D paint app to help me get the scratches placed well, with the heaviest ones on the most exposed edges. Like the dirt map, I paint super quick and rough to start with, and as I do so I try to imagine how the scratches came about. Maybe the scratches on the helmet came from a fall, so they all go in one direction, maybe scratches on the Kevlar forearm pad have built up over time, so they all point in unique directions. Don't paint dumb! Think as you paint.

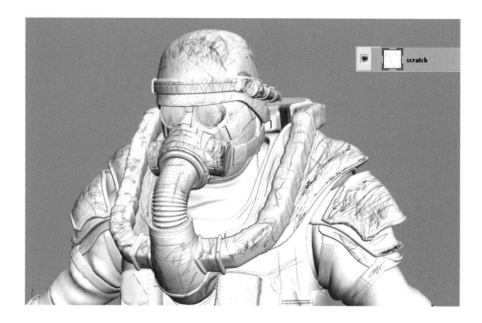

Fabrics don't often scratch sharply like hard surfaces do, so let's blur them out a little.

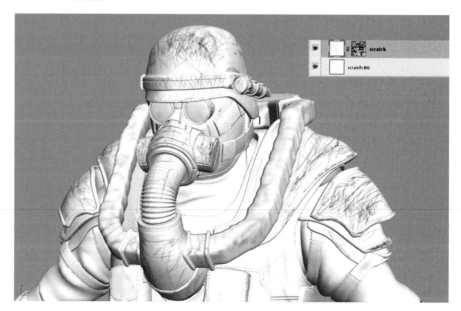

Select all the areas where there are soft fabric materials by holding Shift and Ctrl while clicking each the relevant fabric channels one by one to add them to your selection. Now select Filter > Blur > Gaussian Blur and give these areas a moderate amount of blur. To add more realism, add a mask to the scratch layer and paste in a copy of the AO map, which has the effect of removing the scratches from occluded areas. This newly AO masked scratch layer works well, but we must flatten it so we can use it in another mask…the complexity increases! Add a pure white, scratch background layer below the scratch map, select the two layers together, and then merge them together (Ctrl + E). Now select and copy the contents of this new merged layer to your clipboard for use in the next step.

Layered Scratch Masks

Many surfaces such as the gas tanks have been painted, and will reveal their underlying materials in areas where they have been scratched. Let's create this layered effect by duplicating the Base Colors layer (right-click on the layer and choose Duplicate). Name the top layer: Base Colors and the layer underneath Under Colors. Paste the contents of your clipboard (the merged scratch map from the last section) into a new mask applied to the Base Colors layer.

Now we can paint in the Under Colors layer to create our underlying material colors. The gas tank should reveal bare metal under the paintwork where it has been scratched, so paint a gray color here. Other metals will typically get lighter where they have been scratched, so just lighten those areas. Some plastic areas might be darker where they have been scratched and something has created dirt-filled cavities.

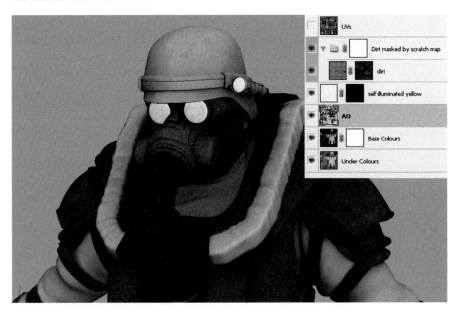

If you export the WIP color map to 3ds Max, it should be easier to see how the colors underneath are shaping up. You can use the channel selections to select specific areas and make sweeping changes to many under-colors at the same time. I have also used the Levels command on the scratch mask itself to tone down the effect a little.

For additional realism, let's remove the dirt from the scratched areas, as it would often be removed by friction as the scratches occurred. I have put the dirt layer in a new folder (group), and masked this new folder with a copy of the scratch mask from the Base Colors layer. Nesting masked folders inside folders is incredibly powerful but can quickly get confusing! Our scratch map will really come alive later, when we can use the spec map to make the scratched areas shinier.

Painting the High-Frequency Detail Layers

Next let's paint the high-frequency (HF) details—the things that crop up again and again across the surface (for example, skin pores, the pattern of the sole of the shoe, the ribbed pattern on the belt, and so on). Details on this small of a scale are much easier to create using texturing rather than modeling. I like to create the HF details as black and white maps; this means that later we can easily pop out these details in the normal map.

The first step is to gather high-resolution images of each fabric type we will use. Many of the surface types, like the rubber and the plastic, are smooth surfaces that don't require HF detail maps, but we will need images to make the micro bumps of the leather, elastic, cloth, NBC suit, and the fire-resistant material on the piping. Like with the dirt, I keep a library of photos of different fabrics; you can buy disks full of fabric textures from the Internet, but I sometimes find it quicker and cheaper to source my own from around the house and quickly take photos/scans of them. Like most reference material you use in your textures, it is much better if it is shot in diffused lighting conditions with no harsh lighting, shadows, or hard contrasts.

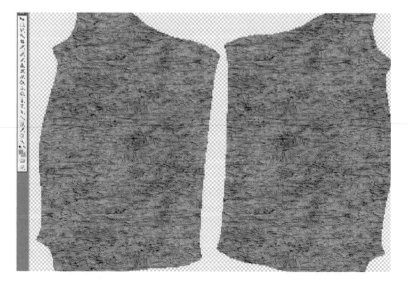

Adjust the maps so that they look similar to how the AO map would look if we had actually modeled every HF micro cavity in to the surface of the object.

Black represents the lowest areas, and white the highest points that are more exposed to the light. The previous image shows my HF detail layer, which describes the creased, wrinkly texture of the leather.

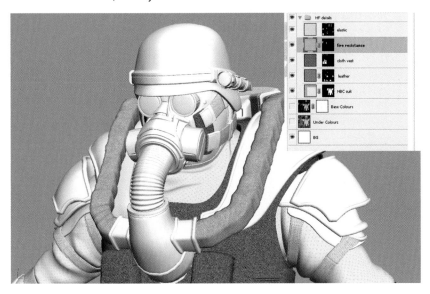

Each type of surface should tile to completely fill its own HF detail layer: to keep things tidy, put all the layers in a folder called "HF details." We can use the channels we saved earlier to quickly create a mask for each layer, Ctrl+click the relevant channel to select the areas it masks, then back in the Layers palette you can click the "Create mask" icon to quickly mask the active layer with your selection.

Set each of the HF detail layers to multiply, so they have a similar effect to how our AO layer works, darkening the occluded areas.

Normal and Specular Maps

Let's add another layer of realism to our creation using Normal and Specular maps. Normal maps are used to fool the eye into believing that there is much more detail than there actually is modeled into the character. They work in a similar way to bump maps, by cheating in the details. Specular maps control how shiny the surface is in different areas; white pixels make the metal look shiny and the black pixels make the dirt look totally matte.

Using DirectX Real-Time Shaders

We can see the effects of the normal and specular maps in real time in the viewport if we use a special DirectX shader written by Ben Cloward. If you visit http://www.bencloward.com/resources_shaders.shtml, you can see that Ben has created a wealth of different shaders that you can use in the Max viewport to simulate various surface effects. He has kindly allowed us to include the Normal Map Specular Shader—3 Lights shader on the book's DVD. You can read all about these shaders at http://www.bencloward.com/shaders_NormalMapSpecular3lights.shtml. Find Ben's shaders on the Web site download under \Chapter 7\Max Files for chapters\7_gamemesh_textured\directx_shaders\ and copy them to somewhere easily accessible on your hard drive. Before we set up the shader, we will need to use Photoshop to make some quick, temporary normal and specular maps to plug into the shader.

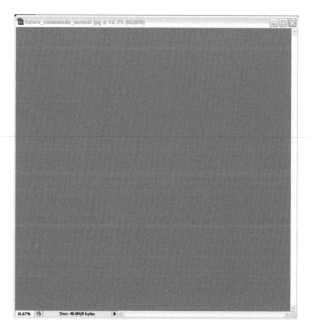

To make a temporary normal map, use the Paint Bucket tool to fill a new 4 K image with RGB color 127,127,255. This purple/blue tone has the effect of perfect flatness in normal maps—it's the normal map's equivalent of black or zero—it has no effect. Save this as something like future_commando_normals.jpg.

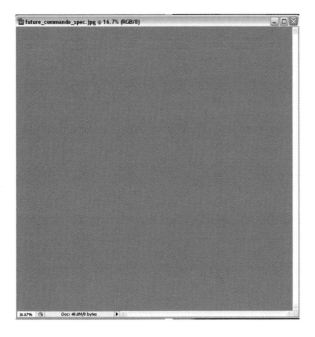

To create a temporary specular map, let's use the Paint Bucket tool to fill a new 4 K image with RGB color: 127,127,127. This is a good medium gray color for a moderate level of shininess. Save the image as something like future_commando_specular.jpg.

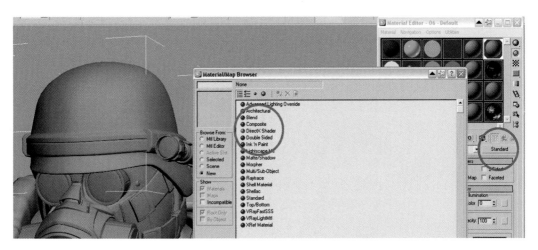

Now we have a color and a normal and a specular map. Let's set up the DirectX shader. In 3ds Max, apply a new material to the character model, then click on the Standard button in the Material Editor to select a DirectX type of material.

Click the top-left box in the DirectX Shader Panel, the one with the long path name in it. This box loads a specific DirectX (FX) shader onto your material. Browse to the folder to where you copied Ben's shaders, and select the one named HLSLnormal_map_specular_3lights_world.fx.

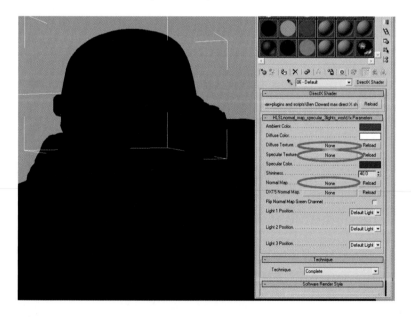

Now Ben's shader is applied to your character. Most likely, the model will turn black, as the maps are not loaded in yet. Click on the slots next to Diffuse Texture, Specular Texture, and Normal Map, and load in the relevant maps.

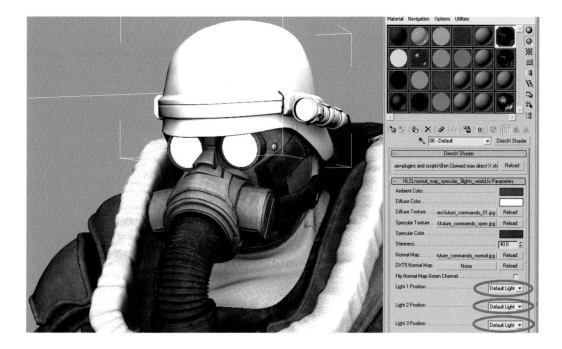

Once you have loaded the three maps into the relevant slots, you should see the shader displaying correctly. The normal and spec maps are just filled with temporary, basic colors, so we are not really getting the benefit from this shader yet. The default settings use the Max Default Light, but it is better if you make three omni lights that surround the character, and load each one into the Light Position slots, as explained below.

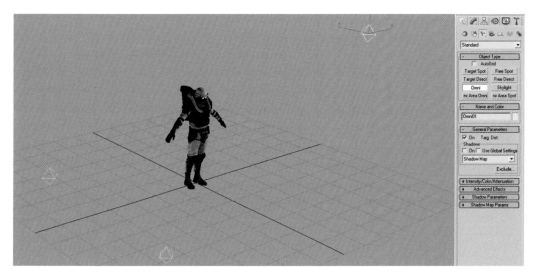

Using Create > Lights > Standard Lights > Omni, make one key light that has an intensity of around 1 and is positioned at the front of the character but a little to one side. At the other side, make a Fill light with an intensity of about 0.5, and at the back a Rim light with an intensity of around 0.5 also.

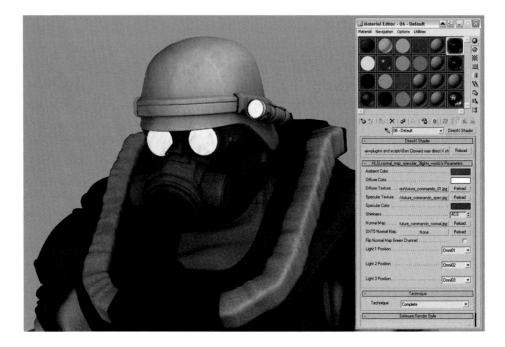

You can tweak the light settings to your own preferences; it's all just to help you see what is going on with the normal mapping later on. You can even animate the intensity and positions of the lights so that you can play the timeline to see the character in different lighting conditions.

Normal Mapping the High-Frequency Details

We can really give the HF details much more punch if we pop them out using a normal map. As it is just a texture-mapping effect this illusion breaks down when viewed up close, especially when seen at angles perpendicular to the viewing angle, where it is obvious that the details are not truly 3D. Normal mapping does not work well as a replacement for modeling the larger geometry, as it does not affect the silhouette of the shape in the way that modeling does.

To follow my style of normal mapping you will need to install the NVIDIA Normal Map Filter for Photoshop, which is available for free download from here: http://developer.nvidia.com/object/photoshop_dds_plugins.html.

One by one, feed the contents of each of the HF Detail layers to the Normal Map Filter. The Normal Map Filter does not work on PSDs with more than one layer, so one at a time, copy the contents of each HF Detail layer and paste each one into a new document, being sure to flatten each image down to just one background layer.

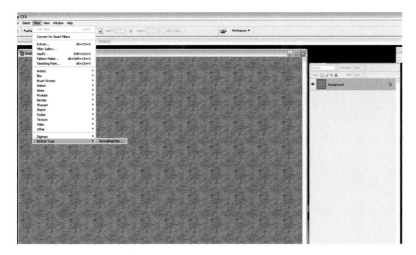

With one of your temporary, one-layer HF detail documents selected, choose Filter > NVIDIA Tools > NormalMapFilter to bring up the options for our normal map.

Although there are lots of options here, all you really need to do is type different numbers into the Scale Box. The Scale setting describes how powerful the effect of the bumpiness of the surface is. I find that 6 works well for me most of the time. You can also press the 3D Preview button if you want to see how your normal map will look in real-time 3D. Press OK to create your normal map.

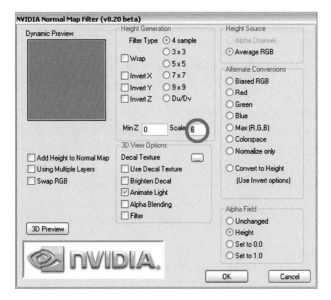

Create a new PSD file called future_commando_normals.psd, and one by one, paste in the normal maps that you have generated for each HF detail layer.

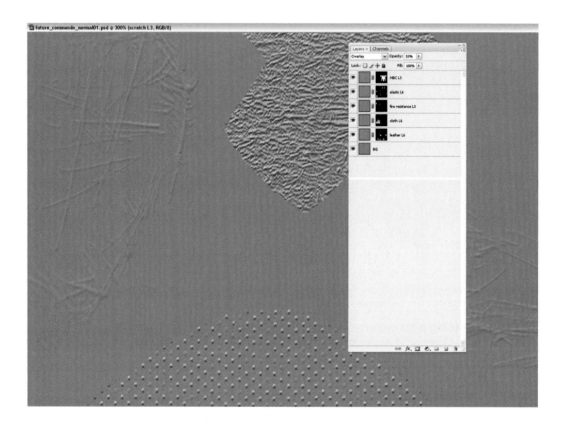

To blend all these maps together, copy over the masks from the original HF detail layers in the color PSD (future_commando_01.psd). Your future_commando_normals.psd should look something like the previous figure. I've zoomed in to 300% to show the details. I like to add a little note for myself on the name of each layer: L3 means that I generated the map with a scale of 3, L6 a scale of 6, and so on. These notes will help us if we decide to tweak the strength of each one later on.

In the normal map PSD document, select "Save As" and overwrite the temporary future_commando_normals.jpg map that we made earlier. If you go back to 3ds Max now, the new map should have automatically loaded into the material, and the normal map should be displaying nicely now. You should export your normal map to 3ds Max frequently, as you work, because reviewing the normal map applied to the character in Max is much easier than staring at a bunch of blue colors in Photoshop.

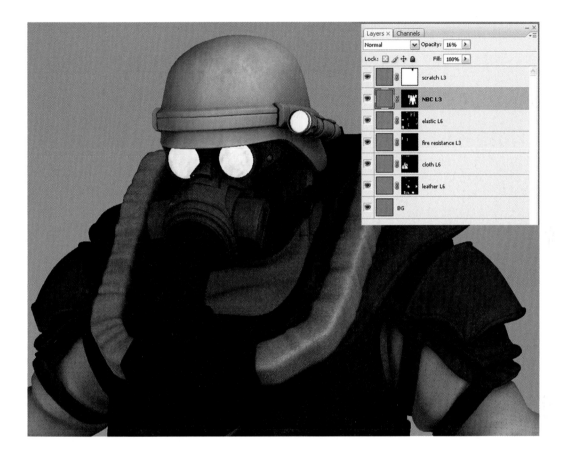

In the previous figure, I've decided that the NBC suit material is way too bumpy, so I've toned that down by changing the opacity of the NBC L3 layer to 6%. I've also gone back to the color PSD and made his vest a little bit lighter.

Adding More Small Details

Before we finish the texturing with the specular map, there are a few finishing touches to add to the color and normal maps. As these details are all very flat, we won't be generating normal maps from them, so they can all be painted on the Base Colors layer.

The Danger Label on the Gas Tank

I drew the shapes for the Danger label using the Rectangle and Polygon Selection tools, using the Brush tool to fill the selections with color and the Edit > Stroke command to outline them where needed. I used the Text tool to create the typography, then merged everything down onto the Base Colors layer, making sure to preserve the (scratch) mask. Be sure to make the yellow tones a slightly desaturated yellow: In the real world, most things are not completely saturated with color, but are usually faded from weathering.

Metal Textures

At the moment, your metal areas are probably looking a little flat and boring; we'd better give them an interesting texture. To build up the texture, use the Filter > Add Noise, then Filter > Blur > Gaussian Blur a number of times, entering smaller numbers into the Size parameter on each iteration.

Glowing Bulbs

If we were working on a character for a feature film that would be viewed close up, I would probably model the inner workings of the glowing eye and torch, and add some cool render effects. However, as this texture will eventually need to be baked down onto a 1 K game mesh, it is probably too much work on this project to get bogged down in this level of detail. In production, you have to draw a line somewhere on the level of detail, or you will make too much work for yourself and miss your deadlines.

I drew the glowing torch and eye lenses by hand using the Brush tool and then overlaid a grid image in Color Burn mode. When I was happy with these layers, I merged them together onto the self-illuminated yellow layer to save a little RAM.

Micro Bumps Layer

Many surfaces are not as perfectly smooth and flat as you might assume. Accidents, daily use, weathering, factory defects and warping caused by sun exposure all lead to small imperfections on surfaces.

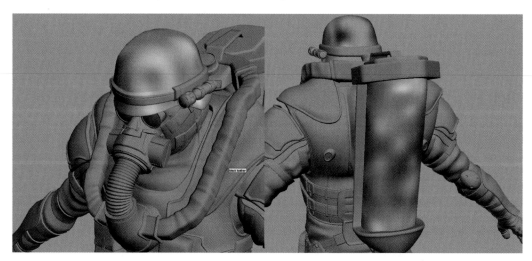

To create this effect of less-than-perfect surfaces, let's paint another black-and-white map that we can feed into the NVIDIA Normal Map Filter. Starting with a mid-gray background, you can use the Burn tool to darken areas that you would like to push down in the normal map. If you hold Alt when using the Burn tool, it will dodge instead, lightening the areas and thus raising them in the normal map. You can paint these micro bump dings onto the helmet, gas tank, shoes, and anywhere else where you'd like to make the surface less regular. Generate a normal map from this black-and-white image using the NVIDIA filter and place it in the top layer in the normals.psd. If you put this micro bumps layer into Overlay mode, it will blend over the top of the existing normal map layers.

The High-Res Specular Textures

Creating the spec map is fairly straightforward; for the most part, we will use existing elements from the color PSD. We will create a number of new "Spec" layers that we can turn on to convert our color PSD texture into a spec map.

The adjustment layers (icon shown in the previous figure), which are found at the bottom of the Layers window, are great for making nondestructive changes. Adjustment layers can be turned on and off and masked, and if you don't like them, you can just delete them to go back to how things were before.

Select the top layer in your PSD (probably the UVs layer), click the "Create new fill or adjustment layer" icon, and Select Hue/Saturation. Drag the Saturation control down to –100 to totally desaturate everything underneath this adjustment layer and press the OK button. Right-click on the new adjustment layer's mask, and choose "Delete layer mask": This will save us a little of our precious RAM, as we don't need the mask. Now give the layer a meaningful name, like Spec Desaturator.

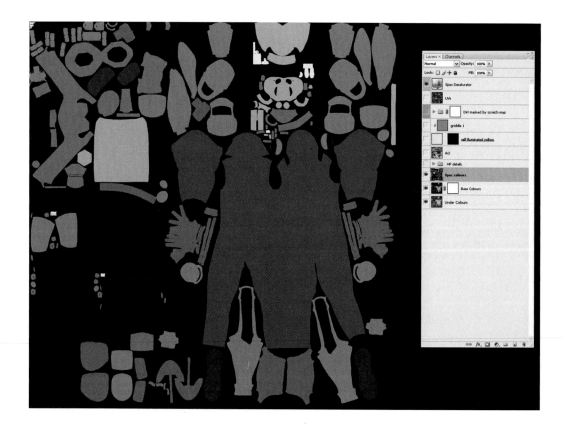

Create a new layer above the Base Colors layer called Spec Colors. One at a time, select each channel that we saved earlier and fill that selection with a color. Fill Spec Colors with black for nonreflective (specular is just a cheated reflection, really) things like cloth. Fill Spec Colors with medium gray for things like the NBC suit and plastics that have a moderate amount of shininess, and fill it with white for very shiny things like metal. This layer should completely block out any layers below it.

My aim when creating the specular map is to break up the highlights; the spec map is where I concentrate the majority of the grime and dirt in the textures. As I've mentioned earlier, if you look at even the newest objects around you, you will notice that the reflections on their surfaces are broken up by imperfections, fingerprints, dirt, and scratches.

Let's improve our spec texture by making the dirty areas less shiny, and the scratched areas shinier. Copy the dirt and scratch masks that we made earlier and paste duplicates of them at the top of the Layers window next to the Spec Desaturator layer. Name them "Spec–dirt is darker" and "Spec–scratches are lighter," respectively. Now if you put the "Spec–dirt is darker" layer into Multiply mode, it will make all the dirty areas not shiny; if you put the "Spec–scratches are lighter" layer into Screen mode, it will make all the scratched areas more shiny. (You might need to invert it also.) I also adjusted the levels of these maps to amplify their effects.

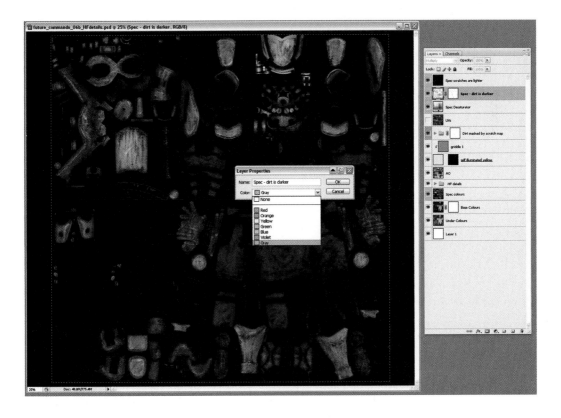

Right-click on all the new spec layers one at a time, selecting Layer Properties and applying a gray color. It will now be easy to identify which layers are for the spec map, an ability that will reduce our user errors when we toggle our PSD between color and spec modes. If you use Save As and save this image over the temporary future_commando_specular.jpg texture, you can check the new spec map in Max.

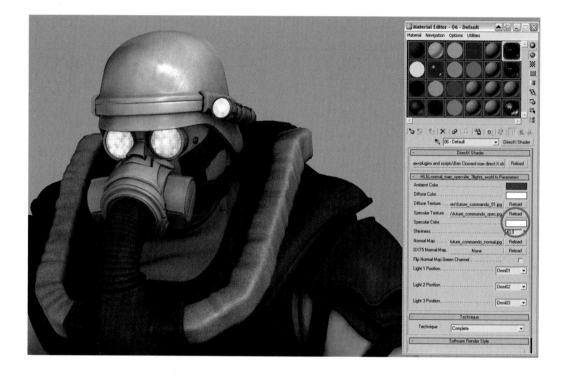

In the DirectX shader, make sure that the Specular Color is set to white, so you can accurately tweak your spec map. It's now just a matter of tweaking the three textures to your taste. When you are finished you can re-export the textures in TIF format to increase the quality.

The Gun

After a discussion with the team, it was decided that an over-the-top, multi-function gun would best suit the battlefield needs of our soldier. As we didn't have a concept image for the gun, I blended together elements from several existing weapons into one design, mixing together a flamethrower and a chain-gun. It had to be big, as we didn't want our soldier to feel inadequate on the battlefield! The weapon required additional fuel tanks to be fitted to the existing gas tank to supply the flamethrower with fuel. As these are detachable items, the gas tanks and the weapon both have their own separate texture sheets.

In-Game-Mesh Modeling

For our game mesh, we have been allocated a polygon budget of 12,000 triangles. This is a reasonable amount for a prominent game character for a first-person shooter on the Xbox 360 or the PlayStation 3. Background characters that don't receive all the limelight might get only 2,000–5,000 triangles, but lead characters that are designed for talking in close-up shots might get 15,000 or more polys.

Earlier, during the modeling of our high-res mesh, we wisely saved a copy of our work-in-progress proxy mesh when it was around 6,000–7,000 triangles (for half the mesh). This basic, approximate form will make an excellent starting point for our game mesh. If we load up this old .OBJ mesh (File > Import…), it should fit perfectly over the top of our high-res character. Add the Symmetry modifier and give this proxy mesh a green material with opacity of 50% so that we can clearly see the high-res mesh underneath it.

Using all the familiar Edit Poly tools, we now need to optimize this mesh for use in videogames, aiming to get the half game mesh to around 6,000 triangles. The core idea when creating real-time assets such as this is that each triangle/polygon is precious. If we can reduce polygons in one area without any detrimental effect, we can spend these elsewhere in the model to improve the overall appearance. Ideally, we can keep a clean, quad-based topology, but a few triangles here and there are fine.

The way I construct my game meshes owes much to my previous experience with using normal maps. Normal maps are great at representing the many small details, but they are very poor when used to fake the larger features, which should always be modeled in. Sometimes we can delete many polygons from a relatively flat area and let the normal map do the work instead, without the surface looking much different.

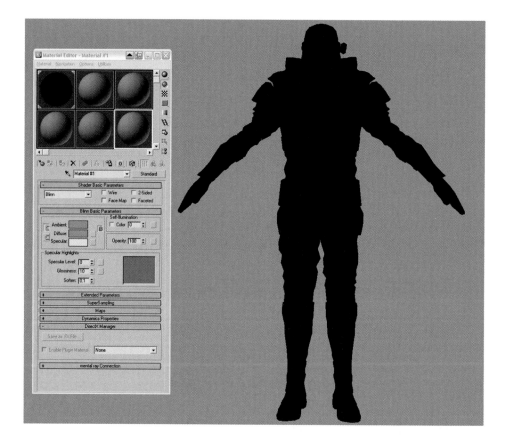

I spend lots of polygons on creating a detailed silhouette, because only geometry can give us a detailed and interesting profile. Sometimes I change the material so that it has 100% self-illumination, which makes it easy to focus on just the silhouette. View your game-mesh model from every angle and see whether its silhouette looks correct. If you press F4 to toggle edged faces, you can see whether there are areas with lots of polygons that are contributing very little to the silhouette, then track them down and delete them.

Typically, an in-game character will be rigged and animated through a wide range of poses, so we must take care that the geometry we build around areas that bend (knees, elbows, shoulder, wrist, and so on) has enough detail to support a full range of movement. The best way to get a feeling for this is to rig your own meshes and test-animate the rigs so you can experience firsthand exactly where geometry is needed, and where you can scrimp on it.

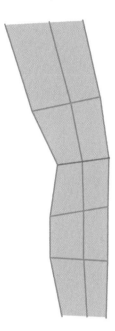
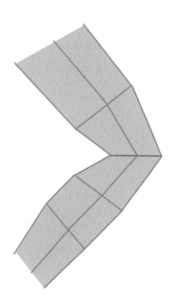

One edge loop on a joint is often not enough once you start animating the character.

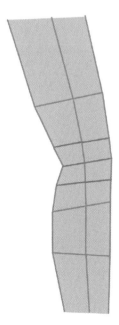
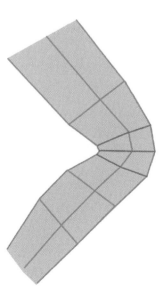

When in doubt, a good rule of thumb is to have at least three edge loops around each joint to allow for correct deformation during animation.

Modeling for games sometimes involves using some low-down dirty tricks! Knowing when you can pull these off and when to do things the proper way is an art form in itself. Some people might tell you to make sure that all areas of your mesh are welded together; granted, this approach works better in some situations, but we can save lots of polys in some areas if we disregard this advice. Andy Gahan showed me the following trick when I first started work on PS2 games, but it's as relevant as ever for the current generation of games.

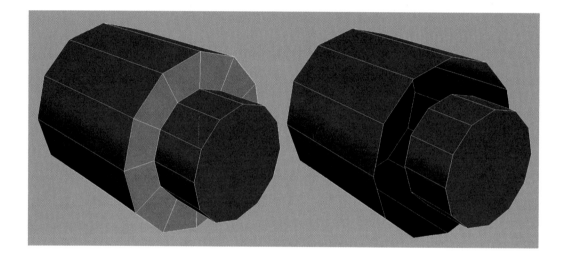

As an example, take your typical cylindrical object with some beveled detail, like the one in the following figure. The highlighted polygons here contain twenty-four triangles; let's delete them.

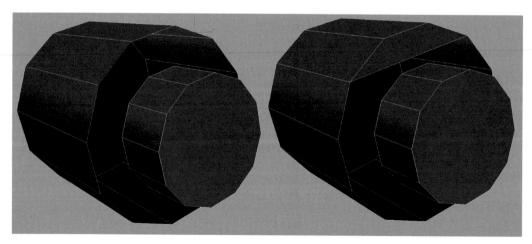

Select two opposite edges and use Edit Polys Bridge command to join them; repeat the Bridge operation for each set of opposite edges.

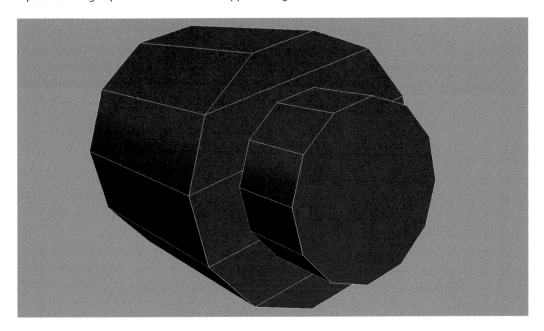

Now we have two overlapping shapes, rather than one whole mesh. The new polygons we have added contain only ten triangles, a savings of almost 60 percent!

If we use this trick on the ends of each cylinder on the gas tank valves, we can reap substantial savings. Here I saved thirty triangles by deleting the old welded polys and replacing them with new bridged edges. There is a gas tank valve on each side of the character, so this is a total savings of sixty triangles. Look for other areas to perform this trick and save additional polys, which we can use to improve the detail in complex areas such as the creases and folds of the NBC suit.

You should avoid the use of this trick in certain deformable areas, as the open edges may get exposed during animation. The only way to get a good feeling for how far you can push this is to get firsthand experience with rigging and animating game meshes.

When finishing off the model, I like to turn on the Edged Faces in the viewport and squint my eyes at it so I get just a hazy general impression of the mesh topology. This makes it easier to see areas where the polygons are denser, and areas that are relatively sparse. Unless there is a special reason (animation, silhouette or mapping) all the meshes should have similar levels of detail. Sometimes I will rob from the rich to give to the poor, taking polygons away from areas that don't need them.

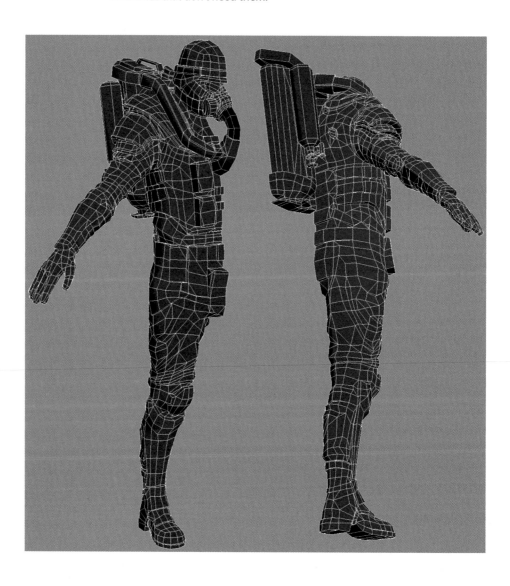

Many games give a bias to the head when it comes to detail. The viewer's eye naturally focuses here, so it is worth spending a bit more of your budget here. Some games feature the characters up close in animated dialog shots, so they are built with lots of detail in the face, designed to smoothly morph between different emotions and mouth shapes.

In-Game-Mesh UVing

Like the high-res mesh, it's good to UV the half game mesh before you mirror it over. You should try to minimize the number of UV shells. The fewer shells, the fewer seams, so join them together whenever possible.

When you have the Unwrap UVW modifier applied to your object, the seams show up as bright green lines. I try to hide the UV seams in areas that won't be seen easily, like the inside of the legs or the inside of the arms. Better still, I like to line up the seams with areas where there are already fabric seams in the high-res mesh (the areas where the garments are stitched together, or the intersection between two different surfaces).

It's worth noting that sometimes developers give a bias to the UVs of the head and the eyes; that is, they make them larger to fit in more detail. But as our character is intended for a fast-paced arcade game with few dialog scenes, this won't be necessary.

Once you're happy with the UV seams, you can add a Symmetry modifier and collapse the stack into an Editable Poly to create the full mesh.

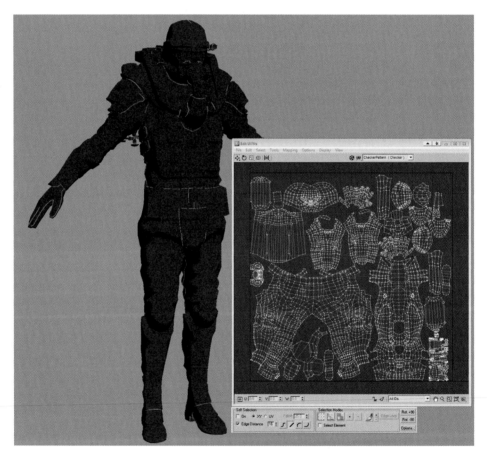

Now that we have the whole mesh, we can create the creases and folds that are unique to the left-hand side of the NBC suit. It is also possible to save some more polys by deleting any edges on the line of symmetry that aren't contributing to the character's form. Once you have finished modeling, you can select the new half of the mesh and horizontally flip the UVs. In UVlayout, it is now straightforward to complete the UVs by welding all the seams that run up the center line and reflattening all the pieces. In the previous figure, I have cut off the codpiece as a separate UV shell to avoid having a seam that runs down the line of symmetry. As always, remember to pack your UV shells as tightly as possible.

Baking Down the High-Res Details

To produce the highest-quality meshes for PlayStation 3 and Xbox 360 games, the colors and details of the high-res mesh are often baked down onto the comparatively low-polygon game mesh. The game mesh's normal map does a great job of faking the high-res details, giving us almost the same effect for a fraction of the system resources of the original multi-million-polygon mesh.

The high-res and in-game meshes should now sit perfectly over the top of each other like the following figure. Be sure that the high-res meshes have standard 3ds Max materials, with the color, specular, and normal maps applied to the relevant map slots. Make sure that no DirectX materials are applied to the high-res objects, as they cannot be baked down onto the game mesh.

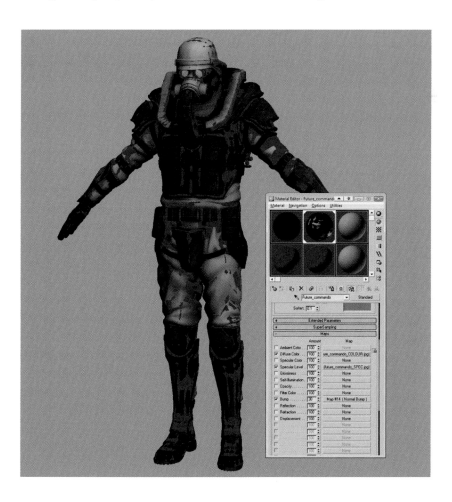

We could go through and bake our maps one by one, but it is easier to bake all three maps (color, spec, and normal) at the same time. Select the game mesh and select Rendering > Render To Texture. In the General Settings tab at the top of the Render To Texture settings, choose an output path for the textures.

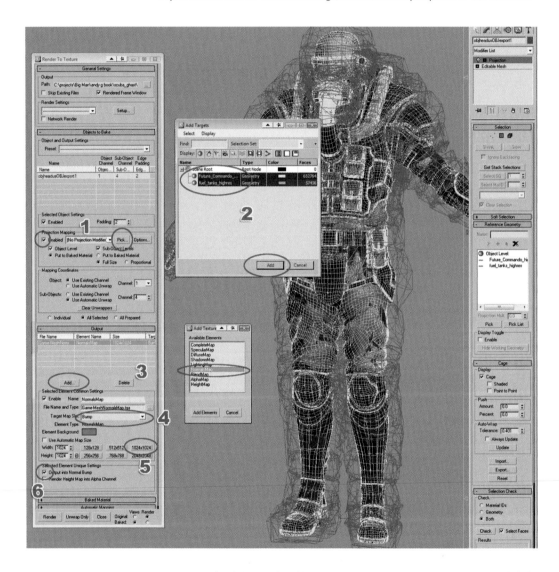

Be sure to check the Enabled box in the Projection Mapping section, and click the Pick button to bring up the Add Targets menu.

In the Add Targets pop-up box, select all of the objects that make up the high-res mesh; in my case, this is the main body of the future commando and the gas tanks. Click Add and a Projection relationship will be set up between the game mesh and the high-res objects.

To set up the normal map output, click Add in the Output section and choose a NormalMap Texture element. Choose Bump for the Target Map Slot to ensure that Render To Texture will plug our new normal map into the Bump slot of the new material that it will apply to our character. Click the 1024 × 1024 button to choose a 1 K map size. Be sure that "Output into Normal Bump" is checked, so the normal map gets plugged into bump slot via a Normal Bump node.

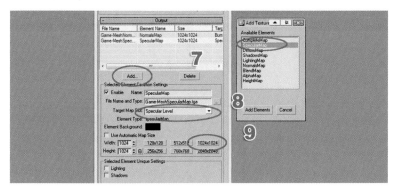

Now that we have the NormalMap output all set up, let's configure the specular map bake. Click Add and choose a SpecularMap Texture element. Choose Specular Level for the target map slot. Click the 1024 × 1024 button to choose a 1 K map size.

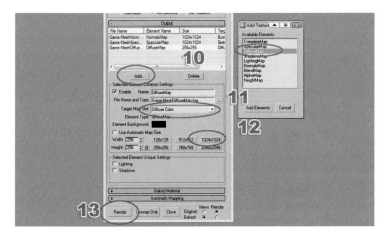

Finally, let's set up the diffuse/color map bake. Click Add and choose a DiffuseMap Texture element. Choose Diffuse Color for the target map slot. Click the 1024 × 1024 button to choose a 1 K map size. Click Render to render out all three maps at the same time and apply them to a new material.

Isolate the game mesh or hide the high-res mesh to view the work so far. In Photoshop, browse to the location where you saved these textures and open them up to take a look at them.

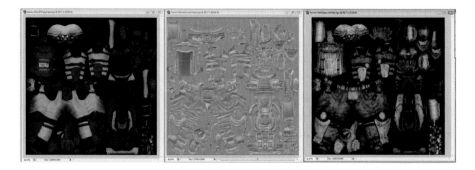

Back in 3ds Max you will notice that a blue cage has appeared around the game mesh, and that a Projection modifier has been added to its stack. The blue Projection cage is a visual tool to help you control how the information is baked down from the high-res target mesh onto the low-res one. During a render, rays are fired out from each point on the game mesh until they get to the cage, from where they take the information from the nearest high-res surface.

When baking from high-res to low-res there are often some problems. Cavities and other complex areas with overlapping details cause problems for the renderer, because when there are many high-res surfaces close to each other the renderer doesn't know which one to take its information from. The Projection cage is designed to solve this problem, as each vertex in the cage can be tweaked by hand, but because we have more than 6,000 vertices in this mesh, the prospect is daunting!

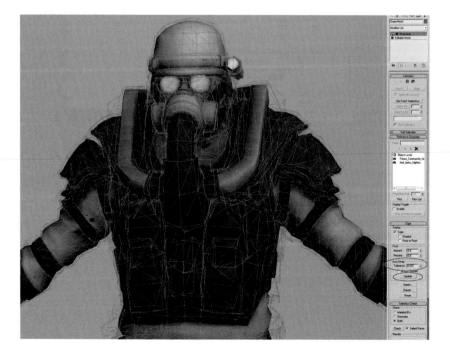

Luckily, there are controls in the Projection modifier that can move each vertex on the cage all together at the same time. If you type various values into the Auto-Wrap parameter and hit the Update button, you will see the cage recalculate at different distances from the game mesh.

My favorite and fastest way to get perfect game mesh maps is to bake each of the maps a number of times, each with a different size cage. Often I will bake a small, medium, and large version of each map, which I can blend together in Photoshop using masks.

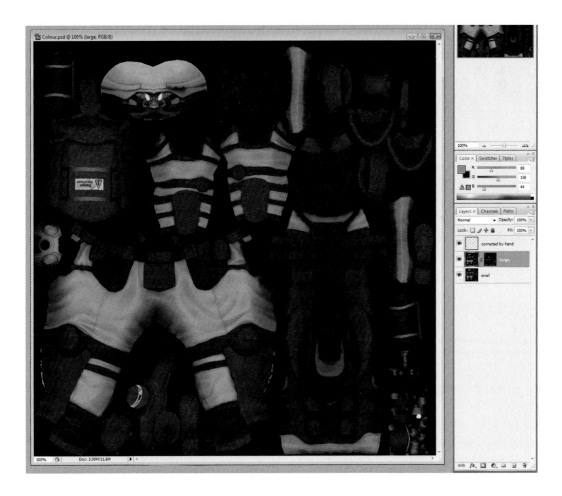

To fix the color map, I rendered first with a small cage, and then, in the areas with missing information, I painted in (using a mask) another version of the map I had rendered with a larger cage. To quickly finish it, I used the Brush tool, Rubber Stamp tool, and Healing Brush tool to make a few quick and dirty fixes on the layer that was corrected by hand. I fixed the problems with the specular map using exactly the same techniques.

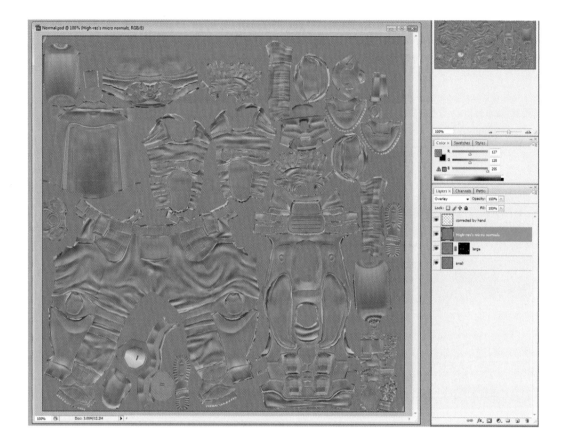

To fix the normal map, I used the same process as I did for the color map, with a couple of additional techniques. I corrected some of the areas that had rendered incorrectly by painting the blue/magenta color R127,G128,B255 on the hand-corrected layer.

The low-frequency normal maps that we obtained from the baking process do not include all the high-frequency details that are in the normal map of the high-res version of the character. To add these details to our mesh, apply the normal map of the high-res character to its diffuse color channel instead of its usual bump channel assignment. Then when you bake the maps again, the high-res normal map has been baked into the DiffuseMap texture. Copy and paste this map into our game mesh normals PSD, and put it in Overlay mode to blend it over the top of the other normal map layers.

It's very useful to apply the DirectX shader that we used earlier, so we can preview the effects of the spec, normal, and diffuse maps all working together in real time. If you keep a sharp eye out, you can make the game mesh incredibly similar to its original high-res counterpart.

Rendering Your Character

So we've finished the character now, and although he looks pretty darn good in the DirectX shader in the viewport, we can make him look nicer still if we render him using the Scanline renderer. True high-end rendering is beyond the scope of this chapter so we will use specular highlights to approximate blurry reflections, and AO maps to approximate the diffuse scattering of light.

I will show you how to render the high-res asset, but I recommend that you render the game mesh, too; potential employers are keen to see what you can do with a restricted polygon count. Dramatic, shadowy lighting looks cool but doesn't give a detailed view of your model, and perfectly flat and even lighting looks unrealistic and doesn't show off the contours of your model. Here we will create a lighting scheme somewhere between these two extremes. To start, delete any old lights from the scene and apply a blank, gray material to the character.

The Studio Wall

Although it will not be the focus of the renders, a simple and well-lit scene can help show off our character and put him in a real-life context. I used the Primitive Plane object and a couple of bend modifiers to make a primitive photography studio wall like you see below. Gradually curved wall-to-floor backdrops like this allow photographers to get the most minimal backgrounds possible, with no hard corners or other visual distractions. To add a little real-world believability to the studio floor, I've added a color texture with some marks on the floor where people have been standing with their dirty shoes on.

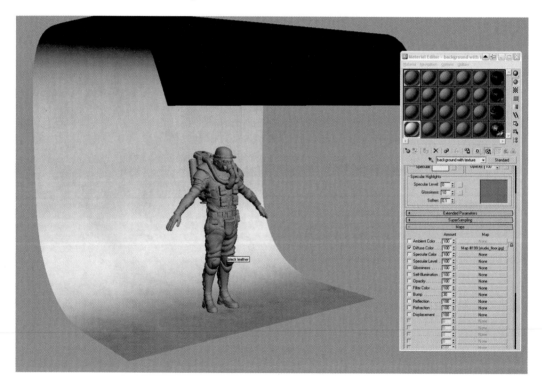

Be sure that the Studio Wall object and the soles of the character's shoes are exactly touching, without penetrating or crossing each other. A floating character or one that sinks through the floor will destroy the illusion of realism.

Using the AO baking, like we rendered previously for the character, we can calculate the lighting for the studio wall. Render the AO map and apply the texture to the diffuse slot of the Studio Wall object.

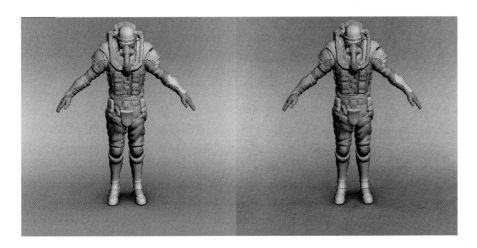

The AO shadow texture on the floor will add a subtle "this character is really standing here" ambient shadow effect. If you take this AO map into Photoshop and multiply it over the top of the dirt-textured floor, you will mix the two for a nice-looking background.

The Camera

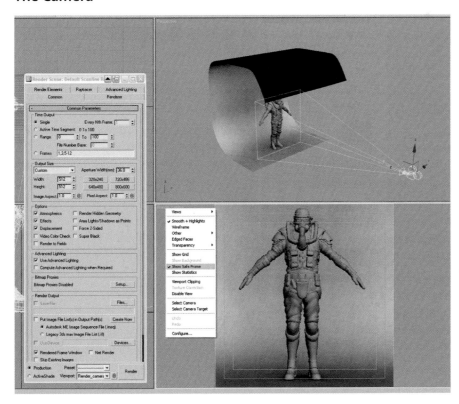

Create a camera a good distance away from our character and point it at him. Now zoom in until he fills the screen in the Camera viewport. Remember, the further away the camera, the less perspective distortion. We will be doing square renders, so in the Render Scene options set a width and height of 512 pixels for our test renders. Right-click on the camera name in the viewport and turn on Show Safe Frame in the options so that you can see the proportions of the camera in the viewport.

Creating the Lights

When creating lights, it is essential to add them one at a time so that you can see the effect each one has on the scene. With lighting, more is less, so make sure that each light you create has a purpose.

To create our key light, go to the Create > Lights panel and choose a Target Spot light; drag to create the light and point it directly at the character—the default intensity of 1 is usually okay. Normally, key lights are in front of the subject, often to one side in order to help show off the form of the shape. Lighting that is too close to the camera makes your objects look flat, so it's better to have this main light off to the right-hand side.

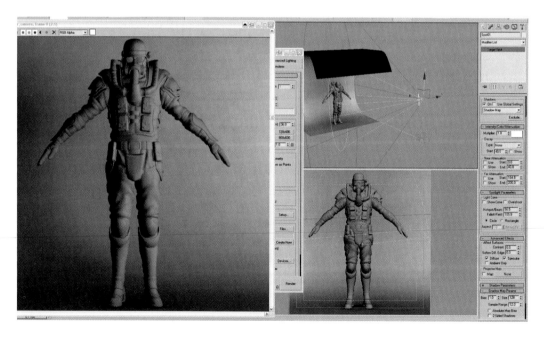

Be sure to check the Shadows On box to turn on the shadows. If you were to render now, you would get the hard-edged shadow look so common in CGI (computer-generated images). Interior light is usually quite soft, as the light bounces around quite a lot compared to outdoor scenes. Photographers often use silk or other translucent materials in front of their harsh studio lights in order to spread out the light and soften the shadows. We can simulate this effect by changing the size of the Shadow map to 128 pixels (a very rough setting) and the Sample Range to 12 (to smooth out the effect).

In the Spotlight parameters, you might also want to increase the Hotspot and Falloff of the lamp. Do a test render and you should get something like the previous image.

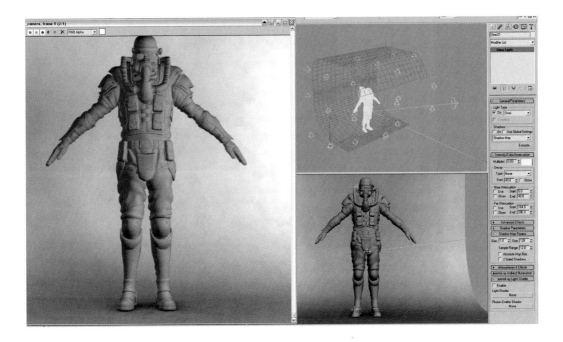

Photographers often use fill lights to fill in the shadowy areas of their subjects; in CG, we use fill lights for similar purposes and also to simulate the effect of bounced light from the environment. Add lots of Omni lights around the character, each with no shadows, and a tiny Multiplier value like 0.03. You might want to give the lights to the left a slightly blue tint to simulate the ambient light of the sky coming in from a large window. It is also a good idea to give the other Omni lights and the main key light a slightly orange tint to simulate the hue of a lightbulb.

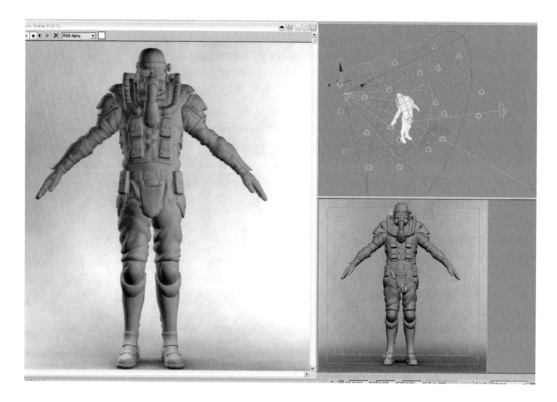

Rim lighting is used in photography to really pop subjects out from their background. Make a copy of the key light and move it to the other side of the character. This process should wrap up an interesting lighting scheme, which shows off the complex modeling that we have done.

Materials in Theory

An object's reflective qualities are dictated by how rough or smooth the object is on a micro scale.

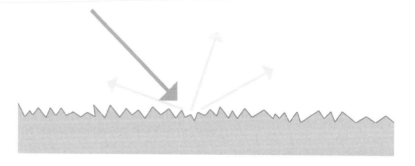

Diffuse reflection occurs when light hits a rough surface and is scattered in many directions. Surfaces with 100% diffuse reflection will look the same no matter which angle you view them from. A good example of a surface with pretty much 100% diffuse reflection would be a dirty, old cardboard box.

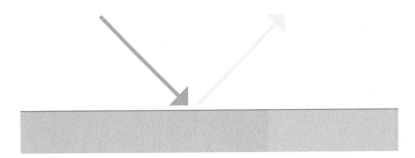

Specular reflection occurs when light hits a smooth object and bounces off at a perfect right angle. Specular reflection is easy to identify, because it changes depending on the viewing angle. A mirror is a good example of an almost perfectly 100% specular reflective surface.

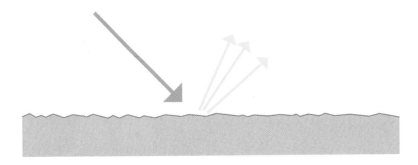

Different ratios of mixed diffuse and specular reflection occur on most surfaces. These surfaces are not flat enough to show perfect reflections like a mirror, but they are smooth enough to ensure that most of the light bounces off in a consistent direction to create blurred reflections. A good example of this would be most metals; they are very shiny, but the details of the reflections are blurred.

Materials in 3ds Max

To simulate these different types of surface in 3ds Max, we will split up the mesh into a number of smaller meshes, each with its own material:

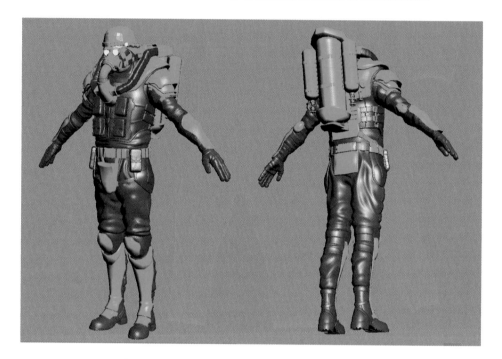

- Blurred Reflections should be applied to all the objects with hard, shiny surfaces like metals and plastics. This material uses the standard Specular effect to fake the look of blurred reflections; true blurred reflections are very computationally expensive and available only on the more advanced renderers, but this cheat will suffice for us here.

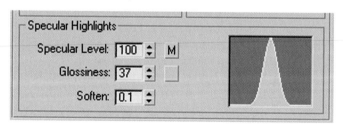

The micro roughness at I talked about earlier can be achieved using the Glossiness control; a value of 37 will give tight, smooth highlights.
- Blurred Reflections Rough should be exactly as Blurred Reflections but with a tweaked Glossiness value of 11. This material should be applied to all the fabrics with fairly rough surfaces, like most of the fairly matte clothes and straps.

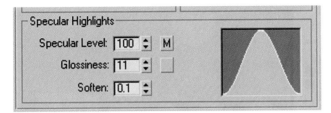

- Blurred Reflections Mid represents the medium-roughness areas and should have a glossiness of something like 21. Apply this material to the NBC suit and leather areas.

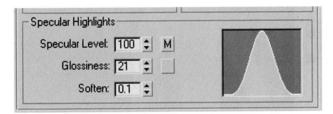

- Self Illuminated should be applied just to the eyes and lens of the torch; it will be just a regular texture, but with the Self Illumination setting at 100%.

Now all that remains is to plug the relevant color and spec maps into the Diffuse Color and Specular Level slots of these four materials. To apply the Normal map, click on the Bump Slot, and Choose Normal Bump, then click on the Normal slot to apply your bump map.

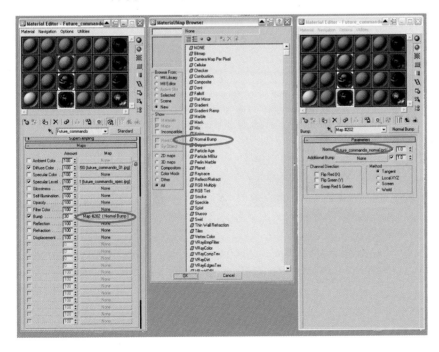

Back in the Maps section of your material, take care to change the bump value from its default of 30 up to the full strength of 100.

The Final Renders

For the final renders, increase the resolution to 1024 × 1024 or more pixels. In the previous figure, I have linked all the objects of the character to a dummy so that I can easily rotate the character (by rotating the parent dummy) for different renders.

As we have modeled some pretty awesome detail into our soldier, you might also want to do some close-up renders to showcase our attention to detail.

The renders I have produced here have a kind of stylized, cartoony feel to them because of the manual cheating we have done in the lighting. Quite often in videogames, this is a good thing, as many projects require a stylized effect. Setting up the lighting manually like this gives you ultimate control.

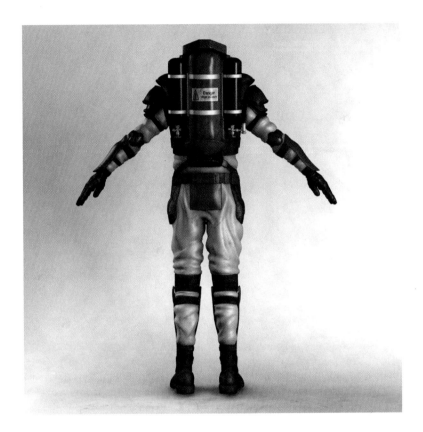

We could have gone further with the rendering to achieve a higher level of realism. To improve the quality of the light, we would have to discard the AO layers from our texture maps and use a true "global illumination" renderer such as Brazil, Mental Ray, or V-Ray. These high-end renderers can accurately render real-world lighting effects such as color bleeding, caustics, area lights (Max's standard lights are infinitely small), and blurry reflections.

As a 3D artist, you must constantly improve your work to keep up with the rapid pace of change. At the end of a project (after a good rest of course!), it's a good habit to perform a little post mortem on your work. What could you have done to make it better? How could you have made the process faster? How does your work compare to that of your peers? If you learn from your experiences, you will build your next character faster, and it will be of higher quality, too.

Index

U